1981

ABOUT PHILOSOPHY

ABOUT PHILO

SOPHY 2nd edition

Robert Paul Wolff

University of Massachusetts

Prentice-Hall, Inc., Englewood Cliffs, New Jersey 07632

Library of Congress Cataloging in Publication Data

WOLFF, ROBERT PAUL.
  About philosophy.

  Includes bibliographies and index.
  1. Philosophy–Introductions. I. Title.
BD21.W64 1981   100   80–19819
ISBN 0–13–000695–5

ABOUT PHILOSOPHY, Second Edition
Robert Paul Wolff

Editorial/production supervision by Virginia Rubens
Cover design by Jerry Pfeifer
Manufacturing buyer: Harry P. Baisley

Printed in the United States of America

10 9 8 7 6 5 4 3 2 1

PRENTICE-HALL INTERNATIONAL, INC., *London*
PRENTICE-HALL OF AUSTRALIA PTY. LIMITED, *Sydney*
PRENTICE-HALL OF CANADA, LTD., *Toronto*
PRENTICE-HALL OF INDIA PRIVATE LIMITED, *New Delhi*
PRENTICE-HALL OF JAPAN, INC., *Tokyo*
PRENTICE-HALL OF SOUTHEAST ASIA PTE. LTD., *Singapore*
WHITEHALL BOOKS LIMITED, *Wellington, New Zealand*

CONTENTS

PREFACE TO THE SECOND EDITION xv

PREFACE TO THE FIRST EDITION xvii

1 WHAT IS PHILOSOPHY? 2

SOCRATES

ADVANCED READING 34
John Wisdom
Philosophical Perplexity

TOPICS FOR FURTHER STUDY 48
SUGGESTIONS FOR FURTHER READING 48

2 ETHICS   50

IMMANUEL KANT

ADVANCED READING   83
Jane English
Abortion and the Concept of a Person

TOPICS FOR FURTHER STUDY   92
SUGGESTIONS FOR FURTHER READING   93

3 SOCIAL PHILOSOPHY   94

JOHN STUART MILL

ADVANCED READING   123
John Rawls
Distributive Justice

TOPICS FOR FURTHER STUDY   134
SUGGESTIONS FOR FURTHER READING   134

4 POLITICAL PHILOSOPHY   136

JEAN-JACQUES ROUSSEAU

ADVANCED READING   166
Hugo Bedau
On Civil Disobedience

TOPICS FOR FURTHER STUDY   176
SUGGESTIONS FOR FURTHER READING   177

5 PHILOSOPHY OF ART   178

PLATO

ADVANCED READING   212
Susanne K. Langer
Problems of Art

TOPICS FOR FURTHER STUDY   220
SUGGESTIONS FOR FURTHER READING   221

6 PHILOSOPHY OF RELIGION 222

SØREN KIERKEGAARD

ADVANCED READING 256
Norman Malcolm
Anselm's Ontological Arguments

TOPICS FOR FURTHER STUDY 266
SUGGESTIONS FOR FURTHER READING 267

7 THEORY OF KNOWLEDGE 268

RENÉ DESCARTES

ADVANCED READING 301
Bertrand Russell
Knowledge by Acquaintance and Knowledge by Description

TOPICS FOR FURTHER STUDY 310
SUGGESTIONS FOR FURTHER READING 311

8 METAPHYSICS AND PHILOSOPHY OF SCIENCE 312

GOTTFRIED LEIBNIZ

ADVANCED READING 353
Clarence Irving Lewis
The Problem of the Categories

TOPICS FOR FURTHER STUDY 363
SUGGESTIONS FOR FURTHER READING 364

GLOSSARY 365

INDEX 371

LIST OF SELECTIONS INCLUDED IN THE TEXT

Chapter 1: What Is Philosophy?

Plato, *Republic*. Thrasymachus on justice.

Lucretius, *On the Nature of Things*. Evidences of the existence of atoms.

Science News: *New theories of the atom*. Steady state versus big bang theories of the universe.

Marcus Aurelius, *Meditations*. Selections on reason in man and nature.

David Hume, *A Treatise of Human Nature*. A plan for a science of human nature.

Immanuel Kant, *A Critique of Pure Reason*. The spirit of criticism.

Ludwig Wittgenstein, *Philosophical Investigations*. Two statements about philosophy.

Plato, *Gorgias*. Callicles on the nature of philosophy.

ADVANCED READING: John Wisdom, *Philosophical Perplexity*.

Chapter 2: Ethics

Ruth Benedict, *Anthropology and the Abnormal*. The relativity of ethical judgments.

Immanuel Kant, *Groundwork of the Metaphysic of Morals*. Man as an end in himself; The principle of autonomy; The dignity of humanity.

Jeremy Bentham, *An Introduction to the Principles of Morals and Legislation*. The principle of utility. Application of utilitarianism to law.

Plato, *Republic*. The virtues of the soul and of the state.

Erik Erikson, *Childhood and Society*. Ego-integrity and despair.

ADVANCED READING: Jane English, *Abortion and the Concept of a Person*.

Chapter 3: Social Philosophy

Adam Smith, *The Wealth of Nations*. The invisible hand.

John Stuart Mill, *Utilitarianism*. Higher and lower pleasures.

John Stuart Mill, *Principles of Political Economy*. Custom and competition; The limits of laissez-faire.

Michael Oakeshott, *Rationalism in Politics*. The nature of the rationalist.

Alexis de Tocqueville, *The Old Régime and the French Revolution*. The spirit of liberty in the old regime.

Karl Marx, *Economic-Philosophic Manuscripts of 1844*. Alienation.

Herbert Marcuse, *One-Dimensional Man*. The irrationality of modern capitalist society.

ADVANCED READING: John Rawls, *Distributive Justice*.

Chapter 4: Political Philosophy

Jean-Jacques Rousseau, *The Social Contract*. The problem; The social contract; The dangers of representation; The problem of majority rule.

David Hume, *"Of the Original Contract."* The non-existence of a contract.

John Locke, *Second Treatise of Civil Government*. Implicit and explicit contracts.

Edmund Burke, *Reflections on the French Revolution*. Society is not a contract.

Benito Mussolini, *The Doctrine of Fascism*. The elements of fascism.

Friedrich Engels, *Herr Eugen Dühring's Revolution in Science*. The withering away of the state.

ADVANCED READING: Hugo Bedau, *On Civil Disobedience*.

Chapter 5: Philosophy of Art

Plato, *Republic*. Art as an imitation of an imitation of the real.
Aristotle, *Poetics*. Catharsis and the positive function of tragedy.
Oscar Wilde, *Intentions*. Art for art's sake.
William Wordsworth, Preface to the *Lyrical Ballads*. The romantic theory of poetry.
Leo Tolstoy, *What Is Art?* The definition of art; The religious function of art.
Herbert Marcuse, *One-Dimensional Man*. The negative function of art.

ADVANCED READING: Susanne Langer, *Problems of Art*

Chapter 6: Philosophy of Religion

Søren Kierkegaard, *Concluding Unscientific Postscript to the Philosophical Fragments*. Truth is subjectivity.
William Paley, *Natural Theology*. The argument from design.
David Hume, *Dialogues Concerning Natural Religion*. Refutation of the argument from design.
St. Thomas Aquinas, *Summa Theologica*. Three proofs for the existence of God.
David Hume, *Dialogues Concerning Natural Religion*. Refutation of the cosmological argument.
St. Anselm, *Proslogion*. The ontological argument.
Immanuel Kant, *Critique of Pure Reason*. Refutation of the ontological argument.
Sigmund Freud, *The Future of an Illusion*. Religious faith as an illusion.

ADVANCED READING: Norman Malcolm, *Anselm's Ontological Arguments*.

Chapter 7: Theory of Knowledge

René Descartes, *Discourse on Method*. Four rules of the mind.
René Descartes, *Meditations on First Philosophy*. The method of doubt and the certainty of my own existence; Clearness and distinctness as criteria of truth; Reason and the senses as sources of knowledge.
Gottfried Leibniz, *The Monadology*. The principles of contradiction and of sufficient reason.
John Locke, *Essay Concerning Human Understanding*. The mind as a blank piece of paper on which experience writes.
David Hume, *A Treatise of Human Nature*. Ideas and impressions. The skeptical critique of causal inference. Nature dispels skeptical doubts.

ADVANCED READING: Bertrand Russell, *Knowledge by Acquaintance and Knowledge by Description*.

Chapter 8: Metaphysics and Philosophy of Science

Gottfried Leibniz, *The Monadology*. The nature of substance.
Samuel Clarke and Gottfried Leibniz, *The Leibniz-Clarke Correspondence*. The possibility of absolute space.

Thomas Hobbes, *Leviathan*. The materialist account of the mind.

J. J. C. Smart, *"Materialism."* An argument for the identity thesis.

Norman Malcolm, *Scientific Materialism and the Identity Theory*. A reply to Smart.

David Hume, *Enquiry Concerning Human Understanding*. Must the future resemble the past?

Carl Hempel and Paul Oppenheim, *The Logic of Explanation*. The deductive model of explanation.

Thomas Kuhn, *The Structure of Scientific Revolutions*. Changes in paradigms.

ADVANCED READING: Clarence Irving Lewis, *The Problem of the Categories*.

ILLUSTRATION CREDITS

Page		
	2	Courtesy Alinari-Scala.
	14	Courtesy New York Public Library Picture Collection.
	22	Courtesy Scala, New York/Florence.
	23	Courtesy The Bettmann Archive, Inc.
	26	Courtesy New York Public Library Picture Collection.
	30	Courtesy The Granger Collection, New York.
	50	Courtesy New York Public Library Picture Collection.
	67	Courtesy The Bettmann Archive, Inc.
	94	Courtesy The Bettmann Archive, Inc.
	99	Courtesy The Bettmann Archive, Inc.
	107	(top) Courtesy The Bettmann Archive, Inc.
	107	(bottom) Courtesy Brown Brothers, Sterling, Pa.
	113	Courtesy The Bettmann Archive, Inc.
	115	Courtesy The Granger Collection, New York.
	118	(left) Courtesy Calogero Cascio/Photo Researchers, Inc.
	118	(right) Courtesy Wide World Photos, Inc.
	136	Courtesy Giraudon, Paris.
	140	Courtesy Brown Brothers, Sterling, Pa.
	151	Courtesy The Bettmann Archive, Inc.
	153	Courtesy The Bettmann Archive, Inc.
	156	Courtesy United Press International.
	178	Courtesy Alinari-Scala.
	189	Courtesy The Bettmann Archive, Inc.
	195	Courtesy Culver Pictures, Inc.
	198	Courtesy The Bettmann Archive, Inc.
	199	Courtesy The Bettmann Archive, Inc.
	201	Courtesy The Bettmann Archive, Inc.
	202	Courtesy Spanish National Tourist Office.
	203	Courtesy Martha Swope, Photographer.
	206	Courtesy University of California, San Diego.
	222	Courtesy The Bettmann Archive, Inc.
	225	Courtesy The Granger Collection, New York.
	227	Courtesy New York Public Library Picture Collection.
	237	Courtesy The Granger Collection, New York.
	242	Courtesy The Bettmann Archive, Inc.
	246	Courtesy The Bettmann Archive, Inc.
	253	Courtesy The Bettmann Archive, Inc.
	268	Courtesy New York Public Library Picture Collection.
	270	Courtesy John Hart and Field Enterprises, Inc.
	291	Courtesy The Bettmann Archive, Inc.
	294	(left) Courtesy Scala, New York/Florence.
	294	(right) Courtesy New York Public Library Picture Collection.
	312	Courtesy The Bettmann Archive, Inc.
	325	Courtesy NASA.
	332	Courtesy John Hart and Field Enterprises, Inc.
	333	Courtesy The Bettmann Archive, Inc.

HUGO BEDAU, "On Civil Disobedience," from *The Journal of Philosophy,* Vol. LVIII (1961). Reprinted by permission of the publisher and the author.

RUTH BENEDICT, "Anthropology and the Abnormal," *Journal of General Psychology,* Vol. X (1934).

JANE ENGLISH, "Abortion and the Concept of a Person," from the *Canadian Journal of Philosophy,* Vol. V., No. 2. Reprinted by permission of the publisher.

ERIK H. ERIKSON, *Childhood and Society,* 2nd ed. Copyright © 1963 by W. W. Norton & Company, Inc. Reprinted by permission of W. W. Norton & Company, Inc.

SIGMUND FREUD, *"The Future of an Illusion,"* trans. by James Strachey. Reprinted with the permission of W. W. Norton & Company, Inc. Copyright © 1961 by James Strachey. To Sigmund Freud Copyrights Ltd., The Institute of Psycho-Analysis and The Hogarth Press Ltd. for permission to quote from *The Future of an Illusion* in Volume XXI of *The Standard Edition of the Complete Psychological Works of Sigmund Freud,* translated and edited by James Strachey.

CARL HEMPEL and PAUL OPPENHEIM, "Studies in the Logic of Explanation," from *Philosophy of Science,* Vol. 15 (1948). Reprinted by permission of Williams & Wilkins.

IMMANUEL KANT, *Groundwork of the Metaphysic of Morals,* trans. by H. J. Paton (New York, Harper & Row, 1964), pp. 94, 98–100. Reprinted by permission of the publisher.

IMMANUEL KANT, *Immanuel Kant's Critique of Pure Reason,* trans. by Norman Kemp Smith. Reprinted by permission of St. Martin's Press, Inc., and Macmillan, London and Basingstoke.

Excerpts from SØREN KIERKEGAARD, *Concluding Unscientific Postscript,* trans. by David F. Swenson and Walter Lowrie (copyright 1941 © 1969 by Princeton University Press; Princeton Paperback, 1968), pp. 287–291. Reprinted by permission of Princeton University Press and the American Scandinavian Foundation.

SUSANNE K. LANGER, *Problems of Art.* Used by permission of Charles Scribner's Sons. Copyright © 1957 Susanne K. Langer.

C. I. LEWIS, *Mind and the World Order* (Dover Publications, Inc., 1956). Reprinted by permission of the publisher.

NORMAN MALCOLM, "Anselm's Ontological Arguments," from *Philosophical Review,* Vol. LXIX (1960). Reprinted by permission of the author.

HERBERT MARCUSE, *One-Dimensional Man.* Copyright © 1964 by Herbert Marcuse. Reprinted by permission of Beacon Press.

MICHAEL OAKESHOTT, *Rationalism in Politics and Other Essays,* pages 1, 2, 3, 7–8. Copyright © 1962 by Michael Oakeshott. Basic Books, Inc., Publishers, New York. Reprinted by permission of Basic Books, Inc. and Methuen & Co. Ltd.

PLATO, *Gorgias,* © 1952 by the Liberal Arts Press. Reprinted by permission of the publishers, The Bobbs-Merrill Company, Inc.

PLATO, *The Republic of Plato,* trans. by F. M. Cornford, 1941, by permission of the Oxford University Press, Oxford.

JOHN RAWLS, "Distributive Justice," from *Philosophy, Politics, and Society,* third series, ed. by Peter Laslett and W. G. Runciman. Reprinted by permission of the author.

BERTRAND RUSSELL, "Knowledge by Acquaintance and Knowledge by Description," from *The Problems of Philosophy,* published by Oxford University Press (1912). Reprinted by permission of Oxford University Press.

SAINT ANSELM, *Saint Anselm: Basic Writings,* trans. by S. N. Deane. Published by Open Court Publishing Company, La Salle, Ill., 1966. Copyright © 1962 by Open Court Publishing Company. Reprinted by permission of the publisher.

SAINT THOMAS AQUINAS, "Summa Theologica," from *Basic Writings of Saint Thomas Aquinas,* ed. by Anton C. Pegis. Reprinted by permission of the publisher, Random House, Inc. Copyright 1945 by Random House, Inc.

J. J. C. SMART, "Materialism," from *The Journal of Philosophy,* Vol. LX, 22 (October 24, 1963). Reprinted by permission of the publisher and the author.

"Supporting Evidence for the Theory of the Steady State," © 1970; and "Headlong for the Breakthrough . . ." © 1968, *Science News.* Reprinted by permission from *Science News,* the weekly news magazine of science and the applications of science. Copyright 1970 and 1968 by Science Service, Inc.

JOHN WISDOM, "Philosophical Perplexity," from *Proceedings of the Aristotelian Society,* 1937, pages 71–88. Reprinted by permission of the publishers.

PREFACE
TO THE SECOND EDITION

In this new edition of *About Philosophy,* I have made a major alteration in the structure and organization of the text, in order to broaden the scope of the materials covered and increase the flexibility of the book as a teaching instrument. At the conclusion of each chapter, a substantial selection has been added from the writings of a twentieth-century author. The selection, accompanied by editorial introductions, topics for further study, and suggested readings, permits instructors and students to explore in greater depth the branch of philosophy dealt with in the chapter. A number of instructors have expressed a desire for material of this sort, as an extension and enrichment of the material already present in the text. By and large, the new selections are somewhat more difficult, as well as considerably longer than the original material. They have been placed at the conclusion of each chapter so that instructors will have maximum freedom to use them or not as their individual pedagogical needs dictate.

Readers familiar with the first edition will find that a great many changes have also been made within the body of the text. Here again, the comments and criticisms of instructors who have actually taught from *About Philosophy* have been invaluable. The response of teachers and students to the first edition encourages me to believe that *About Philosophy* is a teachable text. I hope that this second edition will prove an even better instrument for teaching and learning.

Three of my colleagues—Bruce Aune, Robert J. Ackermann, and Ann Ferguson—made valuable suggestions during the revision of the first edition. Malcolm Reid of Gordon College was kind enough to write to me concerning a problematic passage, and I have benefitted from his comments.

R. P. W.

PREFACE
TO THE FIRST EDITION

This book is the outgrowth of two decades of teaching. I faced my first philosophy class in the fall of 1955, when I was a graduate student not much older than my students. Because I was young, it was easier then for me to put myself in their place and try to see philosophy through their eyes, as an entirely new experience. As the years have passed, I have grown older, but my students remain the same age. So the gap between us widens, and I must work harder each year to recapture their perspective. Long familiarity with the problems and methods of philosophy has led me to take them too much for granted. Again and again, I must remind myself that philosophy is a special way of looking at life, a way that is *natural,* but not therefore obvious. And should I forget this fact, my students will very quickly remind me!

In this introduction to philosophical problems, theories, and personalities, I have tried always to keep the student's point of view central. I imagine my reader to be intelligent, naturally curious, but skeptical. He or she is willing to listen to new ideas, but not to accept them merely on the authority of an author or teacher. My job is to present philosophy as an activity that sensible, intelligent people would *want* to engage in. It is not enough for me to explain what the great philosophers said in a clear, uncluttered way. I must also help my reader to understand *why* they said it, why they felt compelled to think about their moral, scientific, religious, or logical problems as they did.

In writing this book, I have had the help of a great many men and women, and it is a pleasure to have the opportunity to acknowledge my debt to them. My first thanks must go to the several thousand students who have listened to me, argued with me, learned from me, and taught me over the past twenty years. Some of them have become teachers of philosophy themselves; others are craftsmen, lawyers, clerks, doctors, politicians, policemen, and I know not what else. But all have helped me to become a better teacher. I hope their voices echo in these pages.

Several of my colleagues at the University of Massachusetts answered my questions and corrected some of my misconceptions in one or another of the branches of philosophy touched on in this book. First among them is Professor Robert J. Ackermann, an extraordinarily gifted and widely learned man whom I am fortunate to count as my friend. Professor Mary Sirridge guided me through some of the complexities of the philosophy of art, a field in which she is an expert and I am a novice.

The single most important source of assistance was Ms. (soon to be Dr.) Karen Warren, who devoted several months to invaluable research and background work on every chapter of the book. To say that Ms. Warren was my "research assistant" entirely fails to do justice to the nature and magnitude of her contribution. Ms. Warren is, by the common agreement of my colleagues, far and away the most successful teacher among all the graduate students who have come through the Philosophy Department of the University of Massachusetts. Her research for me included beautifully clear analyses of key issues in each field of philosophy, as well as the more conventional mustering of sources and biographical details. Her own teaching skill enabled her to lay out the material for me so that I in turn could present it in what I hope is a coherent and comprehensible manner. I quite literally could not have written this book without her aid.

ROBERT PAUL WOLFF
Northampton, Massachusetts

ABOUT PHILOSOPHY

SOCRATES was tried by the Athenians on charges of "impiety" and "corrupting the young of Athens," but it seems clear that his real offense was opposition to, or even lack of sufficient support for, the leaders of the newly restored democratic regime.

Socrates had associated with the aristocratic families which overthrew the first democracy, and his disciple, Plato, was a member of one of the powerful families which ruled Athens for a while before the restoration. Since an amnesty had been declared, it was legally impossible for the rulers to prosecute Socrates for political

1 WHAT IS PHILOSOPHY?

offenses, so they trumped up the religious accusations and enlisted a religious fanatic, Meletus, to bring charges against the seventy-year-old philosopher.

Socrates could have fled from Athens before the trial, conviction in which could carry a death sentence. Even after his conviction, he could have proposed banishment as an alternative to death, and the Athenian jury of 501 citizens would almost certainly have accepted such a compromise. But Socrates was convinced that he had done Athens no harm by his philosophical questioning. Indeed, he insisted that he had, by his activities, been a benefactor of his native city, and so as an alternative to the death penalty demanded by the prosecution he proposed that Athens pension him off as a respected citizen.

The Athenian rulers, trapped by Socrates' uncompromising integrity, were forced to carry out the sentence of death, though they would probably have been all too happy to allow their prisoner to escape before the execution. One month after the trial, following a long night of philosophical discussion with his friends, Socrates drank the poison hemlock prepared for him by his jailers, and died.

I

When I was a student, one of my professors told us about the conversations he would strike up in the club car on the train from Boston to New York. A group of men would gather around the bar, and each in turn would introduce himself, saying a few words about the line of work he was in. One would announce himself as a lawyer, a second as a traveler in ladies' apparel, a third as an engineer. When it was my professor's turn, he would say, "I am a philosopher." That, he told us, would always bring the conversation to a dead halt. No one knew quite what to say to a man who described himself as a philosopher. The others were too polite to ask, "What does a philosopher do?" But the announcement always cast a pall over the gathering. Eventually, he took to saying, "I am a teacher." That went over all right, and so long as no one asked what he taught, they could get on to more congenial topics, such as the prospects for the Red Sox, or the weather.

What *do* philosphers do? Oddly enough, that is a question philosophers have been asking for as long as there has been a discipline called philosophy. Indeed, as we will see a bit later on, "What do philosophers do?" is probably the most common philosophical question! But all this sounds like double talk, which is just what makes people nervous about philosophy in the first place. You all know what a doctor does; you know what physicists, historians, composers, and sanitation engineers do. Most of you probably even have some sort of idea of what microbiologists do. But philosophers are something else again. Philosophers ask questions—odd questions, like "Could my whole life be a dream?" and dangerous questions, like "What right does the government—any government—have to tell me what to do?"

The best way to find out what philosophers do is to take a look at one of them, and on anybody's list, the natural first choice must be the most famous philosopher of all time, SOCRATES. Socrates was born in 469 B.C. to a stonemason and a midwife in the Greek city-state of Athens. As far as we know, he spent his entire life in and about Athens, serving his time in the army at one point, taking his turn in the government at another. He was a rather homely man in a society that prized manly beauty, and though he was hardly poor, he seems to have managed on much less money than his friends and disciples had. Athens itself was a city of 130,000, busy and prosperous by the standards of the time but small enough so that everyone who was anyone knew everyone else. In his youth, Socrates studied the scientific theories a number of original thinkers had developed in the preceding several centuries, but he soon became convinced that the most important and puzzling subject was the human condition itself. He developed the practice of going into the public squares and meeting places of Athens to cajole, goad, or draw his fellow townsmen into discussions about how men ought to live their lives. (In the Athens of Socrates' day, it was taken for granted that women would play no role in these discussions, or indeed in any other public business.) Socrates was quick-witted, clever, and tenacious. He had a knack for asking hard or embarrassing questions that forced others to think a good deal more than they really wanted to. Because some of the people he quizzed were important politicians and famous teachers, it was fun to watch him trip them up—so long as you weren't one of those made to look foolish. So a number of wealthy young men gathered around Socrates as a band of disciples and as a sort of permanent audience. Sometimes he talked with them, quizzing them in the same way and forcing them to examine their own lives; sometimes they watched as he took on a local bigwig or visiting personage.

If this practice of asking questions were all there was to Socrates' life, we would never have heard of him 2400 years later, and we certainly wouldn't think of him as the first and greatest of all philosophers. But three things transformed Socrates from a local curiosity and general pain in the neck into the patron saint of philosophy and one of the great figures of Western civilization.

The first thing was an accident. Among those who followed Socrates was a brilliantly gifted, wealthy young man named Plato. Plato was only twenty-eight when his teacher died, but he was deeply, permanently affected by his relationship with the aging Socrates, and many years later he began to write his Dialogues, playlets in which the style and personality of Socrates were captured, transformed, and elevated into works of great art. Most of what we believe about Socrates comes to us from these Dialogues, including most importantly our conception of Socrates' techniques of questioning. Scholars still debate how much in the Dialogues is Plato's artistic invention and how much is accurate historical portrayal. But there can be no question that the essential style belonged to Socrates himself.

The second thing that happened was not really an accident, though it may seem so at first glance. The rulers of Athens decided that Socrates was more than an annoyance; he was becoming a threat to their political security. So they trumped up some charges against him and put him on trial. Socrates could have plea-bargained, in effect, and gotten off with a punishment of exile, which would have put him safely out of Athens without making him a martyr. But he chose instead to defend himself and his life without excuses or apologies. He had done nothing wrong, he insisted, and now that he was seventy, Athens should be thinking of giving him a pension rather than threatening to put him to death. In the end, Socrates forced the government's hand, and a sentence of death was handed down. Even then, he could probably have escaped from jail with the help of his friends, but he stayed and took the poison his jailers gave him. And so he became the first martyr to philosophy. It is easy to second-guess the Athenian rulers and conclude that they could have spared themselves a lot of trouble by handling the case a bit more skilfully. But Socrates' persistent questioning of established doctrines and received opinions really was a threat, not only to the government but also to the lifestyle of the families who ruled Athens. In a way, the accident is not that Socrates was put to death at the age of seventy, but rather that he had been permitted to go on for so long before those in power landed on him.

The third and most important reason for Socrates' immortality is no accident at all, but the very essence of his life and calling. Witty though he was, irreverent though he could be, annoying though he certainly became, Socrates was deadly serious about his questioning. His death only confirmed what his life had already proved—that for him, the relentless examination of every human action and belief was more important than survival itself. As Socrates said at his trial, "The unexamined life is not worth living," and by drinking the poison, he showed that he would rather die honorably in the cause of that principle than flee in dishonor to some foreign refuge.

Each of us makes countless decisions which affect our lives and the lives of those around us to some degree. Many of the decisions are of very little importance, such as whether or not to go to the movies, where to have dinner, or what to wear. A few of the decisions are truly momentous—whom to marry, what career to pursue; and for some of us, caught up in a war or facing a personal tragedy, our decisions may literally determine life and death. Socrates believed in his own time (and I think he would still believe if he were alive today) that these decisions must be questioned, examined, and criticized if we are to live truly good and happy lives. Most of us make even the most important decisions without really asking ourselves what principles we are basing our choices on, and whether those principles are truly worthy of our respect and commitment. When war comes, young men go off to fight and die with hardly more than a passing thought about whether it is ever morally right to kill another person. A student spends ten years of his or her life working to become a doctor, simply because mom and dad always wanted it. A man and a woman drift into marriage, have children, buy a house and settle down, and only twenty years later does one of them ask, "What am I doing here?"

Socrates had a theory about how each of us ought to examine his or her life, subjecting it to critical analysis and questioning. This theory, on which he based the special style of teaching and philosophizing that has come to bear his name, rested on four basic principles:

1. The unexamined life is not worth living. To be truly human, and thereby truly happy, each man and woman must subject his or her own life and convictions to critical testing.

2. There are objectively valid principles of thought and action which must be followed if we are to live good lives—lives both happy and just. It isn't true that every person's way of life is as good as every other's. Some people are unjust, self-indulgent, obsessed with worthless goals, estranged from their fellows, confused and blind about what is truly important and what is beneath notice, terrified of shadows, and incapable either of living or of dying with grace and dignity. Such people need to find the truth and live in accordance with it.

3. The truth lies within each of us, not in the stars, or in tradition, or in religious books, or in the opinions of the masses. Each of us has within, however hidden, the true principles of right thinking and acting. In the end, therefore, no one can teach anyone else the truth about life. If that truth isn't within you, you will never find it; if it is within you, then only relentless critical self-examination will reveal it.

4. But though no one can teach anyone else about the fundamental principles of right action and clear thinking, some people—call them teachers, philosophers, gadflies—can ask questions that prod men and women to begin the task of self-examination. These teachers may also be able to guide the process, at least in its early stages, because they have been over the same ground themselves and know where the pitfalls are.

From these four principles, it follows that philosophy consists of a process of question and answer, a *dialogue* between two people, one of whom is seeking rational insight and understanding, the other of whom has already achieved some measure of self-knowledge and wishes to help the novice. The dialogue begins with whatever beliefs the student brings to the quest. If she thoughtlessly repeats the traditional moral sayings of her society, then the philosopher will try to force her to question those sayings; if she takes up the position that everything is relative, that nothing is true or valid for all persons (a stance many students adopt at about the time they leave home and cut loose from their parents), then the philosopher will try a different line of questioning. The end point of the journey is always the same: wisdom, rational insight into the principles of thought and action, and thus a happier, more integrated, more worthwhile life. But the starting points are as many as the students who make the journey.

Socrates discovered that each journey to wisdom has an enormous obstacle blocking the road. Modern psychoanalysts call the roadblock "resistance," but a simpler way of putting it is that no one wants to admit that he or she needs to learn. Certainly the politicians and public figures with whom Socrates talked didn't think of themselves as in need of further wisdom. They were quite convinced they already knew how to run the state and how to order their own lives. Socrates had to discover a trick for getting inside their defenses so that he could make them see—really see—that they were not yet truly wise. What he did was to invent a verbal form of judo. The basic trick of judo is to let your opponent's force and momentum work for you. Instead of launching a frontal attack, you let him swing or grab, and then you roll with his motion so that, in effect, he throws himself on the mat. Socrates achieved the same effect in his debates by means of a literary device called "irony." Although this is a book about philosophy, not literature, it might be worth taking a few moments to explain how irony works, so that we can see what Socrates was trying to accomplish.

Irony is a kind of speech or communication that assumes a *double audience.* When a speaker makes an ironic statement, he seems to be directing it at one group of people. This group is called the first, or superficial, audience. But in reality, he is directing his remarks at a second audience, called the real audience. His statement has a double meaning, and the trick of the irony is that while the first audience understands only the superficial or apparent meaning, the second audience understands *both* meanings. This second audience knows that the first audience has misunderstood, so the irony becomes a private joke between the speaker and the second audience—a joke at the expense of the first audience, which never suspects a thing. The whole complicated relationship is portrayed in the drawing on the next page.

For example, suppose a stranger drives up to the general store in a small town to ask directions. "You there!" he says to a farmer seated on the front porch of the store. "Can you tell me the fastest way to get to the state capital? Be quick about it! I have a very important meeting with the governor." "Yes," replies the farmer, with just the slightest wink to his friends on the porch. "I

can tell you the fastest way." He then proceeds to give the stranger totally wrong directions that will take him hours out of his way.

The farmer is speaking ironically. The stranger is the superficial audience, and the other people on the porch are the real audience. The apparent meaning, as understood by the stranger, is that this country bumpkin, who has been properly impressed with the stranger's importance, can tell him the fastest way and has done so. The real, secret, ironic meaning is of course that the farmer can tell this pompous ass the fastest way, but has no intention of doing so because he has been so rude. The reply is a private joke between the farmer and his friends at the stranger's expense.

When Socrates strikes up a conversation with a self-important, self-confident, but really rather ignorant man, he does not try a frontal attack, arguing directly against his opponent's false beliefs. That would simply lead to an impasse, in which each participant would be asserting his own convictions and neither would engage in critical self-examination. Instead, Socrates says, with a deceptively modest air, "Of course, I don't know anything at all, and you seem to be very wise indeed, so perhaps you would be so good as to enlighten me." His opponent, thinking Socrates means literally what he says, gets all puffed up with his own importance and pontificates on goodness or justice or truth or beauty or piety. Then Socrates goes to work on him, pretending to be puzzled, asking politely for clarification, poking away at just those places in his opponent's position that are most vulnerable. After a while, the poor man is thoroughly deflated. Embarrassed by his inability to give coherent, defensible answers to Socrates' apparently humble questions, he finally reaches the rather painful conclusion that he doesn't know what he thought he knew. Now, and only now, can Socrates help him to set out on the path to wisdom, for as Socrates so often insists, the first act of true wisdom is to admit that you are ignorant.

When Socrates says that he himself is ignorant, he is speaking ironically. In fact, he is uttering what students of literature call a "double irony." In the first place, he is having a private joke with his followers, at the expense of the man with whom he is debating. His opponent thinks Socrates is really being deferential, that Socrates actually wants to sit at the great man's feet and learn great truths. But of course Socrates means that he is "ignorant" of those great "truths" just because they are false, confused, and not worth knowing. We have all met someone who thinks he is an expert on some subject when in fact he doesn't know beans about it. "Tell me more!" we say, and sure enough he does, not realizing that we are kidding him.

At a deeper level, which Socrates' own followers sometimes don't really understand, Socrates genuinely means that he is ignorant, in the sense that *he* doesn't have a truth to teach any more than his puffed-up opponent does. The disciples think that Socrates knows what truth, beauty, justice, goodness, and wisdom really are, and they expect that just as soon as he has deflated his opponent, he will teach them. But Socrates believes that every man must find the truth for himself, and so his followers cannot shortcut their journey by learning the truth from Socrates any more than they could by observing the mistakes and confusions of Socrates' opponents. In this deeper double irony, we, the readers of Plato's dialogue, are the real audience, and both Socrates' opponent *and* his disciples are superficial or apparent audiences.

This *dialectical* method of argument, as it has been called, serves a theoretical purpose as well, for Socrates (or Plato, we don't know which) holds that the key to wisdom is the distinction between things as they appear or seem to us and the reality that lies behind them. Just as the world of the senses is merely an appearance of the true reality to be grasped by reason, just as the apparently true opinions of the mob conceal the genuine truth, so too the superficial meaning of an ironic statement is the apparent meaning which hides the deeper, real meaning intended for the real audience. Thus, the structure of language mirrors the structure of reality. Throughout this book, we shall encounter philosophers who have struggled with this notion that language, thought, and being have

First
Audience

I am
ignorant

SOCRATES

Second
Audience

Third
Audience

First, or superficial audience, thinks Socrates is humbly confessing inferiority to him. Second audience (Socrates' followers), realizing Socrates is making fun of first audience, laughs at first audience. Third audience (the reader) laughs at first audience, smiles at second. Third audience realizes *both* that Socrates is making fun of first audience *and* that Socrates' own followers don't realize the true meaning of his statement.

parallel structures, so that by analyzing one we gain insight into the nature of the others.

We have talked enough about Socrates and his debating tricks. It is time to see him in action. The following passage comes from the most famous of Plato's Dialogues, the *Republic*. Socrates and some friends have been having a discussion about the nature of *justice*, by which they mean the fundamental principles of right and wrong. Several suggestions have been made, which Socrates has disposed of without much trouble, and now a young, very excitable, and very bright member of the party named Thrasymachus jumps into the debate. He has been listening to the others impatiently, barely able to control himself.

> What is the matter with you two, Socrates? Why do you go on in this imbecile way, politely deferring to each other's nonsense? If you really want to know what justice means, stop asking questions and scoring off the answers you get. You know very well it is easier to ask questions than to answer them. Answer yourself, and tell us what you think justice means. I won't have you telling us it is the same as what is obligatory or useful or advantageous or profitable or expedient; I want a clear and precise statement; I won't put up with that sort of verbiage.

This is a shrewd attack on Thrasymachus' part, for if he can get Socrates to advance a definition, then perhaps he can turn the tables on the master. But his own uncontrolled impetuosity gets the better of him. When Socrates turns aside the attack with a few mock-humble words, Thrasymachus cannot resist the temptation to teach the teacher. And that, as we shall see, is his downfall. Thrasymachus is no pushover for Socrates, and in a sense their debate ends in a deadlock. In this passage, however, we can see how Socrates uses Thrasymachus' own self-confidence to trip him up, just like a judo master who allows his opponent to rush at him headlong, and then with a flip of the hip tosses him on his back. Notice the ironic modesty with which Socrates turns aside Thrasymachus' blunt attacks, each time gently showing him that he has not yet thought clearly or deeply enough. The contrast between Socrates' inner quiet and Thrasymachus' tempestuousness is also intended by Plato to teach us a lesson, for he, like Socrates, believed that the truly wise man possesses a tranquility which the ignorant cannot achieve.

> Listen then, Thrasymachus began. What I say is that "just" or "right" means nothing but what is to the interest of the stronger party. Well, where is your applause? You don't mean to give it me.
>
> I will, as soon as I understand, I said. I don't see yet what you mean by right being the interest of the stronger party. For instance, Polydamas, the athlete, is stronger than we are, and it is to his interest to eat beef for the sake of his muscles; but surely you don't mean that the same diet would be good for weaker men and therefore be right for us?
>
> You are trying to be funny, Socrates. It's a low trick to take my words in the sense you think will be most damaging.
>
> No, no, I protested; but you must explain.
>
> Don't you know, then, that a state may be ruled by a despot, or a democracy, or an aristocracy?
>
> Of course.
>
> And that the ruling element is always the strongest?
>
> Yes.

Well then, in every case the laws are made by the ruling party in its own interest; a democracy makes democratic laws, a despot autocratic ones, and so on. By making these laws they define as "right" for their subjects whatever is for their own interest, and they call anyone who breaks them a "wrongdoer" and punish him accordingly. That is what I mean: in all states alike "right" has the same meaning, namely what is for the interest of the party established in power, and that is the strongest. So the sound conclusion is that what is "right" is the same everywhere: the interest of the stronger party.

Now I see what you mean, said I; whether it is true or not, I must try to make out. When you define right in terms of interest, you are yourself giving one of those answers you forbade to me; though, to be sure, you add "to the stronger party."

An insignificant addition, perhaps!

Its importance is not clear yet; what is clear is that we must find out whether your definition is true. I agree myself that right is in a sense a matter of interest; but when you add "to the stronger party," I don't know about that. I must consider.

Go ahead, then.

I will. Tell me this. No doubt you also think it is right to obey the men in power?

I do.

Are they infallible in every type of state, or can they sometimes make a mistake?

Of course they can make a mistake.

In framing laws, then, they may do their work well or badly?

No doubt.

Well, that is to say, when the laws they make are to their own interest; badly, when they are not?

Yes.

But the subjects are to obey any law they lay down, and they will then be doing right?

Of course.

If so, by your account, it will be right to do what is not to the interest of the stronger party, as well as what is so.

What's that you are saying?

Just what you said, I believe; but let us look again. Haven't you admitted that the rulers, when they enjoin certain acts on their subjects, sometimes mistake their own best interest, and at the same time that it is right for the subjects to obey, whatever they may enjoin?

Yes, I suppose so.

Well, that amounts to admitting that it is right to do what is not to the interest of the rulers or the stronger party. They may unwittingly enjoin what is to their own disadvantage; and you say it is right for the others to do as they are told. In that case, their duty must be the opposite of what you said, because the weaker will have been ordered to do what is against the interest of the stronger. You with your intelligence must see how that follows. . . .

Now, Thrasymachus, tell me, was that what you intended to say—that right means what the stronger thinks is to his interest, whether it really is so or not?

Most certainly not, he replied. Do you suppose I should speak of a man as "stronger" or "superior" at the very moment when he is making a mistake?

I did think you said as much when you admitted that rulers are not always infallible.

That is because you are a quibbler, Socrates. Would you say a man deserves to be called a physician at the moment when he makes a mistake in treating his patient and just in respect of that mistake; or a mathematician, when he does a sum wrong and just in so far as he gets a wrong result? Of course we do commonly speak of a physician or a mathematician or a scholar having made a mistake; but really none of these, I should say, is ever mistaken, in so far as he is worthy of the name we give him. So strictly speaking—and you are all for being precise—no one who practises a craft makes mistakes. A man is mistaken when his knowledge fails him; and at the moment he is no craftsman. And what is true of craftsmanship or any sort of skill is true of the ruler: he is never mistaken so long as he is acting as a ruler; though anyone might speak of a ruler making a mistake, just as he might of a physician. You must understand that I was talking in that loose way when I answered your question just now; but the precise statement is this. The ruler, in so far as he is acting as a ruler, makes no mistakes and consequently enjoins what is best for himself; and that is what the subject is to do. So, as I said at first, "right" means doing what is to the interest of the stronger.

Very well, Thrasymachus, said I. So you think I am quibbling?

I am sure you are.

You believe my questions were maliciously designed to damage your position?

I know it. But you will gain nothing by that. You cannot outwit me by cunning, and you are not the man to crush me in the open.

Bless your soul, I answered, I should not think of trying. But, to prevent any more misunderstanding, when you speak of that ruler or stronger party whose interest the weaker ought to serve, please make it clear whether you are using the words in the ordinary way or in that strict sense you have just defined.

I mean a ruler in the strictest possible sense. Now quibble away and be as malicious as you can. I want no mercy. But you are no match for me.

Do you think me mad enough to beard a lion or try to outwit a Thrasymachus?

You did try just now, he retorted, but it wasn't a success.

PLATO, *Republic*

II

I told you that Socrates spent some time when he was young studying the theories about the nature of the universe which had been developed by other Greek thinkers during the 200 years before his own time. The Greek word for world or universe is *kosmos,* so we call the study of the nature of the world *cosmology.* The study of the human condition and the study of the cosmos are the two great branches of philosophy, and there is no division more fundamental in philosophy than that between the philosophers who study the human experience and the philosophers who speculate about the order of the entire universe. (Later on, we shall see that some philosophers have tried to unite

The ancient conception of the universe as a series
of concentric spheres.

the two in a single theoretical framework, but that is getting ahead of our
story.)

The Greeks, like all peoples, had their religious myths about the creation
of the world and the origins of their civilization, but some time roughly 600
years before the birth of Christ, a number of men began to search for a more
rational, more factually well-grounded theory of the composition, order, and
origin of the world. Some of these early scientists—for that is what they were—
flourished in a city-state named Miletus on the coast of what is now Turkey,
in the eastern Mediterranean. They are known as Milesians, after their home
town, and they appear to have been the very first philosophers in what we
are calling the cosmological tradition. For various reasons, only bits and pieces
of what they wrote still survive, and most of what we know about them must
be learned indirectly from what other ancient writers say about them. They
are little more than names to us today, but perhaps it is worth telling you
their names, for we owe them an intellectual debt almost too great to calculate.
There was *Thales*, usually spoken of as the very first philosopher of all. Thales
was what we today would call an astronomer; the story is told that while walking
one evening with his eyes turned to the stars, he fell into a well, and thereby
created the myth of the absent-minded professor. But it is also said of him
that by using his superior knowledge of the weather, acquired by his astronomical

studies, he managed to corner the market in olive oil and make a fortune. Following Thales were the Milesians *Anaximander* and *Anaximenes,* who expanded and developed speculative theories about the basic components of nature and their order. Their names are strange, and we have long since lost almost all of what they wrote and said, but as you study your physics, chemistry, or astronomy, or watch a rocket lift off for yet another space probe, you might just give them a thought, for they started Western civilization on its scientific journey.

The theories of the ancient cosmologists seem odd to modern readers. When we look behind the surface detail, however, we can see some surprisingly modern ideas. The fundamental problem of the Milesians was to determine the basic stuff or component matter from which all the variety of things in the world were composed. The four categories into which they divided all things were earth, water, air, and fire. Thales claimed that at base everything in the universe was water; earth, air, and fire were simply forms of water, or water in other guises. Anaximenes, by contrast, said that everything was air. Now all of this sounds quaint and very peculiar, but suppose that we say solid instead of earth, liquid instead of water, gas instead of air, and energy instead of fire. Then we have the theory that everything in the universe is solid, liquid, gaseous, or some form of energy, and that isn't a bad guess at all! What is more, the search for some underlying element that simply *appears* in one or another of these forms has a distinctly modern ring to it. The nineteenth-century theory of the atom, for example, told us that ninety and more elements found in nature could really be reduced to differing arrangements of three basic building blocks: neutrons, protons, and electrons. The theory of subatomic particles has become much more complicated since that simple model of the atom was proposed, but the Milesian search goes on today for the building blocks of the universe.

The second great theme of the Milesians and their successors was that natural events were to be understood by appeal to natural forces, not by appeal to the actions of the gods or the interventions of some non-natural forces. The keynote of these early philosopher-scientists was that nature is natural, and in their speculations and observations, they showed remarkable shrewdness and good sense. For example, water seems to turn into ice (a solid) when it is very cold, and into steam (a gas) when it is very hot. Solid things (such as iron) which are very solid indeed, actually melt when made hot enough. All of this suggests that there is some underlying stuff which takes on different forms under different conditions.

Here is a short passage from a philosopher who lived very much later in the ancient world, but whose attention to the evidence of his senses is typical of the cosmological frame of mind. Lucretius was a Roman philosopher and poet who lived in the first century before Christ, nearly five centuries after the Milesians. He defended a cosmological theory called atomism, according to which everything in the universe, including even the human soul, is composed of little bits of matter called atoms, which are so small that they cannot be seen by the naked eye (another surprisingly modern doctrine!). As you can see, Lucretius uses a variety of familiar observations to prove that despite appearances to the contrary, all things are composed of tiny, indestructible atoms which themselves have no parts and are absolutely solid.

Now mark me: since I have taught that things cannot be born from nothing, cannot when begotten be brought back to nothing, that you may not haply yet begin in any shape to mistrust my words, because the first-beginnings of things cannot be seen by the eyes, take moreover this list of bodies which you must yourself admit are in the number of things and cannot be seen. First of all the force of the wind when aroused beats on the harbours and whelms huge ships and scatters clouds; sometimes in swift whirling eddy it scours the plains and straws them with large trees and scourges the mountain summits with forest-rending blasts: so fiercely does the wind rave with a shrill howling and rage with threatening roar. Winds therefore sure enough are unseen bodies which sweep the seas, the lands, ay and the clouds of heaven, tormenting them and catching them up in sudden whirls. On they stream and spread destruction abroad in just the same way as the soft liquid nature of water, when all at once it is borne along in an overflowing stream, and a great downfall of water from the high hills augments it with copious rains, flinging together fragments of forests and entire trees; nor can the strong bridges sustain the sudden force of coming water: in such wise turbid with much rain the river dashes upon the piers with mighty force: makes havoc with loud noise and rolls under its eddies huge stones: wherever aught opposes its waves, down it dashes it. In this way then must the blasts of wind as well move on, and when they like a mighty stream have borne down in any direction, they push things before them and throw them down with repeated assaults, sometimes catch them up in curling eddy and carry them away in swift-circling whirl. Wherefore once and again I say winds are unseen bodies, since in their works and ways they are found to rival great rivers which are of a visible body. Then again we perceive the different smells of things, yet never see them coming to our nostrils; nor do we behold heats nor can we observe cold with the eyes nor are we used to see voices. Yet all these things must consist of a bodily nature, since they are able to move the senses; for nothing but body can touch and be touched. Again clothes hung up on a shore which waves break upon become moist, and then get dry if spread out in the sun. Yet it has not been seen in what way the moisture of water has sunk into them nor again in what way this has been dispelled by heat. The moisture therefore is dispersed into small particles which the eyes are quite unable to see. Again after the revolution of many of the sun's years a ring on the finger is thinned on the under side by wearing, the dripping from the eaves hollows a stone, the bent ploughshare of iron imperceptibly decreases in the fields, and we behold the stone-paved streets worn down by the feet of the multitude; the brass statues too at the gates show their right hands to be wasted by the touch of the numerous passers by who greet them. These things then we see are lessened, since they have been thus worn down; but what bodies depart at any given time the nature of vision has jealously shut out our seeing. Lastly the bodies which time and nature add to things by little and little, constraining them to grow in due measure, no exertion of the eyesight can behold; and so too wherever things grow old by age and decay, and when rocks hanging over the sea are eaten away by the gnawing salt spray, you cannot see what they lose at any given moment. Nature therefore works by unseen bodies.

LUCRETIUS, *On the Nature of Things*

Cosmological speculation goes on today, as it did 2500 years ago. From the earliest times, philosophers have been actively involved in the experimental and theoretical advances of what today we call science. Indeed, it is difficult to say just where hard science leaves off and speculative, philosophical cosmology begins. Thales himself, for example, was said to have discovered a method for measuring the height of the Egyptian pyramids, by waiting until the precise hour of the day when a body's shadow was equal to its height. Anaximander devised an instrument known as a gnomon, a rod whose shadow permits us to calculate the direction and height of the sun. The great fourth-century B.C. philosopher Aristotle, pupil and follower of Plato, virtually invented the science of formal logic, and made significant contributions to what we would today call taxonomy. Plato's school of followers, the Academy, did important work in the branch of mathematics known as solid geometry. Two thousand years later, René Descartes, the French philosopher and scientist, invented analytic geometry (which we still study in school today) as a tool for analyzing and giving expression to his theory of the nature of the material universe. His successor, Gottfried Leibniz, invented a version of the differential calculus as part of his dispute with Descartes about the nature of matter. In our own century, the logicians and philosophers Bertrand Russell and Alfred North Whitehead established the modern discipline of mathematical logic with their monumental *Principia Mathematica*. Throughout the entire course of Western civilization, philosophical speculation, scientific experiment, and pure logical and mathematical theorizing have advanced together, often in the writings of the same thinkers, sometimes in the very same works. The philosophical enterprise begun by the ancient Milesians has borne splendid fruit, both in an expanded scientific understanding of nature and in a refined conceptual sophistication about those original questions of the nature and order of the cosmos. Before leaving our discussion of this great tradition of philosophical thought, let us read a few selections of modern cosmology. The first deals with the microcosm—the unimaginably tiny bits of stuff from which all else in the universe is compounded. These speculations, we may imagine, are the lineal descendants of the ancient atomistic theories of Democritus, Epicurus, and the Roman Lucretius. The second deals with the macrocosm, the universe as a whole, and specifically with its origins. It traces its lineage to the inspired guesses of the Milesians and their followers.

In this century it has been possible to describe the atom as a hard core surrounded by orbiting electrons; and then the atomic nucleus appeared as a composite of neutrons and protons held together by a short-range force much stronger than

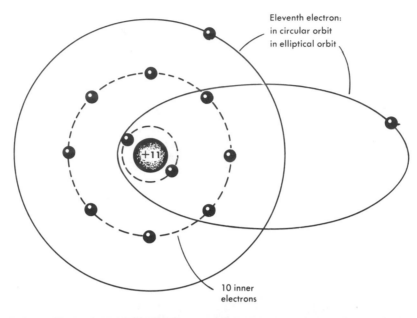

Eleventh electron:
in circular orbit
in elliptical orbit

+11

10 inner
electrons

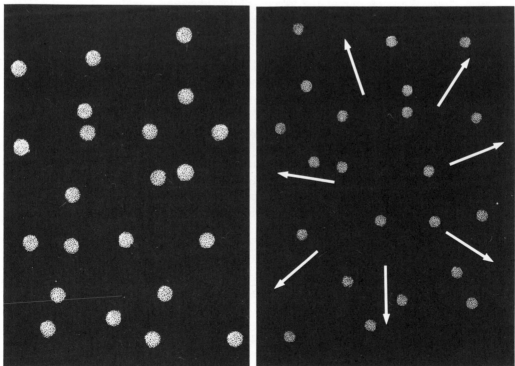

The inner structure of the atom, according to modern physicists.

the electric force which would tend to push them apart. Both these concepts are easy to visualize.

But with the elementary particles, including neutrons and protons, physicists just don't know what the underlying causes of behavior are.

On the other hand, they have discovered more than a hundred particles, many of them created in high-energy accelerators and existing for only a fraction of an instant. They have catalogued them and classified them according to their mass, their electric charge, the way they spin, and various other qualities.

They have found that some of the particles can be organized in groups of eight or ten with similar properties. But understanding, as well as explanations of inconsistencies in the groupings, remain elusive.

One promising concept, which however hasn't yielded very good numerical results, is that the particles that are subject to the strong force binding nucleus are made up out of each other, so that none of them is fundamental.

The basis for this theory, called the bootstrap hypothesis, comes from the way forces are applied between particles. Physicists found they could describe electromagnetic forces by saying that charged particles exchanged another particle, called a photon, and by this means exerted electromagnetic force on each other.

The strong forces are also exerted by exchanging particles other than photons. What the bootstrap theory suggests is that any strongly interacting particle can serve as the means of exerting strong forces between two others. When two particles exert a strong force, they create another, producing a bound system; and that system, according to the theory, is the created particle.

Another theory, easier to visualize but extremely unlikely to be more than a mathematical tool, is the . . . quark model, which holds that the particles are made up of combinations of two or three different kinds of sub-particles.

Developed by Dr. [Murray] Gell-Mann, the quark hypothesis predicts the grouping of particles into already observed sets of eight and ten.

Science News

Cosmology attempts to deduce the history of the universe from astronomical observation. Its great difficulty is that the events concerned take millions or billions of years to work themselves out, and it is therefore hard to observe the history in progress and be exactly sure what one is seeing.

Modern cosmologists are left with two general classes of theory: the so-called big bang or cosmic fireball and the steady-state or continuous creation theories.

In the middle 1960s radio astronomical observations provided evidence that was taken as very dramatic support for the big-bang theory, and the buildup of data became so convincing to many cosmologists that they were ready to bury the rival steady-state theory. Recent observations in infra-red light, which have been possible only in the last few years, give proponents of the steady-state ammunition to strike back.

The difference between the two theories rests on the density of the universe. If the universe has been expanding for any length of time, everyone agrees there must have been a time when it was very small, and the question is: Did it then have the same amount of matter as it has now?

If it did, then the pressure temperature and density were beyond anything imaginable today. This is the cosmic fireball and its physical conditions suggest that it must have exploded and thus given the impetus for the expansion now seen.

The other side says that this did not happen. The matter in the universe was always as dense as it is now, and therefore there was never a hot high-density state. This requires that matter be added as the universe expands. It can be continually created out of nothing or pumped in from some realm beneath the universe, possibly through galaxy centers. . . .

The source of matter for galactic expansion . . . could be some kind of continuous creation or pumping-in process at the centers. Some of the matter is annihilated at or near the source; some survives to build up the galaxy.

Acceptance of this idea immediately raises the problem of antimatter. According to currently accepted laws of particle physics, when matter is created, so is an equal amount of antimatter.

There is no observational evidence for any large amounts of antimatter in the visible universe. On the other hand, there is no observational evidence against its presence. An antistar would look precisely like a star, so there is no way to tell. . . .

Meanwhile the evidence on which the proponents of the big-bang theory based their jubilation a few years ago remains, though its interpretation is more and more questioned. Radio astronomers had found a background of radio waves whose spectrum corresponded to a perfect thermal radiator or blackbody at a temperature of three degrees above absolute zero (SN: 7/5, p. 9). Existence of such a blackbody background is a prediction of the big-bang theory, and the discovery seemed to be evidence for it.

There are other possible interpretations of this radio spectrum, although the blackbody is the simplest. Extension of the observations into the infrared was eagerly awaited since it was in this range that the background's blackbody character should show up unmistakably.

The infrared observations so far have not been happy for the blackbody enthusiasts. The first of them showed background infrared fluxes, which, if they were thermal, were hotter than three degrees. These could be explained away as the background plus something else . . .

The battle between the rival cosmologies is far from over, but with the advent of infrared observations it is becoming clear that the steady-state theory, over which some cosmologists were reading funeral orations a few years ago, is very much alive again.

Science News

One final point before we move on. Thales, Anaximander and the rest are called "philosophers" in dictionaries of biography or histories of Western thought. But if you look up Murray Gell-Mann in *Who's Who,* you will find him listed as a physicist. Why is it that cosmological questions are investigated by scientists today, although they were investigated by philosophers 2000 years ago? Is this just what labor unions call a "jurisdictional dispute" or has some important theoretical change taken place here?

The most common answer to this question is that "philosophy" used to include just about everything that men and women did by way of systematic, reasoned investigation of the heavens, the earth, or the human condition. In the writings of Plato, Aristotle, and the other ancients we find discussions which today would be labeled physics, mathematics, astronomy, biology, psychology, economics, political science, sociology, anthropology, theology, and even engineering. Over the past two millennia, one after another of these branches of human knowledge has pulled itself together, broken off from "philosophy," and established itself as an independent discipline with its own rules of inquiry, objects of investigation, and theoretical framework. Philosophy today, according to this way of looking at things, is what remains after all the intellectual children have left home. Roughly speaking, that reduces philosophy to conceptual analysis plus some armchair speculation on whatever the other sciences haven't laid claim to yet.

There is another view, however, which seems to me to be a good deal closer to the truth. Philosophy, it holds, is the systematic reflection of the mind upon the criteria of right thought and right action which it employs in all of its activities. On this view, there is a "philosophical" component to virtually everything we do. Political scientists (and politicians too), scientists, artists, economists, and astronomers all need to reflect on the nature of their enterprises, and the people officially called philosophers are simply those among us who concentrate their attention on this self-critical or reflective side of our intellectual undertakings.

III

Although the study of the human condition and the study of the cosmos are the two great themes of Western philosophy, it must not be supposed that they developed in an unconnected way. Philosophers are, above all else, seekers after unity. Where human experience presents a manyness, they seek the underlying oneness. In the long history of Western thought, philosophers have tried two basically different strategies for bringing the two branches of philosophy into some interconnected whole.

The first strategy was tried by some of the earliest philosophers, among whom were a group known as Stoics. The Stoics claimed that the natural world exhibited a rational order which could be explained by appeal to the existence and operations of a power of reason, which they called *logos*. (We get our word *logic* from this term, and also the word ending -ology, meaning "study of.") In the cosmos, this logos was often identified with what we today would call God, but it could also be identified with the power of reason in each human being. Therein lies the principle that bridged the gap between the study of human nature and the study of physical nature, for the very same fundamental logos or rational order which made itself known in the order of the planets, the succession of the seasons, and the regular behavior of natural bodies in

To medieval thinkers, as God ruled the world, so the king ruled society, and reason in each individual ruled the passions. The art of that period reflects this hierarchical view of the universe.

space and time also exhibited itself in our capacity for logical reasoning, in our ability to control our passions by the power of our understanding, and in the proper order and arrangement of men and women in a stable, just, and rationally ordered society. Our power of reason was said to be a "spark" or fragment of the divine Logos which informed and governed the universe. Eventually, this ancient Greek doctrine was taken up into the theology of the Christian, Jewish, and Muslim religions, and became the basis for much of the religious theology that flourished in the Middle Ages.

After studying cosmology as a youth, Socrates turned away from it, convinced that the proper study for us is our own nature. But if the Stoics were correct, then a philosopher could study human nature and physical nature together, for the same principles that explained the arrangements of the heavenly bodies would, properly understood, also explain how we should live our lives within a well-ordered set of social arrangements.

The unifying doctrine of the Stoics gave rise to one of the most important philosophical ideas in Western thought—the idea of *natural law.* God, or the power of Reason, created the universe in accordance with a rational idea of the proper form and order of its organization. On the cosmic level, this conception determined the existence, nature, and relative positions of the stars, the sun, the moon, and the earth. At the social level, this same idea determined the appropriate hierarchy of classes and statuses from the king or emperor down to the lowliest serf. Within each individual human being, the same idea determined the relative order and importance of the rational, passional, and appetitive elements of the soul. Human beings were unique in the natural order by virtue of their possession of a spark of that logos or reason, for it permitted them at one and the same time to understand the grand plan and also to live their own lives freely and responsibly in conformity with it.

MARCUS AURELIUS (121–180 A.D.) was one of the most remarkable men to hold the exalted position of Roman Emperor. For almost five centuries, Rome ruled a vast empire stretching from Great Britain through what is now Western Europe, entirely around the shores of the Mediterranean Sea, and deep into northern Africa and the Middle East. Marcus was both a gifted and successful general, winning many battles against the barbarian tribes who repeatedly attacked Rome's border provinces; and also a wise and thoughtful philosopher, learned in the writings of the Greeks and his Roman predecessors, and without illusions about the fleetingness of the power and glory which were his as emperor. During the second century after the birth of Christ, the empire persecuted the followers of that Eastern prophet, and Marcus, despite (or perhaps even because of) his commitment to Stoicism, carried forward these persecutions. It was not until more than a century later, with the conversion of the Emperor Constantine, that Christianity ceased to be the object of official attack, and became instead the established religion of the Roman Empire.

Among the greatest of the ancient Stoics was a Roman emperor who ruled from 161 to 180 A.D. Marcus Aurelius combined great skill as a general and ruler with a contemplative nature. His reflections on the universe and our brief stay in it have come down to us in the form of a series of meditations. Following are a few selections which convey the themes and something of the flavor of his thought.

Constantly regard the universe as one living being, having one substance and one soul; and observe how all things have reference to one perception, the perception of this one living being; and how all things act with one movement; and how all things are the co-operating causes of all things which exist; observe too the continuous spinning of the thread and the contexture of the web.

The intelligence of the universe is social. Accordingly it has made the inferior things for the sake of the superior, and it has fitted the superior to one another. Thou seest how it has subordinated, co-ordinated and assigned to everything its proper portion, and has brought together into concord with one another the things which are the best.

All things are implicated with one another, and the bond is holy; and there is hardly anything unconnected with any other thing. For things have been co-ordinated, and they combine to form the same universe (order). For there is one universe made up of all things, and one God who pervades all things, and one substance, and one law, one common reason in all intelligent animals, and one truth; if indeed there is also one perfection for all animals which are of the same stock and participate in the same reason.

To the rational animal the same act is according to nature and according to reason.

MARCUS AURELIUS, *Meditations*

Thus, the first strategy devised by philosophers for uniting the study of human nature with the study of physical nature was the Stoic doctrine of natural law. The second strategy was worked out 2000 years later by a brilliant group of seventeenth- and eighteenth-century philosophers in the British Isles and on the continent of Europe. We shall be taking a close look at some of their theories in Chapter Seven when we talk about the branch of philosophy known as the "theory of knowledge." In this introductory look at the nature of philosophy in general, we ought nevertheless to try to form some preliminary idea of what they were doing, for their ideas and their writings have been among the most influential in the entire literature of Western thought.

The key to the new strategy was a very simple, very powerful idea: The universe is vast, and ten thousand generations would be too short a time to say everything that can be learned about it; but every single fact, every theory, every insight, guess, hypothesis, or deduction is *an idea in the human mind.* So instead of turning our eyes outward to the universe, let us turn our eyes inward to the nature of the human mind itself. Let us study *the way in which* we know, rather than *what* we know. The universe may be infinite, but the mind is finite. What is more (these philosophers thought), though the universe is infinitely varied, the human mind is everywhere and always exactly the same. (They hadn't yet heard of evolution, or the variation in conceptual frameworks from culture to culture.) Instead of writing many books on cosmology, physics, psychology, politics, morals, and religion they needed to write just one book on the powers, capacities, forms, and limits of the human mind. So during the seventeenth and eighteenth centuries, we find titles like the following cropping up in the philosophical literature: *An Essay Concerning Human Understanding,* by the Englishman John Locke; *Principles of Human Knowledge,* by the Irishman George Berkeley; *A Treatise of Human Nature,* by the Scotsman David Hume; and the greatest of them all, *A Critique of Pure Reason,* by the Prussian Immanuel Kant.

Now, it might look at first glance as though these philosophers had simply taken Socrates' advice to forget about the study of physical nature and seek instead a knowledge of human nature. But that would be a mistake, for the British empiricists (as Locke, Berkeley, Hume, and their lesser compatriots are called) and the Continental rationalists (Descartes, Leibniz, Kant, and their fellow philosophers) had got their hands on a wholly different way of doing philosophy. Socrates never imagined that we could learn something about the natural sciences by studying ourselves. He simply thought that the search for the just and happy life was more important than speculation about the elements of the universe or the origin of the order of the heavenly bodies. The British empiricists and Continental rationalists, by contrast, thought they had found a device for combining the study of human nature and the study of the universe in one single philosophical enterprise. If they could learn *how* we know—whether it is by looking with our eyes, touching with our hands, and listening with our ears, or whether it is by reasoning with our minds and ignoring the evidence of our senses, or perhaps whether it is by some combining of what the senses tell us with what reason tells us—if philosophy could study the process of knowledge rather than getting all tangled up in the details of particular bits of knowledge of this and that, then maybe philosophy could give us some very general answers to such questions as, Can we know anything at all? How much can we know? Can we know about things that happened before we were born, or somewhere else in space? Can we know that things *must* happen the way they do, or must we simply say, "This happens, and then this . . ." and let it go at that? Can we know about things we can't see or feel, like atoms, or the unconscious, or even God? Can one person know for sure that there are other persons in the world, and not just bodies that look like persons? Can I, myself, be sure that the whole world isn't simply my dream? All these questions, and many more besides, might be answered by a systematic study of the human mind itself. In this way, the study of physical nature would be combined with the study of human nature, not through a theory of universal logos or intelligence, as the Stoics thought, but through a theory of how we know.

One of the best statements of the new strategy is to be found in the introduction to David Hume's great work, *A Treatise of Human Nature.* Hume was a Scotsman, born in 1711. The *Treatise,* in three volumes, was published in 1739 and 1740, when Hume was not yet thirty years old! There are three important points to notice in the following passage from Hume's *Treatise.* First, as we have already remarked, the basic idea of Hume's strategy is to turn the multiplic-

DAVID HUME (1711–1776) was one of those precocious philosophers whose greatest work was done early in life. Born and reared near Edinburgh in Scotland, Hume attended Edinburgh University, where he studied the new physics of Isaac Newton and the new philosophy of John Locke. When still a teenager, Hume conceived the idea of developing a full-scale theory of human nature along the lines of Newton's revolutionary theory of physical nature. After what seems to have been some sort of mental breakdown, Hume went to France to rest and recover, and while there he wrote his first and greatest book, the monumental *Treatise of Human Nature*.

Hume went on to become an extremely popular and successful essayist and man of letters. His six-volume *History of England* established his reputation as the first major modern historian. Nevertheless, his sceptical doubts about religion and his attacks on the metaphysical doctrines of his Continental and British predecessors earned him many enemies. One of his most brilliant works, twelve *Dialogues Concerning Natural Religion,* was only published after his death. His friends, including the economist Adam Smith, persuaded him that the book was too controversial, and might permanently damage his reputation.

As you can see from the portrait of Hume, the lightness and quickness of his mind was entirely hidden by the lumpishness of his appearance. Nature often plays such tricks on us!

ity of sciences and fields of study into a unified examination of human nature and the mind's power of knowing. Second, Hume thinks that he shall have to study "the nature of the ideas we employ," for it is from those ideas that we form whatever judgments we wish to make in physics, religion, politics, or morals. And finally, Hume says, he shall have to examine "the operations we perform in our reasonings." In Chapter Seven, we shall see that this distinction between the nature of our ideas, on the one hand, and the nature of our reasonings with our ideas, on the other, is an important weapon in the strategy of the new theorists of knowledge.

● Reading selections from the works of the great philosophers is a bit like watching videotape replays of great football stars. Since we know who made it to stardom, it is easy for us to spot their greatness from the very first. But let us have a little pity for the poor book reviewer who was handed an anonymous work entitled *A Treatise of Human Nature* and told to write a brief review of it in a few weeks. Here is what one nameless unfortunate had to say about Hume's *Treatise,* in a literary journal rather imposingly called *A History of the Works of the Learned.*

. . . A Man, who has never had the Pleasure of reading Mr. Locke's incomparable Essay, will peruse our author with much less Disgust, than those can who have been used to the irresistible Reasoning and wonderful Perspicuity of that admirable Writer.

Poor Hume was so upset by the negative reviews of the *Treatise* that later in life he disowned it, saying that it was merely a first effort of his youth. How many of us, I wonder, would recognize the greatness of a new book of philosophy within months of its publication? ●

It is evident, that all the sciences have a relation, greater or less, to human nature; and that, however wide any of them may seem to run from it, they still return back by one passage or another. Even *Mathematics, Natural Philosophy,* and *Natural Religion,* are in some measure dependent on the science of MAN; since they lie under the cognisance of men, and are judged of by their powers and faculties. It is impossible to tell what changes and improvements we might make in these sciences were we thoroughly acquainted with the extent and force of human understanding, and could explain the nature of the ideas we employ, and of the operations we perform in our reasonings. And these improvements are the more to be hoped for in natural religion, as it is not content with instructing us in the nature of superior powers, but carries its views further, to their disposition towards us, and our duties towards them; and consequently, we ourselves are not only the beings that reason, but also one of the objects concerning which we reason.

If, therefore, the sciences of mathematics, natural philosophy, and natural religion, have such a dependence on the knowledge of man, what may be expected in the other sciences, whose connection with human nature is more close and intimate? The sole end of logic is to explain the principles and operations of our reasoning faculty, and the nature of our ideas; morals and criticism regard our tastes and sentiments; and politics consider men as united in society, and dependent on each other. In these four sciences of *Logic, Morals, Criticism,* and *Politics,* is comprehended almost everything which it can anyway import us to be acquainted with, or which can tend either to the improvement or ornament of the human mind.

Here then is the only expedient, from which we can hope for success in our philosophical researches, to leave the tedious lingering method, which we have hitherto followed, and, instead of taking now and then a castle or village on the frontier, to march up directly to the capital or centre of these sciences, to human nature itself; which being once masters of, we may everywhere else hope for an easy victory.

From this station we may extend our conquests over all those sciences, which more intimately concern human life, and may afterwards proceed at leisure, to discover more fully those which are the objects of pure curiosity. There is no question of importance, whose decision is not comprised in the science of man; and there is none, which can be decided with any certainty, before we become acquainted with that science. In pretending, therefore, to explain the principles of human nature, we in effect propose a complete system of the sciences, built on a foundation almost entirely new, and the only one upon which they can stand with any security.

DAVID HUME, *A Treatise of Human Nature*

The new study of the mind's capacity for knowing came to be called *epistemology,* from the Greek for the study or science (-ology) of knowledge *(episteme).* It was not to be merely descriptive, like psychology, however. Its purpose was to settle some ancient philosophical disputes by finding out what we can legitimately claim to know, and what we can not claim to know because our claims carry us beyond the limits of the powers of the mind. This *critical* dimension of the new strategy extended across the entire spectrum of philosophical investigations, as the passage from Hume's *Treatise* indicates. In a brief excerpt from Immanuel Kant's *Critique of Pure Reason,* you can get some sense of what a dramatic challenge the new critical epistemology was to established ways of thinking.

We often hear complaints of shallowness of thought in our age and of the consequent decline of sound science. But I do not see that the sciences which rest upon a secure foundation, such as mathematics, physics, etc., in the least deserve this reproach. On the contrary, they merit their old reputation for solidity, and, in the case of physics, even surpass it. The same spirit would have become active in other kinds of knowledge, if only attention had first been directed to the determination of their principles. Till this is done, indifference, doubt, and, in the final issue, severe criticism, are themselves proofs of a profound habit of thought. Our age is, in especial degree, the age of criticism, and to criticism everything must submit. Religion through its sanctity, and law-giving through its majesty, may seek to exempt themselves from it. But they then awaken just suspicion, and cannot claim the sincere respect which reason accords only to that which has been able to sustain the test of free and open examination.

IMMANUEL KANT, *A Critique of Pure Reason*

IV

From the very beginning, philosophers have been objects of suspicion and even ridicule. Socrates was satirized in a play by the brilliant comic poet Aristophanes as a man with his head in the clouds who talked in a crazy fashion about nonsensical matters. We have already seen that the very first philosopher, Thales, acquired the reputation of being absent-minded. Usually, philosophers are accused of quibbling about questions so divorced from any genuine human concern that only someone unfit for real life would make his living worrying about them.

Needless to say, I don't think this caricature of philosophy has much truth in it; otherwise, I would hardly have spent my own life thinking about philosophical questions. But it is not hard to see how the notion has gained popularity. Suppose that I say to you: Four is two plus two. Four is also three plus one. Therefore two plus two is three plus one. All right, you would answer. Perfectly reasonable. If A is B and A is C then B must be C. Right? Fine, I go on. Socrates is wise, and Socrates is ugly. Therefore Wisdom must be Ugliness! Now right there, you know you have been had. Something has gone badly wrong.

Here's another one. Yesterday, I remembered seeing a friend of mine, but after thinking about it for a moment, I realized I must have been remembering a dream, because my friend has been in Europe for two years. Last night I dreamed that I was the king of Persia, and at the time it was so real I could fairly smell the incense and hear the court musicians! It would seem that sometimes, when we think we are awake, we are really dreaming; and some of the things we think we actually remember doing are just recollections of dreams. So maybe everything I see, touch, smell, and hear is a dream. Maybe my whole life is a dream, and I have never been awake. Well, there you are again! I start out with some perfectly reasonable premise and end with a conclusion so wild that only a philosopher would take it seriously.

Peculiar puzzles and strange counterintuitive conclusions have been popping up in philosophical books ever since the days of the ancient Milesians, but somehow the arguments of the British empiricists and the Continental rationalists in the seventeenth and eighteenth centuries contained more really puzzling statements than was usual even for philosophers. Somewhat in reaction to their way of doing philosophy, a gifted Austrian mathematician and philosopher named Ludwig Wittgenstein developed a new and extremely controversial theory of what philosophical problems are and what we ought to do about them. Wittgenstein (1889–1951) suggested that a philosophical problem is a sort of cross between a logical confusion, a grammatical mistake, and a neurosis. Philosophers start off using language in a perfectly proper way to talk about the world, and then they formulate a question or propose a thesis which *sounds* all right but is really odd in some way. Instead of realizing that they have gone wrong, however, they press right on, drawing more and more bizarre conclusions, obsessed with the seeming plausibility of their own words.

For example, it makes perfectly good sense to ask, How high is the Empire State Building? How high is the moon? But it makes no sense to ask, How high is up? That is just a child's joke. Well, it also makes perfectly good sense to ask, was that a dream or did I really see my friend? Am I dreaming now,

LUDWIG WITTGENSTEIN (1889–1951) was born in Vienna, and spent his formative years in Austria. He wrote virtually all his philosophical works in German, but his principal influence has been on English and American philosophy, where he is probably the single most important philosophical thinker of the twentieth century. After early training in engineering, Wittgenstein turned to mathematical logic, under the influence of the work of the Englishman Bertrand Russell. Eventually Wittgenstein came to Cambridge, England, where he spent much of his adult life.

His highly original research in logic led Wittgenstein to a theory of language, truth, and meaning which he set forth, in a laconic and distinctive style, in his *Tractatus Logicc—Philosophicus*. This was the only philosophical book published by Wittgenstein during his lifetime, but he wrote great quantities of philosophy which appeared posthumously. Later in life, he thoroughly reversed his own earlier theories, and set forth a new account of language and meaning in his *Philosophical Investigations*. Wittgenstein was an intense, brooding man who made so deep an impression on his students and colleagues that even now, a quarter of a century after his death, there are many distinguished English and American philosophers who still consider themselves his disciples.

or am I really the king of Persia? But perhaps it *doesn't* make sense to ask, Is my whole life a dream? That question *looks* sensible enough, but then, so does How high is up?

Wittgenstein proposed that philosophers treat their problems as symptoms of a conceptual disorder rather than as subjects for investigation and debate. Whenever we come upon someone who is really mesmerized by a philosophical problem, we ought to try to relieve her of her distress by dissolving the problem, by showing her where she went wrong and how she can get back onto the path of talking ordinary common sense. These two statements from Wittgenstein's book, *Philosophical Investigations,* capture the spirit of his approach:

My aim is: to teach you to pass from a piece of disguised nonsense to something that is patent nonsense.

The philosopher's treatment of a question is like the treatment of an illness.

The second statement suggests that philosophers ought really to be in the business of putting themselves out of business! If philosophical puzzles are like illnesses, then the sooner we cure the people who have come down with a bad case of philosophy, the sooner there will be no philosophy left to cure. Odd as it may seem, Wittgenstein is not the only great philosopher to claim that his philosophy would put philosophy out of business. Immanuel Kant thought roughly the same thing.

V

Philosophy is a reflective self-examination of the principles of the just and happy life, says Socrates. Philosophy is a study of the universe, its origins, elements, and laws, say the ancient cosmologists and their modern descendants. Philosophy is a search for the rational principles that bind the universe and human life together into a single, logical whole, say the Stoics and many others. Philosophy is a critique and dissection of the mind's power to know, say the epistemologists of the seventeenth and eighteenth centuries. Philosophy is a conceptual disease of which we should be cured, says Wittgenstein. It would seem that there couldn't be five more dissimilar conceptions of philosophy imaginable. On second look, however, we see that they all have something in common. They all say philosophy is something you *think about,* not something you *do* something about. Philosophers are dreamers, popular opinion has it, even if they don't think that all of life is a dream. Philosophers sit in their cozy studies, or in their ivory towers.

Strange as it may seem, the most devastating criticism of philosophy as mere do-nothing talk that anyone has ever made was written by, of all people, Plato! You will remember that Plato came from a wealthy and powerful Athenian family, and the normal thing for the son of such a family to do was to go into politics, to participate in the public life of Athens. Roughly in middle life, Plato was faced with a hard choice: whether to go on with his philosophical studies, gathering around him the group of followers and fellow thinkers with whom he had been spending his time; or to give up philosophy and take his natural place in the affairs of his city-state. Plato had already begun to write the Dialogues for which he is famous, and so in one of them, *Gorgias,* he talked about the problem indirectly. The Dialogue is really three arguments between Socrates and a series of opponents (a bit like an elimination match). A famous teacher and lecturer, Gorgias, has come to town, bragging that he can give a public speech on any subject his audience wants to hear about. Socrates takes him on, and suggests that Gorgias explain to them what *rhetoric* is. The discussion becomes a more general examination of the nature of the good life, and as we might expect, Gorgias is no match for Socrates. Very quickly, he gets tangled up in his own definitions, and Socrates has little trouble throwing him verbally to the mat. Then one of Gorgias' disciples, a young man named Polus, steps in. He isn't really any brighter than Gorgias, but he is full of self-confident enthusiasm, and he manages a few tussles with Socrates before he too is thrown. Now the real antagonist steps forward. He is a gifted young man named Callicles, with a quick wit, a sharp mind, and much of the same impatience that we saw at the beginning of this chapter in Thrasymachus. The remainder of the Dialogue is a knock-down, drag-out match between Callicles and Socrates, and Plato puts so many good arguments into Callicles' mouth that we cannot really say either man is the final winner. During one of his several long speeches (Callicles tends to talk too long, not answering Socrates' questions), Callicles ridicules Socrates for spending his time philosophizing instead of engaging in grown-up and manly pursuits, such as politics. Dramatically, this passage is an attack by Callicles on Socrates, but because Plato wrote both sides, he is really arguing with himself about what he ought to do in his own life. As you know, Plato decided to continue talking and writing philosophy, but it is a part of his greatness that he can give such witty expression to the opposing point of view.

Here, then, you have the truth of the matter. You will become convinced of it if you only let philosophy alone and pass on to more important considerations. Of course, Socrates, philosophy does have a certain charm if one engages with it in one's youth and in moderation; but if one dallies overlong, it's the ruin of a fellow. If a man, however well endowed, goes on philosophizing throughout his life, he will never come to taste the experiences which a man must have if he's going to be a gentleman and have the world look up to him. You know perfectly well that philosophers know nothing about state laws and regulations. They are equally ignorant of the conversational standards that we have to adopt in dealing with our fellow men at home and abroad. Why, they are inexperienced even in human pleasures and desires! In a word, they are totally innocent of all human character. So, when they come to take part in either a private or a public affair, they make themselves ridiculous—just as ridiculous, I dare say, as men of affairs may be when they get involved in your quibbles, your 'debates.' . . .

But the best course, no doubt, is to be a participant in both. It's an excellent thing to grasp as much philosophy as one needs for an education, and it's no disgrace to play the philosopher while you're young; but if one grows up and becomes a man and still continues in the subject, why, the whole thing becomes ridiculous, Socrates. My own feeling toward its practitioners is very much the same as the way I feel toward men who lisp and prattle like a child. When I see a child, who ought to be talking that way, lisping and prattling, I'm pleased, it strikes me as a pleasant sign of good breeding and suitable to the child's age; and when I hear a little lad speaking distinctly, it seems to me disagreeable and offends my ears as a mark of servile origin. So, too, when I hear a grown man prattling and lisping, it seems ridiculous and unmanly; one would like to strike him hard! And this is exactly the feeling I have about students of philosophy. When I perceive philosophical activity in a young lad, I am pleased; it suits him, I think, and shows that he has good breeding. A boy who doesn't play with philosophy I regard as illiberal, a chap who will never raise himself to any fine or noble action. Whereas when I see an older man still at his philosophy and showing no sign of giving it up, that one seems to me, Socrates, to be asking for some hard knocks! For, as I said just now, such a man, even if he's well endowed by nature, must necessarily become unmanly by avoiding the center of the city and the assemblies where as the Poet says, "men win distinction." Such a fellow must spend the rest of his life skulking in corners, whispering with two or three little lads, never pronouncing any large, liberal, or meaningful utterance.

PLATO, *Gorgias*

Now that you are launched into the study of philosophy, it might help you to know what is coming up in the chapters ahead. Chapters Two, Three, Four, and Five are devoted to philosophical investigations of various aspects of the human condition, including ethics, social philosophy, political philosophy, and the philosophy of art. Chapter Six combines an examination of the nature and existence of God with an analysis of the subjective character of religious experience. Chapter Seven explores the efforts by the great epistemologists to study the nature of the universe through analysis of the cognitive powers of the human mind. Chapter Eight, finally, takes us back to the ancient issues of cosmology and metaphysics, but in a more modern form. As you work through the book, you will get some sense of the enormous variety of ways in which philosophers have grappled with the mysteries of physical and human nature.

During the first twenty-two or twenty-three centuries of its long life, philosophy staked out the largest possible territory for itself. The great philosophers, as we have seen, sought to grasp the inner nature of the physical universe, the fundamental principles of the good life, the foundations of mathematics, and even the nature and existence of God Himself. Beginning in the eighteenth century, however, philosophy's pretensions came under progressively harsher attack. Skeptical doubts about our ability to know anything at all are as old as the ancient Greeks, and they have been revived periodically during the history of philosophy, often with rather devastating effects. In the eighteenth century, however, new and powerful assaults were launched on philosophy's claim to give us knowledge of God. These attacks, as we shall see in Chapter Six, called into question the very possibility of a rational understanding of the transcendent origins of the universe.

At the same time, what we now know as the natural and social sciences began to separate themselves from philosophy, establishing themselves as independent disciplines with their own methodologies, their own traditions, and even—in schools and universities—their own professorships. Sir Isaac Newton, the great seventeenth-century English physicist, was referred to by his contemporaries as a "natural philosopher," and Adam Smith, who founded modern economics a century later, was a professor of "moral philosophy" at Glasgow in Scotland. In the nineteenth century, Newton would have been called a physicist, Smith an economist, and neither would have been thought to be a philosopher at all!

As physics, chemistry, biology, astronomy, mathematics, economics, sociology, anthropology, history, and pyschology split off from philosophy to become separate disciplines, there seemed to be less and less left as the proper territory of philosophy itself. It began to look as though philosophy was simply a staging area for new disciplines, a waiting room in which branches of human knowledge bided their time until they were ready to be born as genuine sciences. Yet surely that could not be true. Were Plato, Aristotle, St. Thomas Aquinas, Bacon, Hobbes, Locke, Berkeley, Hume, Descartes, Spinoza, Leibniz, and Kant nothing more than physicists, mathematicians, sociologists, or psychologists before their time?

Philosophers responded to this challenge in one or another of at least five different ways. Some simply accepted the new intellectual order of things, and plunged into substantive work in one of the new disciplines. Others, especially in the nineteenth century, made a desperate, brilliant last-ditch effort to defend philosophy as an overarching study of the totality of being as such. This, in effect, was a sort of theology without religion, and despite the heroic intellectual performance of such immortal philosophers as Georg Wilhelm Friedrich Hegel, it was doomed to failure. Either a philosophy of *being as such* is theology, in which case it is fatally prone to the skeptical attacks that Hume, Kant, and others had mounted against rational theology; or else it is a science of the universe, in which case astronomers armed with telescopes and physicists armed with linear accelerators and electron microscopes are better equipped to handle the subject.

One school of philosophers (the so-called logical positivists) redefined philosophy as a study of the methodology and logical structure of the natural sciences. This preserved a small territory for philosophy, but it made the once-proud discipline very much of a hanger-on at the scientist's laboratory or study.

Another closely allied school of philosophers defined philosophy, rather more broadly, as a logical analysis of the modes of reasoning and forms of judgment in all the branches of human knowledge, not merely in the natural sciences. "Analytic philosophy," as it came to be called, flourished in Great Britain and the United States, and is now probably the dominant form of philosophizing among professional philosophers in the English-speaking world.

Now, all of these redefinitions of philosophy had deep roots and long histories in traditional philosophy. It was not at all hard to read Plato as a philosopher of being, or as an analytic philosopher. Aristotle clearly could be thought of as a political scientist, a biologist, a psychologist, and an astronomer, and also as a philosopher of being, an analytic philosopher, and as a student of the methodology of the natural sciences. Each of the great philosophers, in fact, could be seen to have grappled with problems that fitted nicely into one or another of these new conceptions of the mission and method of philosophy. And although more than a dozen new independent disciplines sprang up from one or another branch of philosophy, there was certainly no shortage of intellectually curious men and women ready to "do philosophy." By the early twentieth century, the grand old philosophical questions (What is the meaning of life? What is the origin of the universe? What can I truly know? How ought I to act?) had been so chewed over, turned around, dissected, inspected, and reexamined that there scarcely seemed to be any real point in doing philosophy any more at all.

At this point, Ludwig Wittgenstein appeared with a radically new point of view on the nature and purpose of philosophy. Naturally, one could find historical precedents for his approach—there may, after all, be something new under the sun, but there cannot be, after all this time, something *totally* new in philosophy. Nevertheless, Wittgenstein's message was a dramatic departure from all the varieties of philosophizing that had been going on throughout the nineteenth and early twentieth centuries.

The most striking feature of Wittgenstein's approach was the fact that he thought philosophers should do their best to stop philosophizing! Philosophical questions, he suggested, are really not normal questions at all. All of us, for example, have at some time had a dream that was so realistic that we sort of half wondered whether perhaps it wasn't really a dream. But only a *philosopher* (Descartes) would ask seriously how we know that we aren't *always* dreaming! All of us have been tricked by an odd arrangement of shadows and light into thinking that we see an animal in some bushes when it is only the breeze blowing the leaves. But only a philosopher (Hume) would argue that we can never know that there are ordinary physical objects in the world independent of our senses.

Wittgenstein compared philosophical questioning to a kind of illness or derangement, and suggested that the real job of philosophers is to cure us of the compulsion to ask such questions, *not* to try to answer them! How can we cure ourselves? Not by hypnosis, and not by psychoanalysis, and certainly not, as Hume had proposed, by going out, mixing with one's friends, and just trying to forget those odd questions. The solution, rather, is to look at the language in which we ask philosophical questions, patiently tracing out the ways in which philosophers stretch, or distort, or misuse language, so that little by little we come to see that the questions we are trying to ask really make no sense. In the end, if this enterprise is successful, we cease being philosophers, and perhaps start to sleep well at night.

Wittgenstein had an enormous influence on those who met him at Cambridge

University in England. Although he published only one book during his lifetime (several other books have been published posthumously), his impact on other philosophers spread his reputation and his method far beyond Cambridge, and even beyond England. Among the many first-rate philosophers who took up something like the Wittgensteinian method was John T. Wisdom. Wisdom clearly believed that Wittgenstein's attack on philosophy had great merit, but he thought, nonetheless, that there was *some* point to the odd questions philosophers ask. In the essay which has been reproduced here, Wisdom undertakes to show that, despite everything Wittgenstein had said, there remained some legitimate positive tasks for philosophers to perform.

The key to Wisdom's attack can be found in the statement on page 41 that Wittgenstein treats philosophical theories "as merely symptoms of linguistic confusion." By contrast, Wisdom says, "I wish to represent them as also symptoms of linguistic penetration." In short, Wisdom's view is that philosophers are not merely confused or caught up in linguistic mistakes. Philosophers have insights of a logical or substantive nature which they try to express by means of odd, paradoxical, or perplexing statements. If we take those statements literally, we may perfectly well conclude that they are false. But we will not thereby have figured out what prompted the philosopher to utter them in the first place. As Wisdom suggests near the end of his essay, the *usefulness* of philosophical statements may actually depend upon their being paradoxical, and hence, strictly speaking, false.

Wisdom is very close to Wittgenstein in philosophical style; to an American pragmatist or a continental phenomenologist, they might not seem different at all. Yet the move made by Wisdom opens the way for a very broad variety of philosophical questions. Once we recognize the usefulness of the paradoxical, the puzzling, the counterintuitive, we are ready to acknowledge the philosophical legitimacy of thinkers as diverse as Kierkegaard, Berkeley, Heidegger, and Plato.

The last line of Wisdom's essay may be puzzling in itself, since it is a reference to the last line of Wittgenstein's first book (the only one published during his lifetime), *Tractatus Logico-Philosophicus*. Wisdom writes:

"Philosophers should be continually trying to say what cannot be said."

Wittgenstein had written:

"Whereof one cannot speak, thereof one must be silent."

JOHN WISDOM: *Philosophical Perplexity*

1. *Philosophical statements are really verbal.*—I have enquired elsewhere the real nature of philosophical requests such as "Can we know what is going on in someone else's mind?" "Can we really know the causes of our sensations?" "What is a chair?", and of philosophical answers such as "We can never really know the causes of our sensations," "A chair is nothing but our sensations," or "A chair is something over and above our sensations," "The goodness of a man, of a picture, or an argument is something over and above our feelings of approval and over and above those features of the man, the picture or the

argument, which 'determine' its goodness." There is no time to repeat the enquiry here and I have to say dogmatically:

A philosophical answer is really a verbal recommendation in response to a request which is really a request with regard to a sentence which lacks a conventional use whether there occur situations which could conventionally be described by it. The description, for example "I know directly what is going on in Smith's mind," is not a jumble like "Cat how is up," nor is it in conflict with conventional usage like "There are two white pieces and three black so there are six pieces on the board." It just lacks a conventional usage. To call both "Can 2 + 3 = 6?" and "Can I know what is going on in the minds of others?" nonsensical questions serves to bring out the likeness between them. But if one were to deny that there is a difference between them it would be an instance of that disrespect for other people which we may platitudinously say, so often damages philosophical work. A disrespect which blinds one to the puzzles they raise—in this instance the puzzle of the philosophical *can* which somehow seems between "Can 2 + 3 make 6?" and "Can terriers catch hares?" Compare "Can persons be in two places at once?" "Do we have unconscious wishes?" "Can you play chess without the queen?" (W).[1]

Even to say that "I know directly what is going on in Smith's mind" is *meaningless,* is dangerous, especially if you have just said that "There are two white pieces and three black so there are six" is meaningless.

It is not even safe to say that "I know directly what is going on in Smith's mind" lacks a use or meaning and leave it at that. For though it has no meaning it tends to have a meaning, like "All whiffley was the tulgey wood," though of course it is unlike this last example in the important respect that it does not lack a meaning because its constituent words are unknown. Nor does it lack meaning because its syntax is unknown. This makes it puzzling and makes it resemble the logical case. It is clear that for these reasons it would be even more illuminating and more misleading to say that "God exists" and "Men are immortal" are meaningless—especially just after saying 2 + 3 = 6 is meaningless.

2. *Philosophical statements are not verbal.*—I have said that philosophers' questions and theories are really verbal. But if you like we will not say this or we will say also the contradictory.[2] For of course *(a)* philosophic statements usually have not a verbal air. On the contrary they have a non-verbal air like "A fox's brush is really a tail." (W). And their non-verbal air is not an unimportant feature of them because on it very much depends their puzzlingness.

---

[1] Wittgenstein has not read this over-compressed paper and I warn people against supposing it a closer imitation of Wittgenstein than it is. On the other hand I can hardly exaggerate the debt I owe to him and how much of the good in this work is his—not only in the treatment of this philosophical difficulty and that but in the matter of how to do philosophy. As far as possible I have put a W against examples I owe to him. It must not be assumed that they are used in a way he would approve.

[2] I do not wish to suggest that Wittgenstein would approve *this* sort of talk nor that he would disapprove it.

And *(b)* though really verbal a philosopher's statements have not a merely verbal point. Unlike many statements the primary point of uttering them is not to convey the information they convey but to do something else. Consequently all attempts to explain their peculiar status by explaining the peculiar nature of their subject matter, fail. For their subject matter is not peculiar; their truth or falsity, in so far as these are appropriate to them at all, is fixed by facts about words, *e.g.,* Goodness is not approval by the majority, because "The majority, sometimes approve what is bad" is not self-contradictory. But the point of philosophical statements is peculiar. It is the illumination of the ultimate structure of facts, *i.e.,* the relations between different categories of being or (we must be in the mode) the relations between different sub-languages within a language.

The puzzles of philosophical propositions, of fictitional propositions, general propositions, negative propositions, propositions about the future, propositions about the past, even the puzzle about psychological propositions, is not removed by explaining the peculiar nature of the subject matter of the sentences in which they are expressed but by reflecting upon the peculiar manner in which those sentences work. Mnemonic slogan: It's not the stuff, it's the style that stupefies.

3. *The divergence of point from content.*—The divergence of point from content which is found in necessary and near necessary propositions can be explained here only briefly.

Suppose a decoder, though still utterly ignorant of the meaning of both of two expressions "monarchy" and "set of persons ruled by the same king," has after prolonged investigation come to the conclusion that they mean the same in a certain code. He will say to his fellow decoder " 'Monarchy' means the same as 'set of persons ruled by the same king'." The translator, and the philosopher also, may say the same. They all use the same form of words because what they say is the same. But the point of what they say is very different. The decoder's point can be got by anyone who knows the meaning of "means the same as"; the translator does what he wants with the sentence only if his hearer knows the meaning either of "monarchy" or of "set of persons ruled by the same king"; the philosopher does what he wants with the sentence only if his hearer already uses, *i.e.* understands, *i.e.* knows the meaning of, *both* "monarchy" and "set of persons ruled by the same king." This condition makes the case of the philosopher curious; for it states that he can do what he wants with the sentence only if his hearer already knows what he is telling him. But this is true in the required sense. The philosopher draws attention to what is already known with a view to giving insight into the structure of what "monarchy" say means, *i.e.* bringing into connexion the sphere in which the one expression is used with that in which the other is. Compare the man who says "I should have the change from a £1 after spending five shillings on a book, one and sevenpence halfpenny on stamps and two and twopence halfpenny at the grocer's, so I should have eleven shillings and twopence." This is Moore's example and I beg attention for it. It is tremendously illuminating in the *necessary synthetic* group of puzzles and in a far, far wider field than this, because it illuminates the use of "means the same"—a phrase which stops so many. When on first going to France I learn the exchange rate for francs do I know the meaning of "worth 100 francs" or do I come to know this after staying three weeks?

The philosopher is apt to say "A monarchy is a set of people under a king" rather than " 'Monarchy' means the same as 'a set of people under a king.' " By using the former sentence he intimates his point. Now shall we say "A monarchy is a set of people under a king" means the same as " 'Monarchy' means 'a set of people under a king' " or not? My answer is "Say which you like. But if you say 'Yes' be careful, etc., and if you say 'No' be careful, etc."

If we decide to describe the difference between the two as a difference of meaning we must not say that the difference in meaning is a difference of subjective intension, nor that it is a difference of emotional significance merely. For these are not adequate accounts of the difference between the two. And not an adequate account of the difference between the use of "3 plus 5 plus 8" and the use of "16."

4. *Philosophy, truth, misleadingness and illumination.*—Now that we have seen that the philosopher's intention is to bring out relations between categories of being, between spheres of language, we shall be more prepared to allow that false statements about the usage of words may be philosophically very useful and even adequate provided their falsity is realized and there is no confusion about what they are being used for.

The nature of the philosopher's intention explains how it is that one may call a philosophical theory such as *A proposition is a sentence,* certainly false, and yet feel that to leave one's criticism at that is to attend to the letter and not the spirit of the theory criticized.

The nature of the philosopher's intention explains also how it is that one can not say of a philosopher's theory that it is false when he introduces it in his own terminology, while yet one often feels that such theories are somehow philosophically bad. Thus (W) suppose the word "sense-datum" has never been used before and that someone says "When Jones sees a rabbit, has an illusion of a rabbit, has an hallucination of a rabbit, dreams of a rabbit, he has a sense-datum of a rabbit." One can not protest that this is false, since no statement has been made, only a recommendation. But the recommendation purports to be enlightening and one may well protest if it is, on the contrary, misleading. This particular recommendation is liable to suggest that sense data are a special sort of thing, *extremely* thin coloured pictures, and thus liable to raise puzzles, such as "How are sense-data related to material things?" We can abuse a philosopher as much as we like if we use the right adjectives. *Good is an ultimate predicate* is useless, *A proposition is a subsistent entity* is useless and pretentious,[3]

---

[3] Neither of these theories are entirely useless. They are for one thing good antitheses to the naturalistic error.

We can never know the real cause of our sensations is misleading. And we can praise him although he speaks falsely or even nonsensically. People have considered whether it is true that "an event is a pattern of complete, particular, specific facts and a complete, particular, specific fact is an infinitely thin slice out of an event."[4]

You may say "How absurd of them since the statement is nonsense." Certainly the statement is nonsense and so, if you like, it was absurd of them. But it was better than saying it was nonsense and ignoring it. Suppose I say "The thoroughbred is a neurotic woman on four legs." This is nonsense, but it is not negligible.[5]

5. *Provocation and Pacification.*—So far, however, little or nothing has been said to explain what sort of things make a philosophical statement misleading and what make it illuminating. Only a short answer is possible here.

In the first place there is the misleading feature which nearly all philosophical statements have—a non-verbal air. The philosopher *laments* that we can never really know what is going on in someone else's mind, that we can never really know the causes of our sensations, that inductive conclusions are never really justified. He laments these things as if he can dream of another world where we can see our friends and tables face to face, where scientists can justify their conclusions and terriers can catch hares. This enormous source of confusion we can not study now.

Secondly philosophical statements mislead when by the use of like expressions for different cases, they suggest likenesses which do not exist, and by the use of different expressions for like cases, they conceal likenesses which do exist.

Philosophical theories are illuminating in a corresponding way, namely when they suggest or draw attention to a terminology which reveals likenesses and differences concealed by ordinary language.

I want to stress the philosophical usefulness of metaphysical surprises such as "We can never really know the causes of our sensations," "We can never know the real causes of our sensations," "Inductive conclusions are never really justified," "The laws of mathematics are really rules of grammar." I believe that too much fun has been made of philosophers who say this kind of thing. Remember what Moore said about 1924—words to this effect: When a philosopher says that really something is so we are warned that what he says is really so is not so really. With horrible ingenuity Moore can rapidly reduce any metaphysical theory to a ridiculous story. For he is right, they are false—only there *is* good in them, poor things. This shall be explained.

Wittgenstein allows importance to these theories. They are for him expres-

---

[4] *Problems of Mind and Matter,* p. 32.

[5] The matter can be put in terms of truth and falsehood. A philosophical theory involves an explicit claim, an equation, and an implicit claim that the equation is not misleading and is illuminating. The explicit claim may be false and the implicit true on one or both counts, or *vice versa.*

sions of deep-seated puzzlement. It is an important part of the treatment of a puzzle to develop it to the full.

But this is not enough. Wittgenstein allows that the theories are philosophically important not merely as specimens of the whoppers philosophers can tell. But he too much represents them as merely symptoms of linguistic confusion. I wish to represent them as also symptoms of linguistic penetration.

Wittgenstein gives the impression that philosophical remarks either express puzzlement or if not are remarks such as Wittgenstein himself makes with a view to curing puzzlement.

This naturally gives rise to the question "If the proper business of philosophy is the removal of puzzlement, would it not be best done by giving a drug to the patient which made him entirely forget the statements puzzling him or at least lose his uneasy feelings?"

This of course will never do. And what we say about the philosopher's purposes must be changed so that it shall no longer seem to lead to such an absurd idea.

The philosopher's purpose is to gain a grasp of the relations between different categories of being, between expressions used in *different manners*. He is confused about what he wants and he is confused by the relations between the expressions, so he is very often puzzled. But only such treatment of the puzzles as increases a grasp of the relations between different categories of being is philosophical. And not all the philosopher's statements are either complaints of puzzlement or pacificatory. Philosophers who say "We never know the real causes of our sensations," "Only my sensations are real," often bring out these "theories" with an air of triumph (with a misleading air of empirical discovery indeed). True the things they say are symptoms of confusion even if they are not of puzzlement. But they are also symptoms of penetration, of noticing what is not usually noticed. Philosophical progress has two aspects, provocation and pacification.

6. *Example of the pointless doubts: (a) how misleading they are.*—Let us consider this with examples. Take first the philosopher who says to the plain man: "We do not really know that there is cheese on the table; for might not all the sense evidence suggest this and yet there be no cheese. Remember what happened at Madame Tussaud's."

Our assertion with confidence that there is cheese on the table or our assertion that we know that there is cheese on the table raises at least these three puzzles: (1) *the categorial puzzle,* which finds expression in "We ought not to speak of a cheese (of the soul) but of bundles of sense data"; (2) *the knowledge puzzle,* which finds expression in "We ought not to say 'I know there is cheese on the table' but 'Very, very probably there is cheese on the table' "; (3) *the justification puzzle,* which finds expression in "Empirical conclusions are not really justified."

We can not here speak of all these. We are considering (2) the *knowledge* or *pointless doubt* puzzle. There are a group of pointless doubt puzzles including the following: "We don't really know that there is cheese on the table"; "We ought to say only 'It is probable that there is cheese on the table' "; "It is improper to say 'I know that there is cheese on the table' "; "It would be well if we prefixed every remark about material things with 'probably'."

All these suggestions are misleading—they all suggest that it has been discovered that we have been over-confident about material things. They should have slightly different treatment but I have only just *realized* this multiplicity. Let us take the puzzle in the crude form "Couldn't there be no cheese here although all the sense-evidence suggests there is?"

Wittgenstein explains that this sentence though of the verbal form we associate with doubt and though it may be uttered with the intonation, expression and gestures we associate with doubt, is not *used* as a sentence expressing doubt. To utter it is to raise a pseudo doubt. People say "We ought not to say 'There *is* cheese on the table' but 'Probably there is cheese on the table' or 'The sense-evidence suggests ever so strongly that there is cheese on the table.' For whatever we do we never observe a cheese, we have to rely upon our senses. And we may be suffering from a joint hallucination of all the senses or a consistent dream. Remember how people are deceived at Madame Tussaud's. And we may see and touch cheesy patches, smell cheesy smells, obtain cheesy pictures from cameras and cheesy reactions from mice and yet the stuff tomorrow be soap in our mouth. And then tomorrow we shall say 'Yesterday we were mistaken.' So our 'knowledge' today that there is cheese here is not real knowledge. Every one ought really to whisper 'Possibly hallucinatory' after *every* sentence about material things however much he has made sure that he is right."

What those who recommend this should notice is how not merely unusual but pointless a use of words they recommend. As language is at present used, I raise my hungry friends' hopes if I say "There is cheese on the table," and I damp them if I add "unless it is hallucinatory." But this additional clause has its effect only because I do *not always* use it. If a parent adds "be very careful" to everything he says to a child he will soon find his warnings ineffective. If I prefix every statement about material things with "probably" this doubt-raiser will soon cease to frighten hungry friends, that is cease to function as it now does. Consequently in order to mark those differences which I now mark by saying in one case "Probably that is cheese on the table" and in another case "I know that is cheese on the table," I shall have to introduce a new notation, one to do the work the old did. "To do the work the old did"!; that is, to claim what I formerly claimed with "know"!

It may now be said "In the ordinary use of 'know' we may know that that is cheese on the table, but this knowledge is not real knowledge."

This gives the misleading idea that the philosopher has envisaged some kind of knowing which our failing faculties prevent us from attaining. Terriers can not catch hares, men can not really know the causes of their sensations. Nothing of the kind, however. For when we say to the philosopher "Go on, describe this real knowledge, tell us what stamp of man you want and we will see if we can buy or breed one" then he can never tell us.

It may now be said, "No, no, the point is this: There is some inclination to use[6] 'know' strictly so that we do not know that insulin cures diabetes, that the sun will rise tomorrow, because these propositions are only probable inferences from what we have observed. There is some inclination to use 'know' only when what is known is observed or is entailed by something known for certain. Now you do not know in this sense that you will not have to correct yourself tomorrow and say "I was mistaken yesterday, that was not cheese," since nothing you know for certain today is incompatible with this. And if you do not know but what you may have to correct yourself tomorrow you do not know that you are right today."

But what is meant by "certain"? I should claim to know for certain that that is cheese on the table now. And as the objector rightly points out this entails that I shall not have to correct myself tomorrow. I therefore know in the strict sense that I shall not have to correct myself tomorrow.

It will be said that it is not *absolutely* certain that that is cheese on the table. But I should reply that it is.

It will be said that it is not *senseless to doubt* that that is cheese on the table, not even after the most exhaustive tests. I should reply that it is.

But, of course, by now I see what the sceptic is driving at. It is not senseless to doubt that that is cheese on the table, in the sense in which it is senseless to doubt "I am in pain," "I hear a buzzing"—not even after the most exhaustive tests—indeed the exhaustive tests make no difference to this. For, in this sense, it is not senseless to doubt that that is cheese on the table provided only that "He says that that is cheese but perhaps he is mistaken" has a use in English. You see, "He says he is in pain, but perhaps he is mistaken" has no use in English. Hence we may be "absolutely certain" that he is not mistaken[7] about his pain, in the very special sense that "He is mistaken" makes no sense in this connexion.

Thus the sceptic's pretended doubts amount to pointing out that, unlike statements descriptive of sensations, statements about material things make sense with "perhaps he is mistaken." And the sceptic proposes to mark this by an extraordinary use of "know" and "probably." He proposes that we should not say that we know that that is cheese on the table unless it is entailed by statements with regard to which a doubt is not merely out of the question but unintelligible, *i.e.,* such that where S is P is one of them then "S is P unless I am mistaken" raises a titter like "I am in pain unless I am mistaken." "That is cheese on the table" is not such a statement and so of course it does not follow from such statements—otherwise a doubt with regard to it would be unintelligible, *i.e.,* it would be absolutely certain in the strict, philosophic sense.

---

[6] Another form would be: 'It is proper' as opposed to 'usual' to use 'know' so that, etc.

[7] Of course he may be *lying*.

The sceptic's doubts become then a recommendation to use "know" only with statements about sense-experience and mathematics and to prefix *all* other statements with "probably."[8]

This is very different talk and much less misleading. But still it is misleading unless accompanied by the explanation given above of the astounding certainty of statements about sense-experience. Even with the explanation the suggestion is highly dangerous involving as it does a new and *manner* indictating use of the familiar words 'know' and 'probable.' Without the explanation it suggests that there is a difference in degree of certainty between statements about material things and statements about sense data, a difference in certainty dependent upon their subject matter, in a sense analogous to that in which we say "I am certain about what happened in Hyde Park—I was there—but I am not certain about what happened in Spain—I was not an eye-witness." This suggests that I know what it would be like to be an eye-witness of cheese, but am in fact unfortunately obliged to *rely upon the testimony of* my senses.

Now the difference between statements about sense-experiences and statements about material things is not at all like this. The difference is not one of subject-matter (stuff) but of a different manner of use (style). And statements about sense-experiences are certain only because it makes no sense to say that they may be wrong.[9] Notice the connexion between "He says he is in pain but I think he is mistaken" and "He crys 'Ow!' but I think he is mistaken." The difference between sense-statements and thing-statements cannot be adequately explained here. And consequently the full misleadingness of such a use of "probably" as is recommended in what we may call the last form of the pseudo doubt, cannot be adequately explained here.

But I hope I have said enough to bring out in good measure the misleadingness of saying such things as "O dear, we can never know the causes of our sensations," and even "It would be philosophically excellent to put 'probably' before all statements about material things."

7. *Example of the pointless doubts: (b) how importantly illuminating they are.*—But though the recommended use of "probably" would be pointless as a cautionary clause and would thus be extremely misleading, the recommendation to use it so is not pointless, is not prompted wholly by confusion, but partly by penetration. The philosopher says to the plain man "You do not really know that that is a cheese on the table." We have pacified those who are opposed to this statement by bringing out the sources of their reluctance to agree with it. But the philosopher must pacify everyone and we must now pacify those philosophers who are pleased with it and complete the pacification of those who are puzzled by it, being tempted to deny it and at the same time tempted

---

[8] Compare the tendency to use 'what ought to be done' irrevocably. People who do this lament thus: "What one ought to do is always for the best, but unfortunately we never know what we really ought to do." Others lament thus: "We can know what we ought to do but unfortunately this does not always turn out for the best."

[9] This, I realize, stands very much in need of pacifying explanation.

to assert it. What *is* the point behind the misleading statement "We can never know statements about material things"? The answer has been given already by the method of forcing reformulations. But we may now approach the answer by a different route. Under what circumstances are such things usually said?

It is when after considering hallucinations, illusions, etc., one wishes to emphasize (1) the likeness between such cases and cases in which there was "something really there," and to emphasize the continuity between *(a)* cases in which one says "I think that is cheese on the table," "I believe that is a real dagger," "Probably that is a snake, not a branch" and *(b)* cases in which one says "That *is* cheese on the table," "I found that it *was* a snake"; and to emphasize (2) the unlikeness between even so well assured a statement as "This is my thumb" and such a statement as "I see a pinkish patch," "I feel a softish patch," "I am in pain."

It is not at all easy at first to see how in being revocable and correctable by others the most assured statement about a thing is more like the most precarious statement about another thing than it is like a statement descriptive of one's sensations. Ordinary language conceals these things because in ordinary language we speak both of some favourable material-thing-statements and of statements about our sensations, as certain, while we speak of other statements about material things as merely probable. This leads to pseudo-laments about the haunting uncertainty of even the best material thing-statements and pseudo-congratulations upon the astounding certainty of statements about our sensations.

We are all, when our attention is drawn to those cases so often described in which it looks for all the world as if our friend is standing in the room although he is dying two thousand miles away, or in which we think we see a banana and it turns out to be a reflection in a greengrocer's mirror, we are all, in such cases, inclined to say "Strictly we ought always to add" unless it is a queer looking stick and not a banana, or a reflection or an hallucination or an illusion."[10] We do not stop to consider what would happen if we did always add this. Horrified at the deceptions our senses have practised upon us we feel we must abuse them somehow and so we say that they never *prove* anything, that we never *know* what is based on them.

The continuity and the difference which is concealed by ordinary language would be no longer concealed but marked if we used "probably" in the way recommended. But what an unfortunate way of obtaining this result! And in what a misleading way was the recommendation made! I do not really know that this is a thumb. The huntsman's coat is not really pink. A fox's brush is really a tail. (W).

8. *Other Examples.*—Now many other examples should be given. "What is a mathematical proposition?" "Do inductive arguments give any probability to their conclusions?" These other puzzles shoud be re-created, the temptations to give the answers which have been given should be re-created. But this cannot

---

[10] Then every statement would be tautologous but *absolutely* certain!

be done in this paper. Without bringing up the puzzles and temptations the following accounts are half dead, but I offer them for what they are worth.

Take "The laws of mathematics and logic are really rules of grammar." With this instructive incantation people puzzle themselves to death. Is it or isn't it true? And if false what amendment will give us the truth? If not rules then what? The answer is "They are what they are, etc. Is a donkey a sort of horse but with *very* long ears?" People are puzzled because of course it isn't true that the laws of mathematics are rules of grammar (more obvious still that they are not commands). And yet they cannot bring themselves to lose the advantages of this falsehood. For this falsehood draws attention to (1) an unlikeness and (2) a likeness concealed by ordinary language; (1) an unlikeness to the laws of hydraulics and an unlikeness in this unlikeness to the unlikeness between the laws of hydraulics and those of aeronautics; for it is an unlikeness not of subject-matter but of manner of functioning—and (2) a likeness but not an exact likeness to the functioning of rules.

Again "Inductive arguments do not really give any probability to their conclusions" gives the misleading idea that the scientists have been found out at last, that our confidence in our most careful research workers is entirely misplaced, their arguments being no better than those of the savage. Nothing of the kind of course. What is at the back of this lament is this: In ordinary language we speak of Dr. So and so's experiment with a group of 100 children whose teeth improved after six months extra calcium as having very much increased the probability of the proposition that bad teeth are due to calcium deficiency. We also say that my having drawn 90 white balls from a bag which we know to contain 100 balls, each either white or black, has very much increased the probability of the proposition that all the balls in that bag are white. We even speak numerically in connexion with empirical probability—we not only argue a priori and say "There were six runners, there are now only five, we still know nothing of any of them, so it is now 4–1 against the dog from trap 1" but we also argue empirically and say "It was 5–1 against the dog from trap 1; but I hear a rumour that each of the others has been provided with a cup of tea, and I think we may now take 4–1 against him."

The similarity in the way we speak of these cases leads us when asked how empirical arguments give probability to their conclusions to try to assimilate them to the formal cases, balls in bags, dice, etc. But when this attempt is made it begins to appear that the investigation of nature is much less like the investigation of balls in a bag than one is at first apt to think.

At the same time is revealed the shocking continuity between the scientist's arguments by the method of difference and the savage's post hoc ergo propter hoc,[11] between the method of agreement and the reflexes of rats, and struck by the difference and the continuity and how they are concealed by ordinary

---

[11] See Keynes *A Treatise on Probability.*

language we provoke attention to them with "Even the best established scientific results are nothing but specially successful superstitions." We say this although we have made no shocking discovery of scientists faking figures, although the scientist's reasons for his belief in insulin still differ from my landlady's reasons for belief in Cure-all, in exactly the way which, in the ordinary use of language, makes us call the one belief scientifically grounded and the other a superstition. Similarly we may say, having seen a butterfly die or been told the age of an oak "The strongest of us have really only a short time to live." We say this although we have made no discovery of impending disaster, or we may say "Man is nothing but a complicated parasite" when we watch the arrival of the 9.5 at the Metropolis.

Conclusion

The plain man has come to expect of philosophers paradoxical, provoking statements such as "We can never really know the causes of our sensations," "Causation is really nothing more than regular sequence," "Inductive conclusions are really nothing but lucky superstitions," "The laws of logic are ultimately rules of grammar." Philosophers of logic know that the statements are provocative; this is why they so often put in some apologetic word such as "really" or "ultimately."

These untruths persist. This is not merely because they are symptoms of an intractible disorder but because they are philosophically useful. The curious thing is that their philosophical usefulness depends upon their paradoxicalness and thus upon their falsehood. They are false because they are needed where ordinary language fails though it must not be supposed that they are or should be in some perfect language. They are in a language not free from the same sort of defects as those from the effects of which they are designed to free us.

To invent a special word to describe the status of, for example, mathematical propositions would do no good. There is a phrase already, "necessary yet synthetic." It is, of course, perfectly true that mathematical propositions are "necessary synthetics"—it should be true since the expression was made to measure. True but no good. We are as much inclined to ask "What are necessary synthetic propositions?" as we were to ask "What are mathematical propositions?" "What is an instinct?" An innate disposition certainly. But philosophically that answer is useless. No—what is wanted is some device for bringing out the relations between the manner in which mathematical (or dispositional) sentences are used and the manners in which others are used—so as to give their place on the language map. This cannot be done with a plain answer, a single statement. We may try opposite falsehoods or we may say, "Be careful that this expression 'mathematical proposition' does not suggest certain analogies at the expense of others. Do not let it make you think that the difference between mathematical propositions and others is like that between the propositions of hydraulics and those of aeronautics. Do notice how like to rules, etc., and yet, etc."

If you will excuse a suspicion of smartness: Philosophers should be continually trying to say what cannot be said.

TOPICS FOR FURTHER STUDY

1. At one point, Wisdom suggests that the point of philosophical statements is "the illumination of the ultimate structure of facts." What do you suppose he means by this assertion? How might this conception of the point of philosophical statements differ from, say, the conception of philosophy which Socrates had? Does it make sense to speak of the ultimate structure of facts? What must we assume about the world in order to talk this way? What must we assume about our minds, about our capacity to know, in order to investigate the ultimate structure of facts?

2. Wisdom, like Wittgenstein, and also, in a way, like Plato and Aristotle, concentrates a good deal on language as opposed to the world. In what ways could a study of language be a pathway to an understanding of the world? What would we have to assume about the relationship between language, thought, and the world in order for a study of language to be philosophically significant?

3. Socrates, as we have seen, distinguished very sharply between the investigation of nature, which he undertook as a young man and then rejected, and the investigation of the principles of right thought and action, to which he devoted most of his adult life. Is the style of philosophizing employed by Wisdom more appropriate to the first of these enterprises (the investigation of nature) or to the second (the investigation of the principles of right thought and action)? Why? The seventeenth and eighteenth century epistemologists tried to unite the two enterprises through the device of examining the structure of the mind. Can they also be united through an examination of the use of language? Why? Why not?

4. What sorts of philosophical problems, in your judgment, can *not* adequately be handled in the manner employed by Wisdom? What questions do you expect a philosophy course to take up? Now that you have read the first chapter of this text, how do the topics discussed differ from what you expected? Can you see ways in which the methods and approaches employed by the philosophers discussed so far can be adapted to the problems you are concerned about?

SUGGESTIONS FOR FURTHER READING

JOHN AUSTIN, *Sense and Sensibilia*

AFRED J. AYER, *Language, Truth, and Logic*

RENÉ DESCARTES, *Discourse on Method*

ERNEST GELLNER, *Words and Things*

G. W. F. HEGEL, Introduction to *The Philosophy of History*

MARTIN HEIDEGGER, *What is Metaphysics?*

DAVID HUME, "The Epicurean," "The Stoic," "The Platonist," and "The Sceptic" in *Collected Essays*

JEAN-PAUL SARTRE, *Existentialism as a Humanism*

WILFRID SELLARS, "Philosophy and the Scientific Image of Man," in *Frontiers of Science and Philosophy,* ed. by R. Colodny

IMMANUEL KANT (1724–1804) was born, lived out his life, and died in the provincial city of Königsberg in Prussia. Kant's early studies were concentrated in the areas of natural science, mathematics, and philosophy. At the University of Königsberg, he learned the philosophical theories of Leibniz, as they had been interpreted by a widely-read German philosopher, Christian Wolff. After graduating from the University, Kant took a number of jobs as a tutor to children in the houses of Prussian aristocrats. Finally, he returned to the university to become what was called a *privatdozent*. This meant that he was licensed by the university to offer lectures, which the students could attend. But he was not paid by the university;

2 ETHICS

instead, he had to collect fees from the students. The more popular he was, the more money he made! For more than a dozen years, Kant lectured as much as twenty-one hours a week on virtually every subject imaginable, from mathematics and logic to geography and history. Finally, in 1770, he was appointed to the position of Professor of Logic and Metaphysic.

Kant was already well known throughout Germany for his writings on physics, astronomy, and metaphysics, but his important work was still far in the future. For eleven years, from 1770 until 1781, he published virtually nothing. All that time, he was struggling with fundamental problems of human knowledge. Finally, in 1781, there appeared the book that was to revolutionize all philosophy: *The Critique of Pure Reason.* In the next ten years, book after book flowed from his pen. After the *Critique,* Kant published *Prolegomena to any Future Metaphysics* (1783), *The Groundwork of the Metaphysic of Morals* (1785), *Metaphysical Foundations of Natural Science* (1786), *Critique of Practical Reason* (1788), and the *Critique of Judgment* (1790).

Kant continued writing and revising his theories until finally, at the age of eighty, shortly after the start of the new century, he died. Though he had never left his native Königsberg, his mind had spanned all time and all space, and he had left an indelible mark on the thought of his civilization.

I

Irwin Edman, a well-known early twentieth-century Columbia University professor of philosophy, is said to have stopped a student on the street one day. "Excuse me," Edman said. "Can you tell me whether I am walking north or south?" The startled student replied, "You are walking south, Professor." "Ah, good," Edman replied. "Then I have already eaten lunch."

Well, it isn't much of a joke, and it has been told of half the professors in America, but it does capture the popular impression of philosophy professors as rather unworldly characters, out of touch with the real world—people, as American businessmen are fond of saying, who have "never met a payroll."

Immanuel Kant is the greatest philosopher to live and write since the ancient times of Plato and Aristotle; he is the first great philosopher in modern times (after the end of the Middle Ages) to make his living as what we would call a professor of philosophy; and he is also about as close as any great philosopher has ever come to the standard caricature of the professor. Kant is said to have lived so regular and retiring a life that the townspeople of Königsberg, his lifelong home, could set their clocks by him as he went by on his daily walk. One would expect a professorial type like Kant to make contributions to such abstruse technical fields as cosmology, metaphysics, or the theory of knowledge, and so he did. But it is rather surprising to discover that Kant also wrote profound, powerful, and deeply moving books on the problems of morality. Despite the uneventful regularity of his own private life, Kant was able to confront and grapple with the great issues of duty, right, justice, and virtue which have troubled the human soul since the ancient times recorded in the Old Testament. The contrast between his outer life and his inner thoughts serves as a reminder to us that the greatness of a philosopher's insights cannot readily be measured by the external excitements of his life or times.

Kant was born on April 22, 1724 to a north Prussian family of modest means in the port city of Königsberg on the North Sea. Two centuries earlier, Luther had turned Central Europe upside down with his Reformation of the Catholic Church, and out of Luther's challenge to the institution of the papacy and to the rituals of medieval Christianity had sprung a number of Protestant sects. Kant's family belonged to the sect known as Pietism, an extremely individualistic form of Protestant Christianity which rejected the mystery, ritual, and ceremony that the Catholic Church had interposed between the ordinary Christian and his God. Pietism emphasized the direct, inner relationship of the individual worshipper to God. It placed a strong inner conscience and a stern self-control at the center of its religious doctrine. Kant's mother was particularly devout, and it was universally said of him that he owed both his religious faith and his overpowering sense of moral duty to her influence.

Although he was a believing Christian, Kant rejected the notion that religious doctrine could provide a foundation for morality. Quite to the contrary, he insisted that our moral principles must be established on purely rational grounds, open to criticism and capable of a defense as solid as that which philosophers offered for the principles of pure logic itself.

For Kant, the central question of morality was not, What should I do? This he firmly believed was perfectly well-known to every decent man and woman, whether a peasant or a professor. As he remarked at one point in his moral writings, the truths of ethics had been known for thousands of years, so that a moral philosopher could hardly expect to discover something *new* in ethics. Rather, Kant saw the real moral problem in the way that most Puritans and other individualistic Protestants did, as the constant struggle to do what we know is right in the face of temptations and distractions. The soldier who knows that his duty requires him to stand fast even as his fear tempts him to run; the businessman who knows that he should give honest measure for honest measure in the marketplace, but nevertheless secretly wishes to tilt the scales in his own favor; the good husband who knows that his marriage vow is absolutely binding but feels the temptation of adultery—these and others like them are the men and women Kant has in mind when he writes on moral questions.

Kant was a student of the new science of Newton as well as a deeply committed Pietist. He saw a fundamental conflict between the scientific explanation of natural events, which emphasized their subordination to causal laws, and the moral assumption that we are free to choose our actions and hence are morally responsible for what we do. How can we demand that a person resist temptation and hold to the moral law if every action is merely another causally determined event in the universal natural order? How can we conceive of persons as free, responsible beings and yet also acknowledge their place in the system of events and objects studied by science?

Equally important to Kant, how can we prove, absolutely and without the slightest room for doubt or uncertainty, that the fundamental moral beliefs shared by all right-thinking persons are true, and not merely public opinion? As we saw in the first chapter, Kant insisted that even religion and morality submit to the spirit of *criticism*. The simple peasants and proud professors of north Prussia might believe that they knew the truth about ethics, but until they could produce a valid proof of their beliefs, they would have no argument to offer against the skeptic, the relativist, the doubter who said that all opinions were equally good or even that there was no truth about ethics to be known at all.

Kant had some ideas about how to handle these two problems. He thought that he could work out a philosophical truce between ethics and science that would give each its rightful place in the totality of human knowledge; at the same time, he hoped to provide a proof of the fundamental principles of ethics. In this way, he would bring all the parts of his own life and work into harmony with one another. In his philosophical system, there would be a place for the devout faith imparted to him by his mother, a proof of the moral maxims he had grown up with and which to his death he never doubted, and a conceptual framework for the great new achievements of science and mathematics which so dominated the intellectual world of his day and to which he devoted so much of his own life and work. Kant's struggle to achieve a harmonious accommodation among his scientific interests, his moral convictions, and his religious faith was a model for many later struggles by other philosophers. Today more than ever, science seems to encroach upon religion and morality. New developments in behavioral psychology threaten our age-old belief in moral freedom. Though many philosophers have challenged Kant's solution, few would deny that he saw deeply into the problem and forced the rest of us to confront it as philosophers.

II

Having read this far into a chapter on ethics, some of you may have the feeling that you don't quite recognize the subject as one that you can relate yourself to. Perhaps Kant knew perfectly well what was right, but many of *us* are filled with doubts. Furthermore, you may want to say, his single-minded emphasis on duty, on conscience, on doing the *right* thing, misses the real flavor of much of our thinking about how to live our lives. The fact is that although this book contains only one chapter called Ethics, there are many quite different sorts of problems that have been discussed under that name since the time of the ancient Greeks. There is hardly enough room in a single chapter, let alone in one book, to talk about them all, but at least *three* are important enough to demand some extended examination.

Kant has already introduced us to the first reason that people worry about what is called Ethics, namely a desire to discover an absolutely certain, irrefutable proof of the moral principles which we are already convinced are true. This proof serves two purposes: first, it answers the skeptic, who denies that there are any moral truths at all; and second, it answers the relativist, who says, in effect, "Everyone's opinions are as good as everyone else's."

A second reason why people worry about ethics is that sometimes we get into situations in which we want to do the right thing but really don't know what it is. For example, a woman may find that she is pregnant, and feel that to have a baby will simply turn her life inside out. Perhaps she wants to continue her studies in order to prepare for a career; perhaps the pregnancy is the result of a casual affair with a man whom she does not love; perhaps she and her husband already have as many children as they want and feel they can care for. Should she have an abortion? Part of her says that abortion is morally wrong; another part tells her that to have the baby would be wrong. She wants to do what is right, but she just doesn't know what *is* right in the situation.

Or a young man wants to leave home and start a life of his own, despite his parents' pleas that he remain with them and care for them. On the one hand, he feels love for his parents and a debt of gratitude and loyalty for all the years they have given him. On the other hand, he knows that this is his only life, and that it is wrong for him to sacrifice it to the needs or demands of his parents. Again, he wants to do what is right, but he does not know whether he really has an obligation to stay at home, and if he does, for how long.

In philosophy, cases such as these are sometimes called "hard cases." They are real-life moral dilemmas in which ordinary moral opinions are either hopelessly contradictory or else just confused. Many philosophers have sought some method or rule by which we could decide hard cases, either by a process of moral reasoning or even by a sort of calculation. Genuine confusion rather than temptation is the motivation here, and frequently the emphasis is less on an absolutely rock-solid *proof* of things we already believe than it is on some genuinely new insight into an otherwise unsolvable dilemma.

But the oldest tradition of ethical reflection in Western thought has nothing to do with rights and duties, temptations and their denial, hard cases and tortured choices. For Plato, for Epicurus, for the ancient Stoics, and for countless philosophers since their time, Ethics has been concerned with the definition, analysis, search, and achievement of the Good Life. Our stay on this earth is brief, the years pass faster and faster as we grow older, and all too soon we are forever dead. As we grow up and grow old, how shall we live our lives? What set of precepts, what style of inner feelings and outer relationships, what set of commitments will make us truly happy during the short passage of our lives? Should we strive to pile wealth upon wealth? fulfill our talents? aim for power and fame? retire to quiet contemplation? taste every experience, pleasurable or not, before death comes? Can reason and philosophy even help us in this choice? Or is the life of the mind itself just one path among many, and not the happiest at that?

Sometimes, when we say that someone lived a "good life," we mean that he or she experienced a great deal of pleasure—ate, drank, made merry. As the Italians say, such a person lived *"la dolce vita,"* the "sweet life." But just as often, we mean that the life was one of virtue, of service, of honor and dignity, that it was a life in which there was goodness. Many philosophers deliberately preserve this ambiguity because they believe that a truly happy life must also be a virtuous life, a life of goodness. Plato is perhaps the philosopher most often associated with this claim, and we shall read something by him on the subject later on in this chapter. But many other philosophers have, in one way or another, made the same claim, among whom are such unlikely bedfellows as Confucius and Karl Marx.

Here, then, are three reasons for thinking about ethics—or better, three searches which are usually grouped under the heading "Ethics": the search for absolutely certain, universally valid first principles of conduct that can stand against the challenges of the skeptic and the relativist; the search for a method or process of reasoning to help us in deciding hard cases and other real-world moral choices; and the search for the good life, the life that combines virtue and happiness in true human fulfillment. Most of the remainder of this chapter will be devoted to a deeper examination of these three approaches to the subject of ethics.

III

When we are very little, our parents stop us from doing things we shouldn't—hitting baby brother, eating paint, touching a wall plug—by physically pulling us away and saying "No!" in a loud, firm voice. You can't have a philosophical discussion with a two-year-old, as I was forced very quickly to recognize with my own two sons. As we grow older, we internalize those "No's" in the form of some set of rules, or norms, some conception of what is right and wrong. For a very long time, we simply accept these rules as given, a part of the world just as trees and tables, our parents and friends are a part of the world. Pretty early on, of course, we discover that not everyone abides all the time by the rules that our parents have taught us, but we can handle that fact, conceptually, by means of the category "bad." "Why can't I hit my brother? Tommy does." "Because it is wrong. Tommy is a bad boy, and I don't want you to be a bad boy like him."

So we grow older, with a more or less coherent moral code as part of our mental equipment. There are bad guys, naughty children, villains, criminals, but they are the "others," the ones who aren't nice, the sort of people *we* don't want to be like.

Then, one day, somewhere, there comes the great shock. It may be when we are still children, or when we go away to college, or when we move from a tight little homogeneous neighborhood to a big, heterogeneous city. It may simply be something we see on television. But all of a sudden, we encounter a whole group of people who seem to be good, decent, respectable, law-abiding, and upright, except that they call good what we call bad! We think it is good to fight for our country, and they think it is wicked. We think homosexuality is evil, and they think it is a perfectly acceptable lifestyle. They think abortion is a sensible technique for rational family planning and population control, and we call it murder.

This discovery, in whatever form it comes, is a genuine shock. The problem doesn't lie in the realization that some people do bad things. Ever since we saw Tommy hit his brother, we have known that. The real problem is that these people doing "bad" things and living by the "wrong" rules are *good* people. They are responsible; they are respected by their friends and neighbors. They may even be held up to children as models of virtue. And yet they do bad things! A man comes home from a war in which he gunned down two hundred defenseless women and children in a village, and he is paraded along Main Street as a hero. A mother and father refuse to allow their baby to receive medical treatment, the baby dies, and they are praised in their church as pillars of rectitude. A governor calls out the National Guard to shoot striking prison inmates, and he is immortalized in marble in front of the state capitol.

If it is unsettling to encounter men and women within our own society whose moral codes differ markedly from our own, think how much more unsettling it is to discover whole cultures or civilizations in which what we call virtue is despised as vice and what we condemn as wicked is celebrated as noble! Even a study of the history of the literate civilizations of the East and the West provides countless examples of this sort of variation in moral beliefs. When the anthropologists' experiences with nonliterate cultures are added to our stock of information, it begins to appear that there isn't a single rule, precept, or moral belief that has been accepted by decent men and women everywhere. War? Torture? Child murder? Adultery? Suicide? Theft? Lying? Every single one has been condemned by some cultures and accepted, approved, or even praised by others.

There are basically three ways in which a philosopher can deal with the troublesome problem of the variation in moral codes from person to person, group to group, and culture to culture. The first way is to deny that the variation exists, despite appearances to the contrary. The second way is to admit that the variation exists, and conclude that there are therefore no universally valid moral norms applicable to all persons in all places at all times. The third way is to acknowledge the variation, but insist nonetheless that some moral principles are true and other supposed principles are false, no matter how many people believe them. Those who take this last route then do their best to provide some sort of proof for the principles they believe to be valid.

How can philosophers possibly maintain that there is no real disagreement about norms and moral principles, when the evidence of personal and cultural variation is all around them? Essentially, their tactic is to argue that when two people or two cultures seem to disagree about what is right or good, they are *really* only disagreeing about some of the facts of the case. If they could settle that disagreement, then it would turn out that they actually make the same moral judgments. For example, the Christian Scientist, like the nonbeliever, wants what is best for his sick child. But he firmly believes that the body is not real, and that salvation depends upon holding firm to that belief. So for him to consent to an operation for his child would be as irresponsible (on his assessment of the facts) as for another parent to give a diabetic child all the candy she wants. To take another example, the culture that condemns abortion may believe that the fetus is already a person; the culture that approves abortion does not think the fetus is a person until after it is born. Both condemn murder, defined as the wilful killing of a person, but they disagree on the factual question of whether abortion is murder.

A number of philosophers have taken this line, including the Scotsman David Hume whom you encountered in Chapter One. Anthropologists have actually carried out cross-country surveys of norms in an effort to discover any constants. Although it does appear that the ban or taboo on incest is very widespread, the effort has essentially been a failure. There aren't any broad moral principles of justice, charity, equity, or benevolence which can be discovered in the moral systems of all cultures. (There is a much deeper question which we have not touched on yet. Even if there *were* universally accepted norms, what would that fact prove? Does everybody believing something make it right? Don't we need some justification for our moral convictions which goes beyond saying, "Everybody agrees with me?" This problem troubled Kant a great deal, and a bit later on in this chapter, we shall see how he tried to deal with it.)

The second response to moral disagreement—the denial of objective, universal moral norms—has actually been relatively rare in the history of Western ethical theory, but it has had its defenders from the time of the ancient Greeks to the present day. Strictly speaking, there are two different forms of this position; the first, which can be called *ethical skepticism,* denies that we can have the slightest certainty about questions of the right and the good. Sometimes the ethical skeptic says that words like "right," "good," "ought," and "duty" just don't have any meaning; sentences containing them are a bit like incantations or cheers of approval or perhaps just plain gibberish. Because the very words we use to make moral judgments have no meaning, our moral judgments can hardly be called true or false, valid or invalid. At other times, the ethical skeptic merely points out that no valid argument can be found for any particular moral principle. If I doubt that murder is wrong, you cannot find an argument that will prove to me that it is. If I can't see why I should help another person in distress, there is no way it can be demonstrated to me that I should. Philosophers who take either of these lines frequently think that science and scientific language are the models on which we should base all of our knowledge. They point to the nondescriptive character of moral statements (they don't tell us how things are; they claim to tell us how things ought to be). They contrast the orderly experimentation and examination of data in the sciences with the haphazard, intuitive, unfactual character of moral disputes. Sometimes they suggest that moral arguments really come down to disagreements over matters of taste, and as the old saying has it, *de gustibus non disputandem est* (there is no disputing in matters of taste).

The *ethical skeptic* is sometimes joined in the fight against objective moral principles by the *ethical relativist*. How often, in a bull session, have we heard someone say, "Oh well, it's all relative!" Sometimes that means "Everyone *has* his own opinion." Sometimes it means "Everyone *is entitled* to his own opinion." But sometimes it means "Everyone's opinion is true to him, even though it may not be true for someone else." As a student said to me once in class when I asked whether he thought that Hitler had been wrong to kill millions of people in death camps, "Well, it wouldn't be right for me, but I guess it was right for him."

In the following passage, the American anthropologist Ruth Benedict draws on her wide knowledge of the varieties of human culture to argue for the fundamental relativity of moral judgments. There is something very unsettling about the fact that a scientist who has seen so much of human culture and society in all its forms should come to a relativist position.

No one civilization can possibly utilize in its mores the whole potential range of human behavior. . . .

Every society, beginning with some inclination in one direction or another, carries its preference farther and farther, integrating itself more and more completely upon its chosen basis, and discarding those types of behavior that are uncongenial. Most of those organizations of personality that seem to us most incontrovertibly abnormal have been used by different civilizations in the very foundations of their institutional life. Conversely the most valued traits of our normal individuals have been looked on in differently organized cultures as aberrant. Normality, in short, within a very wide range, is culturally defined. . . . The very eyes with which we see the problem are conditioned by the long traditional habits of our own society.

It is a point that has been made more often in relation to ethics than in relation to psychiatry. We do not any longer make the mistake of deriving the morality of our own locality and decade directly from the inevitable constitution of human nature. We do not elevate it to the dignity of a first principle. We recognize that morality differs in every society, and is a convenient term for socially approved habits. Mankind has always preferred to say, "It is morally good," rather than "It is habitual," and the fact of this preference is matter enough for a critical science of ethics. But historically the two phrases are synonymous.

RUTH BENEDICT, *Anthropology and the Abnormal*

Immanuel Kant is the strongest opponent of the ethical relativist position. A major aim of Kant's philosophical efforts was to provide an absolutely solid, totally universal proof of the validity of that moral principle which he considered the foundation of all ethics, the principle which he called the *categorical imperative*. Kant was well aware that there were serious ethical disagreements among philosophers on particular questions of moral judgment, though he was not so impressed as Hume had been by the systematic cultural differences which appeared to divide "cultivated" peoples. But Kant was extremely concerned about the lack of solid foundations for even those ethical beliefs which were more or less broadly agreed upon. In a number of profound and very difficult treatises on ethics, Kant undertook to lay those foundations.

Saying just a few words about Kant's philosophy is like saying just a few words about quantum mechanics or the theory of relativity! Nevertheless, some of the key notions of Kant's moral philosophy can be understood pretty well without plunging into the depths of his argument, and in the remainder of this section, I shall introduce you to those notions through a combination of my exposition and Kant's own words.

Kant first set out his moral philosophy in a little book called *Groundwork of the Metaphysic of Morals* (a rather imposing title). He intended the book to be just an introduction to his theory, and shortly thereafter he published another, longer work called *Critique of Practical Reason*. But as often happens, the short "introductory" book took on a life of its own, and today it is widely viewed as the finest statement of Kant's position.

The aim of *Groundwork* is to discover, analyze, and defend the fundamental principle of morality. As you know, Kant didn't think he had discovered a *new* principle, and he liked to say that his categorical imperative was nothing more than a philosophically more precise statement of the old Golden Rule: Do unto others as you would have others do unto you. Here is the way in which Kant revised and restated that rule:

THE CATEGORICAL IMPERATIVE

Act only on that maxim through which you can at the same time will that it should become a universal law.

That doesn't *look* much like the Golden Rule, but Kant thought it contained the same basic notion, which is that we ought to put aside our own private interests and act instead on the basis of rules that would be equally reasonable for all moral agents to adopt as their own. "Do unto others as you would have others do unto you" doesn't mean "Go ahead and steal from your neighbor so long as you don't squawk when he steals from you." It means something more like "Treat other people with the same respect and dignity that you expect to be treated with." As we shall see, the idea of human dignity plays a central role in Kant's moral philosophy.

There are three ideas that lie at the heart of Kant's ethics. If we can understand something about each of them, we can form at least a preliminary notion of his theory. The ideas are first, that persons are rational creatures, capable of thinking about the choices they face and selecting among them on the basis of reasons; second, that persons have an infinite worth or dignity which sets them above all merely conditionally valuable things in this world, that they are what Kant calls ends-in-themselves; and third, that persons, as rational ends-in-themselves, are the *authors* of the moral law, so that their obedience to duty is not an act of slavish submission but an act of dignified *autonomy*. Persons as rational agents, persons as ends-in-themselves, and persons as autonomous—these are the basic building blocks out of which Kant constructs his proof of the categorical imperative.

When Kant asserts that persons are rational agents, he means more than merely that they are capable of making judgments about the nature of the world, or inferences from one set of propositions to another. A rational agent is a person who is capable of *moving himself or herself to act* by reason. David Hume, like many other philosophers, had thought that reason was incapable of moving us to action. Hume argued that *desire* moved us to act; reason could merely point out the most efficient path to the goal that desire chose. So Hume said, in a much-quoted passage, that "reason is, and ought only to be the slave of the passions, and can never pretend to any other office than to serve and obey them" (*Treatise of Human Nature,* Book III). Kant replied that if we are to make any sense at all out of our condition as creatures capable of choice and deliberation, we must acknowledge that we can be moved by *reasons,* not merely by *desires.*

If Kant is right that we can be moved by reason, then it makes sense to ask whether we have acted wisely or foolishly, whether we have reasoned consistently in our choice of ends and means. It makes sense, also, to ask whether in our reasoning we have taken special account of our own particular wishes and interests, or instead have limited ourselves only to reasons which would be compelling reasons for any person in the same circumstances. In short, it makes sense to ask whether we have acted *rationally.*

This notion of "reasons good for all rational agents" is a difficult one to grasp. Perhaps one way to get some idea of Kant's meaning is to compare a moral agent to a mathematician doing a geometry problem. Suppose the mathematician is trying to show that the square of the hypotenuse of a right triangle is equal to the sum of the squares of the other two sides (the so-called Pythagorean Theorem that some of you studied in high school). Now, the first thing she does in developing the proof is to draw a triangle, and because every triangle has to be some size and shape or other, the particular triangle the mathematician draws will be some particular size (maybe 4½ inches by 6 inches by 7½ inches), and it will also be some particular color (depending upon the color of the paper she draws it on), and so forth. But of course she isn't supposed to pay any attention to the actual size and color of the triangle. They are there, all right, but she is supposed to ignore them. The only thing she is allowed to count in her proof is the fact that the triangle has a right angle in it. If our imaginary mathematician constructs her proof by using only the fact that her triangle is a right triangle, then her conclusions, when she gets them, will apply to *all* right triangles, not just to the one she actually drew.

In the same way, Kant claims that moral agents, when they reason about what they ought to do, should ignore all the particular facts about their own interests, special desires, individual circumstances, and so on, and concentrate just on those facts which hold for *all* rational agents as such. If they do that, he says, then the conclusions they come to will be valid for all rational agents, not just for themselves. In short, their conclusions will be universal laws, not just personal rules. Kant uses the word "maxim" to mean a personal rule on which we actually base our decisions. [In the following selection, he also uses

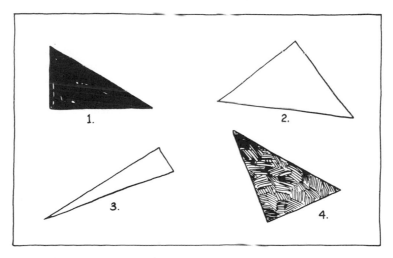

All four triangles have three angles and three sides, though they differ in color, shape, and size. When mathematicians prove geometric theorems, they ignore the irrelevant differences, and make reference only to the properties on which their arguments are based.

the term "subjective principle" with this meaning.] So he is telling us that when we make our decisions, we, like the mathematician, should restrict ourselves to rules, or maxims, that could just as well serve any rational agent. In other words, he tells us to restrict ourselves to maxims that could serve as universal laws. That is what he is trying to say in the categorical imperative: Act only on that maxim through which you can at the same time will that it should become a universal law.

If we do succeed in acting in a genuinely rational way, Kant says, we show ourselves to possess a dignity that sets us above everything else in the world. Indeed, the statement that moral agents, as persons, have an infinite worth or dignity, is, according to Kant just another way of saying what has already been said in the categorical imperative. Here is the famous passage in which Kant develops the notion that persons are ends-in-themselves. Difficult as Kant's argument is, I think you will be able to see in it something of the grandeur and profundity which made Kant so great a moral philosopher:

Now I say that man, and in general every rational being, *exists* as an end in himself, *not merely as a means* for arbitrary use by this or that will: he must in all his actions, whether they are directed to himself or to other rational beings, always be viewed *at the same time as an end.* All the objects of inclination have only a conditioned value; for if there were not these inclinations and the needs grounded on them, their object would be valueless. Inclinations themselves, as sources of needs, are so far from having an absolute value to make them desirable for their own sake that it must rather be the universal wish of every rational being to be wholly free from them. Thus the value of all objects that can *be produced* by our action is always conditioned. Beings whose existence depends, not on our will, but on nature, have none the less, if they are non-rational beings, only a relative value as means and are consequently called *things.* Rational beings, on the other hand, are called *persons* because their nature already marks them out as ends in themselves and consequently imposes to that extent a limit on all arbitrary treatment of them (and is an object of reverence). Persons, therefore, are not merely subjective ends whose existence as an object of our actions has a value *for us:* they are *objective ends*—that is, things whose existence is in itself an end, and indeed an end such that in its place we can put no other end to which they should serve *simply* as means; for unless this is so, nothing at all of *absolute* value would be found anywhere. But if all value were conditioned then no supreme principle could be found for reason at all.

If then there is to be a supreme practical principle and a categorical imperative, it must be such that from the idea of something which is necessarily an end for every one because it is an *end in itself* it forms an *objective* principle of the will and consequently can serve as a practical law. The ground of this principle is: *Rational nature exists as an end in itself.* This is the way in which a man necessarily conceives his own existence: it is therefore so far a *subjective* principle of human actions. But it is also the way in which every other rational being conceives his existence on the same rational ground which is valid also for me; hence it is at the same time an *objective* principle, from which, as a supreme practical ground, it must be possible to derive all laws for the will. The practical imperative will therefore be as follows: *Act in such a way that you always treat humanity, whether in your own person or in the person of any other, never simply as a means, but always at the same time as an end.*

IMMANUEL KANT, *Groundwork of the Metaphysic of Morals*

Hume had described reason as the "slave" of the passions, subservient to their direction. Kant is the sworn foe of such slavery, as he was of slavery in the political realm. If my reason is the slave of my passions, then I forfeit the dignity that I possess in virtue of being an end-in-myself. There is no honor in subservience to passion, any more than in subservience to a king or emperor. In the inner life of each man and woman, as in the public life of the State, honor is to be found only in submission to self-made laws. The citizen of a republic, who makes the laws to which he bows his head, loses no dignity by his obedience, for he is obeying only himself when he abides by the law. His obedience is an act of responsibility rather than of servitude.

The same principle, Kant thought, holds true within the individual soul. When reason bows to passion, it forfeits its claim to honor and dignity. But if reason can itself legislate the laws to which it submits; if reason can itself write the categorical imperative that binds it, then it will perserve its freedom in the very act of submission. To give laws to oneself is, following the Greek, to be *auto-nomos*—giver of law to oneself—in short: autonomous. The principle of the autonomy of reason is, Kant says, yet another version of the categorical imperative. In the following passage, Kant develops this notion of autonomy. Do not be surprised if you find this bit of text hard going. Kant is difficult to understand even in his easier writings, and this statement about autonomy is one of his chewiest bits of argument.

This principle of humanity, and in general of every rational agent, *as an end in itself* (a principle which is the supreme limiting condition of every man's freedom of action) is not borrowed from experience; firstly, because it is universal, applying as it does to all rational beings as such, and no experience is adequate to determine universality; secondly, because in it humanity is conceived, not as an end of man (subjectively) but as an objective end—one which, be our ends what they may, must, as a law, constitute the supreme limiting condition of all subjective ends and so must spring from pure reason. That is to say, the ground for every enactment of practical law lies *objectively in the rule* and in the form of universality which (according to our first principle) makes the rule capable of being a law (and indeed a law of nature); *subjectively,* however, it lies in the *end;* but (according to our second principle) the subject of all ends is to be found in every rational being as an end in himself. From this there now follows our third practical principle for the will namely, the Idea *of the will of every rational being as a will which makes universal law.*

By this principle all maxims are repudiated which cannot accord with the will's own enactment of universal law. The will is therefore not merely subject to the law, but is so subject that it must be considered as also *making the law* for itself and precisely on this account as first of all subject to the law (of which it can regard itself as the author).

Imperatives as formulated above did, by the mere fact that they were represented as categorical, exclude from their sovereign authority every admixture of interest as a motive. They were, however, merely *assumed* to be categorical because we were bound to make this assumption if we wished to explain the concept of duty. That there were practical propositions which commanded categorically could not itself be proved, any more than it can be proved in this chapter generally; but one thing could have been done—namely, to show that in willing for the sake of duty renunciation of all interest, as the specific mark distinguishing a categorical from a hypothetical imperative, was expressed in the very imperative itself by means of some determination inherent in it. This is what is done in the present third formulation of the principle—namely, in the Idea of the will of every rational being as *a will which makes universal law.*

Once we conceive a will of this kind, it becomes clear that while a will *which is subject to law* may be bound to this law by some interest, nevertheless a will which is itself a supreme law-giver cannot possibly as such depend on any interest; for a will which is dependent in this way would itself require yet a further law in order to restrict the interest of self-love to the condition that this interest should itself be valid as a universal law.

Thus the *principle* that every human will is *a will which by all its maxims enacts universal law* would be *well suited* to be a categorical imperative in this respect: that precisely because of the Idea of making universal law it is *based on no interest* and consequently can alone among all possible imperatives be *unconditioned.* Or better still if there is a categorical imperative (that is, a law for the will of every rational being), it can command us only to act always on the maxim of such a will in us as can at the same time look upon itself as making universal law; for only then is the practical principle and the imperative which we obey unconditioned, since it is wholly impossible for it to be based on any interest.

We need not now wonder, when we look back upon all the previous efforts that have been made to discover the principle of morality, why they have one and all been bound to fail. Their authors saw man as tied to laws by his duty, but it never occurred to them that he is subject only to *laws which are made by himself* and yet are *universal,* and that he is bound only to act in conformity with a will which is his own but has as nature's purpose for it the function of making universal law. For when they thought of man merely as subject to a law (whatever it might be), the law had to carry with it some interest in order to attract or compel, because it did not spring as a law from *his own* will: in order to conform with the law his will had to be necessitated by *something else* to act in a certain way. This absolutely inevitable conclusion meant that all the labour spent in trying to find a supreme principle of duty was lost beyond recall; for what they discovered was never duty, but only the necessity of acting from a certain interest. This interest might be one's own or another's; but on such a view the imperative was bound to be always a conditioned one and could not possibly serve as a moral law. I will therefore call my principle the principle of the *Autonomy* of the will in contrast with all others, which I consequently class under *Heteronomy.*

IMMANUEL KANT, *Groundwork of the Metaphysic of Morals*

Having set forth three key principles: (1) the rationality of the will, (2) the infinite worth of persons as ends-in-themselves, and (3) the self-legislating, or autonomous, character of reason, Kant now pulls them all together in the notion of a society of moral agents, all of whom govern their actions by reason, all of whom are ends-in-themselves, and all of whom are autonomous. He calls this society a *kingdom of ends,* and we can imagine it as an ideal community of upright, responsible, rational men and women who base their actions on universally valid laws which they autonomously lay down for themselves. It is a community that lives according to the categorical imperative. In our last passage from Kant, we see all of these themes united:

In the kingdom of ends everything has either a *price* or a *dignity.* If it has a price, something else can be put in its place as an equivalent; if it is exalted above all price and so admits of no equivalent, then it has a dignity.

What is relative to universal human inclinations and needs has a *market price;* what, even without presupposing a need, accords with a certain taste has a *fancy price (Affektionspreis);* but that which constitutes the sole condition under which anything can be an end in itself has not merely a relative value but has an intrinsic value—that is, *dignity.*

Now morality is the only condition under which a rational being can be an end in himself; for only through this is it possible to be a law-making member in a kingdom of ends. Therefore morality, and humanity so far as it is capable of morality, is the only thing which has dignity. Skill and diligence in work have a market price; wit, lively imagination, and humour have a fancy price; but fidelity to promises and kindness based on principle (not on instinct) have an intrinsic worth. In default of these, nature and art alike contain nothing to put in their place; for their worth consists, not in the effects which result from them, not in the advantage or profit they produce, but in the attitudes of mind which are ready in this way to manifest themselves in action even if they are not favoured by success. Such actions too need no recommendation from any subjective disposition or taste in order to meet with immediate favour and approval; they need no immediate propensity or feeling for themselves; they exhibit the will which performs them as an object of immediate reverence; nor is anything other than reason required to *impose* them upon the will, nor to *coax* them from the will—which last would anyhow be a contradiction in the case of duties. This assessment reveals as dignity the value of such a mental attitude and puts it infinitely above all price, with which it cannot be brought into reckoning or comparison without, as it were, a profanation of its sanctity.

What is it then that entitles a morally good attitude of mind to make claims so high? It is nothing less than the *share* which it affords to a rational being *in the making of universal law,* and which therefore fits him to be a member in a possible kingdom of ends. For this he was already marked out in virtue of his own proper nature as an end in himself and consequently as a maker of laws in the kingdom of ends—as free in respect of all laws of nature, obeying only those laws which he makes himself and in virtue of which his maxims can have their part in the making of universal law (to which he at the same time subjects himself). For nothing can have a value other than that determined for it by the law. But the law-making which determines all value must for this reason have a dignity for the appreciation of which, as necessarily given by a rational being, the word *'reverence'* is the only becoming expression. *Autonomy* is therefore the ground of the dignity of human nature and of every rational nature.

IMMANUEL KANT, *Groundwork of the Metaphysic of Morals*

IV

How shall we deal with those terrible situations in which we want very much to do the right thing but simply cannot figure out what it is? Sometimes, there are two different and conflicting things, both of which seem right in the situation. Sometimes the situation is such a tangle that we are just at a loss. The source of our uncertainty is not temptation, or skepticism, or relativism, but the genuine moral difficulty of the case itself. One of the most ancient attempts to deal with such hard cases, and also to lay down a rule for action which will always tell us what we ought to do, is the moral philosophy which these days goes under the name of *utilitarianism.* In this section, we are going to take a look at several varieties of utilitarianism, see what the theory says and how it works, and also consider some serious objections to it.

Utilitarianism is simply the rule that we should always try to make as many people as happy as possible. Indeed, it is sometimes called "The greatest happiness principle" for this reason. The cosmologist Lucretius was a utilitarian, and so was the man whose teachings he followed, Epicurus. In the modern world, the most famous utilitarian, generally credited with establishing the doctrine as a serious contender in moral philosophy, was the eighteenth-century Englishman Jeremy Bentham.

Bentham argues that however people may appear to use the words "good" and "evil," we really just mean "pleasant" or "pleasurable" when we say "good," and "painful" when we say "evil." More good is better than less, which is to say that more pleasure is better than less. And of course, less pain is better than more. The only good reason for doing anything is to increase the amount of pleasure that human beings experience, or at least to reduce the amount of pain. What is more, pleasures and pains can, in a manner of speaking, be added to and subtracted from one another. I can ask myself, Which gave me more pleasure: the good movie I saw last week, or the mediocre movie I saw last night plus the really good pizza I had afterward? I can also ask myself, which will be more painful: three dentist's visits now, complete with drillings, or a toothache followed by an extraction followed by the annoyance of a missing tooth later? If the mediocre movie plus the pizza gave me more pleasure, then the next time I have to choose between a good movie and no pizza, or a mediocre movie and pizza, I ought to take the mediocre movie plus pizza. And more seriously, if the dentist's visits, bad as they are, add up to less pain than the

JEREMY BENTHAM (1748–1832)* was the founder of the ethical doctrine now known as utilitarianism. He began his long life during the reign of King George II, and died in the year of the Reform Bill that extended the franchise to virtually all of middle-class England. He lived through the American Revolution, the French Revolution, the Napoleonic Wars, and the rise of parliamentary government in England, and nearly survived into the reign of Queen Victoria. He was the godfather of John Stuart Mill, son of his friend and colleague James Mill. John Stuart was, in his own turn, the godfather of Bertrand Russell, the great English philosopher who ended his own long and distinguished life by leading the British campaign for nuclear disarmament in the 1960s. So in three generations of great English philosophers, we move from the mid-eighteenth century world of wigs, carriages, and kings, to the mid-twentieth century world of jets, nuclear weapons, and popular democracy.

Bentham's primary concern as a philosopher was with legal and social reform. The law in the eighteenth century was a crazy quilt of precedents, quibbles, hanging offenses, and rank injustices. Several of Bentham's books were devoted to the attempt to sort things out and find some rational system of principles to put in place of the tangle that had grown up over so many centuries. He hoped that his simple, intuitively appealing principle of utility—the Greatest Happiness of the Greatest Number—would serve as the basis for a thoroughgoing reform of the law.

rotting of my tooth, then I ought to go to the dentist even though I don't want to, because the only rational thing to do is to minimize the total amount of pain in my life.

Bentham announced the doctrine now known as utilitarianism in a book entitled *Introduction to the Principles of Morals and Legislation,* first printed in 1780 and formally published in 1789. Here is a selection from the opening chapter. Notice the complete identification of pleasure with good and pain with evil. This is the heart and soul of Bentham's utilitarian doctrine.

Nature has placed mankind under the governance of two sovereign masters, *pain* and *pleasure.* It is for them alone to point out what we ought to do, as well as to

* In his will, Jeremy Bentham left his whole estate to the University of London provided that his remains be present at all board meetings. The University stuffed his body, shown above. The head here is wax, but the actual head, preserved in the tradition of South American headhunters, lies between his feet.

determine what we shall do. On the one hand the standard of right and wrong, on the other the chain of causes and effects, are fastened to their throne. They govern us in all we do, in all we say, in all we think: every effort we can make to throw off our subjection, will serve but to demonstrate and confirm it. In words a man may pretend to abjure their empire: but in reality he will remain subject to it all the while. The *principle of utility* recognizes this subjection, and assumes it for the foundation of that system, the object of which is to rear the fabric of felicity by the hands of reason and law. Systems which attempt to question it, deal in sounds instead of sense, in caprice instead of reason, in darkness instead of light.

But enough of metaphor and declamation: it is not by such means that moral science is to be improved.

The principle of utility is the foundation of the present work: it will be proper therefore at the outset to give an explicit and determinate account of what is meant by it. By the principle of utility is meant that principle which approves or disapproves of every action whatsoever, according to the tendency which it appears to have to augment or diminish the happiness of the party whose interest is in question: or, what is the same thing in other words, to promote or to oppose that happiness. I say of every action whatsoever; and therefore not only of every action of a private individual, but of every measure of government.

By utility is meant that property in any object, whereby it tends to produce benefit, advantage, pleasure, good, or happiness, (all this in the present case comes to the same thing) or (what comes again to the same thing) to prevent the happening of mischief, pain, evil, or unhappiness to the party whose interest is considered: if that party be the community in general, then the happiness of the community: if a particular individual, then the happiness of that individual.

The interest of the community is one of the most general expressions that can occur in the phraseology of morals: no wonder that the meaning of it is often lost. When it has a meaning, it is this. The community is a fictitious *body,* composed of the individual persons who are considered as constituting as it were its *members.* The interest of the community then is, what?—the sum of the interests of the several members who compose it.

It is in vain to talk of the interest of the community, without understanding what is the interest of the individual. A thing is said to promote the interest, or to be *for* the interest, of an individual, when it tends to add to the sum total of his pleasures: or, what comes to the same thing, to diminish the sum total of his pains.

An action then may be said to be conformable to the principle of utility, or, for shortness sake, to utility, (meaning with respect to the community at large) when the tendency it has to augment the happiness of the community is greater than any it has to diminish it.

A measure of government (which is but a particular kind of action, performed by a particular person or persons) may be said to be conformable to or dictated by the principle of utility, when in like manner the tendency which it has to augment the happiness of the community is greater than any which it has to diminish it.

JEREMY BENTHAM,
An Introduction to the Principles of Morals and Legislation

The crucial step in Bentham's argument is his move from the total pleasure and pain experienced by one person to the total pleasure or pain experienced by all the members of the community taken together. This is the device which permits Bentham to extract a moral principle from his theory. The point is that whenever I do anything at all, my action has effects which impinge on the lives of other people. Sometimes I cause them pleasure, sometimes I cause them pain, and sometimes of course I cause some of them pleasure and others pain. For example, if the young man we mentioned earlier decides to stay at home with his parents rather than leave and set out on his own, he will probably cause himself pain and his mother and father pleasure. That is just why he doesn't know what to do! If his staying at home caused his parents pain too (they, after all, might want to live their own lives), then the decision would be an easy one for him.

Whenever we face hard choices, Bentham tells us, we can translate an impossible moral dilemma into a problem of addition and subtraction. For the young man, the choice is between staying home with his parents and leaving. He adds up all the pleasure and pain (negative values for pain, of course) that anybody in the situation will experience as the result of his staying, and compares it with the total pleasure and pain that everyone will experience as a result of his leaving home. He then chooses the alternative with the highest positive

TO MARRY OR NOT TO MARRY
A UTILITARIAN CALCULATION

IF I MARRY	UNITS OF PLEASURE	IF I DON'T MARRY	UNITS OF PLEASURE
1. A secure sex life	+ 1000	1. Freedom to enter new relationships	+ 500
2. But no playing the field	− 300	2. Loneliness	− 300
3. The joy of children	+ 700	3. No children, no grand-children	− 800
4. The expense of children	− 500	4. But no responsibilities	+1000
5. Companionship in old age	+ 400	5. No ties to hold me in one job, one place	+ 400
6. Responsibilities, ties, burdens	− 600	6. But no roots, no one who really cares whether I live or die	− 500
THE UTILITY OF MARRYING	+ 700	THE UTILITY OF NOT MARRYING	+ 300
+700 IS GREATER THAN +300, THEREFORE: I DO			

According to Bentham, the rational man or woman will choose the alternative which offers the greatest total of pleasure. Does anyone ever make an important decision this way? Would you?

total (or, if it is one of those "least of evils" situations, the alternative with the smallest negative total). For example, suppose that the young man desperately wants to leave home. Then we can assume that he will suffer great pain if he must stay, and he will gain great pleasure if he goes. Let us also assume that his parents would like him to stay at home, but they are not dead set on it. They will manage all right if he leaves. Now we have great pain plus moderate pleasure on the side of staying, and great pleasure plus moderate pain on the side of going. Obviously, this adds up to a decision to go.

A great many objections can be raised to utilitarianism, and I am about to raise several of the more serious ones. But before we start chopping this theory down, it is worth taking a few moments to look at its very considerable strengths. In the first place, utilitarianism assumes that everyone wants to be happy, and it is hard to argue with that. But even more important, utilitarianism explains happiness in terms that everyone can understand. It doesn't say that happiness is oneness with the infinite, or self-fulfillment, or the integration of adult roles with childhood ego formations, or what have you. It says that happiness is pleasure, unhappiness is pain, and the more pleasure or the less pain the better.

Nor does utilitarianism demand strange, painful sacrifices from its believers. Kant believed, for example, that we should keep our promises and tell the truth no matter who got hurt. That is a dark saying, fraught with potentiality for terrible choices where lives are lost or hideous pain inflicted simply because someone will not violate an absolute moral rule. But Bentham says nothing of that sort. By all means lie, he says, if the total pain produced by the truth is greater than that produced by the lie. Make sure to add in the side effects of the lie, such as the likelihood that the next time you tell the truth it won't be believed. But when all those long-term, short-term, direct, and indirect effects have been calculated, then just choose the course promising the greatest happiness for the greatest number of people.

The most impressive strength of utilitarianism is its ability to transform seemingly impossible problems of moral deliberation into manageable empirical problems of investigation and addition. To see what that means, imagine that we lived a long time ago in an agricultural society which had not yet discovered geometry. Each year, as the flood waters from the river receded, it would become necessary to divide up the land again for the spring planting. The plots all must be triangular (owing to some religious belief, we may suppose). The high priest would stake out each family's land, and then the arguing would begin over whose plot was bigger, and who had been slighted in the dividing up. The wise men would gather, great deliberations would ensue, with much prayer and meditation, and in the end no one would really be satisfied with the high priest's decisions. Now just think what it would mean, in such a society, for someone to discover the simple geometric theorem that the area of a triangle is equal to one-half the base times the height! All those moral and religious disputes would be dissolved in an instant into a process of calculation. The royal surveyor would just measure the bases of the family plots, multiply by their heights, (the plots', not the family's), and then make adjustments until each family had the same area. It would put the royal moral philosopher and the royal priest out of business!

Well, Bentham had hopes that his great happiness principle would do the same for the modern wizards who in his own society did the job of the ancient priests and moral philosophers—namely the judges and lawyers. He believed that rational legislators, with the principle of utility to guide them, could replace the hideous tangle of laws and punishments of the English common law with a single reasonable schedule of punishments designed to produce the greatest happiness for the greatest number. Where the legislators lacked enough facts to make a sensible decision, instead of digging around in their law books for precedents and corollary cases, they could go out and collect some facts to settle the matter. Here is another selection from Bentham's *Principles* which shows how he hoped to use the Greatest Happiness Principle in practice:

1. The general object which all laws have, or ought to have, in common, is to augment the total happiness of the community; and therefore, in the first place, to exclude, as far as may be, every thing that tends to subtract from that happiness: in other words, to exclude mischief.

2. But all punishment is mischief: all punishment in itself is evil. Upon the principle of utility, if it ought at all to be admitted, it ought only to be admitted in as far as it promises to exclude some greater evil.

3. It is plain, therefore, that in the following cases punishment ought not to be inflicted.

1. Where it is *groundless;* where there is no mischief for it to prevent: the act not being mischievous upon the whole.

2. Where it must be *inefficacious:* where it cannot act so as to prevent the mischief.

3. Where it is *unprofitable,* or too *expensive;* where the mischief it would produce would be greater than what it prevented.

4. Where it is *needless:* where the mischief may be prevented, or cease of itself, without it: that is, at a cheaper rate. . . .

CASES WHERE PUNISHMENT IS UNPROFITABLE

These are,

1. Where, on the one hand, the nature of the offence, on the other hand, that of the punishment, are, *in the ordinary state of things,* such, that when compared together, the evil of the latter will turn out to be greater than that of the former.

Now the evil of the punishment divides itself into four branches, by which so many different sets of persons are affected. 1. The evil of *coercion* or *restraint:* or the pain which it gives a man not to be able to do the act, whatever it be, which by the apprehension of the punishment he is deterred from doing. This is felt by those by whom the law is *observed.* 2. The evil of *apprehension:* or the pain which a man, who has exposed himself to punishment, feels at the thoughts of undergoing it. This is felt by those by whom the law has been *broken,* and who feel themselves in *danger* of its being executed upon them. 3. The evil of *sufferance:* or the pain which a man feels, in virtue of the punishment itself, from the time when he begins to undergo it. This is felt by those by whom the law is broken, and upon whom it comes actually to be executed. 4. The pain of sympathy, and the other *derivative* evils resulting to the persons who are in *connection* with the several classes of original sufferers just mentioned. Now of these four lots of evil, the first will be greater or less, according to the nature of the act from which the party is restrained: the second and third according to the nature of the punishment which stands annexed to that offence.

On the other hand, as to the evil of the offence, this will also, of course, be greater or less, according to the nature of the offence. The proportion between the one evil and the other will therefore be different in the case of each particular offence. The cases, therefore, where punishment is unprofitable on this ground, can by no other means be discovered, than by an examination of each particular offence; which is what will be the business of the body of the work.

2. Where, although in the *ordinary state* of things, the evil resulting from the punishment is not greater than the benefit which is likely to result from the force with which it operates, during the same space of time, towards the excluding the evil of the offence, yet it may have been rendered so by the influence of some *occasional circumstances.* In the number of these circumstances may be, 1. The multitude of delinquents at a particular juncture; being such as would increase, beyond the ordinary measure, the *quantum* of the second and third lots, and thereby also of a part of the fourth lot, in the evil of the punishment. 2. The extraordinary value of the services of some one delinquent; in the case where the effect of the punishment would be to deprive the community of the benefit of those services. 3. The displeasure of the *people;* that is, of an indefinite number of the members of the *same* community, in cases where (owing to the influence of some occasional incident) they happen to conceive, that the offence or the offender ought not to be punished at all, or at least ought not to be punished in the way in question. 4. The displeasure of *foreign powers;* that is, of the governing body, or a considerable number of the members of some *foreign* community or communities, with which the community in question, is connected.

JEREMY BENTHAM,
An Introduction to the Principles of Morals and Legislation

Utilitarianism has probably had more words written about it than all the other moral theories put together. It is a clear, simple, natural-sounding moral philosophy, and it has a thousand things wrong with it as a theory! That is a perfect formula for a philosophical argument. Two sorts of objections turn up over and over again in philosophical discussions. First, critics say that although utilitarianism looks clear and simple, it is actually so confused that we can't tell exactly what it says. And second, these same critics argue that, even after we have decided what utilitarianism says, we find that it tells us to do things that most of us would consider deeply immoral. Let us take a look at both of these objections.

What does utilitarianism say? Very simple: maximize happiness. But what exactly does that mean? The most natural answer is, add up all the pleasure experienced by all the people in the world, subtract all the pain they suffer, and that is the total. Then anything that increases the total is good, anything that decreases it is bad, and if two actions promise to increase the total, the one that offers a bigger increase is just that much better. What could be clearer?

Ah well. A little philosophy teaches us that a trap very often lurks in even the simplest-looking statement. If *total* happiness is all that counts, then a world with a *billion* marginally happy people will be morally better than a world with a *million* extremely happy people. The point is that if the very happy people are only five hundred times happier than the marginally happy people, then one billion times the small happiness in the first world will be a bigger total than one million times the tremendous happiness in the second world. Something is obviously wrong with that conclusion. In an already over-crowded world, it makes no sense to go on increasing the population as long as each additional person can be said to experience a slight balance of pleasure over pain. Surely Bentham wasn't merely arguing for a population explosion.

So maybe what he really meant was to maximize the *average* happiness experienced by the people already on this earth. That makes a good deal more sense. A world of a million very happy people is obviously preferable to a world of a billion marginally happy people, because in the first world, the *level* of happiness—in other words, the average—is higher. And it is the level of happiness we are really interested in.

But once again, serious problems arise. Suppose we can make some people very happy indeed by making other people miserable. That isn't an implausible hypothesis at all. Slavery is a social system which lays the burden of work and suffering on one group—the slaves—so that another group—the masters—can lead easy, comfortable lives. (So is capitalism, but we shall get to that in the next chapter.) Is Bentham really in favor of slavery?

Bentham has an answer, of sorts. His principle, he claims, calls for "the greatest happiness of all those whose interest is in question." Because everyone (even a slave) is someone whose interest is in question, it follows that utilitarian-ism calls for the greatest possible happiness for everyone, not just the greatest happiness for the slave-owners, or the capitalists, or the rulers. Now the trouble with this interpretation of the Principle of Utility is that on closer examination, it turns out not to be any sort of rule at all. The proof for this is a trifle technical, involving as it does the mathematical theorem that in general two or more independent functions cannot be maximized simultaneously. But the real point—if that last sentence hasn't caused you all to close your books—is rather simple.

Sometimes, life offers me a way to make everybody happier at the same time, and obviously when a chance like that comes along, I take it. Too often, life offers me a way to make everybody unhappier at the same time, and if I have any sense at all, I stay away from chances like that. But most of the time, what I do will make some people happier and other people unhappier.

Remember the young man trying to decide whether to leave his parents? His first choice, to stay home, makes his parents happier and him unhappier. His second choice, to leave, makes him happier and his parents unhappier. There just isn't any way to make all of them happier at the same time. That is precisely why it is a hard case. Now, we don't need Bentham to tell us what to do on those rare occasions when we can make everyone happier simultaneously. But utilitarianism is supposed to give us a rule, a method, for handling just the hard-to-decide cases in which one person's happiness has to be balanced off against another person's unhappiness. Plausible as "the greatest happiness for the greatest number" sounds, it doesn't work out in practice to be a rule that is going to settle any hard cases for us.

Suppose we go back therefore to the notion of the greatest average happiness. (Notice, by the way, that if you keep the population stable, greatest average happiness is exactly equal to greatest total happiness, so that is probably what Bentham has in mind.) How does that stand up as a rule for deciding what to do? At least it is unambiguous; if we have enough information to predict the outcomes of our actions, then we can add up the pleasures, subtract the pains, divide by the total population, and get some sort of average. But now we run into the second sort of objection to utilitarianism—namely that it tells us to do things that seem immoral.

Once again, the problem is making some people suffer so that others may be happy. Let me sketch out a bizarre example that will help to make this point. Suppose Americans, like the ancient Romans, positively enjoyed watching people being tortured. (Naturally, such an assumption is totally contrary to the real facts, because American taste in movies, television shows, and novels shows that we are all kindly, peace-loving, sympathetic creatures who hate the sight of violence!) Now Bentham will obviously believe that torture is an evil to the person who suffers it, for torture is painful, and pain is evil. But the pleasure that a group of sadists get from watching the torture is good, for pleasure, says Bentham, is good. So for a utilitarian, torture can be justified if and only if the total pleasure produced outweighs the total pain produced, including side effects, long-run effects, and so forth. What is more, if torture produces, in total and on balance, greater happiness than any other alternative open to us, then it is the positively right thing to do, according to utilitarianism.

We shall therefore institute a new TV show called "Torture of the Week." This is a live show in which real victims really do get tortured. (Sadists get little or no pleasure from watching simulated torture.) The victims are simply snatched off the street by force (no one except a masochist is going to offer himself as a victim, and real sadists don't enjoy watching masochists undergo torture). According to utilitarianism, if there are enough viewers who are ecstatic at the sight of this torture, then their pleasure must outweigh the pain suffered by the victim. And if no other show on television has anything resembling its high ratings, then we can assume that putting on the torture show is not only justified, but positively morally obligatory!

Just to handle an obvious objection, let us also assume that a board of social psychologists concludes that the torture show does not increase the probability of violent crime in the society. Indeed, it may even decrease such crime, by offering an outlet for sadistic desires. In short, assume that from any point of view, this torture show meets the criterion of the Principle of Utility.

What is wrong with this proposal? Don't tell me that there aren't enough people around who would enjoy the show. The point of the example was to show that according to utilitarianism the show *would* be right if there *were* such people in America. Besides, we could always increase the pleasure product by beaming the show overseas so that sadists all over the world could watch it. And don't tell me that the pain of the victim's suffering outweighs the pleasure of millions of sadistic viewers. That is just plain implausible, and what is more, I can always adjust the torture inflicted on the victim downward until the pleasure of the viewers outweighs it.

No, what really convinces me that my proposal is immoral (and I suspect many of you feel the same way) is that society has *no right* to make one man or woman suffer for the mere amusement of others. This is one of those cases, something inside me says, where adding up pleasures and pains is the wrong way to find out what we ought to do. If America's sadists have to suffer the pain and frustration of losing their favorite show, then so much the worse for them!

We have opened up a very large and complicated subject with this appeal to the notion of *rights,* and a few words can only begin to indicate some of its ins and outs. Nevertheless, let's explore it for a bit, just to see what makes Bentham's pleasure-pain calculus seem such an inadequate expression of our moral convictions. To begin with, we must not go overboard and say that society never has the right to derive benefits from the suffering of one of its members. Leaving aside obvious but controversial cases like wars, we can simply recall that every time a major bridge or tunnel is built, several workmen lose their lives. It may seem callous when we put it into words, but all of us employ a rough utilitarian calculation in judging the social desirability of large-scale public works. We try hard to minimize the loss of life in heavy construction, but we refuse to bring it to a dead halt simply because we know that men lose their lives on the job. If a project is going to cost hundreds of lives, we will probably veto it. If only a few men are likely to be killed, we will give it the go-ahead. Aren't we weighing one man's life against the convenience of the motorists who will use the bridge? How does that differ from weighing the pain of the victim against the pleasure of the sadistic viewers?

Well, one answer is that the construction men choose voluntarily to work on the bridge, knowing that it is a risky job, whereas the torture victim is forced into his role. That certainly is part of the difference, for I imagine we would take a *somewhat* different view of the show if we knew that the victims were volunteers.

But there still seem to be other differences. The motorist benefits from the suffering of the construction worker, to be sure. But that suffering isn't the object of his or her pleasure. The sadist, on the other hand, takes pleasure in the victim's pain. Now, it seems to me that there are some pleasures that are evil in and of themselves. They are bad pleasures, pleasures which people should not have; and pleasure taken in the pain of another person is one of those evil pleasures. So the torture example suggests, at least to me, that Bentham's original assumption was wrong. Not all pleasures are equal, save for quantity or intensity. And "good" does not simply mean "pleasant." So when we perform Bentham's social arithmetic, adding up pleasures and pains in order to evaluate a social policy, we most certainly ought not to put the sadist's pleasure on the plus side. He or she doesn't have a right to that pleasure, and if it is to be weighed at all, it ought to be put on the negative side with the pains. (Needless to say, there may be some pains which ought to go on the positive side! As you can see, this subject gets more and more complicated the deeper into it you go.)

It may even be, as Immanuel Kant thought, that there are some considerations more important than pleasure and pain—considerations of justice and freedom. Kant would argue that the torture show degrades both the victim and the viewers, that it treats them—in his famous phrase—as means merely and not as ends in themselves.

But when all is said and done, when examples like my torture show have been brought forward to refute utilitarianism, when the unclarities in the very meaning of the principle have been exposed to view, there still remains a natural appeal of Bentham's theory that will not go away. In the next chapter, when we meet John Stuart Mill, Bentham's most famous follower, we shall try once again to discover the kernel of truth that seems to lie inside the moral philosophy of utilitarianism.

V

The Greeks spoke of the search for the principles of the good life. The Romans had a phrase, *mens sana in corpore sano*—a sound mind in a sound body. Psychoanalysts today talk about an integrated ego. Marx wrote of "alienation" and a future of "unalienated labor." The idea is essentially the same in each case, even though the emphasis, the underlying theory, or the viewpoint differs. For ages, men and women have been seeking for a style of life and spirit that achieves a wholeness, an integration, an authenticity of mind and body, of reason, passion, and desire. These days, the search is left to psychologists and the religious, at least in England and America, but in the tradition of Western thought, it is philosophers who have given the most sustained and thoughtful attention to the search for the good life.

Everyone who has reflected for even a short while on the problem of achieving an integrated, fulfilled, virtuous life agrees that the key to a solution lies in the discovery of the proper internal order of the self itself (what the Greeks call the "soul" or *psyche*). And needless to say, there are almost as many theories about the precise nature of that desirable inner order as there are writers on the subject. But on one fundamental issue, the philosophers of the good life divide into two distinct camps. One group, which includes Stoics like Marcus Aurelius, claims that inner peace and harmony can be achieved regardless of the character of the society in which we live, regardless of the external circumstances of peace or war, tyranny or justice, health or disease. The other group emphasizes the interplay between the individual personality and the larger society, claiming that not even a wise man or woman can be truly happy save in a truly just and virtuous society. In this latter category we find Plato, Aristotle, Karl Marx, and such modern psychological theorists as Eric Fromm and Erik Erikson. You have already had an opportunity to read a bit of what Marcus Aurelius wrote about the good life. In this last section, we shall explore the view of Plato and others that the inner harmony of the self must be integrated with a proper order of society before a truly good life can be achieved.

In philosophy, we return to the same great books again and again. In Chapter One, you read a selection from an early section of Plato's immortal dialogue, the *Republic*. Now we shall jump ahead more than a hundred pages to the point at which Plato pulls together the long argument he has been developing. The official subject of the *Republic* is a search for a definition of "justice," a word to which Plato gives a broader meaning than we do today. Plato suggests two analogies or comparisons as aids in discovering the nature of justice, or true morality. The first analogy is between the soul (i e., the personality) and the body. He argues that we can speak of a healthy body and also of a healthy soul, of a diseased body and also of a diseased soul. Health of the body rests on a proper harmony or order of the bodily elements, and health of the soul in like manner consists of the correct ordering of the psychic elements. In this Dialogue, Plato distinguishes three functional parts of the soul. (I say "in this Dialogue" because Plato didn't really have a fully worked out theory of psychology, and in other Dialogues he divided the human personality up in other ways. Don't just memorize "the parts of the soul in Plato"—Try to see what he is driving at, and put his thought into your own words if you can.) The three elements are reason, or the power to deliberate, compare alternatives, suppress unwise impulses, and make sensible choices; the "spirited element," or the aggressive, warlike, wilful part of one's personality; and appetite or desire. Each of these elements has a role to play in the healthy, virtuous soul, but each must learn its proper function and perform it willingly and in harmony with the other elements. Reason must rule, governing the spirited element and directing its aggression in wise, nondestructive ways. The healthy, necessary appetites must be regulated by reason and satisfied in the proper proportion and to the appropriate degree. Too much indulgence of one or many desires may produce superficial and short-lived pleasure, but in the end it causes inner conflict and unhappiness. A well-integrated soul is a smoothly functioning whole in which each element performs its proper function and all together maintain balance, health, and true happiness.

The second of Plato's analogies is between the individual soul and the society as a whole. Just as there are several elements in the soul with special functions and a just order of subordination to one another, so there are several classes of citizens in the society with special functions and a proper social relationship to one another. The wisest citizens must rule in society, as reason does in the soul, for they possess at one and the same time the knowledge of what is truly good for the society and the rational self-control to resist the temptation of harmful desires.

In this passage from the *Republic,* Socrates is summarizing his argument. Thrasymachus and most of the others have dropped out of the conversation, and there remain only two young men, Glaucon and Adeimantus (in real life, Plato's older brothers).

And so, after a stormy passage, we have reached the land. We are fairly agreed that the same three elements exist alike in the state and in the individual soul.

That is so.

Does it not follow at once that state and individual will be wise or brave by virtue of the same element in each and in the same way? Both will possess in the same manner any quality that makes for excellence.

That must be true.

Then it applies to justice: we shall conclude that a man is just in the same way that a state was just. And we have surely not forgotten that justice in the state meant that each of the three orders in it was doing its own proper work. So we may henceforth bear in mind that each one of us likewise will be a just person, fulfilling his proper function, only if the several parts of our nature fulfil theirs.

Certainly.

And it will be the business of reason to rule with wisdom and forethought on behalf of the entire soul; while the spirited element ought to act as its subordinate and ally. The two will be brought into accord, as we said earlier, by that combination of mental and bodily training which will tune up one string of the instrument and relax the other, nourishing the reasoning part on the study of noble literature and allaying the other's wildness by harmony and rhythm. When both have been thus nurtured and trained to know their own functions, they must be set in command over the appetites, which form the greater part of each man's soul and are by nature insatiably covetous. They must keep watch lest this part, by battening on the pleasures that are called bodily, should grow so great and powerful that it will no longer keep to its own work, but will try to enslave the others and usurp a dominion to which it has no right, thus turning the whole of life upside down. At the same time, those two together will be the best of guardians for the entire soul and for the body against all enemies from without: the one will take counsel, while the other will do battle, following its ruler's commands and by its own bravery giving effect to the ruler's designs.

Yes, that is all true.

And so we call an individual brave in virtue of this spirited part of his nature, when, in spite of pain or pleasure, it holds fast to the injunctions of reason about what he ought or ought not to be afraid of.

True.

And wise in virtue of that small part which rules and issues these injunctions, possessing as it does the knowledge of what is good for each of the three elements and for all of them in common.

Certainly.

And, again, temperate by reason of the unanimity and concord of all three, when there is no internal conflict between the ruling element and its two subjects, but all are agreed that reason should be ruler.

Yes, that is an exact account of temperance, whether in the state or in the individual.

Finally, a man will be just by observing the principle we have so often stated.

Necessarily.

Now is there any indistinctness in our vision of justice, that might make it seem somehow different from what we found it to be in the state?

I don't think so.

Because, if we have any lingering doubt, we might make sure by comparing it with some commonplace notions. Suppose, for instance, that a sum of money were entrusted to our state or to an individual of corresponding character and training, would anyone imagine that such a person would be specially likely to embezzle it?

No.

And would he not be incapable of sacrilege and theft, or of treachery to friend or country; never false to an oath or any other compact; the last to be guilty of adultery or of neglecting parents or the due service of the gods?

Yes.

And the reason for all this is that each part of his nature is exercising its proper function, of ruling or of being ruled.

Yes, exactly.

Are you satisfied, then, that justice is the power which produces states or individuals of whom that is true, or must we look further?

There is no need; I am quite satisfied.

And so our dream has come true—I mean the inkling we had that, by some happy chance, we had lighted upon a rudimentary form of justice from the very moment when we set about founding our commonwealth. Our principle that the born shoemaker or carpenter had better stick to his trade turns out to have been an adumbration of justice; and that is why it has helped us. But in reality justice, though evidently analogous to this principle, is not a matter of external behaviour, but of the inward self and of attending to all that is, in the fullest sense, a man's proper concern. The just man does not allow the several elements in his soul to usurp one another's functions; he is indeed one who sets his house in order, by self-mastery and discipline coming to be at peace with himself, and bringing into tune those three parts, like the terms in the proportion of a musical scale, the highest and lowest notes and the mean between them, with all the intermediate intervals. Only when he has linked these parts together in well-tempered harmony and has made himself one man instead of many, will he be ready to go about whatever he may have to do, whether it be making money and satisfying bodily wants, or business transactions, or the affairs of state. In all these fields when he speaks of just and honourable conduct, he will mean the behaviour that helps to produce and to preserve this habit of mind; and by wisdom he will mean the knowledge which presides over such conduct. Any action which tends to break down this habit will be for him unjust; and the notions governing it he will call ignorance and folly.

That is perfectly true, Socrates.

Good, said I. I believe we should not be thought altogether mistaken, if we claimed to have discovered the just man and the just state, and wherein their justice consists.

Indeed we should not.

Shall we make that claim, then?

Yes, we will.

So be it, said I. Next, I suppose, we have to consider injustice.

Evidently.

This must surely be a sort of civil strife among the three elements, whereby they usurp and encroach upon one another's functions and some one part of the soul rises up in rebellion against the whole, claiming a supremacy to which it has no right because its nature fits it only to be the servant of the ruling principle. Some turmoil and aberration we shall, I think, identify with injustice, intemperance, cowardice, ignorance, and in a word with all wickedness.

Exactly.

And now that we know the nature of justice and injustice, we can be equally clear about what is meant by acting justly and again by unjust action and wrongdoing.

How do you mean?

Plainly, they are exactly analogous to those wholesome and unwholesome activities which respectively produce a healthy or unhealthy condition in the body; in the same way just and unjust conduct produce a just or unjust character. Justice is produced in the soul, like health in the body, by establishing the elements concerned in their natural relations of control and subordination, whereas injustice is like disease and means that this natural order is inverted.

Quite so.

It appears, then, that virtue is as it were the health and comeliness and well-being of the soul, as wickedness is disease, deformity, and weakness.

True.

And also that virtue and wickedness are brought about by one's way of life, honourable or disgraceful.

That follows.

So now it only remains to consider which is the more profitable course: to do right and live honourably and be just, whether or not anyone knows what manner of man you are, or to do wrong and be unjust, provided that you can escape the chastisement which might make you a better man.

But really, Socrates, it seems to me ridiculous to ask that question now that the nature of justice and injustice has been brought to light. People think that all the luxury and wealth and power in the world cannot make life worth living when the bodily constitution is going to rack and ruin; and are we to believe that, when the very principle whereby we live is deranged and corrupted, life will be worth living so long as a man can do as he will, and wills to do anything rather than to free himself from vice and wrongdoing and to win justice and virtue?

Yes, I replied, it is a ridiculous question.

PLATO, *Republic*

For the first two millennia of Western philosophy, the wise understanding of the human condition was the province of philosophers and poets. In the past three-quarters of a century, however, their intuitive insight has been supplemented, though not supplanted, by the systematic scientific investigations of countless theorists of human personality. Plato's brilliant recognition of the analogy between the health of the body and the health of the mind has been embodied in a branch of medicine called psychiatry, whose practitioners study the forms, causes, symptoms, and cures for what we now routinely call "mental illness." With psychiatrists, as with philosophers, there is a fundamental split between those who examine the individual psyche in separation from its social setting and those who study the connections between individual mental health or illness and the network of social and institutional relationships which surround the patient.

Sigmund Freud (1856–1939), the founder of modern psychoanalytic theory and practice, tended toward the first method of investigation. Although he wrote several provocative essays on the psychic roots of social phenomena, his primary interest was in the inner dynamics of the psyche itself. Among all those who have followed Freud's lead in developing a science of psychiatry, perhaps no figure comes closer to Plato both in spirit and in fineness of sensibility than the contemporary analyst, historian, author, and philosopher Erik H. Erikson. Erikson has sought to build on Freud's investigation of the infantile stages of personality development by analyzing the later stages through which each of us passes in coming either well or badly to maturity and old age. It was Erikson who actually coined the now familiar phrase "identity crisis" in an essay on the emotional upheaval that so many young men and women go through in late adolescence and early adulthood. But Erikson was also interested in the continuing development of personality later in life. He discovered from his clinical practice with patients of all ages that as an individual grew through infancy, childhood, adolescence, young adulthood, mature adulthood, and old age, he or she faced a series of turning points, or crises. At each stage, the individual might resolve the crisis successfully and grow into a stronger, more fulfilled person, or fail to handle the crisis well and bear ever after the scars of that failure. In old age, those who have lived the cycle of childhood, adulthood, and maturity well achieve thereby an inner harmony which Erikson calls "ego integrity." It is very much like what Plato calls wisdom. This ego integrity gives meaning to the life that has been lived, and permits the individual to face impending death with acceptance, dignity, and pride. Here is Erikson's description of this final stage of the life cycle.

Only in him who in some way has taken care of things and people and has adapted himself to the triumphs and disappointments adherent to being the originator of others or the generator of products and ideas—only in him may gradually ripen the fruit of these seven stages. I know no better word for it than ego integrity. Lacking a clear definition, I shall point to a few constituents of this state of mind. It is the ego's accrued assurance of its proclivity for order and meaning. It is a post-narcissistic love of the human ego—not of the self—as an experience which conveys some world order and spiritual sense, no matter how dearly paid for. It is the acceptance of one's one and only life cycle as something that had to be and that, by necessity, permitted of no substitutions: it thus means a new, a different love of one's parents. It is a comradeship with the ordering ways of distant times and different pursuits, as expressed in the simple products and sayings of such times and pursuits. Although aware of the relativity of all the various life styles which have given meaning to human striving, the possessor of integrity is ready to defend the dignity of his own life style against all physical and economic threats. For he knows that an individual life is the accidental coincidence of but one life cycle with but one segment of history; and that for him all human integrity stands or falls with the one style of integrity of which he partakes. The style of integrity developed by his culture or civilization thus becomes the "patrimony of his soul," the seal of his moral paternity of himself. . . . In such final consolidation, death loses its sting.

The lack or loss of this accrued ego integration is signified by fear of death: the one and only life cycle is not accepted as the ultimate of life. Despair expresses the feeling that the time is now short, too short for the attempt to start another life and to try out alternate roads to integrity. Disgust hides despair, if often only in the form of "a thousand little disgusts" which do not add up to one big remorse. . . .

Each individual, to become a mature adult, must to a sufficient degree develop all the ego qualities mentioned, so that a wise Indian, a true gentleman, and a mature peasant share and recognize in one another the final stage of integrity. But each cultural entity, to develop the particular style of integrity suggested by its historical place, utilizes a particular combination of these conflicts, along with specific provocations and prohibitions of infantile sexuality. Infantile conflicts become creative only if sustained by the firm support of cultural institutions and of the special leader classes representing them. In order to approach or experience integrity, the individual must know how to be a follower of image bearers in religion and in politics, in the economic order and in technology, in aristocratic living and in the arts and sciences. Ego integrity, therefore, implies an emotional integration which permits participation by followership as well as acceptance of the responsibility of leadership.

Webster's Dictionary is kind enough to help us complete this outline in a circular fashion. Trust (the first of our ego values) is here defined as "the assured reliance on another's integrity," the last of our values. I suspect that Webster had business in mind rather than babies, credit rather than faith. But the formulation stands. And it seems possible to further paraphrase the relation of adult integrity and infantile trust by saying that healthy children will not fear life if their elders have integrity enough not to fear death.

ERIK H. ERIKSON, *Childhood and Society*

We began our discussion of ethics with an extremely abstract topic: Kant's search for universally valid first principles of action. We then descended just a bit out of the clouds to look for a method for handling so-called "hard cases" of moral decision, and to reflect on the nature of the genuinely good life. But even these last two approaches to ethics are very far removed from the actual day-to-day life situations that confront us. It may be obvious to a philosopher what the connection is between the Categorical Imperative, or the Greatest Happiness Principle, or the Doctrine of the Just Soul, and my personal choices. But even the philosopher, when off duty, so to speak, may find it hard to connect up ethical theories with life.

It might be challenging, therefore, to turn in this portion of our discussion of ethics to a very real problem indeed—the problem of abortion. In recent years, no issue of public policy has engaged the moral convictions, the religious faith, the sympathy and the anger of the American people so powerfully as the permissibility of abortion. By an accident of history and law, the moral legitimacy of abortion has become tangled up with the quite separate question of whether public money should be used to pay for the medical costs of abortion. The real point of dispute, however, is over the rightness or wrongness of abortion itself.

On one side are millions of men and women who insist that women have a right to control their own bodies, that overwhelmingly male state legislatures, congresses, and judiciaries have no right to require a woman to bring a pregnancy to term. On the other side are millions of men and women who fervently believe that abortion is murder, plain and simple. Since we live in a democracy, the issue may ultimately be decided by counting votes, in order to see which side has the greater millions. But no one, surely, can be happy at the thought that so fundamental an issue of morality will be settled at the ballot box.

The moral status of abortion is a "philosophical" issue, if ever there was one. Like the other great disputes of public policy, such as the legitimacy of representative government, the justice of taxation, capital punishment, and the right of the state to make war, abortion is an issue that mixes together factual, legal, moral, and even metaphysical considerations in a way that is almost impossible to disentangle. If we leave to one side purely religious arguments, which rely upon an appeal to sacred texts, the debate turns on such matters as the nature of a person, and the moral rights and duties of persons with respect to one another.

What can Kant, or Bentham, or Plato tell us about the rights and wrongs of abortion? As soon as we try to think about this question, we come up against a fundamental and very peculiar problem. All the great systems of moral theory, however much they may disagree on everything else, agree on one point. They all assume that each of us is a separate, distinct moral agent. They all assume, in a sense, that the individual person is the basic unit, or building block, of the moral world. Kant argues that each of us is an autonomous rational agent; Bentham says that each of us is a rational pleasure-maximizer; Plato says that each of us has a soul whose internal harmony or disharmony determines whether we can live the good life. But all three agree that the individual is the starting point of moral reasoning.

Now the immediate, obvious, un-get-over-able fact about an unborn infant is that it is *not* a separate being. We do not come into this world fully grown, nor do we hatch out of eggs. Each of us is conceived in the womb of our mother, where we are at first so totally dependent upon that natural environment that it hardly makes sense to speak of us as independent at all. Little by little we grow and develop, until at some point, before actual birth, we can be thought of as capable of living independently of the mother—as "viable," in the medical jargon. It is then a good long time more before we can plausibly be described as autonomous rational agents, or as rational pleasure-maximizers, or as healthy souls.

So the problem is this: philosophical theories of ethics tell us what the moral relationships ought to be between fully developed moral agents; or they tell us what principles should govern the choices of fully developed moral agents; or they tell us what the good life is for fully developed moral agents. But by and large, no philosophical theory of ethics tells much of anything about what the moral relationships ought to be between fully developed moral agents (the mother, the doctor) and something that is neither a moral agent nor not a moral agent (the fetus). Nor does any moral theory tell us how to weigh the pleasures and pains of a fetus, which is not yet conscious; or how to evaluate the inner harmony of what is not yet a soul. In the essay by Jane English reproduced here, a variety of philosophical techniques and insights are brought to bear on the very concrete question of when and whether abortion is morally justified.

As English points out, the debate between the pro- and anti-abortion forces has focussed on the question whether the fetus is a *person*. Everyone seems to agree that if the fetus is *not* a person, then the moral restrictions on what we do to it are, at the very least, much less stringent than if it *is* a person. But how do we decide whether a fetus is *a person?* Obviously, this is not a verbal dispute about the dictionary definition of a word. When we say that persons have rights that must be respected, we have in mind, however unclearly thought through, some conception of what it is to be a person. If we hold certain religious beliefs, we may think that being a person means having a *soul.* Leaving religious doctrine to one side, we may think of a person as a being that is conscious, or that can reason, or that can make plans, or suffer pain, or learn language. Very soon, we realize that we are engaged in a *philosophical* analysis of the concept of personhood. This apparently abstract philosophical debate has direct, immediate implications for the way we write our laws, practice medicine, and distribute government funds.

Even after we determine whether, or in what sense, a fetus of a certain age is a person, we still have a very tangled philosophical problem, because we must then decide what the rights of the fetus are as against the rights of the mother or of other moral persons. The intimate dependence of the fetus on the mother—a dependence virtually unique in human experience—raises especially complicated questions about how far the mother can legitimately go in placing her interests or well-being above that of the fetus, and how far doctors or the law can legitimately go in placing the well-being of the fetus above that of the mother.

Once again, a great deal seems to turn on when, or whether, we judge the fetus to be a person. Almost everyone who puzzles over this problem agrees that the newly-fertilized egg, a single cell, is not in any recognizable sense a person. Virtually everyone agrees, as well, that the newborn baby is a person. So apparently, the disagreement is "simply" over where, in between, what isn't a person becomes a person. But isn't there something fundamentally crazy about looking at so important a question in this way? Can the difference between a legitimate medical procedure and a murder be merely a subtle matter of degree?

The most careful philosophical intelligence must be combined with considerable factual knowledge and a goodly measure of human wisdom if this issue is to be resolved satisfactorily. The philosophical literature on the subject draws heavily on all of the traditions in moral theory which we have studied in this chapter. In the present essay, Jane English argues that the discussion thus far has been confused, with both sides arguing fruitlessly over just exactly when the fetus becomes a person. By means of hypothetical thought experiments, she tries to lead us to a better understanding of the relationship between our other, less controversial moral beliefs and our beliefs about abortion.

JANE ENGLISH: *Abortion and the Concept of a Person*

The abortion debate rages on. Yet the two most popular positions seem to be clearly mistaken. Conservatives maintain that a human life begins at conception and that therefore abortion must be wrong because it is murder. But not all killings of humans are murders. Most notably, self defense may justify even the killing of an innocent person.

Liberals, on the other hand, are just as mistaken in their argument that since a fetus does not become a person until birth, a woman may do whatever she pleases in and to her own body. First, you cannot do as you please with your own body if it affects other people adversely.[1] Second, if a fetus is not a person, that does not imply that you can do to it anything you wish. Animals, for example, are not persons, yet to kill or torture them for no reason at all is wrong.

At the center of the storm has been the issue of just when it is between ovulation and adulthood that a person appears on the scene. Conservatives draw the line at conception, liberals at birth. In this paper I first examine our concept of a person and conclude that no single criterion can capture the concept of a person and no sharp line can be drawn. Next I argue that if a fetus is a person, abortion is still justifiable in many cases; and if a fetus is not a person, killing it is still wrong in many cases. To a large extent, these two solutions are in agreement. I conclude that our concept of a person cannot and need not bear the weight that the abortion controversy has thrust upon it.

I

The several factions in the abortion argument have drawn battle lines around various proposed criteria for determining what is and what is not a person. For example, Mary Anne Warren[2] lists five features (capacities for reasoning, self-awareness, complex communication, etc.) as her criteria for personhood and argues for the permissibility of abortion because a fetus falls outside this

Author's Note: I am deeply indebted to Larry Crocker and Arthur Kuflik for their constructive comments.

[1] We also have paternalistic laws which keep us from harming our own bodies even when no one else is affected. Ironically, anti-abortion laws were originally designed to protect pregnant women from a dangerous but tempting procedure.

[2] Mary Anne Warren, "On the Moral and Legal Status of Abortion," *Monist* 57 (1973), p. 55.

concept. Baruch Brody[3] uses brain waves. Michael Tooley[4] picks having-a-concept-of-self as his criterion and concludes that infanticide and abortion are justifiable, while the killing of adult animals is not. On the other side, Paul Ramsey[5] claims a certain gene structure is the defining characteristic. John Noonan[6] prefers conceived-of-humans and presents counterexamples to various other candidate criteria. For instance, he argues against viability as the criterion because the newborn and infirm would then be non-persons, since they cannot live without the aid of others. He rejects any criterion that calls upon the sorts of sentiments a being can evoke in adults on the grounds that this would allow us to exclude other races as non-persons if we could just view them sufficiently unsentimentally.

These approaches are typical: foes of abortion propose sufficient conditions for personhood which fetuses satisfy, while friends of abortion counter with necessary conditions for personhood which fetuses lack. But these both presuppose that the concept of a person can be captured in a strait jacket of necessary and/or sufficient conditions.[7] Rather, 'person' is a cluster of features, of which rationality, having a self concept and being conceived of humans are only part.

What is typical of persons? Within our concept of a person we include, first, certain biological factors: descended from humans, having a certain genetic make-up, having a head, hands, arms, eyes, capable of locomotion, breathing, eating, sleeping. There are psychological factors: sentience, perception, having a concept of self and of one's own interests and desires, the ability to use tools, the ability to use language or symbol systems, the ability to joke, to be angry, to doubt. There are rationality factors: the ability to reason and draw conclusions, the ability to generalize and to learn from past experience, the ability to sacrifice present interests for greater gains in the future. There are social factors: the ability to work in groups and respond to peer pressures, the ability to recognize and consider as valuable the interests of others, seeing oneself as one among "other minds," the ability to sympathize, encourage, love, the ability to evoke from others the responses of sympathy, encouragement, love, the ability to work with others for mutual advantage. Then there are legal factors: being subject to the law and protected by it, having the ability to sue and enter contracts, being counted in the census, having a name and citizenship, the ability to own property, inherit, and so forth.

Now the point is not that this list is incomplete, or that you can find counterinstances to each of its points. People typically exhibit rationality, for instance, but someone who was irrational would not thereby fail to qualify as

---

[3] Baruch Brody, "Fetal Humanity and the Theory of Essentialism," in Robert Baker and Frederick Elliston (eds.), *Philosophy and Sex* (Buffalo, N.Y., 1975).

[4] Michael Tooley, "Abortion and Infanticide," *Philosophy and Public Affairs* 2 (1971).

[5] Paul Ramsey, "The Morality of Abortion," in James Rachels, ed., *Moral Problems* (New York, 1971).

[6] John Noonan, "Abortion and the Catholic Church: a Summary History," *Natural Law Forum* 12 (1967), pp. 125–131.

[7] Wittgenstein has argued against the possibility of so capturing the concept of a game, *Philosophical Investigations* (New York, 1958), §66–71.

a person. On the other hand, something could exhibit the majority of these features and still fail to be a person, as an advanced robot might. There is no single core of necessary and sufficient features which we can draw upon with the assurance that they constitute what really makes a person; there are only features that are more or less typical.

This is not to say that no necessary or sufficient conditions can be given. Being alive is a necessary condition for being a person, and being a U.S. Senator is sufficient. But rather than falling inside a sufficient condition or outside a necessary one, a fetus lies in the penumbra region where our concept of a person is not so simple. For this reason I think a conclusive answer to the question whether a fetus is a person is unattainable.

Here we might note a family of simple fallacies that proceed by stating a necessary condition for personhood and showing that a fetus has that characteristic. This is a form of the fallacy of affirming the consequent. For example, some have mistakenly reasoned from the premise that a fetus is human (after all, it is a human fetus rather than, say, a canine fetus), to the conclusion that it is a human. Adding an equivocation on 'being', we get the fallacious argument that since a fetus is something both living and human, it is a human being.

Nonetheless, it does seem clear that a fetus has very few of the above family of characteristics, whereas a newborn baby exhibits a much larger proportion of them—and a two-year-old has even more. Note that one traditional anti-abortion argument has centered on pointing out the many ways in which a fetus resembles a baby. They emphasize its development ("It already has ten fingers . . .") without mentioning its dissimilarities to adults (it still has gills and a tail). They also try to evoke the sort of sympathy on our part that we only feel toward other persons ("Never to laugh . . . or feel the sunshine?"). This all seems to be a relevant way to argue, since its purpose is to persuade us that a fetus satisfies so many of the important features on the list that it ought to be treated as a person. Also note that a fetus near the time of birth satisfies many more of these factors than a fetus in the early months of development. This could provide reason for making distinctions among the different stages of pregnancy, as the U.S. Supreme Court has done. . . .[8]

For these reasons I believe our concept of a person is not sharp or decisive enough to bear the weight of a solution to the abortion controversy. To use it to solve that problem is to clarify *obscurum per obscurius*.

II

Next let us consider what follows if a fetus is a person after all. Judith Jarvis Thomson's landmark article, "A Defense of Abortion,"[9] correctly points

---

[8] Not because the fetus is partly a person and so has some of the rights of persons, but rather because of the rights of person-like non-persons. This I discuss in part III below.

[9] J. J. Thomson, "A Defense of Abortion," *Philosophy and Public Affairs* 1 (1971).

out that some additional argumentation is needed at this point in the conservative argument to bridge the gap between the premise that a fetus is an innocent person and the conclusion that killing it is always wrong. To arrive at this conclusion, we would need the additional premise that killing an innocent person is always wrong. But killing an innocent person is sometimes permissible, most notably in self defense. Some examples may help draw out our intuitions or ordinary judgments about self defense.

Suppose a mad scientist, for instance, hypnotized innocent people to jump out of the bushes and attack innocent passers-by with knives. If you are so attacked, we agree you have a right to kill the attacker in self defense, if killing him is the only way to protect your life or to save yourself from serious injury. It does not seem to matter here that the attacker is not malicious but himself an innocent pawn, for your killing of him is not done in a spirit of retribution but only in self defense.

How severe an injury may you inflict in self defense? In part this depends upon the severity of the injury to be avoided: you may not shoot someone merely to avoid having your clothes torn. This might lead one to the mistaken conclusion that the defense may only equal the threatened injury in severity; that to avoid death you may kill, but to avoid a black eye you may only inflict a black eye or the equivalent. Rather, our laws and customs seem to say that you may create an injury somewhat, but not enormously, greater than the injury to be avoided. To fend off an attack whose outcome would be as serious as rape, a severe beating or the loss of a finger, you may shoot; to avoid having your clothes torn, you may blacken an eye.

Aside from this, the injury you may inflict should only be the minimum necessary to deter or incapacitate the attacker. Even if you know he intends to kill you, you are not justified in shooting him if you could equally well save yourself by the simple expedient of running away. Self defense is the purpose of avoiding harms rather than equalizing harms.

Some cases of pregnancy present a parallel situation. Though the fetus is itself innocent, it may pose a threat to the pregnant woman's well-being, life prospects or health, mental or physical. If the pregnancy presents a slight threat to her interests, it seems self defense cannot justify abortion. But if the threat is on a par with a serious beating or the loss of a finger, she may kill the fetus that poses such a threat, even if it is an innocent person. If a lesser harm to the fetus could have the same defensive effect, killing it would not be justified. It is unfortunate that the only way to free the woman from the pregnancy entails the death of the fetus (except in very late stages of pregnancy). Thus a self defense model supports Thomson's point that the woman has a right only to be freed from the fetus, not a right to demand its death.[10]

The self defense model is most helpful when we take the pregnant woman's point of view. In the pre-Thomson literature, abortion is often framed as a

---

[10] *Ibid.*, p. 52.

question for a third party: do you, a doctor, have a right to choose between the life of a woman and that of the fetus? Some have claimed that if you were a passer-by who witnessed a struggle between the innocent hypnotized attacker and his equally innocent victim, you would have no reason to kill either in defense of the other. They have concluded that the self defense model implies that a woman may attempt to abort herself, but that a doctor should not assist her. I think the position of the third party is somewhat more complex. We do feel some inclination to intervene on behalf of the victim rather than the attacker, other things equal. But if both parties are innocent, other factors come into consideration. You would rush to the aid of your husband whether he was attacker or attackee. If a hypnotized famous violinist were attacking a skid row bum, we would try to save the individual who is of more value to society. These considerations would tend to support abortion in some cases.

But suppose you are a frail senior citizen who wishes to avoid being knifed by one of these innocent hypnotics, so you have hired a bodyguard to accompany you. If you are attacked, it is clear we believe that the bodyguard, acting as your agent, has a right to kill the attacker to save you from a serious beating. Your rights of self defense are transferred to your agent. I suggest that we should similarly view the doctor as the pregnant woman's agent in carrying out a defense she is physically incapable of accomplishing herself.

Thanks to modern technology, the cases are rare in which a pregnancy poses as clear a threat to a woman's bodily health as an attacker brandishing a switchblade. How does self defense fare when more subtle, complex and long-range harms are involved?

To consider a somewhat fanciful example, suppose you are a highly trained surgeon when you are kidnapped by the hypnotic attacker. He says he does not intend to harm you but to take you back to the mad scientist who, it turns out, plans to hypnotize you to have a permanent mental block against all your knowledge of medicine. This would automatically destroy your career which would in turn have a serious adverse impact on your family, your personal relationships and your happiness. It seems to me that if the only way you can avoid this outcome is to shoot the innocent attacker, you are justified in so doing. You are defending yourself from a drastic injury to your life prospects. I think it is no exaggeration to claim that unwanted pregnancies (most obviously among teenagers) often have such adverse life-long consequences as the surgeon's loss of livelihood.

Several parallels arise between various views on abortion and the self defense model. Let's suppose further that these hypnotized attackers only operate at night, so that it is well known that they can be avoided completely by the considerable inconvenience of never leaving your house after dark. One view is that since you could stay home at night, therefore if you go out and are selected by one of these hypnotized people, you have no right to defend yourself. This parallels the view that abstinence is the only acceptable way to avoid pregnancy. Others might hold that you ought to take along some defense such as Mace which will deter the hypnotized person without killing him, but that if this defense fails, you are obliged to submit to the resulting injury, no matter how severe it is. This parallels the view that contraception is all right but abortion is always wrong, even in cases of contraceptive failure.

A third view is that you may kill the hypnotized person only if he will actually kill you, but not if he will only injure you. This is like the position that abortion is permissible only if it is required to save a woman's life. Finally we have the view that it is all right to kill the attacker, even if only to avoid a very slight inconvenience to yourself and even if you knowingly walked down the very street where all these incidents have been taking place without taking along Mace or protective escort. If we assume that a fetus is a person, this is the analogue of the view that abortion is always justifiable, "on demand."

The self defense model allows us to see an important difference that exists between abortion and infanticide, even if a fetus is a person from conception. Many have argued that the only way to justify abortion without justifying infanticide would be to find some characteristic of personhood that is acquired at birth. Michael Tooley, for one, claims infanticide is justifiable because the really significant characteristics of person are acquired some time after birth. But all such approaches look to characteristics of the developing human and ignore the relation between the fetus and the woman. What if, after birth, the presence of an infant or the need to support it posed a grave threat to the woman's sanity or life prospects? She could escape this threat by the simple expedient of running away. So a solution that does not entail the death of the infant is available. Before birth, such solutions are not available because of the biological dependence of the fetus on the woman. Birth is the crucial point not because of any characteristics the fetus gains, but because after birth the woman can defend herself by a means less drastic than killing the infant. Hence self defense can be used to justify abortion without necessarily thereby justifying infanticide.

III

On the other hand, supposing a fetus is not after all a person, would abortion always be morally permissible? Some opponents of abortion seem worried that if a fetus is not a full-fledged person, then we are justified in treating it in any way at all. However, this does not follow. Non-persons do get some consideration in our moral code, though of course they do not have the same rights as persons have (and in general they do not have moral responsibilities), and though their interests may be overridden by the interests of persons. Still, we cannot just treat them in any way at all.

Treatment of animals is a case in point. It is wrong to torture dogs for fun or to kill wild birds for no reason at all. It is wrong Period, even though dogs and birds do not have the same rights persons do. However, few people think it is wrong to use dogs as experimental animals, causing them considerable suffering in some cases, provided that the resulting research will probably bring discoveries of great benefit to people. And most of us think it all right to kill birds for food or to protect our crops. People's rights are different from the consideration we give to animals, then, for it is wrong to experiment on people, even if others might later benefit a great deal as a result of their suffering. You might volunteer to be a subject, but this would be supererogatory; you certainly have a right to refuse to be a medical guinea pig.

But how do we decide what you may or may not do to non-persons? This is a difficult problem, one for which I believe no adequate account exists. You do not want to say, for instance, that torturing dogs is all right whenever the sum of its effects on people is good—when it doesn't warp the sensibilities of the torturer so much that he mistreats people. If that were the case, it would be all right to torture dogs if you did it in private, or if the torturer lived on a desert island or died soon afterward, so that his actions had no effect on people. This is an inadequate account, because whatever moral consideration animals get, it has to be indefeasible, too. It will have to be a general proscription of certain actions, not merely a weighing of the impact on people on a case-by-case basis. . . .

The similarity of a fetus to a baby is very significant. A fetus one week before birth is so much like a newborn baby in our psychological space that we cannot allow any cavalier treatment of the former while expecting full sympathy and nurturative support for the latter. Thus, I think that anti-abortion forces are indeed giving their strongest arguments when they point to the similarities between a fetus and a baby, and when they try to evoke our emotional attachment to and sympathy for the fetus. An early horror story from New York about nurses who were expected to alternate between caring for six-week premature infants and disposing of viable 24-week aborted fetuses is just that—a horror story. These beings are so much alike that no one can be asked to draw a distinction and treat them so very differently.

Remember, however, that in the early weeks after conception, a fetus is very much unlike a person. It is hard to develop these feelings for a set of genes which doesn't yet have a head, hands, beating heart, response to touch or the ability to move by itself. Thus it seems to me that the alleged "slippery slope" between conception and birth is not so very slippery. In the early stages of pregnancy, abortion can hardly be compared to murder for psychological reasons, but in the latest stages it is psychologically akin to murder.

Another source of similarity is the bodily continuity between fetus and adult. Bodies play a surprisingly central role in our attitudes toward persons. One has only to think of the philosophical literature on how far physical identity suffices for personal identity or Wittgenstein's remark that the best picture of the human soul is the human body. Even after death, when all agree the body is no longer a person, we still observe elaborate customs of respect for the human body; like people who torture dogs, necrophiliacs are not to be trusted with people.[11] So it is appropriate that we show respect to a fetus as the body continuous with the body of a person. This is a degree of resemblance to persons that animals cannot rival. . . .

Even if a fetus is not a person, abortion is not always permissible, because of the resemblance of a fetus to a person. I agree with Thomson that it would be wrong for a woman who is seven months pregnant to have an abortion just to avoid having to postpone a trip to Europe. In the early months of pregnancy when the fetus hardly resembles a baby at all, then, abortion is permissible whenever it is in the interests of the pregnant woman or her family. The reasons would only need to outweigh the pain and inconvenience of the abortion itself. In the middle months, when the fetus comes to resemble a person, abortion would be justifiable only when the continuation of the pregnancy or the birth of the child would cause harms—physical, psychological, economic or social—to the woman. In the late months of pregnancy, even on our current assumption that a fetus is not a person, abortion seems to be wrong except to save a woman from significant injury or death.

The Supreme Court has recognized similar gradations in the alleged slippery slope stretching between conception and birth. To this point, the present paper has been a discussion of the moral status of abortion only, not its legal status. In view of the great physical, financial and sometimes psychological costs of abortion, perhaps the legal arrangement most compatible with the proposed moral solution would be the absence of restrictions, that is, so-called abortion "on demand."

So I conclude, first, that application of our concept of a person will not suffice to settle the abortion issue. After all, the biological development of a human being is gradual. Second, whether a fetus is a person or not, abortion is justifiable early in pregnancy to avoid modest harms and seldom justifiable late in pregnancy except to avoid significant injury or death.

TOPICS FOR FURTHER STUDY

1. Kant tells us that every rational creature exists as an end in itself, and not merely as a means for arbitrary use by some other will. A pregnant woman is a rational creature. A fetus is at least potentially a rational creature. What then does Kant's great principle tell us about the rights and wrongs of abortion? Clearly, the rights of rational creatures can conflict—never more directly or intimately than in the case of a pregnant woman and her unborn child. Can Kant help us to resolve such conflicts?

2. All of the leading moral philosophers in western civilization, up to the twentieth century, have been men. All of the child-bearers, up to the present and for the

---

[11] On the other hand, if they can be trusted with people, then our moral customs are mistaken. It all depends on the facts of psychology.

foreseeable future, have been, are, and will be women. To what extent, do you think, has this biassed the discussion of the morality of abortion?

3. Utilitarianism instructs us to strive for the greatest happiness of the greatest number. Should the future happiness of the unborn be taken into account in this calculation? What about the possible happiness of the as yet unconceived? Since young women have more years ahead of them, on average, than older women, utilitarianism would seem to suggest that the future interests of young women should be weighed more heavily and hence that an abortion of the fetus of a young mother is morally better than the abortion of the fetus of an older mother. Does this way of reasoning make any sense at all?

4. All of the ethical theories discussed in this chapter approach the subject from the point of view of the individual moral agent. But surely nothing reminds us more of our total involvement with, and dependence upon, the human community than the fact of pregnancy. Can ethical questions really be analyzed as though we were all separate, individual rational creatures?

5. Moralists tend to look down on private interests as selfish or egoistic, but the nice thing about two selfish people is that they can, if they must, compromise. What compromise can there possibly be between the two sides on the abortion issue? If abortion is an absolute right, then a little infringement of it is like a little slavery. On the other hand, if abortion is murder, how can even a single abortion be acceptable?

SUGGESTIONS FOR FURTHER READING

KURT BAIER, *The Moral Point of View*

MICHAEL D. BAYLES, ed., *Contemporary Utilitarianism*

JOHN DEWEY, *Human Nature and Conduct*

ERIK H. ERIKSON, *Childhood and Society*

W. K. FRANKENA, *Ethics*

IMMANUEL KANT, *Groundwork of the Metaphysic of Morals*

——————————— , "On a Supposed Right to Lie from Altruistic Motives"

C. I. LEWIS, *Values and Imperatives*

JOHN STUART MILL, *Utilitarianism*

G. E. MOORE, *Principia Ethica*

W. D. ROSS, *The Right and the Good*

BERTRAND RUSSELL, "What I Believe" in *Why I Am Not a Christian and Other Essays*

M. G. SINGER, *Generalization in Ethics*

S. F. TOULMIN, *The Place of Reason in Ethics*

EDWARD WESTERMARCK, *Ethical Relativity*

JOHN STUART MILL (1806–1873) was the most important English philosopher during the 125 years between the death of David Hume in 1776 and the turn of the twentieth century. Trained from his youth by his father, James Mill, to be a defender of the utilitarian doctrine of Jeremy Bentham and the Philosophical Radicals, Mill devoted his early years to an unquestioning support of his father's principles. After undergoing a severe emotional crisis in his twenties, Mill gave up the narrow doctrine of Bentham, and became instead an eclectic synthesizer of the views of such diverse schools as the French utopian socialists and the German romantics.

3 SOCIAL PHILOSOPHY

Mill was active in the public life of England, first as an officer (and eventually head) of the great East India Company, a principal instrument of English economic expansion during the nineteenth century, and later as a member of parliament. In addition to the books on moral and political topics which have established him as one of the leading spokesmen of liberalism, Mill also wrote a number of highly influential works on logic and the theory of knowledge, including *A System of Logic* and *An Examination of Sir William Hamilton's Philosophy.*

As a young man, Mill befriended Mrs. Harriet Taylor, with whom he maintained a close relationship until, after her husband's death, they were married in 1851. Mill believed Mrs. Taylor to be an enormously gifted thinker, and he was convinced that she would have made her mark on English letters had it not been for the powerful prejudice against women that operated then, as it does now. His relationship with Mrs. Taylor made Mill sensitive to the discrimination against women, with the result that he became one of the few philosophers to speak out on the matter. His discussion of the problem appears in a late work, *The Subjection of Women,* published four years before his death.

I

Some, it is said, are born great; some achieve greatness; and some have greatness thrust upon them. To that saying we might add, and some are trained from birth for greatness. Of all the philosophers who have won for themselves a place in the ranks of the great, none was more carefully groomed, schooled, prodded, and pushed into greatness than the English empiricist and utilitarian thinker of the nineteenth century, John Stuart Mill. Never has a child been given less chance to "do his own thing," and never has a man defended with greater eloquence the right of every man and woman to be left free from the intrusions of well-meaning parents, friends, and governments. Though it would be wrong to reduce Mill's mature philosophical views to the level of mere psychological reflections on his childhood experiences, the temptation is irresistible to see in his adult career a reaction to the pressures of his youth.

Mill was born in 1806, at a time when a strong movement was developing to reform the political life of England. The intellectual leader of the movement was the same Jeremy Bentham whose utilitarian doctrines you encountered in Chapter Two. We took our first look at utilitarianism in its guise as a moral philosophy designed to lay down a principle for calculating what actions are right for an individual facing a decision. But as your reading on the reform of the penal code makes clear, Bentham's primary interest was in social issues, not in private morality. He conceived the Principle of Utility as a weapon in the attack on the traditions, privileges, laws, and perquisites of the English upper classes. So long as courts and governments could hide behind precedent, or immemorial custom, it was extremely hard to force them to admit the injustices and irrationalities of the social system. But once those ancient customs were put to the test of the Principle of Utility, it was immediately clear how badly they failed to produce the greatest happiness for the greatest number.

● JAMES MILL (1773–1836) was a close friend and colleague of Jeremy Bentham, the founder of the doctrine known as utilitarianism. Mill led a group of English political reformers who believed that social justice and wise government required a broadening of the franchise to include the industrial middle classes in England, and a thoroughgoing overhaul of the antiquated laws and governmental machinery which, in Mill's day, strongly favored the landed interests in England. Mill and the Philosophical Radicals, as his circle of supporters were called, succeeded in generating enough support to carry through a number of major reforms, culminating in the sweeping Reform Bill of 1832. Mill's son, the great John Stuart Mill, had this to say about his father's position in *The Autobiography of John Stuart Mill:*

> So complete was my father's reliance on the influence of reason over the minds of mankind, whenever it is allowed to reach them, that he felt as if all would be gained if the whole population were taught to read, if all sorts of opinions were allowed to be addressed to them by word and by writing, and if by means of the suffrage they could nominate a legislature to give effect to the opinions they adopted. ●

One of Bentham's close friends and associates in the reform movement was a philosopher named James Mill; Mill was a thinker of considerable distinction, although he has long since been eclipsed by his more famous son. His writings on economics and moral philosophy erected a system, on Benthamite foundations, which served as a fortress from which the "philosophical radicals," as they were called, sallied forth to do battle with the last remnants of the aristocratic hosts. Shortly after the birth of his son John Stuart, James Mill met Bentham and joined forces with him. Mill decided to train his son up as a soldier in the reform movement, and no medieval squire ever had a more rigorous preparation for combat. Little John Stuart began studying Greek at the age of three. His father surrounded him with Latin-speaking servants so that by the age of eight he could dig into that other ancient tongue. Logic was young John Stuart's fare at twelve, to be followed shortly by the study of the new science of political economy. Formal religion was deliberately omitted from the curriculum, but the poor lad may be forgiven for having somewhat formed the notion that he was being raised an orthodox utilitarian.

By the time he reached adulthood, John Stuart Mill was a brilliant, finely honed logical weapon in the armory of his father's political battles. He wrote attacks on the antiquated legal and political institutions of England, defending his points with straight utilitarian dogma.

Not surprisingly, Mill finally broke under the strain of this rigid doctrinaire discipline. At the age of twenty, he suffered an internal emotional crisis, and began what was to be a lifelong reevaluation of the Benthamism of his father and his father's allies. Though it is always a mistake to sum up a great philosopher's work in a single phrase, we can get some general overview of Mill's subsequent intellectual development by saying that he spent his life struggling to broaden, deepen, and complicate the extremely simple philosophical theory into which he was initiated as a boy.

The doctrine of the reformers was clear, coherent, and attractively free from the mystifications which clouded the writings of the conservative defenders of the old order. As Bentham had laid it down, the only good in this world is pleasure, the only evil pain. Human actions are goal-oriented, purposeful actions. Our desires determine what objects or experiences we choose as our goals, and reason aids us in discovering the most efficient path to those goals. The question, What ought I to do? is either a question of goals—What should I desire?—or else it is a question of means—How can I reach my goal most easily? But there is no point in disputing about desires. We either want something or we don't, and whatever pleasure we experience comes to us as the result of satisfying a desire. So the only questions worth debating are factual questions of means: is this the best way to satisfy my desire, or would that way be quicker, cheaper, easier?

If abstruse questions of natural rights and absolute goodness are to be disputed, then common men and women will be hard put to keep up with trained philosophers, lawyers, or theologians. But if Bentham is right, then the fundamental moral question is simply, Does it feel good? Is this experience pleasurable? Now each one of us is the best judge of whether he or she is feeling pleasure or pain, so utilitarianism has the effect of eliminating expertise and putting all men and women on an equal footing in moral debates. What is more, Bentham insisted, the only morally relevant distinction between pleasures and pains is a quantitative distinction of more and less. As Bentham put it, pushpin (a child's game) is as good as poetry, so long as it gives you an equal amount of pleasure. This doctrine too had the effect of leveling the social distinctions between the high- and low-born, for it had been easy for the cultivated upper classes to insist that they were privy to joys and sorrows too refined for the lower classes even to imagine. In these ways—by making each person the judge of his or her own happiness and by making quantity the only significant variable—utilitarianism provided a philosophical justification for a democratic, social program.

All persons are basically prudent, rationally self-interested actors. That is to say, we seek to satisfy our desires in the most extensive and pleasurable way, and we use the resources available to us—money, talent, power—in the most efficient manner possible. But there are two great obstacles to fully rational self-interested action. The first of these, the target of the eighteenth-century enlightenment, is superstition. So long as people falsely believe that they have no right to satisfy their desires; so long as religion, or ancient custom, or class distinctions inhibit common men and women from using the resources they have for the achievement of their own happiness; so long, in short, as the reasoning power of the mind is clouded by fear, awe, and false belief, then just so long will the injustices and inequalities of society continue. The second obstacle is the ignorance which even enlightened men and women suffer of the facts of science and public affairs, ignorance of the most efficient means for pursuing legitimate satisfactions.

Education was the weapon utilitarians aimed at these twin enemies, superstition and ignorance. Education was to perform two tasks: first, to liberate enslaved minds from the superstitious religious and political dogmas of the past; and second, to introduce the liberated minds to the facts of science and society. An educated population could then be counted on to support wise public policy, for such policy would aim at the greatest happiness of the greatest number, and that simply meant their own happiness as private citizens. Thus utilitarianism combined a psychological theory of individual motivation with a moral theory of the good and an educational theory of enlightenment to produce what we today call a political theory of liberal democracy.

It remains to mention one last element of the utilitarian system, an element which may well have been the most important of all, namely the laissez-faire economic theory created by Adam Smith and David Ricardo and deployed by James Mill and his son in the great debates over public policy. This is not an economics textbook, and philosophy is hard enough all by itself, but at least a few words must be said about the laissez-faire theory in order to fill out Mill's position and set the stage for the powerful attacks which Karl Marx launched against it a very few years later.

The major fact of the end of the eighteenth century and the beginning of the nineteenth was, of course, the growth of mercantile and industrial capitalism. The key to the new capitalism was the systematic investment of accumulated wealth, or "capital," for the purpose of producing goods which could be sold at a profit in the marketplace. The individual who set the economic activity in motion was called an "entrepreneur," which is French for "undertaker" and means someone who undertakes to do something, not someone who buries someone (although critics of capitalism might have argued that there was indeed a connection between the two meanings). The capitalist undertook to rent the land, hire the labor, buy the raw materials, and bring together these factors of production in a process which resulted in finished goods. The goods were put on sale in a market where no law fixed the prices that must be paid or the profits that could be made. Adam Smith, in his famous treatise *The Wealth of Nations,* argued that if everyone were permitted to do the best he could for himself—worker, capitalist, merchant, and consumer—then the net result would be the most efficient use of the resources of the nation for the production of goods designed to satisfy human desires. The consumers would spend their money in the marketplace in such a way as to get the greatest pleasure for value. If one sort of product rose too high in price, they would shift to another, for paying all your money for a single piece of meat would be foolish when the same money could buy you fish, eggs, shoes, and a coat. The capitalists would pull their capital out of areas where too much was being produced, because as supply exceeded demand, they would be forced to drop their prices in order to unload their inventory, and profits would tumble. In the same way, if there were customers clamoring for a commodity that wasn't being produced, they would bid up the price in the market, drive up profits in that branch of business, and attract profit-seeking capitalists who would open new factories to "capitalize" on the unsatisfied demand.

ADAM SMITH (1723–1790) was born in Scotland at a time when that small country was one of the liveliest intellectual centers in Europe. Like his countryman, David Hume, Smith wrote on a wide variety of problems in what we would now call the social sciences. His masterwork was a long, difficult, revolutionary study of the foundations of economic activity in a free market capitalist economy, entitled *Inquiry into the Nature and Causes of the Wealth of Nations*. With this book, Smith created the field of economics, and laid the theoretical basis for the doctrine of laissez faire which still has wide support two centuries later. *The Wealth of Nations* was published in 1776, just at the time when the American colonies were declaring their independence of the English crown, and it is fitting that history should have linked these two events, for the Founding Fathers were deeply imbued with the laissez-faire spirit of individual freedom, minimal government, and the pursuit of rational self-interest.

Since happiness is pleasure, and pleasure results from the satisfaction of desire, and consumers buy goods to satisfy desires, it follows that the capitalists trying to make a profit are at the same time actually working to make the consumers happy. They aren't *trying* to make them happy, of course! The capitalists, like all men and women, are rationally *self*-interested pleasure-maximizers. But the genius of the new capitalist free market system was precisely that each person, seeking only his or her own good, automatically advanced the good of others. Thus selfishness could be counted on to do rationally and efficiently what altruism never quite managed—namely, to produce the greatest happiness possible for the greatest number of people. Here is how Adam Smith puts it in a passage that is much quoted and copied. Smith is actually in the midst of a discussion of restrictions on imports, but the thesis he enunciates has a quite general application:

> But the annual revenue of every society is always precisely equal to the exchangeable value of the whole annual produce of its industry, or rather is precisely the same thing with that exchangeable value. As every individual, therefore, endeavours as much as he can both to employ his capital in the support of domestic industry, and so to direct that industry that its produce may be of the greatest value; every individual necessarily labours to render the annual revenue of the society as great as he can. He generally, indeed, neither intends to promote the public interest, nor knows how much he is promoting it. By preferring the support of domestic to that of foreign industry, he intends only his own security; and by directing that industry in such a manner as its produce may be of the greatest value, he intends only his own gain, and he is in this, as in many other cases, led by an invisible hand to promote an end which was no part of his intention. Nor is it always the worse for the society that it was no part of it. By pursuing his own interest he frequently promotes that of the society more effectually than when he really intends to promote it. I have never known much good done by those who affected to trade for the public good. It is an affectation, indeed, not very common among merchants, and very few words need be employed in dissuading them from it.
>
> ADAM SMITH, *The Wealth of Nations*

Mill read widely in authors whose views were far removed from those of Bentham and his father. He learned from the Romantic critics of the reform movement even as he sought to counter their arguments. He studied the writings of such acute conservative observers as Alexis de Tocqueville, and even absorbed the lessons of the French socialists, though he seems not to have read or appreciated the more powerful theoretical assault mounted by the great German socialist Karl Marx. The breadth of his learning and his personal dissatisfaction with the narrow dogma of his father led Mill to doubt or even to deny some of the central tenets of utilitarian philosophy and social policy. Nevertheless, to the end of his life, his mind remained trapped within the confines of the principles he had been taught as a youth.

In at least *three* important ways, Mill questioned the theses of the orthodox reform doctrine. First, he denied Bentham's egalitarian insistence that any pleasure, in and of itself, was as good as any other (which, as we have seen, was a roundabout way of saying that any person was as good as any other). As far back as Plato, philosophers had argued that some pleasures were simply finer, higher, morally better than other pleasures. Usually, as we might expect, they claimed that the pleasures of the mind were superior to the pleasures of the body. Bentham was prepared to admit that some pleasures were more intense, or more long-lasting, or had more pleasant after-effects than others. A quart of bad wine might give less pleasure than a sip of fine brandy. A night of drinking might be followed by such a horrendous morning after that the total experience would add up to a minus rather than a plus. Some pleasures, like some foods, might be acquired tastes, requiring knowledge and long practice before they could be properly appreciated. But after all this had been taken into account—and Bentham carefully did take it into account—utilitarianism still insisted that only quantity and not quality of pleasure mattered. Mill could not accept this teaching, fundamental though it was to the philosophy he had been trained to defend. He was stung by the critics of utilitarianism who made it out to be a brutish or degraded philosophy, a philosophy of the base appetites. In replying to their charge, he drew a distinction between higher and lower pleasures which fundamentally altered the significance and logical force of utilitarianism. Here is the passage, taken from an essay called "Utilitarianism" which Mill first published in a magazine and later as a short book:

Now such a theory of life excites in many minds, and among them in some of the most estimable in feeling and purpose, inveterate dislike. To suppose that life has (as they express it) no higher end than pleasure—no better and nobler object of desire and pursuit—they designate as utterly mean and groveling, as a doctrine worthy only of swine, to whom the followers of Epicurus were, at a very early period, contemptuously likened; and modern holders of the doctrine are occasionally made the subject of equally polite comparisons by its German, French, and English assailants.

When thus attacked, the Epicureans have always answered that it is not they, but their accusers, who represent human nature in a degrading light, since the accusation supposes human beings to be capable of no pleasures except those of which swine are capable. If this supposition were true, the charge could not be gainsaid, but would then be no longer an imputation; for if the sources of pleasure were precisely the same to human beings and to swine, the rule of life which is good enough for the one would be good enough for the other. The comparison of the Epicurean life to that of beasts is felt as degrading, precisely because a beast's pleasures do not satisfy a human being's conceptions of happiness. Human beings have faculties more elevated than the animal appetites and, when once made conscious of them, do not regard anything as happiness which does not include their gratification. . . .

 . . . It is quite compatible with the principle of utility to recognize the fact that some kinds of pleasure are more desirable and more valuable than others. It would be absurd that, while in estimating all other things quality is considered as well as quantity, the estimation of pleasure should be supposed to depend on quantity alone.

If I am asked what I mean by difference of quality in pleasures, or what makes one pleasure more valuable than another, merely as a pleasure, except its being greater in amount, there is but one possible answer. Of two pleasures, if there be one to which all or almost all who have experience of both give a decided preference, irrespective of any feeling of moral obligation to prefer it, that is the more desirable pleasure. If one of the two is, by those who are competently acquainted with both, placed so far above the other that they prefer it, even though knowing it to be attended with a greater amount of discontent, and would not resign it for any quantity of the other pleasure which their nature is capable of, we are justified in ascribing to the preferred enjoyment a superiority in quality so far outweighing quantity as to render it, in comparison, of small account.

Now it is an unquestionable fact that those who are equally acquainted with and equally capable of appreciating and enjoying both do give a most marked preference to the manner of existence which employs their higher faculties. Few human creatures would consent to be changed into any of the lower animals for a promise of the fullest allowance of a beast's pleasures; no intelligent human being would consent to be a fool, no instructed person would be an ignoramus, no person of feeling and conscience would be selfish and base, even though they should be persuaded that the fool, the dunce, or the rascal is better satisfied with his lot than they are with theirs. They would not resign what they possess more than he for the most complete satisfaction of all the desires which they have in common with him. If they ever fancy they would, it is only in cases of unhappiness so extreme that to escape from it they would exchange their lot for almost any other, however undesirable in their own eyes. A being of higher faculties requires more to make him happy, is capable probably of more acute suffering, and certainly accessible to it at more points, than one of an inferior type; but in spite of these liabilities, he can never really wish to sink into what he feels to be a lower grade of existence.

JOHN STUART MILL, *Utilitarianism*

There are a number of tricky logical problems with the position Mill defends here, the complete analysis of which would carry us into some rather dry and technical regions of the theory of utility. But one problem springs instantly from the page at us. If not all pleasures are equal in quality, if some persons of more refined sensibility are better able to judge of the quality of pleasures, then the basic democratic one-person-one-vote thrust of utilitarianism is lost. Instead of giving every person, however low in station or meagre in education, an equal voice in the choice of the ends of social policy, special weight shall have to be accorded to the opinions of that educated minority who have tasted the elevated pleasures of the mind—to those who claim, from the height of their culture, that Bach is better than rock, and cordon bleu better than cheeseburgers. The fact is that Mill does indeed exhibit just such an aristocratic bias in his political writings, both in regard to the privileged position of the upper classes within England and also in regard to England's privileged position in her colonies vis-à-vis the "subject races" not yet raised to her own level of culture. The cultural imperialism of Mill, as we may call it, is of course interesting as a fact about the man and his times. But it is also a first-rate example of the way in which an apparently trivial philosophical argument about a technical point can carry with it very large consequences for the most practical questions of politics.

Mill's second revision of his father's faith concerned the rationality and predictability of the laborers, capitalists, and consumers who interacted in the marketplace. The doctrine of laissez-faire, with its emphasis on limited government intervention in the market and a removal of all regulations on trade and commerce, depended upon two assumptions, as we have already seen. The first was that economic actors would be counted on to behave in a rationally self-interested manner, buying as cheaply as possible, taking the highest wages available, always looking for a profit; the second, which depended for its plausibility on the first, was that an economy run along laissez-faire lines and populated by rationally self-interested persons would maximize growth and production and thereby create the greatest happiness possible, within the limits of natural resources and technology, for the greatest number of people. In one of his major works, *The Principles of Political Economy,* Mill denied the first of these two assumptions, and thereby laid the theoretical groundwork for the rejection of the second.

First let us look at Mill's argument. Then we will consider its significance.

> Under the rule of individual property, the division of the produce is the result of two determining agencies: Competition, and Custom. It is important to ascertain the amount of influence which belongs to each of these causes, and in what manner the operation of one is modified by the other.
>
> Political economists generally, and English political economists above others, have been accustomed to lay almost exclusive stress upon the first of these agencies; to exaggerate the effect of competition, and to take into little account the other and conflicting principle. They are apt to express themselves as if they thought that competition actually does, in all cases, whatever it can be shown to be the tendency of competition to do. This is partly intelligible, if we consider that only through the principle of competition has political economy any pretension to the character of a science. So far as rents, profits, wages, prices, are determined by competition, laws may be assigned for them. Assume competition to be their exclusive regulator, and principles of broad generality and scientific precision may be laid down, according to which they will be regulated. The political economist justly deems this his proper business: and as an abstract or hypothetical science, political economy cannot be required to do, and indeed cannot do, anything more. But it would be a great misconception of the actual course of human affairs, to suppose that competition exercises in fact this unlimited sway. I am not speaking of monopolies, either natural or artificial, or of any interferences of authority with the liberty of production or exchange. Such disturbing causes have always been allowed for by political economists. I speak of cases in which there is nothing to restrain competition; no hindrance to it either in the nature of the case or in artificial obstacles; yet in which the result is not determined by competition, but by custom or usage; competition either not taking place at all, or producing its effect in quite a different manner from that which is ordinarily assumed to be natural to it.
>
> Since custom stands its ground against competition to so considerable an extent, even where, from the multitude of competitors and the general energy in the pursuit of gain, the spirit of competition is strongest, we may be sure that this is much more the case where people are content with smaller gains, and estimate their

pecuniary interest at a lower rate when balanced against their ease or their pleasure. I believe it will often be found, in Continental Europe, that prices and charges, of some or of all sorts, are much higher in some places than in others not far distant, without its being possible to assign any other cause than that it has always been so: the customers are used to it, and acquiesce in it. An enterprising competitor, with sufficient capital, might force down the charges, and make his fortune during the process; but there are no enterprising competitors; those who have capital prefer to leave it where it is, or to make less profit by it in a more quiet way.

JOHN STUART MILL, *Principles of Political Economy*

Mill is saying that although the behavior of men and women in the market may be *predictable,* it is not *calculable.* The difference is fundamental, so perhaps we should take a moment to explain it more clearly. Suppose I want to open a snack shop, and I am trying to decide whether to locate downtown or in a new mall just being built on the edge of town. I know that the mall will have a number of discount outlets selling well-known brands at very low prices. If I can assume that consumers will be motivated solely by a desire to minimize their expenditures for the goods they buy, then I can calculate *a priori* (without any special information about shopping habits in this area) that the mall will be crowded with bargain-hunters. Since I want my snack shop to be where the shoppers are, I will choose the mall.

But if Mill is right (as in fact he is), then a certain proportion of the shoppers will go on shopping downtown, whether out of habit or because they care enough about such non-monetary things as the familiarity of the stores. There is no way in the world that I can foresee just how many shoppers will be influenced enough by these factors to go downtown instead of to the mall. I can observe shopping behavior in other towns and extrapolate to this case, or do an opinion survey of shoppers, or in some other fashion try to base my prediction on experience. With enough data, I may be able to *predict* what the shoppers will do, so that I can decide where to put my snack shop. But there is no way that I can calculate their behavior *a priori.*

So long as economic actors in the marketplace act in a rationally self-interested way, I can calculate their actions without any prior knowledge of their individual character, without elaborate collections of information about their past behavior. All I need know is (1) that they seek to maximize profits or enjoyments, and (2) that they will make use of the available information in a rational attempt to achieve that maximization. I can then carry out in my own head the same calculation they will carry out, and so I can calculate their actions. But if they are influenced by what Mill calls *custom,* which is to say by *irrational* tastes, habits, and preferences that deviate from the strict rationality of profit maximization, then I can only predict their behavior on the basis of vast quantities of systematically collected data about their past behavior. I cannot count on the "invisible hand" of the marketplace to direct their economic activities into the most productive areas. Capitalists may refrain, out of irrational habits or aversions, from shifting their capital into sectors of unfulfilled market demand. Consumers may go on shopping at a more expensive store when identical goods are offered more cheaply next door. Workers may fail to quit low-paying jobs and move to better-paying jobs in labor-short industries.

The result will be a breakdown of the automatic mechanisms of the market and a need for scientifically controlled management of the economy by a central authority possessing both the information and the power to implement its judgments. In short, the slight revision which Mill makes in the classical theory of laissez-faire leads directly, although not immediately, to the modern managed economy of welfare-state capitalism.

Mill's third alteration in the radical philosophy of James Mill follows directly from the first, and concerns the government's right to interfere with the private lives of its citizens. In his famous essay, *On Liberty,* Mill argues for an absolute ban on all state or social intervention in the inner life of thoughts and feelings. But in the last chapter of the *Principles,* he takes a somewhat different line. To be sure, he says, *"Laisser-faire . . .* should be the general practice: every departure from it, unless required by some great good, is a certain evil." But in considering permissible departures, Mill concedes a very great deal indeed. Listen to him in this suggestive passage:

> We have observed that, as a general rule, the business of life is better performed when those who have an immediate interest in it are left to take their own course, uncontrolled either by the mandate of the law or by the meddling of any public functionary. The persons, or some of the persons, who do the work, are likely to be better judges than the government, of the means of attaining the particular end at which they aim. Were we to suppose, what is not very probable, that the government has possessed itself of the best knowledge which had been acquired up to a given time by the persons most skilled in the occupation; even then, the individual agents have so much stronger and more direct an interest in the result, that the means are far more likely to be improved and perfected if left to their uncontrolled choice. But if the workman is generally the best selector of means, can it be affirmed with the same universality, that the consumer, or person served, is the most competent judge of the end? Is the buyer always qualified to judge of the commodity? If not, the presumption in favour of the competition of the market does not apply to the case; and if the commodity be one, in the quality of which society has much at stake, the balance of advantages may be in favour of some mode and degree of intervention, by the authorized representatives of the collective interest of the state.
>
> Now, the proposition that the consumer is a competent judge of the commodity, can be admitted only with numerous abatements and exceptions. He is generally the best judge (though even this is not true universally) of the material objects produced for his use. These are destined to supply some physical want, or gratify some taste or inclination, respecting which wants or inclinations there is no appeal from the person who feels them; or they are the means and appliances of some occupation, for the use of the persons engaged in it, who may be presumed to be

judges of the things required in their own habitual employment. But there are other things of the worth of which the demand of the market is by no means a test; things of which the utility does not consist in ministering to inclinations, nor in serving the daily uses of life, and the want of which is least felt where the need is greatest. This is peculiarly true of those things which are chiefly useful as tending to raise the character of human beings. The uncultivated cannot be competent judges of cultivation.

JOHN STUART MILL, *Principles of Political Economy*

Despite all his qualifications and revisions in the utilitarian creed, Mill remained faithful to its spirit. But powerful intellectual attacks were mounted on laissez-faire liberalism and utilitarianism from both the right and the left. In the next two sections of this chapter, we shall listen to some of the voices of dissent. The attacks began as soon as industrial capitalism and its liberal defenders appeared. In the very first decades of the nineteenth century, Romantic conservative critics of industrialism and socialist critics of the capitalist organization of that industrialism appeared in England and on the Continent. But I do not want you to think that this is an ancient dispute, buried in dusty books written by men long dead. The very same argument continues today, and so we shall hear from a few of the contemporary philosophers who have questioned the foundations of both the theory and the practice of traditional liberal social philosophy.

II

Living as we do two centuries after industrial capitalism burst its bonds and rose to a position of domination in the economy and society of England, we tend to think of capitalists and capitalism as the Establishment, as the old order, entrenched in its position of superiority even though under attack from socialism and communism. But in its infancy, capitalism was a revolutionary social force which assaulted the bastions of landed wealth and power, toppled kings, and thrust a new class into the arena of politics. The philosophy that rationalized this emergence of a new ruling class was also a revolutionary philosophy, and its celebration of prudential rationality, its insistence upon the rights of the individual, its denial of immemorial custom, privilege, and inherited status grated on the philosophical sensibilities of the old order's defenders as much as the accents of the new industrial barons must have grated on their ears.

The conservative counterattack took many literary forms. It appeared in the speeches of Edmund Burke, in the poetry of Shelley, in the essays and history of Carlyle. Needless to say, there is no single "conservative" position, any more than there was or is a single "liberal" or "radical" position. But

Industrialism changed the lives and the work experiences of millions of men and women. The cultural gap between the fields and the factory can scarcely be imagined by those of us who have not known them both.

the critics from the right tended to concentrate their fire on two strong points of the liberal philosophy. These were the nature and role of *reason* in human affairs, and the legitimacy of *tradition* as a source of the bonds that united men and women in society. In each case, the conservatives argued that the liberals had got the matter badly wrong and had produced thereby a philosophy that was both false and socially harmful.

The prime target of conservative arguments was the utilitarian conception of human reason. By now you will have noted how often this matter of the nature of reason comes up in philosophical disputes. Cosmologists, epistemologists, moralists, and political theorists all argue about our peculiar capacity of reason, about what role it should play in our personality, in our study of nature, and in our social arrangements. Bentham, Mill, and company had made two claims about reason. First, they said that human beings are fundamentally rational creatures, despite the overlay of irrationality which is from time to time produced by superstition, ignorance, or religious faith. By saying that we are rational, they meant that we have it within our power to deliberate, to weigh alternatives, and to make choices guided by knowledge and calculation. Second, they said that this power of reason had the function of selecting the efficient means for the achievement of those ends which had already been set by desire. So to the utilitarians, and to liberal philosophers in general, "rational agent" essentially meant "prudent agent."

The conservatives denied both of these theses about reason. First of all, they denied that reason should take the ruling place in the soul. The poets insisted that the power of imagination was actually a higher faculty than reason. It had the capacity to put us in touch with eternal truths, with the ideal of beauty, with a deeper reality that mere sensation and calculation could never reveal. They considered the utilitarians' prudent man to be a vulgar, uninspired, diminished creature, capable only of adding up pleasures and pains, profits and losses. The mystery, awe, wonder, majesty, and sanctity of the human experience were reduced by a Bentham to the level of "pleasures," to be traded off against a good meal or a soft bed. One might as well use a Rembrandt masterpiece as a scratch pad or melt down a statue of the Blessed Virgin to make paperweights. Better by far to lift the masses, by even a little, through the exercise of the unquestioned authority of their cultivated betters, rather than reduce all art, all culture, all society to the lowest common denominator of popular taste.

I do not know of any philosopher who has attacked this celebration of reason more wittily, profoundly, and effectively than the modern English conservative Michael Oakeshott. In his essay, "Rationalism in Politics," Oakeshott takes on virtually the entire corpus of Western philosophers as he ridicules their conception of rationality. The principal target of Oakeshott's criticism is the familiar distinction between ends and means, a distinction which can be found in the writings of Aristotle, Hobbes, Bentham, Mill, Kant, and countless other philosophers of widely different theoretical persuasions. When a person acts, according to the most common view, first he identifies the state of affairs he wishes to bring about—his goal or *end*—and then he selects what seems to him, given his beliefs about the world, the best or most efficient way of bringing it about—his *means*. So when I mow my lawn, first I identify my end, which is to shorten the length of the grass on my lawn to a height that looks nice to me and also keeps the grass growing, and then I select the means available to me that seems likely to accomplish my end in the most efficient manner, according to my personal evaluation of the relative values or costs of the different means. In short, I tell my son to get out the lawnmower and mow the lawn. Or, if my son has gone off with his friends, I do it myself.

According to this analysis, my choice of ends is determined either by the mere, unanalyzable fact that I desire some thing (maybe I just *like* the look of short grass), or by some set of moral convictions (I may, for peculiar reasons, think that it is immoral to have long grass), or by the fact that I desire something else which this particular end is a means to getting (I may want to impress my neighbors, and past experience tells me that they are really impressed by a well-kept lawn). My choice of means is determined by my knowledge of the world taken together with what Defense Department planners call a "cost-bene-fit" calculation. I figure out the most efficient way to achieve my goal, and then decide whether the payoff is worth the price (if I have to mow the lawn myself, I may decide to pass up my neighbor's praise!).

The interesting thing about Oakeshott's position is that he thinks it is literally impossible for anyone to act in this ends-means way! He sometimes talks as though he thinks it is merely a foolish way to act, but his real claim is that we couldn't act that way even if we tried. What is more, though we always fail, the effort invariably makes things worse than they need be. Here is his argument.

The general character and disposition of the Rationalist are, I think, not difficult to identify. At bottom he stands (he always *stands*) for independence of mind on all occasions, for thought free from obligation to any authority save the authority of 'reason.' His circumstances in the modern world have made him contentious: he is the *enemy* of authority, of prejudice, of the merely traditional, customary or habitual. His mental attitude is at once sceptical and optimistic: sceptical, because there is no opinion, no habit, no belief, nothing so firmly rooted or so widely held that he hesitates to question it and to judge it by what he calls his 'reason'; optimistic, because the Rationalist never doubts the power of his 'reason' (when properly applied) to determine the worth of a thing, the truth of an opinion or the propriety of an action. . . .

He has no sense of the cumulation of experience, only of the readiness of experience when it has been converted into a formula: the past is significant to him only as an encumbrance. He has none of that *negative capability* (which Keats attributed to Shakespeare), the power of accepting the mysteries and uncertainties of experience without any irritable search for order and distinctness, only the capability of subjugating experience; he has no aptitude for that close and detailed appreciation of what actually presents itself which Lichtenberg called *negative enthusiasm,* but only the power of recognizing the large outline which a general theory imposes upon events . . . the mind of the Rationalist impresses us as, at best, a finely-tempered, neutral instrument, as a well-trained rather than as an educated mind. Intellectually, his ambition is not so much to share the experience of the race as to be demonstrably a self-made man. And this gives to his intellectual and practical activities an almost preternatural deliberateness and self-consciousness, depriving them of any element of passivity, removing from them all sense of rhythm and continuity and dissolving them into a succession of climacterics, each to be surmounted by a *tour de raison*. His mind has no atmosphere, no changes of season and temperature; his intellectual processes, so far as possible, are insulated from all external influence and go on in the void. And having cut himself off from the traditional knowledge of his society, and denied the value of any education more extensive than a training in a technique of analysis, he is apt to attribute to mankind a necessary inexperience in all the critical moments of life, and if he were more self-critical he might begin to wonder how the race had ever succeeded in surviving. With an almost poetic fancy, he strives to live each day as if it were his first, and he believes that to form a habit is to fail. And if, with as yet no thought of analysis, we glance below the surface, we may, perhaps, see in the temperament, if not in the character, of the Rationalist, a deep distrust of time, an impatient hunger for eternity and an irritable nervousness in the face of everything topical and transitory.

Every science, every art, every practical activity requiring skill of any sort, indeed every human activity whatsoever, involves knowledge. And, universally, this knowledge is of two sorts, both of which are always involved in any actual activity. It is not, I think, making too much of it to call them two sorts of knowledge, because (though in fact they do not exist separately) there are certain important differences between them. The first sort of knowledge I will call technical knowledge or knowledge of technique. In every art and science, and in every practical activity, a technique is involved. In many activities this technical knowledge is formulated into rules which are, or may be, deliberately learned, remembered, and, as we say, put into practice; but whether or not it is, or has been, precisely formulated, its chief characteristic is that it is susceptible of precise formulation, although special skill and insight may be required to give that formulation. The technique (or part of it) of driving a motor car on English roads is to be found in the Highway Code, the technique of cookery is contained in the cookery book, and the technique of discovery in natural science or in history is in their rules of research, of observation and verification. The second sort of knowledge I will call practical, because it exists only in use, is not reflective and (unlike technique) cannot be formulated in rules. This does not mean, however, that it is an esoteric sort of knowledge. It means only that the method by which it may be shared and becomes common knowledge is not the method of formulated doctrine. And if we consider it from this point of view, it would not, I think, be misleading to speak of it as traditional knowledge. In every activity this sort of knowledge is also involved; the mastery of any skill, the pursuit of any concrete activity is impossible without it. . . .

Now, as I understand it, Rationalism is the assertion that what I have called practical knowledge is not knowledge at all, the assertion that, properly speaking, there is no knowledge which is not technical knowledge. The Rationalist holds that the only element of *knowledge* involved in any human activity is technical knowledge, and that what I have called practical knowledge is really only a sort of nescience which would be negligible if it were not positively mischievous. The sovereignty of 'reason', for the Rationalist, means the sovereignty of technique.

MICHAEL OAKESHOTT, *Rationalism in Politics*

The second utilitarian thesis about reason got equally short shrift from the conservatives. Though they denied the primacy of reason, they insisted that reason could do more than merely select efficient means to any end desire might throw up before us. That, they thought, was a shopkeeper's conception of reason, a bookkeeper's notion of what it meant to be rational. "Two tickles on this side of the ledger, a twinge on that. Let us see how it balances out." Was this the highest peak to which we could aspire in the exercise of our rational powers? Hardly. Reason was far better employed in a reflection upon the truths of revealed religion, in a just appreciation of the wise ordering of statuses and classes in established society, in a contemplation of the eternal form of beauty.

Conservative critics were especially vigorous in their defense of the traditions which the utilitarians lumped together as "superstitions." A tradition is a way of acting, a style of personality, a form of human relationships, which has been enacted and reenacted over many generations, and has acquired through long usage an authority that exceeds any justification a calculating reason can produce. To a utilitarian, tradition is simply a polite name for thoughtless repetition, for the doing once more of something that could not be justified the first time. This harsh view of tradition assumes that we can know enough about our social affairs to make reliable calculations of the best institutions and policies. But if our capacity to discover the underlying nature of society is limited at best; if the power of reason within each of us is only a feeble check against powerful, destructive passions lurking beneath the surface of civilization; if the experiences of past generations are a fund of unspoken wisdom on which the present can draw through the reenactment of the old ways; if all of this be the case, then tradition will be our best guide rather than our worst. It will preserve for us what is soundest in the history of the human race, while also containing, through its authority, those antisocial passions which mere calculative reason cannot adequately suppress.

One way to bring the dispute between the liberals and the conservatives into focus is to embody their abstract philosophies in concrete human form, to try to imagine what the ideal utilitarian liberal would be like and what the ideal conservative would be like. This is a risky business, and I will probably end up by offending both liberals and conservatives, but let me have a go at it anyway. I think it will help you to see what is at stake. The ideal utilitarian liberal can be imagined as a solid, cautious, open-minded, prudent businessman. He is self-made, having earned his present position by hard work, self-denial, and a shrewd calculation of advantage. He is not public-spirited, if by that is meant a desire to help others at the expense of himself. But since his own interests are best advanced in the marketplace by satisfying the desires of his customers, he manages to do good for others in the process of doing well by himself.

The ideal conservative is an aristocrat, born into a family with wealth, tradition, and a name to uphold. He is quirky, individualistic, disdainful of the opinions of anyone not in his own social class, but fiercely proud of his honor and determined to uphold it at all costs. He scorns calculation, and considers a good head for business to be a somewhat degrading trait. He has a cultivated mind, and is at ease with great art and great literature, though he does not work at it like a dry professor. His morals are sometimes a trifle loose, but his word is his bond, and in a war he can be counted on to stand his position until the death. His life has style, a certain flamboyance, and it is his own style, not purchased at a clothing store or copied from the pages of a magazine.

Each one—the businessman and the aristocrat—has his strengths, and each has his weaknesses. The businessman is practical, open to experiment, willing to try new ways to solve intractable problems. He is flexible, capable of compromise, able to deal with men and women of all classes and backgrounds. He is respectful of the manners and mores of others (for he never knows when they will be his customers). If you need a railroad constructed, a new technology exploited, or a dispute settled between labor and management, he is your man.

But the same instrumental calculation that stands the businessman in such good stead when he is faced with a problem of resource management can be his downfall when hard choices of honor and morality come his way. The utilitarian mentality tends to lead to the subversion of principle in the interest of some "larger" end. Benjamin Franklin said in his autobiography that the *appearance* of honesty was more important in business than honesty itself, and such an attitude easily degenerates into an obsessive concern with public relations, with the salability of a policy or a product rather than its soundness. Liberals are long on practical proposals for benevolent social management, but short on backbone when it comes to defending basic principles against attack.

The conservative's strengths and weaknesses are the mirror opposites of the businessman's. The conservative is set in his ways, unwilling to experiment with new industrial or social programs, uninterested in compromise, unable to accommodate himself to the manners of those from different social backgrounds. But he has the capacity to take offense, to feel that his honor has been insulted, and when that happens he will stand and fight, not out of a rational calculation of future advantage but simply from an irrational conviction that certain things are "not done."

These sentiments were expressed with great elegance a century and a half ago by the brilliant French historian and observer of social affairs, Alexis de Tocqueville. In his eloquent book, *The Old Régime and the French Revolution,* de Tocqueville analyzed the paradoxical connection between the presence of an aristocracy in the old regime and the preservation of true—though not in the liberal sense *rational*—freedom. This selection from his book should provide us with some second thoughts about our own tendency to identify class inequality with a loss of freedom.

Many of the prejudices, false ideas, and privileges which were the most serious obstacles to the establishment of a healthy, well-ordered freedom had the effect of maintaining in the minds of Frenchmen a spirit of independence and encouraging them to make a stand against abuses of authority. The nobility had the utmost

ALEXIS DE TOCQUEVILLE (1805–1859) was a French writer, politician, and commentator on public affairs. After a visit to the United States in 1831, he wrote a two-volume study of American politics and national character, *Democracy in America,* which remains to this day the most penetrating analysis of the distinctive American contribution to democratic culture. Tocqueville was one of a number of mid-nineteenth-century writers who believed that complete social and economic equality could be a threat to individual liberty.

contempt for the administration properly so called, though now and again they addressed petitions to it. Even after the surrender of their former power they kept something of their ancestral pride, their traditional antipathy to servitude and subordination to the common law. True, they gave little thought to the freedom of the populace at large and were quite ready to let the authorities rule those around them with a heavy hand. But they refused to let that hand weigh on themselves and were prepared to run the greatest risks in the defense of their liberties if and when the need arose. When the Revolution broke out, the nobility, destined as they were to be swept away with the throne, still maintained in their dealings with the King an attitude vastly more arrogant and a freedom of speech far greater than those of the Third Estate, who were soon to overthrow the monarchy. Almost all the safeguards against the abuse of power which the French nation had possessed during its thirty-seven years of representative government were vigorously demanded by the nobles. When we read the *cahiers* they presented to the Estates-General, we cannot but appreciate the spirit and some of the high qualities of our aristocracy, despite its prejudices and failings. It is indeed deplorable that instead of being forced to bow to the rule of law, the French nobility was uprooted and laid low, since thereby the nation was deprived of a vital part of its substance, and a wound that time will never heal was inflicted on our national freedom. When a class has taken the lead in public affairs for centuries, it develops as a result of this long, unchallenged habit of pre-eminence a certain proper pride and confidence in its strength, leading it to be the point of maximum resistance in the social organism. And it not only has itself the manly virtues; by dint of its example it quickens them in other classes. When such an element of the body politic is forcibly excised, even those most hostile to it suffer a diminution of strength. Nothing can ever replace it completely, it can never come to life again; a deposed ruling class may recover its titles and possessions but nevermore the spirit of its forebears. . . .

. . . We must be chary of regarding submission to authority as *per se* a sign of moral abjection—that would be using a wrong criterion. However subservient was the Frenchman of the old régime to the King's authority there was one kind of subservience to which he never demeaned himself. He did not know what it was to bend the knee to an illegitimate or dubious authority, a government little honored and sometimes heartily despised, which it is well to truckle to because it has power to help or harm. This degrading form of servitude was something quite unknown to our forefathers. Their feeling for the King was unlike that of any other modern nation for its monarch, even the most absolute; indeed, that ancient loyalty which was so thoroughly eradicated by the Revolution has become almost incomprehensible to the modern mind. The King's subjects felt towards him both the natural love of children for their father and the awe properly due to God alone. Their compliance with his orders, even the most arbitrary, was a matter far less of compulsion than of affection, so that even when the royal yoke pressed on them most heavily, they felt they still could call their souls their own. To their thinking, constraint was the most evil factor of obedience; to ours, it is the least. Yet is not that type of obedience which comes of a servile mind the worst of all? Indeed, we should be ill advised to belittle our ancestors; and would do better to regain, even if it meant inheriting their prejudices and failings, something of their nobility of mind.

ALEXIS DE TOCQUEVILLE, *The Old Régime and the French Revolution*

Incidentally, Mill read Tocqueville and sought to incorporate his insights into the utilitarian position. Whether he succeeded is a question that I can leave to you for a decision.

III

The conservative reaction to industrialism and liberalism was powerful, and it gave rise in the social sciences to an enormous body of impressive theory and research. But more powerful still was the attack from the left. The misery of the workers in the early factories, the squalor of the slums in which they and their families suffered, the gross contrast between their poverty and the wealth of the entrepreneurs provoked a flood of scathing condemnations of the new industrial order. Some of the criticisms were merely cries from the heart, but especially in France, a number of philosophers and economists made an effort to discover the underlying causes of the suffering created by capitalism. It was the German Karl Marx, however, who mounted the most sustained, thorough-going, and intellectually impressive critique of the institutions, economic theories, and philosophical rationalizations of industrial capitalism.

The genius of Marx's critique was that it met the liberal philosophy head on at its strongest point, and turned its own arguments against itself. Liberalism and laissez faire claimed to be rational doctrines, stripped of all superstitious mystification. The conservatives had denied the primacy of reason, and attempted instead to elevate imagination or tradition to the first place. But Marx accepted the challenge of liberalism. Industrial capitalism, he insisted, was not rational. Instead, it was profoundly irrational, and its claims to rationality, expressed in its economic theory and in its philosophy, were no more than an ideological rationalization designed to conceal the inner illogic of capitalism and thereby preserve a system which favored the interests of a few at the expense of the lives of the many.

Marx argued that industrial capitalism was irrational in two different ways.

KARL MARX (1818–1883) is the founder of modern socialism. Born in Prussia, he studied philosophy, and in his twenties joined a circle of young radical social critics and philosophers known as the Young Hegelians. After a number of years as a pamphleteer and intellectual agitator in Germany and France, Marx moved to London to escape political persecution. Once in England, he settled into a rather quiet life of scholarship, reflection, writing, and political organization. Throughout a lifetime of collaboration with Friedrich Engels, Marx systematically elaborated a full-scale economic, political, philosophical, historical, and moral critique of the industrial capitalist system which had developed first in England and then throughout the rest of Europe.

As a young man, Marx was inflamed with the revolutionary conviction that the capitalist order was on the brink of total collapse. After the failure of the workers' uprisings in 1848, and the reactionary turn of most continental governments, Marx developed a deeper and more long-term analysis of the internal weaknesses of capitalism. Though his writings fill many volumes, there can be no doubt that the masterpiece of his life was the book called, simply, *Capital.*

Unlike many of his followers, Marx was always ready to alter his theories in the face of new evidence. Although he was certain in his youth that socialism could only come by way of a violent revolutionary overthrow of capitalist society and government, later in his life he concluded that in such countries as England and America socialism might come through the relatively peaceful avenue of political agitation and election.

First of all, it was instrumentally irrational. That is to say, it systematically chose inefficient means to attain the ends it claimed to set for itself. The triumphant claim of Smith and the other capitalist apologists had been that a free market profit system would make maximally efficient use of the resources and technology available to a society at any moment, and generate new economic production more expeditiously than any system of government management or tradition. Marx agreed that capitalism was unequaled at the task of production, but the very same capitalism was unable to solve the even more important problem of distributing what its factories had produced. In a capitalist system, production is for profit, not for use. If the capitalist cannot make a good return on his investment, he is forced to close up shop, even though there may be men and women in the society crying for the goods he produces. By the same token, as long as he is making a good profit, he goes on churning out goods regardless of whether they are high on society's list of genuine needs. The market is the distribution mechanism, which means that only consumers with cash in hand can buy what the capitalists have produced. But in order for the capitalist to make a high profit, he must keep his wages down, for—Marx argues—profits come out of the difference between the value of what the workers produce and the wages they are paid by their employers. So the same capitalist who cuts his workers' wages to the bone finds no one in the market with money to buy his products.

Competition with other capitalists pushes each producer to cut prices and increase volume, in an attempt to seize a larger share of the market. The result is a cycle of overproduction, leading to layoffs, recession, depression, general misery, and then an upswing into new overproduction. Now, ever since people have been on this earth, natural disasters have afflicted them, blighting their crops, flooding their homes, striking them down with disease. But the depressions produced periodically in the nineteenth and twentieth centuries by capitalism were not natural disasters; they were man-made disasters, arising out of the inner irrationality of the capitalist system. Hunger resulted not from crop failures, but from the inability of the market system to distribute what had been produced. There was famine in the midst of plenty, until in America in the great Depression of the 1930s, farmers were literally forced to plow piglets under with their tractors while millions hovered on the brink of malnutrition and actual starvation. These "inner contradictions" of capitalism, as Marx called them, were living evidence of the irrationality of that social system which the utilitarians had proclaimed the reign of reason.

Even this terrible instrumental irrationality of capitalism, however, was merely a means, as it were, to the substantive irrationality, the debasing inhumanity of capitalism as it was actually lived by industrial workers. You have all heard the term "alienation." These days it has become a catchword, and is used to apply to everything from psychic disorder to mere boredom. The term was invented by the German philosopher Georg F. W. Hegel, and was taken over by Marx to describe what happens to men and women who labor under capitalism. Marx held that man is by nature a productive animal who lives in this world by intelligently, purposefully transforming nature, in cooperation with his fellow men, into commodities that can satisfy his needs and desires. In the process of production, men and women "externalize" themselves; that is, they make what was first a mere idea in their minds external to themselves in the form of an object or state of affairs which they create by their labor. The most important act of such self-externalizing creation is birth itself, but the same structure of creativity can be seen in the farmer's planning, planting, tending, and harvesting of a field of grain, in the carpenter's conceiving, cutting, fashioning, and finishing of a piece of furniture, and also in an artist's sculpting of a statue or a poet's forming of a sonnet.

Men and women need productive, fulfilling labor in order to be truly happy, Marx thought. He rejected the utilitarian notion that happiness consists simply in the satisfaction of desire. But the process of "externalization," by which men and women embody themselves in their creations, in their transformations of nature and in their interactions with one another, can be corrupted and perverted. If the products of our labor are taken out of our control, if the very laboring process itself is turned into a kind of submission to superior force, then what we make will come to appear to us not as fulfillments of our needs but as oppressive enemies thwarting our human nature. What has been externalized will become *alien*. In short, healthy externalization will become destructive *alienation*.

Capitalism systematically frustrates our need for satisfying labor in every possible way, according to Marx. There is plenty of labor, to be sure. But it is not autonomous labor, it is not labor directed at satisfying genuine human needs, it is not healthful, fulfilling labor; it is competitive labor that sets worker against worker, worker against capitalist, and capitalist against capitalist. The very productivity of capitalism makes it a hell on earth, for at the moment in history when we first achieved the technology to raise ourselves above famine, sickness, and misery, the inner contradictions of our system of property plunged us into depths of suffering worse than anything that was known in the Middle Ages.

Here is just a short selection from Marx's essay on alienated labor from the unpublished and unfinished papers which are known today as the *Economic-Philosophic Manuscripts of 1844*.

What constitutes the alienation of labour? First, that the work is *external* to the worker, that it is not part of his nature; and that, consequently, he does not fulfil himself in his work but denies himself, has a feeling of misery rather than well-being, does not develop freely his mental and physical energies but is physically exhausted and mentally debased. The worker, therefore, feels himself at home only during his leisure time, whereas at work he feels homeless. His work is not voluntary but imposed, *forced labour*. It is not the satisfaction of a need, but only a *means* for satisfying other needs. Its alien character is clearly shown by the fact that as

Marx insists that unalienated work is the fulfillment
of human existence. Would you prefer a world with
no work, or one with demanding, satisfying work?

soon as there is no physical or other compulsion it is avoided like the plague.
External labour, labour in which man alienates himself, is a labour of self-sacrifice,
of mortification. Finally, the external character of work for the worker is shown
by the fact that it is not his own work but work for someone else, that in work
he does not belong to himself but to another person.

KARL MARX, *Economic-Philosophic Manuscripts of 1844*

What could be done about the irrationality and dehumanization of capitalism? Marx's answer, as you all know, was a revolution, a socialist revolution
made by the workers against the capitalists. The revolution, Marx believed,

would accomplish several things. First of all, it would overthrow the system of ownership of the means of production which, under capitalism, placed in the hands of a few the accumulated technology, factories, raw materials, and machinery that had been produced collectively by the labor of generations of working men and women. Second, it would replace the system of production for profit in the marketplace by a system of production for the satisfaction of human needs. Men and women would collectively determine what they needed, and put their talents to work to produce it. The mere accident of profitability would no longer be permitted to govern decisions about capital investment and economic growth. It might be, for example, that a large profit could be made in the United States by building luxury housing for which there was no burning need, but that little or no profit could be made from the production of well-made, gracefully designed, low-cost housing. No matter. If the low-cost housing were needed, it would get first call on the available building materials and construction work force. Finally, the capitalist system of distribution through the market would be replaced by a rational and humane system of distribution for human need. Under capitalism, the ruling slogan might be "From each as much as you can get out of him; to each as little as you can get away with giving him." Under socialism, however, the ruling slogan would be "From each according to his ability; to each according to his work." When the final stage of communism was reached, Marx said, the slogan on society's banner would be "From each according to his ability; to each according to his needs."

Collective ownership of the means of production, production for use rather than for profit, distribution for need rather than for ability to pay. With these changes, socialism would overcome the instrumental and substantive irrationality of capitalism, and eliminate the alienation of human beings from their product, their labor, their own human nature, and their fellow workers.

But Marx wrote in the middle of the nineteenth century, and it is now more than one hundred years later. The last great depression was a half-century ago. In the major industrial nations, despite continuing inequalities of wealth, the workers enjoy a standard of living beyond Marx's wildest dreams. Governments have stepped in with active policies of budget management and monetary control to dampen the boom-to-bust swings which Marx saw as proof of the unstable inner nature of capitalism. Despite the fact that half the world calls itself Marxist, despite the existence of something purporting to be communism in the Soviet Union, in the People's Republic of China, and in a dozen smaller nations, hasn't Marx simply been proved wrong by the passage of time and the flow of events? Is his critique of capitalism relevant today?

No question generates more heated dispute in economics, in political science, or in philosophy. One of the social critics who has defended a modern version of Marx's argument is the German-born philosopher Herbert Marcuse. Marcuse (1898–1979) was educated at Berlin and Freiburg, and then joined the Institute for Social Research at Frankfurt. He came to the United States in 1934 to escape the Nazi persecution of Jews and intellectuals. He taught at Brandeis

University for many years, and then at the University of California at San Diego. Marcuse belongs to a group of twentieth-century social thinkers who have sought to fuse the social insights of Marx with the psychological insights of Freud, in an attempt to arrive at an integrated critical social theory. In *One-Dimensional Man,* which is perhaps his most influential book, Marcuse insists that the managed economy and increased material well-being of workers under modern capitalism do not in the slightest diminish the fundamental substantive and instrumental irrationality that Marx perceived more than a century ago. He argues that the satisfaction of the needs of workers under advanced capitalism is apparent rather than real. Through the manipulation of desire in advertising, in popular culture, in television, and in education, workers are conditioned to like what they get, rather than to insist on getting what they would truly like. To avoid inflation and recession, capitalism pours wasteful trillions into needless defense spending while inner cities rot and human potential goes unfulfilled. The very smoothness of the surface of modern capitalist society is only an added measure of irrationality, for whereas nineteenth-century capitalism was visibly inhuman, and thereby at least made manifest its own inadequacy, modern capitalism has successfully concealed its inhumanity from the very persons it dehumanizes. To call that progress is to suppose that slaves have been made free when they finally are forced to love their chains. This selection comes from the introduction to Marcuse's book. It sets the stage for his critique of capitalist society, philosophy, and ideology.

Does not the threat of an atomic catastrophe which could wipe out the human race also serve to protect the very forces which perpetuate this danger? The efforts to prevent such a catastrophe overshadow the search for its potential causes in contemporary industrial society. These causes remain unidentified, unexposed, unattacked by the public because they recede before the all too obvious threat from without—to the West from the East, to the East from the West. Equally obvious is the need for being prepared, for living on the brink, for facing the challenge. We submit to the peaceful production of the means of destruction, to the perfection of waste, to being educated for a defense which deforms the defenders and that which they defend.

If we attempt to relate the causes of the danger to the way in which society is organized and organizes its members, we are immediately confronted with the fact that advanced industrial society becomes richer, bigger, and better as it perpetuates the danger. The defense structure makes life easier for a greater number of people and extends man's mastery of nature. Under these circumstances, our mass media have little difficulty in selling particular interests as those of all sensible men. The political needs of society become individual needs and aspirations, their satisfaction promotes business and the commonweal, and the whole appears to be the very embodiment of Reason.

And yet this society is irrational as a whole. Its productivity is destructive of the free development of human needs and faculties, its peace maintained by the constant threat of war, its growth dependent on the repression of the real possibilities for pacifying the struggle for existence—individual, national, and international. This repression, so different from that which characterized the preceding, less developed stages of our society, operates today not from a position of natural and technical immaturity but rather from a position of strength. The capabilities (intellectual and material) of contemporary society are immeasurably greater than ever before— which means that the scope of society's domination over the individual is immeasurably greater than ever before. Our society distinguishes itself by conquering the centrifugal social forces with Technology rather than Terror, on the dual basis of an overwhelming efficiency and an increasing standard of living. . . .

The fact that the vast majority of the population accepts, and is made to accept, this society does not render it less irrational and less reprehensible. The distinction between true and false consciousness, real and immediate interest still is meaningful. But this distinction itself must be validated. Men must come to see it and to find their way from false to true consciousness, from their immediate to their real interest. They can do so only if they live in need of changing their way of life, of denying the positive, of refusing. It is precisely this need which the established society manages to repress to the degree to which it is capable of "delivering the goods" on an increasingly large scale, and using the scientific conquest of nature for the scientific conquest of man.

HERBERT MARCUSE, *One-Dimensional Man*

Marcuse's critique of American society raises political and moral questions, of course, but it also raises very deep metaphysical issues which have been the subject of philosophical debate ever since the time of Plato. Marcuse knows that Americans are, at least legally speaking, free to accept or reject the economic and social arrangements which he condemns as "one-dimensional." He is even willing to concede that most Americans, if asked by a pollster, would say that they like the consumer goods they buy with their money and the amusements with which they fill up their leisure hours. But Marcuse insists that despite their legal freedom and their apparent contentment with the politics and culture of American society, Americans are really fundamentally *unfree,* because their reasoning has been corrupted and their very desires twisted by the repressive institutions of capitalist society.

Does it make any sense to say that a person is unfree when he thinks he is free? Can a person really *not* desire something although consciously he believes that he does desire it? Bentham and the utilitarians say not. Desire is a conscious state of mind which I am immediately and unmistakably aware of. I may be wrong to believe that the thing I desire is going to give me pleasure, but I cannot be wrong about whether I really do desire it. What is more, the utilitarians go on, happiness or pleasure is also a conscious state of mind, and I can simply not be mistaken about whether I am happy. Other people may be wrong about how I feel—I may have the peculiar habit of frowning when I feel good—but I myself can never be wrong about my own happiness.

Plato doesn't agree, and neither does Marcuse. Both of them, and many other philosophers as well, hold that a man or woman can actually be unhappy without knowing it. People deceive themselves, they lie to themselves, they sometimes refuse to recognize the misery they are experiencing, because it is too hard to face the fact of that misery. And deceiving themselves about their own happiness, men and women can be slaves to passion, to ideology, to habit, or to fantasy, while all the time imagining that they are free.

This is a powerful argument, but a dangerous one. As we have already seen, the simple psychology of Bentham serves as a foundation for the democratic political philosophy of the liberal movement. Once we start arguing that ordinary men and women cannot judge whether they are truly happy, it is only a short step to the conclusion that some wise and powerful dictator had better make their decisions for them. That way lies tyranny and the totalitarianism of the twentieth-century state. But if we reject the notion of false pleasures and self-deception, then we lose all critical purchase on our society. We are forced to accept the superficial notion that whatever *seems* pleasant to people really is enjoyable. We rule out the possibility that men and women grow in self-knowl-edge.

My own judgment is that Plato, Marx, Marcuse, and the rest are correct in their fundamental claim that people can be unhappy and yet not "know" it—not admit it even to themselves. But like all powerful critical arguments, this one is dangerous and must be used carefully. Solid empirical evidence is needed (such as the evidence used by a psychiatrist in diagnosing mental illness) before we are justified in claiming that someone is deceiving himself about his own state of happiness. And even after we have made a solidly based judgment, we may still have no right to *force* someone to do what will really make him happy.

Social philosophy during the past two centuries has been a three-cornered debate among liberals, conservatives, and radicals. By and large, liberals have been defenders of the bourgeois capitalist social order that emerged in the late eighteenth and early nineteenth century, though they have been as critical as one could be of what they saw as the failings or shortcomings of that order. The conservatives and radicals, from different sides, have assailed bourgeois society as, in one way or another, inhumane, mechanical, corrupting, or unjust.

Not all social philosophers focussed their attention on the economic side of bourgeois capitalism, of course. For some, the decline in the authority of the traditional state, or the sweeping changes in art, literature, manners, and morals, loomed larger than the doings of the factory and the marketplace. Nevertheless, the dominant fact of the new society was the enormous expansion of economic activity, the sheer mass of goods spewed forth into the market, and it is therefore not surprising that social philosophy should have paid so much more attention to matters economic than it had ever done before.

The central question of social philosophy, to paraphrase the American logician Willard van Orman Quine, can be stated in three Anglo-Saxon monosyllables: *Who gets what?* The story of human history may be a story of the unending struggle to wrest a living from nature, but the principal sub-plot of that story is the struggle over how the fruits of human labor will be shared out among the members of society. A good deal of what is grown, or dug out of the ground, or crafted, or sewn, or spun must be used simply to replace what is used up and to keep those of us who work going for another season. The farmer needs to keep some wheat as seed for planting; the miner will need iron and steel to replace the shovels that wear out; the weaver will need more thread, and so forth. But there is some left over—a surplus, as economists call it—and the real fights in human history tend to be over how that extra, that surplus, gets divided up.

From a philosopher's point of view, there are really two questions here, not just one. The central question, to be sure, is: Who gets what? But logically prior to that question is another, rather more philosophical question: How shall we decide who gets what? A good deal of social philosophy turns out, when we look at it closely, to be about how to decide who gets what, rather than directly about who gets what.

Consider utilitarianism, for example. As we have seen, the principle of utility does not state a principle for dividing up the social surplus. It does not say, "Give each person exactly what she has produced," or "Give each person what he needs," or "Give each person what she can get by fair exchange in the market." The principle of utility, instead, gives us a rule for picking rules. It says, Choose a rule of social division that will produce the greatest happiness for the greatest number. Presumably, it is for social scientists, or politicians, or perhaps for each of us personally through the polls, to decide what that rule of social division is.

Conservatives, by and large, reject the notion that we can rationally lay down some *rule* for dividing the social surplus, and then follow it as though we were engaged in cutting a cake. To Oakeshott, such a procedure is not merely absurd, it is literally impossible. We may *try* to proceed in that rational manner, but willynilly, we will act out the traditions, the habits, and the culture of our society. Blueprints for the just society, he holds, are crack-brained schemes hatched by uprooted intellectuals who have lost touch with their origins.

Marx, of course, lays his views right on the line. He gives us a method of analysis, to be sure, but he also gives us straight out an answer to the question, Who gets what? According to him, workers should seize control of the factories and farms, the mines and warehouses, and put an end to the private ownership of the means of production. Then, a socialist society can be established in which the principle of distribution will be: From each according to his ability, to each according to his work. Eventually, Marx claims, it will become possible to transcend even the necessity of apportioning reward to performance, and at that time in the future, the true communist society can come into existence, based upon the principle: From each according to his ability, to each according to his need.

For the first half of the twentieth century, the philosophers who worked in the Anglo-American analytic style pretty much ignored social philosophy. They were primarily concerned with problems growing out of the new mathematics and science of the modern era, in what philosophers call the fields of "epistemology" and "metaphysics." In the past thirty years, however, more and more analytic philosophers in the United States have been bringing their technical skills to bear on the grand old questions of social philosophy, so that there is now a genuine rebirth of this branch of philosophy.

The most popular position among modern social philosophers is some form of utilitarianism, and in colleges across the country, Mill's famous essay on that subject is perhaps the most widely read book in courses on ethics and social philosophy. But utilitarianism, as we have seen, poses a number of serious theoretical problems which turn out to be very difficult to solve. It was only a matter of time, therefore, before a major challenge to the utilitarian school would arise. *A Theory of Justice*, by the Harvard philosopher John Rawls, is precisely that challenge.

Rawls' work unites a number of themes which we have been studying in this chapter. It is, first of all, an attempt to answer the basic question: Who should get what? As you will see, Rawls has a rather subtle principle of distribution, which is based on the idea that equality of distribution is the just rule, and that inequalities must be defended by showing that they indirectly benefit the worst-off members of society.

But Rawls also has a new and striking answer to the philosopher's question: How shall we decide who gets what? Rawls proposes a complicated game, or bargaining situation, in which the members of a society imagine themselves to be choosing a rule of distribution by unanimous agreement. Since the agreement must be unanimous, according to the rules of this imaginary game, no majority can tyrannize over a minority. The underlying aim of Rawls' imaginary game is to capture the notion that basic social rules must have a universal acceptability not tied to the peculiarities of one time, or place, or culture, or moment in history.

Finally, Rawls, by means of his theory of choosing a distribution rule, speaks to the central issue of the role of reason in social life. As you shall see, Rawls takes a very strong view—he himself has on occasion called it a Kantian view—about the *rational* character of the fundamental rules of social intercourse. Rawls deliberately sets up his imaginary bargaining situation so as to eliminate the influence of the nonrational sides of human nature. He is not denying the existence of those nonrational elements in personality, of course. But like Kant, and unlike Oakeshott, Rawls believes that only the rational side of our nature should come into play when we are deciding on the basic principles of social justice.

This selection is an essay by Rawls in which he laid out the basic elements of the theory which he later elaborated in his very long book, *A Theory of Justice*. There are two points to which you should pay special attention. First, make sure you understand Rawls' fundamental principle of distribution, the so-called "difference principle," according to which inequalities in the distribution of wealth must somehow work to the advantage of the least well-off members of society. Second, look carefully at Rawls' hypothetical thought experiment, the "original position," by means of which he tries to persuade us that his difference principle is the rationally most defensible principle of social justice.

JOHN RAWLS: *Distributive Justice*

We may think of a human society as a more or less self-sufficient association regulated by a common conception of justice and aimed at advancing the good of its members. As a co-operative venture for mutual advantage, it is characterized by a conflict as well as an identity of interests. There is an identity of interests since social co-operation makes possible a better life for all than any would have if everyone were to try to live by his own efforts; yet at the same time men are not indifferent as to how the greater benefits produced by their joint labours are distributed, for in order to further their own aims each prefers a larger to a lesser share. A conception of justice is a set of principles for choosing between the social arrangements which determine this division and for underwriting a consensus as to the proper distributive shares.

Now at first sight the most rational conception of justice would seem to be utilitarian. For consider: each man in realizing his own good can certainly balance his own losses against his own gains. We can impose a sacrifice on ourselves now for the sake of a greater advantage later. A man quite properly acts, as long as others are not affected, to achieve his own greatest good, to advance his ends as far as possible. Now, why should not a society act on precisely the same principle? Why is not that which is rational in the case of one man right in the case of a group of men? Surely the simplest and most direct conception of the right, and so of justice, is that of maximizing the good. This assumes a prior understanding of what is good, but we can think of the good as already given by the interests of rational individuals. Thus just as the principle of individual choice is to achieve one's greatest good, to advance so far as possible one's own system of rational desires, so the principle of social choice is to realize the greatest good (similarly defined) summed over all the members of society. We arrive at the principle of utility in a natural way: by this principle a society is rightly ordered, and hence just, when its institutions are arranged so as to realize the greatest sum of satisfactions.

The striking feature of the principle of utility is that it does not matter, except indirectly, how this sum of satisfactions is distributed among individuals, any more than it matters, except indirectly, how one man distributes his satisfactions over time. Since certain ways of distributing things affect the total sum of satisfactions, this fact must be taken into account in arranging social institutions; but according to this principle the explanation of common-sense precepts of justice and their seemingly stringent character is that they are those rules which experience shows must be strictly respected and departed from only under exceptional circumstances if the sum of advantages is to be maximized. The precepts of justice are derivative from the one end of attaining the greatest net balance of satisfactions. There is no reason in principle why the greater gains of some should not compensate for the lesser losses of others; or why the violation of the liberty of a few might not be made right by a greater good shared by many. It simply happens, at least under most conditions, that the greatest sum of advantages is not generally achieved in this way. From the standpoint of utility the strictness of common-sense notions of justice has a certain usefulness, but as a philosophical doctrine it is irrational.

If, then, we believe that as a matter of principle each member of society has an inviolability founded on justice which even the welfare of everyone else cannot over-ride, and that a loss of freedom for some is not made right by a greater sum of satisfactions enjoyed by many, we shall have to look for another account of the principles of justice. The principle of utility is incapable of explaining the fact that in a just society the liberties of equal citizenship are taken for granted, and the rights secured by justice are not subject to political bargaining nor to the calculus of social interests. Now, the most natural alternative to the principle of utility is its traditional rival, the theory of the social contract. The aim of the contract doctrine is precisely to account for the strictness of justice by supposing that its principles arise from an agreement among free and independent persons in an original position of equality and hence reflect the integrity and equal sovereignty of the rational persons who are the contractees. Instead of supposing that a conception of right, and so a conception of justice, is simply an extension of the principle of choice for one man to society as a whole, the contract doctrine assumes that the rational individuals who belong to society must choose together, in one joint act, what is to count among them as just and unjust. They are to decide among themselves once and for all what is to be their conception of justice. This decision is thought of as being made in a suitably defined initial situation one of the significant features of which is that no one knows his position in society, nor even his place in the distribution of natural talents and abilities. The principles of justice to which all are forever bound are chosen in the absence of this sort of specific information. A veil of ignorance prevents anyone from being advantaged or disadvantaged by the contingencies of social class and fortune; and hence the bargaining problems which arise in everyday life from the possession of this knowledge do not affect the choice of principles. On the contract doctrine, then, the theory of justice, and indeed ethics itself, is part of the general theory of rational choice, a fact perfectly clear in its Kantian formulation.

Once justice is thought of as arising from an original agreement of this kind, it is evident that the principle of utility is problematical. For why should rational individuals who have a system of ends they wish to advance agree to a violation of their liberty for the sake of a greater balance of satisfactions enjoyed by others? It seems more plausible to suppose that, when situated in an original position of equal right, they would insist upon institutions which returned compensating advantages for any sacrifices required. A rational man would not accept an institution merely because it maximized the sum of advantages irrespective of its effect on his own interests. It appears, then, that the principle of utility would be rejected as a principle of justice, although we shall not try to argue this important question here. Rather, our aim is to give a brief sketch of the conception of distributive shares implicit in the principles of justice which, it seems, would be chosen in the original position. The philosophical appeal of utilitarianism is that it seems to offer a single principle on the basis of which a consistent and complete conception of right can be developed. The problem is to work out a contractarian alternative in such a way that it has comparable if not all the same virtues.

In our discussion we shall make no attempt to derive the two principles of justice which we shall examine; that is, we shall not try to show that they would be chosen in the original position.[1] It must suffice that it is plausible that they would be, at least in preference to the standard forms of traditional theories. . . . The significance of these principles is that they allow for the strictness of the claims of justice; and if they can be understood so as to yield a consistent and complete conception, the contractarian alternative would seem all the more attractive.

The two principles of justice which we shall discuss may be formulated as follows: first, each person engaged in an institution or affected by it has an equal right to the most extensive liberty compatible with a like liberty for all; and second, inequalities as defined by the institutional structure or fostered by it are arbitrary unless it is reasonable to expect that they will work out to everyone's advantage and provided that the positions and offices to which they attach or from which they may be gained are open to all. These principles regulate the distributive aspects of institutions by controlling the assignment of rights and duties throughout the whole social structure, beginning with the adoption of a political constitution in accordance with which they are then to be applied to legislation. It is upon a correct choice of a basic structure of society, its fundamental system of rights and duties, that the justice of distributive shares depends.

[1] This question is discussed very briefly in 'Justice as Fairness', see pp. 138–41. The intuitive idea is as follows. Given the circumstances of the original position, it is rational for a man to choose as if he were designing a society in which his enemy is to assign him his place. Thus, in particular, given the complete lack of knowledge (which makes the choice one under uncertainty), the fact that the decision involves one's life-prospects as a whole and is constrained by obligations to third parties (e.g. one's descendants) and duties to certain values (e.g. to religious truth), it is rational to be conservative and so to choose in accordance with an analogue of the maximin principle.

The two principles of justice apply in the first instance to this basic structure, that is, to the main institutions of the social system and their arrangement, how they are combined together. Thus this structure includes the political constitution and the principal economic and social institutions which together define a person's liberties and rights and affect his life-prospects, what he may expect to be and how well he may expect to fare. The intuitive idea here is that those born into the social system at different positions, say in different social classes, have varying life-prospects determined, in part, by the system of political liberties and personal rights, and by the economic and social opportunities which are made available to these positions. In this way the basic structure of society favours certain men over others, and these are the basic inequalities, the ones which affect their whole life-prospects. It is inequalities of this kind, presumably inevitable in any society, with which the two principles of justice are primarily designed to deal.

Now the second principle holds that an inequality is allowed only if there is reason to believe that the institution with the inequality, or permitting it, will work out for the advantage of every person engaged in it. In the case of the basic structure this means that all inequalities which affect life-prospects, say the inequalities of income and wealth which exist between social classes, must be to the advantage of everyone. Since the principle applies to institutions, we interpret this to mean that inequalities must be to the advantage of the representative man for each relevant social position; they should improve each such man's expectation. Here we assume that it is possible to attach to each position an expectation, and that this expectation is a function of the whole institutional structure: it can be raised and lowered by reassigning rights and duties throughout the system. Thus the expectation of any position depends upon the expectations of the others, and these in turn depend upon the pattern of rights and duties established by the basic structure. But it is not clear what is meant by saying that inequalities must be to the advantage of every representative man.

One possibility is to say that everyone is made better off in comparison with some historically relevant benchmark. An interpretation of this kind is suggested by Hume.[2] He sometimes says that the institutions of justice, that is, the rules regulating property and contracts, and so on, are to everyone's advantage, since each man can count himself the gainer on balance when he considers his permanent interests. Even though the application of the rules is sometimes to his disadvantage, and he loses in the particular case, each man gains in the long-run by the steady administration of the whole system of justice. But all Hume seems to mean by this is that everyone is better off in comparison with the situation of men in the state of nature, understood either as some primitive

---

[2] For this observation I am indebted to Brian Barry.

condition or as the circumstances which would obtain at any time if the existing institutions of justice were to break down. While this sense of everyone's being made better off is perhaps clear enough, Hume's interpretation is surely unsatisfactory. For even if all men including slaves are made better off by a system of slavery than they would be in the state of nature, it is not true that slavery makes everyone (even a slave) better off, at least not in a sense which makes the arrangement just. The benefits and burdens of social co-operation are unjustly distributed even if everyone does gain in comparison with the state of nature; this historical or hypothetical benchmark is simply irrelevant to the question of justice. In fact, any past state of society other than a recent one seems irrelevant offhand, and this suggests that we should look for an interpretation independent of historical comparisons altogether. Our problem is to identify the correct hypothetical comparisons defined by currently feasible changes.

Now the well-known criterion of Pareto[3] offers a possibility along these lines once it is formulated so as to apply to institutions. Indeed, this is the most natural way of taking the second principle (or rather the first part of it, leaving aside the requirement about open positions). This criterion says that group welfare is at an optimum when it is impossible to make any one man better off without at the same time making at least one other man worse off. Applying this criterion to allocating a given bundle of goods among given individuals, a particular allocation yields an optimum if there is no redistribution which would improve one individual's position without worsening that of another. Thus a distribution is optimal when there is no further exchange which is to the advantage of both parties, or to the advantage of one and not to the disadvantage of the other. But there are many such distributions, since there are many ways of allocating commodities so that no further mutually beneficial exchange is possible. Hence the Pareto criterion, as important as it is, admittedly does not identify the best distribution, but rather a class of optimal, or efficient, distributions. Moreover, we cannot say that a given optimal distribution is better than any nonoptimal one; it is only superior to those which it dominates. The criterion is at best an incomplete principle for ordering distributions.

Pareto's idea can be applied to institutions. We assume, as remarked above, that it is possible to associate with each social position an expectation which depends upon the assignment of rights and duties in the basic structure. Given this assumption, we get a principle which says that the pattern of expectations (inequalities in life-prospects) is optimal if and only if it is impossible to change the rules, to redefine the scheme of rights and duties, so as to raise the expectations of any representative man without at the same time lowering the expectations of some other representative man. Hence the basic structure satisfies this principle when it is impossible to change the assignment of fundamental rights

[3] Introduced by him in his *Manuel d'économie politique* (1909) and long since a basic principle of welfare economics.

and duties and to alter the availability of economic and social opportunities so as to make some representative man better off without making another worse off. Thus, in comparing different arrangements of the social system, we can say that one is better than another if in one arrangement all expectations are at least as high, and some higher, than in the other. The principle gives grounds for reform, for if there is an arrangement which is optimal in comparison with the existing state of things, then, other things equal, it is a better situation all around and should be adopted.

The satisfaction of this principle, then, defines a second sense in which the basic structure makes everyone better off; namely, that from the standpoint of its representative men in the relevant positions, there exists no change which would improve anyone's condition without worsening that of another. Now we shall assume that this principle would be chosen in the original position, for surely it is a desirable feature of a social system that it is optimal in this sense. In fact, we shall suppose that this principle defines the concept of efficiency for institutions, as can be seen from the fact that if the social system does not satisfy it, this implies that there is some change which can be made which will lead people to act more effectively so that the expectations of some at least can be raised. Perhaps an economic reform will lead to an increase in production with given resources and techniques, and with greater output someone's expectations are raised.

It is not difficult to see, however, that while this principle provides another sense for an institution's making everyone better off, it is an inadequate conception of justice. For one thing, there is the same incompleteness as before. There are presumably many arrangements of an institution and of the basic structure which are optimal in this sense. There may also be many arrangements which are optimal with respect to existing conditions, and so many reforms which would be improvements by this principle. If so, how is one to choose between them? It is impossible to say that the many optimal arrangements are equally just, and the choice between them a matter of indifference, since efficient institutions allow extremely wide variations in the pattern of distributive shares.

Thus it may be that under certain conditions serfdom cannot be significantly reformed without lowering the expectations of some representative man, say that of landowners, in which case serfdom is optimal. But equally it may happen under the same conditions that a system of free labour could not be changed without lowering the expectations of some representative man, say that of free labourers, so that this arrangement likewise is optimal. More generally, whenever a society is relevantly divided into a number of classes, it is possible, let's suppose, to maximize with respect to any one of its representative men at a time. These maxima give at least this many optimal positions, for none of them can be departed from to raise the expectations of any man without lowering those of another, namely, the man with respect to whom the maximum is defined. Hence each of these extremes is optimal. All this corresponds to the obvious fact that, in distributing particular goods to given individuals, those distributions are also optimal which give the whole stock to any one person; for once a single person has everything, there is no change which will not make him worse off.

We see, then, that social systems which we should judge very differently from the standpoint of justice may be optimal by this criterion. This conclusion is not surprising. There is no reason to think that, even when applied to social systems, justice and efficiency come to the same thing. These reflections only show what we knew all along, which is that we must find another way of interpreting the second principle, or rather the first part of it. For while the two principles taken together incorporate strong requirements of equal liberty and equality of opportunity, we cannot be sure that even these constraints are sufficient to make the social structure acceptable from the standpoint of justice. As they stand the two principles would appear to place the burden of ensuring justice entirely upon these prior constraints and to leave indeterminate the preferred distributive shares.

There is, however, a third interpretation which is immediately suggested by the previous remarks, and this is to choose some social position by reference to which the pattern of expectations as a whole is to be judged, and then to maximize with respect to the expectations of this representative man consistent with the demands of equal liberty and equality of opportunity. Now, the one obvious candidate is the representative man of those who are least favoured by the system of institutional inequalities. Thus we arrive at the following idea: the basic structure of the social system affects the life-prospects of typical individuals according to their initial places in society, say the various income classes into which they are born, or depending upon certain natural attributes, as when institutions make discriminations between men and women or allow certain advantages to be gained by those with greater natural abilities. The fundamental problem of distributive justice concerns the differences in life-prospects which come about in this way. We interpret the second principle to hold that these differences are just if and only if the greater expectations of the more advantaged, when playing a part in the working of the whole social system, improve the expectations of the least advantaged. The basic structure is just throughout when the advantages of the more fortunate promote the well-being of the least fortunate, that is, when a decrease in their advantages would make the least fortunate even worse off than they are. The basic structure is perfectly just when the prospects of the least fortunate are as great as they can be.

In interpreting the second principle (or rather the first part of it which we may, for obvious reasons, refer to as the difference principle), we assume that the first principle requires a basic equal liberty for all, and that the resulting political system, when circumstances permit, is that of a constitutional democracy in some form. There must be liberty of the person and political equality as well as liberty of conscience and freedom of thought. There is one class of equal citizens which defines a common status for all. We also assume that there is equality of opportunity and a fair competition for the available positions on the basis of reasonable qualifications. Now, given this background, the differences to be justified are the various economic and social inequalities in the basic structure which must inevitably arise in such a scheme. These are the inequalities in the distribution of income and wealth and the distinctions in social prestige and status which attach to the various positions and classes. The difference principle says that these inequalities are just if and only if they are part of a larger system in which they work out to the advantage of the most unfortunate representative man. The just distributive shares determined by the basic structure are those specified by this constrained maximum principle.

Thus, consider the chief problem of distributive justice, that concerning the distribution of wealth as it affects the life-prospects of those starting out in the various income groups. These income classes define the relevant representative men from which the social system is to be judged. Now, a son of a member of the entrepreneurial class (in a capitalist society) has a better prospect than that of the son of an unskilled labourer. This will be true, it seems, even when the social injustices which presently exist are removed and the two men are of equal talent and ability; the inequality cannot be done away with as long as something like the family is maintained. What, then, can justify this inequality in life-prospects? According to the second principle it is justified only if it is to the advantage of the representative man who is worst off, in this case the representative unskilled labourer. The inequality is permissible because lowering it would, let's suppose, make the working man even worse off than he is. Presumably, given the principle of open offices (the second part of the second principle), the greater expectations allowed to entrepreneurs has the effect in the longer run of raising the life-prospects of the labouring class. The inequality in expectation provides an incentive so that the economy is more efficient, industrial advance proceeds at a quicker pace, and so on, the end result of which is that greater material and other benefits are distributed throughout the system. Of course, all of this is familiar, and whether true or not in particular cases, it is the sort of thing which must be argued if the inequality in income and wealth is to be acceptable by the difference principle.

We should now verify that this interpretation of the second principle gives a natural sense in which everyone may be said to be made better off. Let us suppose that inequalities are chain-connected: that is, if an inequality raises the expectations of the lowest position, it raises the expectations of all positions in between. For example, if the greater expectations of the representative entrepreneur raises that of the unskilled labourer, it also raises that of the semi-skilled. Let us further assume that inequalities are close-knit: that is, it is impossible to raise (or lower) the expectation of any representative man without raising (or lowering) the expectations of every other representative man, and in particular, without affecting one way or the other that of the least fortunate. There is no loose-jointedness, so to speak, in the way in which expectations depend upon one another. Now, with these assumptions, everyone does benefit from an inequality which satisfies the difference principle, and the second principle as we have formulated it reads correctly. For the representative man who is better off in any pairwise comparison gains by being allowed to have his advantage, and the man who is worse off benefits from the contribution which all inequalities make to each position below. Of course, chain-connection and close-knitness may not obtain; but in this case those who are better off should not have a veto over the advantages available for the least advantaged. The stricter interpretation of the difference principle should be followed, and all inequalities should be arranged for the advantage of the most unfortunate even if some inequalities are not to the advantage of those in middle positions. Should these conditions fail, then, the second principle would have to be stated in another way.

It may be observed that the difference principle represents, in effect, an original agreement to share in the benefits of the distribution of natural talents and abilities, whatever this distribution turns out to be, in order to alleviate as far as possible the arbitrary handicaps resulting from our initial starting places in society. Those who have been favoured by nature, whoever they are, may gain from their good fortune only on terms that improve the well-being of those who have lost out. The naturally advantaged are not to gain simply because they are more gifted, but only to cover the costs of training and cultivating their endowments and for putting them to use in a way which improves the position of the less fortunate. We are led to the difference principle if we wish to arrange the basic social structure so that no one gains (or loses) from his luck in the natural lottery of talent and ability, or from his initial place in society, without giving (or receiving) compensating advantages in return. (The parties in the original position are not said to be attracted by this idea and so agree to it; rather, given the symmetries of their situation, and particularly their lack of knowledge, and so on, they will find it to their interest to agree to a principle which can be understood in this way.) And we should note also that when the difference principle is perfectly satisfied, the basic structure is optimal by the efficiency principle. There is no way to make anyone better off without someone else worse off, namely, the least fortunate representative man. Thus the two principles of justice define distributive shares in a way compatible with efficiency, at least as long as we move on this highly abstract level. If we want to say (as we do, although it cannot be argued here) that the demands of justice have an absolute weight with respect to efficiency, this claim may seem less paradoxical when it is kept in mind that perfectly just institutions are also efficient.

TOPICS FOR FURTHER STUDY

1. Rawls formulates his fundamental principle of justice in two parts. The first part guarantees equal basic liberty to all, in the form, Rawls assumes, of a constitutional democracy. The second part permits inequalities so long as they work to the benefit of the least advantaged. According to Rawls, the equal liberty clause takes absolute priority over the so-called "difference principle." What implications does this have for the amount of relative economic inequality that would be permitted in society? Can the citizens of a democracy truly be equally free so long as there is a significant gap between the income of the best-off and the worst-off segments of the society?

2. The "original position" hypothesis is a version of what is known in political philosophy as the theory of the social contract. Rawls does not think such a contract has ever actually been agreed to, nor does he think it need be in order for the two principles of justice to be adopted. Suppose an entire society did get together to forge a social contract. Would they have a moral right to adopt any principles they wished? Suppose they *chose* utilitarianiam rather than Rawls' principles. Would they be bound to live by utilitarianism? Would they be right to do so?

3. Rawls seems to believe that his principles are neutral as between capitalism and socialism. Could a capitalist economy and society actually live by the "difference principle"? Could a socialist society do so? Can you spell out the ways in which this might happen in the one case or the other?

4. Rawls' principles are designed to overcome inherited inequalities of wealth and of talent. But why ought men and women to have children at all if they are not allowed to pass on to those children something of what they have themselves worked for? Once we sever the direct blood-ties between generations, what would prompt anyone to keep the human race going?

SUGGESTIONS FOR FURTHER READING

MILTON FRIEDMAN, *Capitalism and Freedom*

JOHN KENNETH GALBRAITH, *Economics and the Public Purpose*

FRIEDRICH VON HAYEK, *The Road to Serfdom*

WALTER LIPPMANN, *The Public Philosophy*

HERBERT MARCUSE, *An Essay on Liberation*
_____, *Eros and Civilization*

KARL MARX, *Capital,* Volume I

KARL MARX and FRIEDRICH ENGELS, *The Communist Manifesto*

JOHN STUART MILL, *On Liberty*
_____, *Utilitarianism*

KENNETH MINOGUE, *The Liberal Mind*

ROBERT NOZICK, *Anarchy, State, and Utopia*

MICHAEL OAKESHOTT, *Rationalism in Politics*

GEORGE BERNARD SHAW, *The Intelligent Woman's Guide to Socialism and Capitalism*

ROBERT PAUL WOLFF, *Understanding Rawls*

JEAN-JACQUES ROUSSEAU (1712–1778) is one of the most paradoxical figures in modern European letters. Born in Geneva, Switzerland, he spent his early years in a succession of homes (his mother having died only a few days after his birth). At the age of sixteen he converted to Catholicism, though he seems not to have been devout in any orthodox manner. After trying his hand at such tasks as music teacher and tutor, Rousseau finally found his true calling, which was to be a writer, a man of letters.

Rousseau's writings fall into two groups which seem entirely to contradict each other in their teachings. His autobiographical *Confessions,* his

4 POLITICAL PHILOSOPHY

novels *Émile* and *La Nouvelle Heloise,* and his *Discourse on the Sciences and the Arts,* all set forth in the most moving and powerful way the sentimental doctrine that our nature is inherently good, that civilization is the great corrupter, that feeling rather than reason is the proper guide to life, and that men and women will be naturally moral if only the impediments of cultivated life can be cleared away. But in his greatest work, *Of the Social Contract,* Rousseau argues in a spare and rigorously logical way for the proposition that the just state and morality itself arise from the exercise of our rational powers. Rousseau is thus an apostle both of sentiment—of feeling, of tears and sympathy—and also of reason.

Rousseau was a highly sensitive man; as his novels and his autobiography make clear, he was also a deeply troubled man, and in the last two years of his life, he appears to have suffered progressively more serious mental disorder, culminating in genuine insanity. In the world of fiction, he is the first and perhaps the greatest of the sentimentalists; countless eighteenth- and nineteenth-century novels echo his celebration of the feeling heart and the natural goodness of human nature. In political philosophy, he is a classic articulator of the doctrine of the social contract, on which modern democratic theory is built.

The literary world loves to gossip, and in Jean-Jacques Rousseau, the *enfant terrible* of eighteenth-century letters, it found a subject of endless speculation and titillation. Not since the great medieval logician Abelard married his young ward, Heloise, and got himself castrated for his trouble, has there been a philosopher whose personal turmoil contrasted so perfectly with the clarity and rigor of his thought. Rousseau's life and writings offer us an endless series of paradoxes and contradictions. He is the greatest apostle of what the eighteenth century called "sentiment," the feeling heart, the weeping eye, the rhapsodical outpouring of unstructured emotion. And yet his works deeply influenced that stern champion of pure reason, Immanuel Kant. Rousseau celebrated nature, the pastoral countryside; he condemned civilization and city life as a corrupter and destroyer of man's innate goodness. And yet he was born in Geneva, one of the great city-states of the eighteenth century, and spent some of his most productive years in the capital of all Europe, Paris. His political philosophy, his novels, even his famous autobiography, at once so revealing and so misleading, all conspire to create for us the image of the eternal adolescent, in rebellion against the grown-up world, chafing against the restrictions of discipline and responsibility. Yet surprisingly, Rousseau did not begin to make his mark in the world of European letters until close to his fortieth year, and the most fruitful decade of his life, his forties, is the time when most philosophers and authors put behind them their youthful fantasies and accept the compromises of adult maturity.

Rousseau was born in 1712 in the extremely Calvinist city of Geneva. His youth and young adulthood were chaotic. His mother died almost immediately after his birth, his rather irresponsible father looked after him only fitfully until his tenth birthday, and not at all thereafter. He had little formal education, even by the standards of his day, and throughout his twenties and thirties he drifted about, trying to make his mark as a music theoretician among other things. Finally, at the age of thirty-eight, he entered a contest held by the Academy of the French city of Dijon. The topic was a popular one in enlightenment circles at that time—namely whether the revival of the sciences and arts after their decline during the Middle Ages had helped to corrupt or to purify morals. Rousseau defended the unpopular position that the revival of ancient

*"First of all, I would like to express my gratefulness to all those wonderful ancestors of mine who helped to make this glorious day possible."**

* Drawing by W. Miller; © 1969 The New Yorker Magazine, Inc.

culture had corrupted morals! He won first prize, and his name was made; so too was his reputation as an iconoclast, a destroyer of received opinions and accepted doctrines.

Rousseau nursed a veritable storehouse of resentments throughout his lifetime, and as he grew older and more famous, he also grew more paranoid. The high point of his madness generated one of the great teapot tempests of the cultivated world, and demonstrated, if indeed any demonstration was needed, that even philosophers are not immune from childish bickering. The story, in brief, is this. Rousseau's writings in the late 1750s and early 1760s had brought him into considerable disfavor with the governments of Switzerland and France, both because of his attacks on organized orthodox religion and because of his dangerous republican political sympathies. At that time there was close contact and communication between the literary worlds of England and France. David Hume, the great Scottish philosopher, had many friends in the circle of French *"philosophes,"* as they were called, and he offered to arrange a deal to help Rousseau. It was the practice for kings to give pensions to prominent literary and artistic figures, and Hume wanted to work out such a pension for Rousseau from the English King George III. Rousseau came to England, but he was convinced that Hume was actually secretly plotting against him to destroy his reputation. So he began to make scurrilous attacks on Hume's name and writings in letters to a number of the prominent people of literary London. Now David Hume was one of the sweetest, gentlest, most decent human beings imaginable except where one subject was concerned—his own literary reputation. You could attack his morals, ridicule his fat, bear-shaped body, tease him at a dinner party or laugh at him in a salon, and he would merely respond with a smile or a gentle witticism. But criticize the quality and originality of his writings, and you aroused him to fury! So Hume struck back with a series of letters of his own, defending himself and attacking Rousseau. Jean-Jacques, now convinced that his life was in danger, leaped into a carriage, fled from the country house where Hume had arranged for him to stay, and raced toward the English Channel to catch a boat back to France before Hume and his supposed fellow conspirators could finish him off. Meanwhile, all literary Europe roared with laughter, and wrote Rousseau off as a madman.

Could such a creature actually write philosophy? Could he indeed! Judgments differ among philosophers, as much as they do among the compilers of all-time baseball or football teams, but in my personal judgment, Jean-Jacques Rousseau is the greatest political philosopher who has ever lived. His claim to immortality rests upon one short book, *Of the Social Contract,* an essay scarcely more than a hundred pages long. In that brief, brilliant work, Rousseau formulates the fundamental question of the philosophy of the state, and makes a valiant although ultimately unsuccessful effort to solve it. Why such fame, you might ask, if he failed to solve the problem? In philosophy, as in the sciences, the most important step frequently is to ask the right question, and although philosophers had been analyzing the nature of the state for more than 2000 years before Rousseau, he was the first to see exactly what the problem was and to recognize how difficult it would be to solve.

In the last chapter, we took a look at some of the ways in which philosophers have answered the general question: What is the good society? We saw that moral problems of the just distribution of wealth are central to this subject. In a way, social philosophy, as Plato suggested long ago, is ethics writ large— it is ethics in a social, rather than an individual, setting. But there are a very special set of questions associated with the study of the *state,* and these are best explored separately from the general investigations of ethics and social philosophy.

Political philosophy is, before all else, the philosophical study of the state, so before we go any further, we had best determine what we mean by a *state,* and what philosophical problems are raised by states. Everywhere we look, across historical time and around the globe, men and women are organized into social groupings within defined territorial limits or borders. Within each one of these geographical units, there is some smaller group of people who rule, who give orders, run things, use force to get others to obey—some group

The United States was the first state actually to be brought into existence by a social contract. We call it our Constitution.

who make and enforce laws. This smaller group is what we call *the state*. Sometimes the group that rules consists of a single person and his or her personal followers: a king or queen, a general or dictator, a priest or pope, plus a group of loyal underlings. Sometimes the group consists of a hereditary class, such as a military aristocracy. The group may be a political clique or party which has led a successful revolution against the previous rulers. It may even, as in our own country, be a large group of men and women who have been chosen in an election by a much larger group of citizens. But whoever makes the laws, gives the commands, and enforces them on everyone living within that territory *is* the state.

States may exist for any number of purposes: they may exist to carry out the tenets of a religious faith, to maintain general peace and security, to see to the well-being of some or all of the people within the territory, or to ensure justice and tranquility. The state may even exist merely for the purpose of lining the pockets and satisfying the desires of itself, regardless of what the rest of the population wants or needs. There are so many different purposes for which states have existed that it is not much use to look for some basic or underlying function which all states perform insofar as they are states. Philosophers express this fact by saying that the state cannot be defined *teleologically*. That simply means that we cannot explain what a state is in terms of the goals (*telos* is Greek for end or goal) at which it aims. But all states, regardless of who comprises them and no matter what purposes they pursue, have *two* characteristics in common. Once you understand these two characteristics, you will know what a state *is,* and also what the fundamental problem is of political philosophy.

First of all, states everywhere and always use force to obtain obedience to their commands. Sometimes force takes the form of armed troops, policemen, jails, and death rows. Sometimes merely the threat of force is enough to bring recalcitrant citizens into line. Economic threats can be used as effectively as the whip or the club. But behind the judge there always stands the policeman, and he is not there for ceremony only.

But force alone does not make a group of people into a state, for a band of robbers, an invading army, even a lone gunman holding you up on a dark street all use force to make you obey, and no one would call robbers, an army, or a mugger "the state." The second, and more important mark of the state is that as it issues its commands and shows its sword, it also claims to have the *right* to command and the *right* to be obeyed. Now a mugger does not claim the *right* to rob you. He says, "Your money or your life!"; he does not say, "Your money, for I have a right to it." But when the state sends you a bill for taxes, or commands you to report for induction into the armed forces, or orders you to stop at red lights and drive only with a valid license, it claims to have a right to your obedience. In the language of political philosophy, the state claims to be *legitimate*.

There is a wonderful scene in one of Shakespeare's plays (*Henry IV,*

Part I) in which a group of conspirators are planning their attack on the forces of the king. One of the group is a flamboyant Welsh chieftain named Glendower, who claims to have some magical powers in addition to some usable troops. At one point, in an effort to impress his fellow conspirators with the wonderfulness of his powers, he brags, "I can call spirits from the vasty deep." The leader of the conspiracy, Hotspur, is not very impressed, and he answers, "Why so can I, and so can any man / but will they come when you do call them?" The point, of course, is that it is one thing to make a claim, and quite another to get anybody to believe it.

Now the really remarkable thing about human beings is that they are so prone to accept the claims of legitimacy made by the states that rule the territories in which they live. From time to time, people rebel against the state, and a few philosophers called *anarchists* have denied the state's claim to have a right to rule. But by and large, when states make laws and claim the right to enforce them, people believe their claim and obey *even when they aren't actually being forced to do so.* Those last few words are crucial, of course, for most of us "obey" a gunman who holds us up or an army that invades our city and points its guns at us. We "obey" because we don't want to get shot. Cynics might say that that is really the only reason anyone ever obeys the law, but all the historical and sociological evidence points in the opposite direction. Save in the most unusual circumstances, men and women obey the law far more faithfully than the threat of punishment requires. They obey from habit, to be sure, but they also obey because they genuinely believe that the state has the right to command them. After all, they think, it is *the law.* How often has each of us done something or refrained from doing something merely because the law says that we must or mustn't? How, save by playing on this belief in the legitimacy of the law, could a single official or policeman control the behavior of a large crowd? How could several thousand overworked employees of the Internal Revenue Service collect taxes from two hundred million Americans? How could a lieutenant lead a platoon of frightened soldiers into withering enemy fire? How, indeed, could an old and feeble king bend young, vigorous, ambitious dukes, princes, and generals to his will?

The belief in the legitimacy of the authority of the state is the glue that holds a political society together. It is, more even than armies or police or jails, the means by which the state gets its laws obeyed. So we may sum up the universal characteristics of states by saying that the state is *a group of people who claim the right to enforce obedience to their commands within a territory, and succeed in getting most of the people in the territory to accept that claim.* A group of people who make a claim of this sort are said to be claiming *political authority.* So a state is a group of people who claim political authority, and have their claim accepted by most of those against whom the claim is made.

Well, states claim political authority, and they get their claims accepted. But it is one thing to get other people to accept something you say; it is quite another to be right. I may claim to be a doctor, and if enough people believe me, I can open an office and start prescribing medicine. But that doesn't make me a doctor. My "patients" may fail to notice that I am not curing them, but even that does not make me a doctor. So too, a group may claim the right to rule, and the people may accept their claim, but that does not make their claim *true*.

The fundamental question of all political philosophy is obviously: When does a group calling itself the state really have a *right* to command? Or, since that way of putting the question seems to assume that states sometimes have such a right, we can ask: Does any group of persons ever have the right to command?

The same question can be turned around to focus our attention on the person doing the obeying rather than the people doing the commanding. From my point of view as citizen, a state is a group of people who command me. If I believe that I have an obligation to obey their commands, then I consider them as constituting a legitimate state. Otherwise, I consider them tyrants. To the citizen, the fundamental question of political philosophy is: Do I ever have an obligation to obey the commands issued by some group calling itself the state?

In ancient and medieval times, the citizen's obligation to the ruler was considered to be limited and conditioned upon the ruler's just performance of his or her sovereign duties. But in the sixteenth and seventeenth centuries, in response to fundamental shifts in the relative power of the aristocracy, the monarchy, and the new middle class, the theory began to be put forward that the authority of the ruler was absolute. The king, it was said, was the sole possessor of the ultimate political authority—"sovereignty," as it was called. All others in the society were unconditionally obligated to obey his commands. Usually, a religious justification was advanced for this claim—the king was considered God's representative on earth—but sometimes the theory of an original agreement or contract was also appealed to.

The unqualified claim of absolute kingly authority was unacceptable to the philosophers of the Enlightenment. A person who bows his head to God or his knee to the king merely makes himself the slave of another. In the words of Immanuel Kant, who was, as we have seen, deeply influenced by Rousseau, submission to the commands of another means a loss of autonomy, a denial of one's own reason.

So for the political philosophers of the seventeenth and eighteenth centuries, the question of obligation to the state became a new and more complicated question: Is there any way in which I can submit to the commands of a legitimate state without giving up my freedom and autonomy? It was the special genius of Rousseau that he saw this question more clearly than anyone before him, and expressed it with greater precision and force. Here are the words in which he framed the problem, taken from the sixth chapter of *The Social Contract:*

> Where shall we find a form of association which will defend and protect with the whole common force the person and the property of each associate, and by which

every person, while uniting himself with all, shall obey only himself and remain as free as before?

For the philosophers of the state who struggled with the question of legitimate authority in the seventeenth and eighteenth centuries, the standard solution to the problem was the device which they called the "social contract." The authority of the state, it was argued, could only be founded upon an agreement among all the persons who were to be ruled by the state. The idea of a contract, of course, was taken from the law, where it applied to an agreement between two parties for their mutual advantage. A buyer and a seller in the marketplace made a contract with one another, according to which the seller would supply goods in such and such a quantity, and of so and so quality, and the buyer would pay so much money for them at a particular time. The heart and soul of a contract is what the lawyers called a *quid pro quo* or a "this for that"; each side must stand to benefit from the deal in order to make the contract binding. The right of either party to have the contract enforced on the other derives from *two* things: first of all, each party has freely promised to abide by the contract, and so is bound by his or her word; second, each party benefits from the contract, and so has an obligation to return the benefit to the other according to the agreed terms.

The social contract theorists, as they have become known, conceived the idea of tracing political obligation back to a contract or social agreement between the citizen and all the other members of the society. If each citizen could be imagined to have actually made such an agreement, then the riddle of legitimate state authority would be solved. First, it would then be possible to explain why, and under what conditions, the citizen had a duty to obey the law. Very simply, he would have a duty to obey laws made by a state which he had freely contracted or agreed to bring into existence. If he said to the judge, "Who are you to command me? Who are you to threaten me with punishment if I fail to obey?" the judge would answer, "I am a representative of that state which you yourself promised to obey, when you signed the social contract." And if the citizen, still resistant, went on to ask, "What have I received from my fellow citizens that I should keep the agreement I made with them?" the judge could answer, "You have received peace, social order, even-handed justice, and the benefits of a civilized society."

But even more important, if the citizen asked, "How can I obey this state I have brought into existence without forfeiting my autonomy and giving up my freedom?" the judge could answer, "In this state, and only in this state, those who obey remain free. For the state that makes the laws consists not of *some* of the people who live in this nation, but of all the people. The commands you obey are the very commands which you, as a citizen, have issued in your role as a law-maker. In this state, the law-obeyers and the law-makers are one! Through the device of a social contract, the people become the rulers." Indeed, since the traditional word for ruler is "sovereign," the social contract theory is a doctrine of people's sovereignty, or, as it is usually known, "popular sovereignty." (That doesn't mean that people like it! It means that the people are sovereign. This is what Lincoln meant when he said that we live under a government that is by the people, as well as of and for the people.)

Here is how Rousseau describes the social contract. This passage directly follows the question quoted earlier:

The articles of this contract are so unalterably fixed by the nature of the act that the least modification renders them vain and of no effect; so that they are the same everywhere, and are everywhere tacitly understood and admitted, even though they may never have been formally announced; until, the social compact being violated, each individual is restored to his original rights, and resumes his native liberty, while losing the conventional liberty for which he renounced it.

The articles of the social contract will, when clearly understood, be found reducible to this single point: the total alienation of each associate, and all his rights, to the whole community; for, in the first place, as every individual gives himself up entirely, the condition of every person is alike; and being so, it would not be to the interest of any one to render that condition offensive to others.

Nay, more than this, the alienation being made without any reserve, the union is as complete as it can be, and no associate has any further claim to anything: for if any individual retained rights not enjoyed in general by all, as there would be no common superior to decide between him and the public, each person being in some points his own judge, would soon pretend to be so in everything; and thus would the state of nature be continued and the association necessarily become tyrannical or be annihilated.

Finally, each person gives himself to all, and so not to any one individual; and as there is no one associate over whom the same right is not acquired which is ceded to him by others, each gains an equivalent for what he loses, and finds his force increased for preserving that which he possesses.

If, therefore, we exclude from the social contract all that is not essential, we shall find it reduced to the following terms:

Each of us places in common his person and all his power under the supreme direction of the general will; and as one body we all receive each member as an indivisible part of the whole.

From that moment, instead of as many separate persons as there are contracting parties, this act of association produces a moral and collective body, composed of as many members as there are votes in the assembly, which from this act receives its unity, its common self, its life, and its will. This public person, which is thus formed by the union of all other persons, took formerly the name of "city," and now takes that of "republic" or "body politic." It is called by its members "State" when it is passive, "Sovereign" when in activity, and whenever it is compared with other bodies of a similar kind, it is denominated "power." The associates take collectively the name of "people," and separately, that of "citizens," as participating in the sovereign authority, and of "subjects," because they are subjected to the laws of the State. But these terms are frequently confounded and used one for the other; and it is enough that a man understands how to distinguish them when they are employed in all their precision.

JEAN-JACQUES ROUSSEAU, *The Social Contract*

Two problems arise immediately. First, it is going to be difficult to get everyone together when laws need to be made. How can the people obey only themselves if they don't personally make the laws? The usual solution both in political theory and in political practice is to institute a system of elected representatives. But Rousseau will have none of that. If the state is not kept small enough for everyone to participate in the law-making, then so far as he is concerned, tyranny replaces liberty. Of course, that means that all citizens, and not just a few professionals, are going to have to pay attention to public affairs. But that is the price of freedom, Rousseau insists. As he says later on in *The Social Contract:*

As soon as men cease to consider public service as the principal duty of citizens, and rather choose to serve with their purse than with their persons, we may pronounce the State to be on the very verge of ruin. Are the citizens called upon to march out to war? They pay soldiers for the purpose, and remain at home. Are they summoned to council? They nominate deputies, and stay at home. And thus, in consequence of idleness and money, they have soldiers to enslave their country, and representatives to sell it.

It is the hurry of commerce and of the arts, it is the greedy thirst of gain, and the effeminate softness and love of comfort, that occasion this commutation of money for personal service. Men give up a part of the profits they acquire in order to purchase leisure to augment them. Give money, and you will soon have chains. The word "finance" is a term of slavery; it is unknown in the true city. In a State truly free, the citizens do all with their own arms and nothing with their money; and, instead of purchasing exemption from their duty, they would even pay for fulfilling it themselves. My ideas on this subject are indeed very different from those commonly received; I even think the *corvées* are less an infringement upon liberty than taxes.

The better a State is constituted, the more do public affairs intrude upon private affairs in the minds of the citizens. Private concerns even become considerably fewer, because each individual shares so largely in the common happiness that he has not so much occasion to seek for it in private resources. In a well-conducted city, each member flies with joy to the assemblies; under a bad government, no one is disposed to bend his way thither, because no one is interested in proceedings where he foresees that the general will will not prevail, and in the end every man turns his attention to his own domestic affairs. Good laws lead on to better, and bad ones seldom fail to generate still worse. When once you hear some one say, when speaking of the affairs of the State, "What is it to me?" you may give over the State for lost.

It was the decline of patriotism, the activity of private interest, the immense extent of States, the increase of conquests, and the abuses of government, that suggested the expedient of having deputies or representatives of the people in the assemblies of the nation. These representatives are the body to which, in certain countries, they have dared to give the name of the "Third Estate," as if the private interest of the two other orders deserved the first and second rank, and the public interest should be considered only in the third place.

Sovereignty cannot be represented for the same reason that it cannot be alienated; its essence is the general will, and that will must speak for itself, or it does not exist: it is either itself or not itself: there is no intermediate possibility. The deputies of the people, therefore, are not and cannot be their representatives; they can only be their commissioners, and as such are not qualified to conclude anything definitively. No act of theirs can be a law, unless it has been ratified by the people in person; and without that ratification nothing is a law. The people of England deceive themselves when they fancy they are free; they are so, in fact, only during the election of members of parliament: for, as soon as a new one is elected, they are again in chains, and are nothing. And thus, by the use they make of their brief moments of liberty, they deserve to lose it.

The second problem is how to make decisions when there is disagreement. The natural solution that springs to our minds is to take a vote and let the majority rule. We have become so accustomed to deciding questions by majority vote that it sometimes seems as though little children learn to vote in school before they learn how to count the votes. But Rousseau had the clarity of mind to see that majority rule presented a very serious obstacle to freedom. I might promise, in the original unanimous contract, to abide by the vote of the majority. But in so doing, I seem simply to be agreeing to a sort of voluntary slavery. If I have voted against a proposed law, believing that it is a bad law, contrary to the national interest, then how can I be said to "obey only myself, and remain as free as before," when I am forced to submit to it? Rousseau has an extremely subtle answer to this question. First read what he has to say, and then we can talk about it a bit.

There is one law only which, by its nature, requires unanimous consent; I mean the social compact: for civil association is the most voluntary of all acts; every man being born free and master of himself, no person can under any pretense whatever subject him without his consent. To affirm that the son of a slave is born a slave is to pronounce that he is not born a man.

Should there be any men who oppose the social compact, their opposition will not invalidate it, but only hinder their being included: they are foreigners among citizens. When the State is instituted, residence constitutes consent; to inhabit a territory is to submit to the sovereignty.

Except in this original contract, a majority of votes is sufficient to bind all the others. This is a consequence of the contract itself. But it may be asked how a man can be free and yet forced to conform to the will of others. How are the opposers free when they are in submission to laws to which they have never consented?

I answer that the question is not fairly stated. The citizen consents to all the laws, to those which are passed in spite of his opposition, and even to those which sentence him to punishment if he violates any one of them. The constant will of all the members of the State is the general will; it is by that they are citizens and free. When any law is proposed in the assembly of the people, the question is not precisely to enquire whether they approve the proposition or reject it, but if it is conformable or not to the general will, which is their will. Each citizen, in giving his suffrage, states his mind on that question; and the general will is found by counting the votes. When, therefore, the motion which I opposed carries, it only proves to me that I was mistaken, and that what I believed to be the general will was not so. If my particular opinion had prevailed, I should have done what I was not willing to do, and, consequently, I should not have been in a state of freedom.

Something very tricky is going on in this passage. How can I be free when I don't get what I voted for? Earlier in *The Social Contract,* Rousseau put his point even more dramatically. A citizen who refuses to obey the general will, he said, must be compelled to do so. "This in fact only forces him to be free." What on earth can Rousseau have meant?

The full answer would take a book by itself, but we can say a few things to clear away some of the mystery. Rousseau believed that the people had a right to make laws only as long as they were all genuinely attempting to legislate in the public interest rather than in their own individual and private interests. Now, if the majority could be counted on always to be right about the general good, then no one in the minority would want his or her view to become law. For if I want what is for the general good, and if the majority is always right about the general good, and if I am in the minority, then what I mistakenly wanted is *not* for the general good, and hence not what I really want. And if freedom is getting what you really want, then only by being forced to abide by the majority can I really be free!

There is a flaw in the argument, of course. The majority may always aim at the general good, but it does not always aim accurately. More often than not, even when every citizen is public-spiritedly seeking what is best for all, the truth will be seen only by one citizen or a few. Rousseau confused aiming at and hitting the target.

Americans have a vested interest in the theory of the social contract, with all its flaws, because we are the first nation ever actually to bring itself into existence as a state by means of a real, historical, explicit contract. We call it our Constitution, but what the Founding Fathers actually wrote was the first operative social contract. When it was ratified in 1788, there came into being for the first time in Western history a state truly founded upon a contract.

Although the theory of the social contract has dominated liberal political theory since the seventeenth century, it has been subjected to a number of powerful criticisms. The most obvious objection is that, save for the special case of the United States, no actual state has ever been brought into existence by such an explicit contractual agreement among the citizens-to-be. Hence, the theory just does not provide any justification at all for the claims of even the most "democratic" governments. David Hume was one of the earliest anti-contract writers to make this point. In an essay entitled "Of The Original Contract," he presents the following critique:

Philosophers . . . assert, not only that government in its earliest infancy arose from consent or rather the voluntary acquiescence of the people; but also, that, even at present, when it has attained its full maturity, it rests on no other foundation. They affirm, that all men are still born equal, and owe allegiance to no prince or government, unless bound by the obligation and sanction of a promise. And as no man, without some equivalent, would forego the advantages of his native liberty, and subject himself to the will of another; this promise is always understood to be conditional, and imposes on him no obligation, unless he meet with justice and protection from his sovereign. These advantages the sovereign promises him in return; and if he fail in the execution, he has broken, on his part, the articles of engagement, and has thereby freed his subject from all obligations to allegiance. Such, according to these philosophers, is the foundation of authority in every government, and such the right of resistance, possessed by every subject.

But would these reasoners look abroad into the world, they would meet with nothing that, in the least, corresponds to their ideas, or can warrant so refined and philosophical a system. On the contrary, we find, every where, princes, who claim their subjects as their property, and assert their independent right of sovereignty from conquest or succession. We find also, every where, subjects who acknowledge this right in their prince, and suppose themselves born under obligations of obedience to a certain sovereign, as much as under the ties of reverence and duty to certain parents. These connections are always conceived to be equally independent of our consent, in Persia and China; in France and Spain; and even in Holland and England, wherever the doctrines above-mentioned have not been carefully inculcated. Obedience or subjection becomes so familiar, that most men never make any enquiry about the principle of gravity, resistance, or the most universal laws of nature. Or if curiosity ever move them; as soon as they learn, that they themselves and their ancestors have, for several ages, or from time immemorial, been subject to such a form of government or such a family; they immediately acquiesce, and acknowledge their obligation to allegiance. Were you to preach, in most parts of the world, that political connections are founded altogether on voluntary consent or a mutual promise, the magistrates would soon imprison you, as seditious, for loosening the ties of obedience; if your friends did not before shut you up as delirious for advancing such absurdities. It is strange, that an act of the mind, which every individual is supposed to have formed, and after he came to the use of reason too, otherwise it could have no authority; that this act, I say, should be so much unknown to all of them, that, over the face of the whole earth, there scarcely remain any traces or memory of it.

But the contract, on which government is founded, is said to be the *original contract;* and consequently may be supposed too old to fall under the knowledge of the present generation. If the agreement, by which savage men first associated and conjoined their force, be here meant, this is acknowledged to be real; but being so ancient, and being obliterated by a thousand changes of government and princes, it cannot now be supposed to retain any authority. If we would say any thing to the purpose, we must assert, that every particular government, which is lawful, and which imposes any duty of allegiance on the subject, was, at first, founded on consent and a voluntary compact. But besides that this supposes the consent of the fathers to bind the children even to the most remote generations, (which republican writers will never allow) besides this, I say, it is not justified by history or experience, in any age or country of the world.

Almost all the governments, which exist at present, or of which there remains any record in story, have been founded originally, either on usurpation or conquest, or both, without any pretence of a fair consent, or voluntary subjection of the people. When an artful and bold man is placed at the head of an army of faction, it is often easy for him, by employing, sometimes violence, sometimes false pretences, to establish his dominion over a people a hundred times more numerous than his partizans. He allows no such open communication, that his enemies can know, with certainty, their number or force. He gives them no leisure to assemble together in a body to oppose him. Even all those, who are the instruments of his usurpation, may wish his fall; but their ignorance of each other's intention keeps them in awe, and is the sole cause of his security. By such arts as these, many governments have been established; and this is all the *original contract,* which they have to boast of.

DAVID HUME, *Of The Original Contract*

But the mere historical absence of a contract is not the worst of the problems confronting social contract theories. Even if a group of men and women had indeed contracted together, some time in the dim past, to submit themselves to the collective will of all, that would still leave those of us in the present generation without any reason for obeying the commands of the state. After all, I am not bound by the marriage contracts or the business contracts made by my ancient ancestors; why should I be bound by whatever political contracts they may have made?

To this, the social contract theorists answer that each of us, upon reaching the legal age of adulthood, implicitly signs his or her name to that original contract by remaining in the country, living under its laws, and entering actively into its legal arrangements. John Locke, the spiritual father of our Constitution, especially emphasizes the owning of property in this selection from his most famous political work, the *Second Treatise of Civil Government.*

Every man being, as has been shown, naturally free, and nothing being able to put him into subjection to any earthly power but only his own consent, it is to be considered what shall be understood to be sufficient declaration of a man's consent to make him subject to the laws of any government. There is a common distinction of an express and a tacit consent, which will concern our present case. Nobody doubts but an express consent of any man entering into any society makes him a perfect member of that society, a subject of that government. The difficulty is, what ought to be looked upon as a tacit consent, and how far it binds, *i.e.,* how far any one shall be looked on to have consented, and thereby submitted to any government, where he has made no expressions of it at all. And to this I say that every man that hath any possession or enjoyment of any part of the dominions of any government doth thereby give his tacit consent, and is as far forth obliged to obedience to the laws of that government during such enjoyment as any one under it; whether this his possession be of land to him and his heirs for ever, or a lodging only for a week; or whether it be barely travelling freely on the highway; and in

JOHN LOCKE (1632–1704) had a philosophical career which was, in a sense, the reverse of David Hume's. Locke's great works were not published until close to his sixtieth year, and they were received almost immediately with great acclaim. During the troubled times in England which followed the restoration of the Catholic monarchy (in 1660) after the English Civil War, Locke sided with the moderate faction which sought to limit the power of the King and bring the throne under some control by Parliament. In 1689, one year after the so-called Glorious Revolution which established a limited monarchy in England, Locke published a pair of long essays on the subject of the foundations of the authority of the state. The second of these essays, known now as the *Second Treatise of Civil Government,* is the most important single document in the literature of constitutional democracy. Appearing when it did, the *Second Treatise* naturally was interpreted as a justification for the new regime of William and Mary, for it defended the sort of limited monarchy, hedged round with parliamentary restraints, which the English people adopted as their form of government in 1688. Actually, we now know that the two *Treatises* were written in the early 1680s, some years before the change in government took place.

The next year, 1690, Locke published a massive work on the foundations of human knowledge, the *Essay Concerning the Human Understanding.* (See Chapter 7.) The *Essay* is the foundation-stone of the school of philosophy known as empiricism. Locke's arguments profoundly affected Berkeley, Hume, and the other British philosophers who followed him. The work was very soon translated into French, and had a major influence as well on continental thought. A century later, Immanuel Kant was to acknowledge it as one of the most important influences on his own thinking.

effect it reaches as far as the very being of any one within the territories of that government.

To understand this the better, it is fit to consider that every man when he at first incorporates himself into any commonwealth, he, by his uniting himself thereunto, annexes also, and submits to the community those possessions which he has or shall acquire that do not already belong to any other government; for it would be a direct contradiction for any one to enter into society with others for the securing and regulating of property, and yet to suppose his land, whose property is to be regulated by the laws of the society, should be exempt from the jurisdiction of that government to which he himself, and the property of the land, is a subject. By the same act, therefore, whereby any one unites his person, which was before free, to any commonwealth, by the same he unites his possessions, which was before free, to it also; and they become, both of them, person and possession, subject to the government and dominion of that commonwealth as long as it hath a being. Whoever therefore from thenceforth by inheritance, purchases, permission, or otherwise, enjoys any part of the land so annexed to, and under the government of that commonwealth, must take it with the condition it is under, that is, of submitting to the government of the commonwealth under whose jurisdiction it is as far forth as any subject of it.

But since the government has a direct jurisdiction only over the land, and reaches the possessor of it (before he has actually incorporated himself in the society), only as he dwells upon, and enjoys that: the obligation any one is under, by virtue of such enjoyment, to submit to the government, begins and ends with the enjoyment; so that whenever the owner, who has given nothing but such a tacit consent to the government, will by donation, sale, or otherwise, quit the said possession, he is at liberty to go and incorporate himself into any other commonwealth, or to agree with others to begin a new one *(in vacuis locis)* in any part of the world they can find free and unpossessed. Whereas he that has once by actual agreement and any express declaration given his consent to be of any commonweal is perpetually and indispensably obliged to be and remain unalterably a subject to it, and can never be again in the liberty of the state of nature; unless, by any calamity, the government he was under comes to be dissolved, or else by some public acts cuts him off from being any longer a member of it.

JOHN LOCKE, *Second Treatise of Civil Government*

You may wonder how a person can enter into a contract by "tacit consent." Don't I have to actually *say* that I am making a contract in order to do so? Locke here is relying on the ancient legal principle that when a person, over a period of time, acts in such a way as to give other persons a reasonable expectation that he will continue so to act, and if he benefits from that unspoken understanding, then he has made a "quasi-contract," which the law will enforce just as it will an explicit, spoken contract.

But Locke's argument depends on the assumption that a citizen can pick up and leave if he or she is dissatisfied with the laws of the state under which he or she lives. In Locke's day (the late 1600s) that was still possible. The Pilgrims who came to America, and many millions who followed them, were exercising precisely that option. Today, however, emigration requires visas and passports, no matter where you want to go. Every square foot of inhabitable earth is claimed by some state or other, so that the most anyone can do is to go from the rule of one state to the rule of another. Under this condition, it is harder and harder to see what truth there is in the theory of the implicit, or tacit, contract.

II

The liberal theory of the state dominates early modern political theory, but the nineteenth and twentieth centuries have seen the rise to intellectual prominence and political importance of significant alternatives on both the right and the left of the political spectrum. (In Chapter Three, you encountered this same phenomenon of the central liberal philosophy flanked by right-wing and left-wing countertheories. That is really the basic story of social and political thought in the West for the last two hundred years.) In this section, we will look at the historically most important right-wing attack on liberal philosophy—fascism. In order to prepare the way, we must go all the way back to the late eighteenth century and consider a criticism of the liberal conception of society and the state articulated by the English philosopher Edmund Burke. Burke argued that the notion of a contract, and with it the notion of a society of rationally self-interested pleasure-maximizers, could not do justice to the true nature of the human experience. A business partnership might be founded upon a contract, entered into by a pair of self-interested entrepreneurs who estimated that they would profit from the deal. But it was monstrous and inhumane, Burke insisted, to suppose that the association of men and women in the ongoing social intercourse of life rested upon a similar calculation. It was equally absurd, he said, to reduce a citizen's submission to the majesty of the state to such a contract. Loyalty, honor, love of one's nation, all disappear in the double-entry

EDMUND BURKE (1729–1797) is the father of modern conservative political thought, and its most eloquent spokesman. During his long political career in England, he defended a moderate position on political liberties and the rights of the American colonies, but turned violently against the French Revolution, which he saw as a subversion of the just and natural order of human society. In a moving message to his constituency, Burke defended the duty of a representative to vote his conscience, even against the wishes of the electorate which had put him in office.

bookkeeping of the social contract theories. Here, in a passage from his essay attacking the French Revolution, is Burke's most famous statement of the anti-contract conception of society and the state.

Society is indeed a contract. Subordinate contracts for objects of mere occasional interest may be dissolved at pleasure—but the state ought not to be considered as nothing better than a partnership agreement in a trade of pepper and coffee, callico or tobacco, or some other such low concern, to be taken up for a little temporary interest, and to be dissolved by the fancy of the parties. It is to be looked on with other reverence; because it is not a partnership in things subservient only to the gross animal existence of a temporary and perishable nature. It is a partnership in all science; a partnership in all art; a partnership in every virtue, and in all perfection. As the ends of such a partnership cannot be obtained in many generations, it becomes a partnership not only between those who are living, but between those who are living, those who are dead, and those who are to be born. Each contract of each particular state is but a clause in the great primeval contract of eternal society, linking the lower with the higher natures, connecting the visible and invisible world, according to a fixed compact sanctioned by the inviolable oath which holds all physical and all moral natures, each in their appointed place. This law is not subject to the will of those, who by an obligation above them, and infinitely superior, are bound to submit their will to that law. The municipal corporations of that universal kingdom are not morally at liberty at their pleasure, and on their speculations of a contingent improvement, wholly to separate and tear asunder the bands of their subordinate community, and to dissolve it into an unsocial, uncivil, unconnected chaos of elementary principles. It is the first and supreme necessity only, a necessity that is not chosen but chooses, a necessity paramount to deliberation, that admits no discussion, and demands no evidence, which alone can justify a resort to anarchy. This necessity is no exception to the rule; because this necessity itself is a part too of that moral and physical disposition of things to which man must be obedient by consent or force; but if that which is only submission to necessity should be made the object of choice, the law is broken, nature is disobeyed, and the rebellious are outlawed, cast forth, and exiled, from this world of reason, and order, and peace, and virtue, and fruitful penitence, into the antagonist world of madness, discord, vice, confusion, and unavailing sorrow.

EDMUND BURKE, *Reflections on the French Revolution*

This passage is an early expression of what later came to be known as the "organic" theory of the state. A business partnership or contractual association is a coming together of independent individuals, each of whom has his or her own interests, desires, plans, and standards of judgment. The association combines their efforts but it does not merge them into a single entity. Even a marriage, which in the eyes of the law is a contract, cannot obliterate the distinction between the husband and wife, though the usual talk of "making two one" sounds as though it does.

According to another philosophical tradition, however, society is more accurately compared to a living organism than to a business partnership. In an organism, the "parts" are merged into, and exist for, the whole. The feet, heart, hands, brain, and liver do not have separate interests, plans, or purposes. Indeed, when one organ of the body starts aggrandizing itself at the expense of the others, doctors suspect that the body is sick. An organism is an interconnected system of parts, all of which subserve the interests of the total living thing. There is proper subordination, not equality, among the parts. The brain gives orders which the nerves transmit to the muscles. If the survival of the organism requires it, a part may be amputated or removed, for each part exists only for the whole, not for itself.

Ever since Plato drew a double analogy between body and soul, and soul and state, some philosophers have said that a society is really like an organism. Men and women take their existence and their purpose from their role in the totality; the ruler, like the brain, gives the orders which the subordinate members of the whole must obey. Sacrifice for the good of the state, not self-interested calculation of personal advantage, is the fundamental principle of the organic state. Just as a healthy individual has a coherent personality that gives form and style to his life, so a healthy state has a culture that unites its people and gives their social life a distinctive style. Societies may enter into alliances with one another, just as individuals may enter into contracts with one another. But no alliance between disparate social organisms can overcome the organic wholeness of each.

In the early expressions of this theory, by de Tocqueville, Burke, and others, great emphasis is placed upon the traditions of the society, on its religious faith, and on its hierarchical political and social structure. As Oakeshott makes clear (though he is writing in our own century), the entry of new men and women onto the political scene is a violation of those traditions, a potentially destructive intrusion into the settled style of the politics of the society. But in the nineteenth century, great social and economic changes destroyed the old pre-industrial patterns of life and politics. First the rising capitalist class, then the new working class formed by industrialism, thrust into the political life of nation after nation.

At the same time, the political rearrangements produced by Napoleon's wars released cultural forces which had been pent up by the old imperial order. Nationalities—that is to say, peoples with a common language, culture, and history—began to insist upon political independence. Czechs, Poles, Slovaks, Hungarians, Serbians, Rumanians, Estonians, Lithuanians, Croatians—each group with its special style of culture and society—demanded the chance to determine their own destiny. In the nineteenth century, there was a great surging up of interest in the music and literature of the people, and with it a rejection of the tradition of high Latin culture going back to the time of the Roman Empire. The Grimms' fairy tales, the études of Chopin, the rediscovery of Aryan or Teutonic culture, all were manifestations of this same search for the indigenous culture of the peoples of Central Europe.

BENITO MUSSOLINI (1883–1945) was the founder and leader of the Italian fascist movement. He ruled Italy, first as premier, later as dictator, from 1922 until his overthrow in 1943. Two years later he was captured by Italian underground fighters and assassinated. Mussolini was the first fascist leader in Europe, though he took a back seat to Adolf Hitler in the German–Italian alliance which started and waged the European portion of World War II.

Like Hitler, Mussolini was an enemy of the liberal politics, life style, and economic policies which flourished in much of Europe and America after World War I. Italy was a devoutly religious country, and Mussolini concluded an agreement with the papacy which gained him the support, or at least the acquiescence, of that major force in Italian life.

In the early years of this movement, the doctrine of the folk or people was a progressive and liberating influence in Europe. But the turning point was the unimaginable upheaval of the World War I. In the aftermath of that "war to end all wars," the political unity of Europe was permanently shattered and its economic health gravely damaged. The search for cultural unity took on the darker color of political absolutism. Economic depression and social disintegration fostered a powerful desire for unity, together with a hatred of foreigners and a rejection of the individualistic doctrines of liberalism. The most famous form of this new organicism, of course, was the National Socialism of Adolf Hitler in Germany. But a full decade before Hitler's rise to power, Benito Mussolini gave the doctrine a name, fascism, and a home, Italy. Mussolini cannot really be called a political philosopher, but he stated the fundamental teachings of fascism as clearly and unambiguously as any political leader ever has. In this lengthy section from Mussolini's *The Doctrine of Fascism,* we find all the key elements of fascism: the exaltation of the state, the antiliberalism, the totalitarianism, and the celebration of war rather than peace, struggle rather than accommodation.

Fascism is a religious conception in which man is seen in his immanent relationship with a superior law and with an objective Will that transcends the particular individual and raises him to conscious membership of a spiritual society. Whoever has seen in the religious politics of the Fascist regime nothing but mere opportunism has not understood that Fascism besides being a system of government is also, and above all, a system of thought.

Fascism is a historical conception, in which man is what he is only in so far as he works with the spiritual process in which he finds himself, in the family or social group, in the nation and in the history in which all nations collaborate. From this follows the great value of tradition, in memories, in language, in customs, in the standards of social life. Outside history man is nothing. Consequently Fascism is opposed to all the individualistic abstractions of a materialistic nature like those of the eighteenth century; and it is opposed to all Jacobin utopias and innovations. It does not consider that "happiness" is possible upon earth, as it appeared to be in the desire of the economic literature of the eighteenth century, and hence it rejects all teleological theories according to which mankind would reach a definitive stabilized condition at a certain period in history. This implies putting oneself outside history and life, which is a continual change and coming to be. Politically, Fascism wishes to be a realistic doctrine; practically, it aspires to solve only the problems which arise historically of themselves and that of themselves find or suggest their own solution. To act among men, as to act in the natural world, it is necessary to enter into the process of reality and to master the already operating forces.

Against individualsim, the Fascist conception is for the State; and it is for the individual in so far as he coincides with the State, which is the conscience and universal will of man in his historical existence. It is opposed to classical Liberalism, which arose from the necessity of reacting against absolutism, and which brought its historical purpose to an end when the State was transformed into the conscience and will of the people. Liberalism denied the State in the interests of the particular individual; Fascism reaffirms the State as the true reality of the individual. And if liberty is to be the attribute of the real man, and not of that abstract puppet envisaged by individualistic Liberalism, Fascism is for liberty. And for the only liberty which can be a real thing, the liberty of the State and of the individual within the State. Therefore, for the Fascist, everything is in the State, and nothing human or spiritual exists, much less has value, outside the State. In this sense Fascism is totalitarian, and the Fascist State, the synthesis and unity of all values, interprets, develops and gives strength to the whole life of the people.

Outside the State there can be neither individuals nor groups (political parties, associations, syndicates, classes). Therefore Fascism is opposed to Socialism, which confines the movement of history within the class struggle and ignores the unity of classes established in one economic and moral reality in the State; and analogously it is opposed to class syndicalism. Fascism recognizes the real exigencies for which the socialist and syndicalist movement arose, but while recognizing them wishes to bring them under the control of the State and give them a purpose within the corporative system of interests reconciled within the unity of the State.

Individuals form classes according to the similarity of their interests, they form syndicates according to differentiated economic activities within these interests; but they form first, and above all, the State, which is not to be thought of numerically as the sum-total of individuals forming the majority of a nation. And consequently Fascism is opposed to Democracy, which equates the nation to the majority, lowering it to the level of that majority; nevertheless it is the purest form of democracy if the nation is conceived, as it should be, qualitatively and not quantitatively, as the most powerful idea (most powerful because most moral, most coherent, most true) which acts within the nation as the conscience and the will of a few, even of One, which ideal tends to become active within the conscience and the will of all—that is to say, of all those who rightly constitute a nation by reason of nature, history or race, and have set out upon the same line of development and spiritual formation as one conscience and one sole will. Not a race, nor a geographically determined region, but as a community historically perpetuating itself, a multitude unified by a single idea, which is the will to existence and to power: consciousness of itself, personality.

This higher personality is truly the nation in so far as it is the State. It is not the nation that generates the State, as according to the old naturalistic concept which served as the basis of the political theories of the national States of the nineteenth century. Rather the nation is created by the State, which gives to the people, conscious of its own moral unity, a will and therefore an effective existence. The right of a nation to independence derives not from a literary and ideal consciousness of its own being, still less from a more or less unconscious and inert acceptance of a *de facto* situation, but from an active consciousness, from a political will in action and ready to demonstrate its own rights: that is to say, from a state already coming into being. The State, in fact, as the universal ethical will, is the creator of right.

The nation as the State is an ethical reality which exists and lives in so far as it develops. To arrest its development is to kill it. Therefore the State is not only the authority which governs and gives the form of laws and the value of spiritual life to the wills of individuals, but it is also a power that makes its will felt abroad, making it known and respected, in other words, demonstrating the fact of its universality in all the necessary directions of its development. It is consequently organization and expansion, at least virtually. Thus it can be likened to the human will which knows no limits to its development and realizes itself in testing its own limitlessness.

The Fascist State, the highest and most powerful form of personality, is a force, but a spiritual force, which takes over all the forms of the moral and intellectual life of man. It cannot therefore confine itself simply to the functions of order and supervision as Liberalism desired. It is not simply a mechanism which limits the sphere of the supposed liberties of the individual. It is the form, the inner standard and the discipline of the whole person; it saturates the will as well as the intelligence. Its principle, the central inspiration of the human personality living in the civil community, pierces into the depths and makes its home in the heart of the man of action as well as of the thinker, of the artist as well as of the scientist: it is the soul of the soul.

Fascism, in short, is not only the giver of laws and the founder of institutions, but the educator and promoter of spiritual life. It wants to remake, not the forms of human life, but its content, man, character, faith. And to this end it requires discipline and authority that can enter into the spirits of men and there govern unopposed. Its sign, therefore, is the Lictors' rods, the symbol of unity, of strength and justice.

Benito Mussolini, *The Doctrine of Fascism*

To Karl Marx and his lifelong collaborator Friedrich Engels, the liberal social contract theory of the state was merely a convenient fiction designed to justify the rise to power of the new capitalist class. In order to understand the Marxist conception of the state, we must get at least a preliminary picture of Marx's doctrine of *historical materialism.*

As we saw in Chapter Three, Marx began with the fact of the sheer misery of the working class in England during the first part of the nineteenth century, and added to this the instability of industrial capitalism as he observed it. Out of these elements, and the philosophical theories he had studied in his youth, Marx constructed a full-scale theory about the human condition, society, and history. The theory explained past history, analyzed the situation of industrial capitalism in the mid-nineteenth century, and predicted the future course of economic, social, and political developments. Simplifying somewhat, we can see Marx's theory as consisting of three parts: a theory of human nature; a theory of social organization; and a theory of social change, historical development, and revolution.

You have already studied Marx's theory of human nature in Chapter Three. The keynote is the concept of *alienation.* Human beings are considered by Marx to be socially productive creatures who find fulfillment and happiness through the free, productive, healthful exercise of their natural powers in cooperative labor with their fellow men and women. Capitalism thwarts that exercise, causing an alienation of men and women from the product of their labor, from the labor itself, from their own human nature, and from their fellow workers. The result is misery in the midst of plenty, unreason in the midst of technical rationality.

The second element of Marx's theory is his conception or model of social and economic organization. At first inspection, society at any one time seems an unorganized beehive of multifarious activities, without any system, pattern, or rationale. Agriculture, the arts, science, industry, government, religion, entertainment, marketing, war, charity, crime—the things men and women do are endless in number and variety. Merely to list all the categories of jobs being performed by someone or other is to lose oneself in a confusion of diversity. But Marx saw order in the chaos. He argued that in order to make sense of social life, we must distinguish a certain group of activities which are basic to the survival and reproduction of the human race. Each day, men and women work to transform nature into the food, clothing, and shelter they need to live. These economic activities form the base, or foundation, on which all else in the society rests. In order to distinguish the productive economic activities from the philosophical theorizing which his German idealist predecessors had made so much of, Marx called the productive elements of the society its *material base.* In calling the base "material" he did not mean to suggest that it consisted of physical bodies rather than human thoughts, purposes, and plans, for even productive activities are intelligent, purposeful activities involving "ideas." Rather, Marx wanted to emphasize the fundamental role of economic production as opposed to philosophy, religion, or art.

The material base of a society consists of three subelements. The first is the *means* of production—the raw materials, land, and energy resources with which men and women work. The second is the *forces* of production, which includes the factories, machinery, technology, industrial knowledge, and accumulated skills of those who transform the means of production by their labor. The third and by far the most important subelement of the material base is what Marx called the *social relationships of production.* Since everything in Marx's theory depends on this last element, we must take a few paragraphs to explain it in some detail.

Human beings are productive creatures, to be sure. But according to Marx, they are *socially* productive creatures. Men and women divide the labor among themselves, differentiating the process of production into a series of sub-jobs or specialties and then parceling these pieces of the total productive process out among different workers. Some people raise grain, others dig iron ore out of the ground. Others bake the grain into bread, and still others work the ore into tools and weapons. This *division of labor* requires also a system of exchange, for no one can live on the products of his or her own labor alone. The farmer needs the products of the carpenter, the carpenter needs the products of the metal worker, and the metal worker needs the grain grown by the farmer. The market is the system by which a never-ending chain of trades, or purchases and sales, distributes the products of labor among the members of the society.

Although productive activity is cooperative, in the sense that there is a division of function and an exchange of products, it is by no means harmonious, equitable, or universally beneficent. Very early in human history, according to Marx, some men by force of arms succeed in seizing control over the vital means of production. They take the land, the streams, the mines, and the forests, and they prevent others from using them. Once these men have successfully asserted ownership of the means of production, they are in a position to extract a ransom from the rest of the men and women in the society. Pay me half of all you grow, the landholder says to the farmer, or I will not allow you to farm the land. The farmer has no choice, for if he does not farm, he starves. So two classes of people crystallize out of the social situation: the ruling class, which controls the means of production, and the underclass, which is forced to give up a part of the product of its labor in order to survive.

At first, of course, the naked force which holds the underclass down is obvious to all. But as time passes and generations succeed one another, sheer custom and familiarity confer legitimacy on what was originally mere might. The rulers pass on the control of the means of production to their sons and daughters, who grow up believing that it is theirs by right. The free time which the rulers have—because they eat and drink and wear what they do not have

Marx's theory of the structure of society.

to produce—permits them to develop a culture and style of life quite different from that of the laboring majority. Small wonder that even those in the underclass soon come to believe that the rulers are "different." They may not have been originally, but their descendants have certainly become so! As regular patterns of work, exchange, land ownership, and personal subordination develop, the rulers hold periodic courts to settle disputes that may have arisen in the enactment of those patterns. The decisions of these courts become the law of the land. Needless to say, the decisions rarely threaten the interests of the rulers, for it is they who convene the courts, they who sit on the bench, and they who enforce the orders of the courts with their soldiers. Nor is it surprising that the religious men and women of the society bless the rulers and their dominance. Churches are economically unproductive institutions, and they can survive only by sharing in that portion of the product which the rulers have taken from the laborers.

The system of relationships connecting those who control the means of production and those who do not is called the *social relationships of production.* It is the basic fact about a society, and from it grow such other, secondary facts as the structure of the law, the dogmas of the dominant religion, the underlying themes of the art and literature, *and also the form and organization of the state.* Marx calls these subordinate or secondary features of a society its *superstructure,* conveying by this metaphor the notion that a society rests on, or is built on, that portion of it which is the "base." A more modern way of putting the same idea would be to say that the means, forces, and social relationships of production are the idependent variables in a society; and the law, politics, art, religion and philosophy are the dependent variables.

In the superstructure, the state occupies a central place, for it is the instrument the ruling class uses to maintain its domination of the rest of the society. As the character of the social relationships of production changes, so does the character of the state. Under feudalism, which is a system of production based on ownership of land, the state is controlled by the landed aristocracy, which employs it to maintain control of the agricultural workers (or "serfs") and to regulate the relationships between the great land holders (or "lords") and their subordinate tenants (or "vassals"). This same system of landholding also forms the basis for the military organization of the society, thereby combining the control of the means of production with the supply of the force to maintain that control. In an industrial system of production, where capital rather than land is central to the productive process, the class that owns the capital (the "capitalists") also controls the state. As Marx and Engels say in their most famous work, *The Communist Manifesto,* "The executive of the modern state is but a committee for managing the common affairs of the whole bourgeoisie."

Political philosophers claim that they are disinterestedly pursuing eternal truth when they write their treatises, essays, and dialogues, but Marx pointed to the curious fact that in each era, quite intelligent and reasonable philosophers just happened to argue for precisely that system of politics and law which best served the interests of the ruling class. Aristotle enunciated the dictum that man is a rational animal, and then proceeded to conclude that because some men are more rational than others, nature has obviously created "natural slaves" and "natural masters." That Greek society was at that time built on slave labor was, presumably, irrelevant. St. Thomas Aquinas contemplated the infinite, and came to the conclusion that God had intended a hierarchical organization of the universe remarkably similar to the feudal system then flourishing in Aquinas' Europe. John Locke examined the law of nature, and deduced from it a justification for the contractual freedom and legal equality necessary to the growth of the rising capitalist class of England. In an early essay intended as a review of a book by Bruno Bauer, Marx took the Declaration of the Rights of Man and the Citizen which had been proclaimed by the French Revolution, and showed in a clause-by-clause analysis that it was nothing more than a rationalization for bourgeois capitalism.

The same analysis could be given for Marx's own philosophy, as he himself realized. His theory of historical materialism was a justification for the working-class revolution which he hoped for, predicted, and confidently expected. The intellectual superstructure, as a reflection of the economic or material base, could not be expected to achieve a transhistorical truth. At best, it could give expression to the real social relationships of production and distribution through which men and women, day by day, labored to transform nature into the means for human life.

The third part of Marx's theory was his account of the way in which societies change over time. At any given moment, we may speak of the ruling class and the underclass. But as new technology develops, as the division of labor is carried further and further, slow shifts take place in the material base. Within the feudal order, capitalism begins to grow. New ways of production and exchange give rise to new systems of relationships. At first, the changes seem minute by comparison with the overwhelming preponderance of economic activity. But little by little, more men and women are drawn into the new patterns of economic activity. The economically progressive group, or class, is at first disadvantaged, for the rules have all been made to favor the dominant class. But as the real economic power of the progressive class grows, it begins to demand a place in the ruling circles of the society. It wants laws changed to help rather than hinder its economic interests. It wants a share of the power that comes from controlling the means of production.

Now Marx was an optimist, if by that we mean that he thought the human race was heading toward better times. But he was not a fool. It was perfectly obvious to him that whenever a growing class challenged the dominance of a ruling class, there was going to be violence. There was no way that capitalists could compromise their interests with the landed aristocrats of the old order; one of them was going to have to go. According to Marx and Engels, the two centuries of civil war and social upheaval beginning with the English Civil War, continuing on through the French and American Revolutions, and ending with the American Civil War, were simply the protracted struggle between the landed aristocracy of the precapitalist order and the capitalist class which controlled the new industrial means of production.

In exactly the same way, he predicted that the new rising class of industrial workers, the proletariat, would one day do battle with the ruling class, the capitalists. Out of that revolutionary struggle would emerge a post-capitalist society in which a new system of social relationships of production would replace the old. No longer would there be a small group that controlled the means of production and a large group forced to work for it in an unjust, exploitative, alienated manner. Instead, the entire society would collectively take control of the means of production, and the division of labor would serve the interests of all, not merely the interests of the few. Under this new system of society, called socialism, there would be no domination of one person by another. Hence, there would be no need for a *state,* for the function of the state in every previous society had been to enforce the domination of the ruling class. There would, of course, be some sort of central direction of economic activity, for in a highly complex industrial economy, a sophisticated coordination of millions of workers would be indispensable. But this would merely be an "administration of things," not the "domination of men."

What then would become of the state? The answer, Engels stated, was that it would cease to exist as any unnecessary organ ceases to exist. It would "wither away." Here is Engels' analysis of the future of the state after the proletarian revolution.

> The proletariat takes control of the State authority and, first of all, converts the means of production into State property. But by this very act it destroys itself, as a proletariat, destroying at the same time all class differences and class antagonisms, and with this, also, the State. Past and present Society, which moved amidst class antagonisms, had to have the State, that is, an organization of the exploiting class for the support of its external conditions of production, therefore, in particular, for the forcible retention of the exploited class in such conditions of oppression (such as slavery, serfdom, wage-labor), as are determined by the given methods of production. The State was the official representative of the whole of Society, its embodiment in a visible corporation; but it was only in so far as it was the State of that class which, in the given epoch, alone represented the whole of society. In ancient times it was the State of the slave owners—the only citizens of the State; in the middle ages it was the State of the feudal nobility: in our own times it is the State of the capitalists. When ultimately, the State really becomes the representative of the whole of society, it will make itself superfluous. From the time when, together with class domination and the struggle for individual existence, resulting from the present anarchy in production, those conflicts and excesses which arise from this struggle will all disappear—from that time there will, therefore, be no need for the State. The first act of the State, in which it really acts as the representative of the whole of Society, namely, the assumption of control over the means of production on behalf of society, is also its last independent act as a State. The interference of the authority of the State with social relations will then become superfluous in one field after another, and finally will cease of itself. The authority of the Government over persons will be replaced by the administration of things and the direction of the processes of production. The State will not be 'abolished'; it will wither away. It is from this point of view that we must appraise the phrase, "a free popular State"—a phrase which, for a time, had a right to be employed as a purely propaganda slogan, but which in the long run is scientifically untenable. It is also from this point of view that we must appraise the demand of the so-called anarchists that the State "should be abolished overnight."

> FRIEDRICH ENGELS, *Herr Eugen Dühring's Revolution in Science*

Engels wrote these words just about a century ago (in 1878). Since then, something calling itself a "proletarian revolution" has taken place in a dozen countries, including two of the largest in the world. Were Marx and Engels correct? Has the state withered away?

The question is a tricky one, because neither Russia nor China was an advanced bourgeois capitalist industrial society at the time of its communist revolution. Nevertheless, a number of modern political philosophers, sympathetic with Marx but skeptical of much of his theory, have argued that even in a truly socialist society, the state will not disappear. Marx and Engels based their prediction on the expectation that after the revolution, there would be no further class divisions within society. But the evidence of Russia (and to some extent, of China) suggests that even when the means of production are, technically speaking, owned by everyone collectively, there still springs up a distinction between those who labor and those who manage, those who are on the receiving end of decisions and those who issue the orders. In the Soviet Union, this distinction has given rise to systematic inequalities in the distribution of wealth, educational opportunities, status, and power.

Mao Tse-Tung, the political and philosophical leader of the Chinese revolution, was throughout his long career especially concerned about this tendency for class distinctions to reappear after the official elimination of private ownership of the means of production. The People's Republic of China has tried a number of tactics to overcome the tendency, including the quite unusual practice of requiring technical experts and industrial managers to spend time in the fields or on the production line doing ordinary labor. It remains to be seen whether Marx's dream of a classless society can be achieved. And even if it can be, we shall still have to wait to see whether in such a society, the state will wither away.

If you hit a rock with your shovel when you are digging in the garden, and you want to know just how big the rock is, you feel around until you find its edges. If you want to test some fishing line to see how strong it is, you put enough weight on it to break it. By a sort of analogy, if you want to know the limits of the legitimate authority of the state, you must ask: Where does that authority end? How much strain may the state place on its authority over the citizen before the lines of authority break? At what point does a citizen have the right *not* to obey the law? If we can locate the edges of the state's authority, find out how far its writ ought to run, then we will have a clearer idea of the nature and magnitude of state authority.

We have already seen that there is a very profound difference between the question, How much can a state get away with? and the question, How much does a state have the *right* to demand of its subjects? The first question is a factual question, and in recent years, it has been much studied by social scientists. There seems to be a limit to what a state can impose on its subjects before they either openly rebel or else simply get mulishly stubborn and uncooperative. Can the United States government get Americans to fight and die in a great world war for which powerful, widely accepted justifications can be given? The answer is obviously yes. Can that same government get Americans to fight and die in an unpopular war whose reason for existing is never clear to the great majority of Americans? The experience of the Vietnam era suggests that the answer is: yes for a time, but then, no. Will American citizens continue to obey the laws and pay the taxes of a government which permits soaring inflation and unemployment to go on year after year? That is a question whose answer is emerging as these words are being written.

But all of this concerns only the question of *fact.* Much deeper, and in a way more important, is the question of *right.* Most of us genuinely wish to be good citizens, to act publicly and politically in a manner that is morally defensible. As the citizens of a democracy, we reject the notion that the state, any state, has a right to command whatever it wishes, and that we, as citizens, have an obligation to obey any law, however harsh or unjust. So the fundamental issue facing any politically alert citizen must be: When am I morally obligated to obey the state, *and when have I the right, nay the duty, to resist the commands of the state?*

All three schools of political thought discussed in this chapter offer answers to this question, either explicitly or implicitly. The liberal, contractarian school traces political obligation to the consent of those governed. If the citizens of a democracy ask why they ought to obey the law, the ultimate answer can only be: because that law is, in a manner of speaking, an expression of their own collective will. The fascist ideology, which in one form or another has exercised a very widespread appeal in twentieth-century world politics, teaches that the state takes precedence over the individual, that the individual finds true human fulfillment only in submission to, and incorporation into, the larger ends and activities of the state. By an odd twist of fate and logic, one of the most liberal presidents of recent American history, John F. Kennedy, echoed that fascist thesis when he said, in his 1960 inaugural address, "Ask not what your country can do for you. Ask rather what you can do for your country." Marxist political ideology places greater emphasis on economic issues than on questions of state authority, but it seems to follow rather directly from Marx's theories that the bourgeois state has no moral authority whatsoever over the members of the working class. The Party, however, the Communist Party which leads the working class to a socialist revolution, *does* have such authority—or so the Russian Communists argued—because the party is a leader, the vanguard, of an historical movement, and as such occupies an objectively progressive position in the political world.

The issue of the limits of state authority has taken a rather special form in the United States, as a consequence of our particular history. The Founding Fathers, in an effort to avoid the deep religious conflicts which had torn England and other European nations apart, wrote the Constitution in such a way that no one religious doctrine received any favored political treatment. At the same time, they were, almost without exception, believing Christians of one sort or another. Consequently, they wrote into our fundamental law certain protections of religious freedom. The net effect of these compromises was to make *private* religious conviction privileged. The way was opened to a legal struggle between the commands of the state and the inner demands of individual conscience.

In recent decades, this struggle has taken the form of a continuing legal, moral, and political dispute over the rights of the private citizen whose religious or moral convictions come into direct conflict with the legal commands of the state. Most often, of course, the conflict has emerged in times of war, when certain groups of devout believers, motivated frequently by their adherence to the biblical command, "Thou shalt not kill," have claimed that their obedience to the Bible takes precedence over their obligation to register for the draft or serve in the Armed Forces. But other conflicts between religious belief and state law have played an important role in the development of the doctrine of conscientious objection. For example, some Christians have refused to salute the flag on the grounds that to do so is incompatible with the commandments of God.

Eventually, a number of conscientious citizens began to put forward the claim that moral objections, not merely religious convictions, constituted a legitimate basis for resistance to what they considered to be unjust laws. Whereas the religious dissenters insisted that they owed an absolute allegiance to an authority higher than the state (namely, God), these secular dissenters claimed that the inner commands of one's own conscience must be placed ahead of state commands.

Some secular dissenters, of course, merely reject the claims of state authority absolutely. They deny that the state has any moral right at all to command its subjects. This position is usually called "anarchism," from the Greek root meaning "no rule" or "lack of rule." But most secular dissenters adopt an in-between position which has come to be known as *civil disobedience.*

The central idea of the doctrine of civil disobedience is that the state *does* have a certain right to command its subjects, but that the individual also has a certain right to follow the dictates of conscience rather than the commands of the law. Now, on the face of it, that would seem to be a straight-out contradiction. If the state has the right to command me to go to war, how can I also have the right to say no? Conversely, if I have the right to refuse to serve, how can the state have the right to draft me? The state may have the power. No one disputes *that.* But how can it have the *right?*

In recent years, a very large philosophical literature has grown up on the subject of civil disobedience. Like the debate over abortion, which we looked at in Chapter Two, this is an issue where abstract philosophical doctrines come to bear on a matter of the most immediate practical concern. Hugo Bedau, a philosopher who teaches at Tufts University in Massachusetts, has for a long time been one of the leading voices in the debates on civil disobedience. In this classic essay, he brings the skills of analytic philosophy to bear on the problem of determining just when, and for what reasons, an individual has the moral right to adopt the position of the civil disobedient.

HUGO BEDAU: *On Civil Disobedience*

I

1. A dissenter performs an act of civil disobedience only if he acts *illegally;* i.e., if he violates some positive law, because of (one of) the laws, policies, or decisions of his government which he finds objectionable. Acts of protest directed at government, no matter how conscientious or effective, in which no law is violated (as is usually the case with a poster parade, voluntary boycott, or refusal to accept government employment), are not acts of civil disobedience.[1] Civil disobedience, after all, is not just done; it is committed. It is always the sort of thing that can send one to jail.

As with any disobedience, it seems possible to distinguish between positive acts, which are the doing of something prescribed by law (e.g., trespassing on government property), and negative acts, which are the refusal to do something prescribed by law (e.g., not taking cover when directed to do so during an air raid drill). It has been suggested[2] that acts of the latter sort are almost always likely to be justified, perhaps on the ground that the consequences of abstaining from obedience can seldom be so disruptive as those of committing active disobedience. I am not convinced of this. For instance, widespread refusal of draft calls for military service would have a far greater effect on any "defense" establishment than would widespread trespassing on military bases. Nor do I see how doing something illegal by not going out of one's way to do something in particular is any more likely to be justified than doing something illegal by going out of one's way to do something in particular. . . .

Since all civil disobedience involves illegal activity, it has usually been supposed[3] that such acts could not receive legal protection; i.e., that there could

[1] It has been suggested that work stoppages in arms factories are an ideal form of civil disobedience. But unless quitting a "defense" job is illegal, this is impossible. See Alan Lovell, "Direct Action," *New Left Review,* no. 8 (March–April, 1961): 20. As for the special problems of conscientious disobedience of military orders, which I have totally ignored, see Guenter Lewy, "Superior Orders, Nuclear Warfare, and the Dictates of Conscience," *American Political Science Review,* **55** (March, 1961): 3–23.

[2] A. C. Ewing, *The Individual, the State and World Government* (New York, 1947), p. 69. The terms 'negative' and 'positive' as used in the text are borrowed from Ewing.

[3] See Ewing, *op. cit.,* p. 73, and David Spitz, "Democracy and the Problem of Civil Disobedience," *American Political Science Review,* **48** (June, 1954): 342. See also Franz Newmann, "On the Limits of Justifiable Disobedience," reprinted in his *The Democratic and the Authoritarian State* (Glencoe, 1958), p. 154; he refers to Article 947 of the Constitution of Hesse (1946), which provides for "the right and the duty" of "resistance to unconstitutionally exercised public authority."

be a legal right of civil disobedience (or of any form of resistance to government). What has not been noticed is that, by extending a practice already in use, civil disobedience could be lawfully eliminated. The law has long managed to obviate much civil disobedience by clauses providing exemption for conscientious objectors. There is no logical reason why every law could not have a rider to the effect that anyone who violates it on conscientious grounds shall be exempt from prosecution and penalty. . . .

2. There would clearly be something odd about a policeman's reporting that he had surprised several persons in the act of committing civil disobedience or about employing detectives to root out conspiracies to commit civil disobedience. For this would suggest, contrary to fact, that these illegal acts were an embarrassment to the dissenter and that he might wish them to be kept secret from the public and especially from the government. Usually, though not always, it is essential to the purpose of the dissenter that both the public and the government should know what he intends to do. At least, it is essential that the government know of his act if it is intended that the government shall change its policy because of the act. This is one reason why the authorities are customarily notified in advance by those intending to commit civil disobedience. More fundamental still is the fact that the dissenter views what he does as a civic act, an act that properly belongs to the public life of the community. This derives from the fact that he thinks of himself as acting to thwart some law, policy, etc., that deviates from the true purpose of government as he sees it. Thus, his act draws attention to something he thinks the whole community should be brought to consider, since the community has as much interest in the act as he does. For these reasons, civil disobedience is necessarily *public*.

3. Not every illegal act of public resistance to government, however, is an act of civil disobedience. Anytime the dissenter resists government by deliberately destroying property, endangering life and limb, inciting to riot (e.g., sabotage, assassination, street fighting), he has not committed *civil* disobedience. The pun on 'civil' is essential; only *nonviolent* acts thus can qualify.[4] By 'nonviolent act' one means, I take it, that the agent does not try to accomplish his aim either by initiating or by threatening violence, that he does not respond with violence or violent resistance during the course of his disobedience, regardless of the provocation he may have, and thus that he is prepared to suffer without defense the indignities and brutalities that often greet his act. Even if the reaction to his act is a violent one, whether by the police or by a hostile public, I do not think this negates the civility of his act; it is not a logical consequence of anyone's attempt to act nonviolently that anyone else should respond with violence.

[4] Bentham is typical of the classic philosophers from Bacon to Mill, all of whom tend to ignore civil disobedience. His sole conception of "open disobedience" to government is of "forcible" resistance, as though 'open' meant something other than 'public'. See his *Fragment of Government* (1776), F. C. Montague, ed. (Oxford, 1931), pp. 147 f. Not even Thoreau, who seems to have coined the phrase 'civil disobedience', stressed its nonviolent character. The matter has become obvious only since the writings of Gandhi. See his *Non-violent Resistance* (New York, [1951] 1961), pp. 3–4.

4. The typical act of civil disobedience is not only directed against the government because of some objectionable law, policy, or decision and not only undertaken in order to frustrate that law, etc., but also so designed that the act itself does frustrate that law, etc. If this were the rule, no act could qualify for the title of civil disobedience unless it was the sort of act that, if it were committed by everyone (or even by a large minority), would hamper and perhaps prevent the government from enforcing the law, etc., at issue.

Here we meet an important distinction. Some acts of civil disobedience intend to achieve this aim by directly violating the objectionable law (e.g., refusing to register for the military draft), whereas other acts, like Thoreau's, intend to achieve this aim by violating some other law and are thus aimed at the objectionable law only indirectly (e.g., withholding from payment that portion of one's income taxes used to support the "defense" establishment). Since there are severe limitations to the circumstances in which certain laws are open to direct resistance by anyone except those who administer them (e.g., no ordinary citizen is in a position to resist directly his government's decision to launch a nuclear missile strike or to execute a condemned prisoner), it is only by acts of indirect resistance that it is possible for everyone to commit civil disobedience because of any of his government's laws. On the other hand, an act often allows of no more than a remote connection to the objectionable law, with the result that it appears ineffective and absurd. Hence, the preference among dissenters of cool head and stout heart for direct resistance.

What I have called 'direct resistance' must not be confused with what is popularly called 'direct action'. Direct action is a special form of direct resistance, in which the dissenter uses his own body as the lever with which to pry loose the government's policy. Nonviolent direct action takes either of two forms: "nonviolent obstruction" and "nonviolent interjection."[5] Since the former involves a kind of physical coercion, albeit passive (e.g., climbing onto construction equipment and sitting there), it raises problems for those who scruple at the least suggestion of physical force in the act of disobedience. Thus, it is nonviolent interjection that is generally recognized to constitute the paradigm of every aspect of civil disobedience. Perhaps the most striking example in recent years was the voyage of The Golden Rule in the spring of 1958 into the Central Pacific, to try to force the United States government to abandon its nuclear-weapons testing program or to deliberately expose several of its citizens to a probably fatal dosage of radioactive fallout, since the crew intended to sail the ship directly into the testing area.[6] The fashion in which such an act, without involving any conceivable physical coercion on the government, might force it to change (or at least to reappraise) its policy, is quite plain.

There is a difficulty, however, in treating such cases as definitive, because

---

[5] This distinction and terminology I have taken from Bradford Lyttle, *Essays on Nonviolent Action* (Chicago [1959]), pp. 30 f.

[6] See Albert Bigelow, *The Voyage of The Golden Rule* (New York, 1959).

not all illegal nonviolent public resistance to government constitutes even token frustration of the objectionable law that occasions the resistance. There is a whole class of acts, undertaken in the name of civil disobedience, which, even if they were widely practiced, would in themselves constitute hardly more than a nuisance (e.g., trespassing at a nuclear-missile installation). These acts may well serve as public witness to the integrity of the dissenter's convictions and may well lead to the commission of other acts that will frustrate the objectionable law. But overrunning a missile site with trespassers who only trespass and refuse to cooperate in their own arrest cannot really interfere with the construction of a single launching pad or with the launching of a single missile. Therefore, such acts are often just a harrassment and, at least to the bystander, somwhat inane. I am inclined, therefore, to treat this class of cases almost as border-line. . . .

It is worth noticing at this point that the civil disobedient need not be an anarchist. Contrary to some opinions, the decision to resist nonviolently a certain law does not logically presuppose or entail the belief that all laws (or all this government's laws) ought to be resisted, or that governments and police forces are unnecessary, or that it is a sufficient condition for justifiably resisting the government on any occasion that it sanctions a manifestly unjust law. It may be that civil disobedience tends to encourage anarchism, as the classic Utilitarians believed, because respect for law may be weakened in the public at large (not to mention among the dissenters) even by an isolated act of resistance. Since it is true that habitual respect for the law is needed to allow the enforcement of manifestly just and beneficial laws, the conscientious dissenter will hesitate to undertake any act that would undermine this habit. But if worry about cultivating this habit figures prominently in government chancelleries, why is it that we continue to have incidents where even "democratic" governments complacently murder, kidnap, incite to rebel, lie, and break their solemn promises?

5. Civil disobedience is, finally, a *conscientious* act. That is, the dissenter proposes to justify his disobedience by an appeal to the incompatibility between his political circumstances and his moral convictions. Usually, this requires that he be convinced that it would be worse for everyone to suffer the consequences of the objectionable law than it would be for everyone to suffer the consequences of his (and, conceivably, of everyone else's) civil disobedience. This requirement is reminiscent of Utilitarianism and one of its later variants[7] in that what is involved is a weighing of consequences against one another. But it is different in that such weighing is regarded here not as providing the criterion of justifiable civil disobedience but only as a condition of its conscientiousness. For not every conscientious act is justified, i.e., the right thing for the agent to do. Conscientiousness also usually requires that the dissenter

---

[7] See Bentham, *op. cit.,* pp. 211, 215, 220, 227, and Ernest Barker, *Principles of Social and Political Theory* (Oxford, 1951), p. 224.

acknowledge that the law, no matter what it is, makes some claim on his obedience, no matter how readily this claim may be overridden by other claims. Only an anarchist could think that his resistance was conscientious when he knew that he had taken nothing into account to justify himself except the fact that by this law the government sanctioned manifest injustice.[8] Why anyone should think a law is objectionable enough to deserve his resistance and why he should think his resistance ought to be nonviolent are quite independent considerations; there are any number of reasons why he might come to such conclusions. So the conscientiousness of the decision seems to lie in the way it is reached rather than in the nature of the convictions used to reach it.

It is not even necessary that the law because of which the disobedience is committed effect substantial injustice, violate basic rights, suffocate liberty, or otherwise work to the public disadvantage, though some such claim is almost invariably put forward. Though it may be highly improbable, there is no logical reason why a United States citizen could not commit acts of civil disobedience because of racial desegregation in the public schools, the Fifth Amendment, or foreign economic aid. A government, after all, can be subjected to conscientious resistance on account of *any* of its laws, policies, or decisions; and if anyone can have the right to resist conscientiously whatever he chooses, everyone else can have an equal right. I am even doubtful whether a civil disobedient must justify his resistance by appeal to the belief that the government sanctions manifest injustice, etc. I do not see any contradiction in his having no interest in that issue and still believing that his act is justified. It is true that disobedience that is mainly and patently self-serving raises doubts about its conscientiousness. But it is not a *logical* truth that people are easily self-deceived about their own motives, especially for those of their acts which benefit themselves. About the only moral convictions, therefore, we can assume in advance that a civil disobedient must have are that it is better to suffer violence than to inflict it and that law and order are not lightly to be disturbed. But since even these convictions need obtain only *ceteris paribus* (one need not, after all, be a Gandhian *Satyagrahi*), this is not saying much. Any number of circumstances might arise to override them, and there are any number of other convictions one might have with which they could conflict. I can conclude only and somewhat lamely that probably no one holds moral convictions that would rule out civil disobedience for him in every conceivable situation.

6. Are there specifiable political circumstances in which civil disobedience rather than another form of resistance or rather than no resistance at all is so unexceptionably justified that these circumstances constitute, as it were, part of the necessary context of any such act? I am not sure. Whenever legal devices for redress of grievances or for orderly change of laws and government personnel do not exist at all (e.g., the predicament of the dissenter in a totalitarian state)

---

[8] Thus, when it is said that a bill of attainder provides its victim with a sufficient condition for having "the right to resist," I suppose one would want to introduce some further considerations to determine when and how the agent ought to exercise this right. See Neumann, *op. cit.*, p. 158.

or when these devices have been exhausted for the foreseeable future (e.g., the predicament of the segregationist since the Supreme Court decision in Brown vs. Board of Education) or when it would take so much time to pursue these remedies that the objectionable law would meanwhile take its effect (e.g., the predicament of the crew of The Golden Rule), some sort of direct resistance to government is likely to be contemplated by the aggrieved parties. One is almost bound to insist that whenever such legal devices still obtain and civil disobedience or any other form of resistance is nevertheless committed, either the dissenter is acting irresponsibly, or his politics are anarchical, or both.[9] But even if these legal devices do not obtain, that fact alone does not ordinarily suffice to justify resistance[10] nor to determine whether it should be direct or indirect, violent or nonviolent.

7. In the light of the foregoing examination, I suggest the following definition: Anyone commits an act of civil disobedience if and only if he acts illegally, publicly, nonviolently, and conscientiously with the intent to frustrate (one of) the laws, policies, or decisions of his government.

II

8. The radical possibility arises that whenever one is confronted by a law, one ought to disobey it—partly, as H. A. Prichard once suggested, because "after all the mere receipt of an order backed up by a threat seems, if anything, to give rise to the duty of resisting rather than of obeying"[11] but mainly just because "the certification of something as legally valid is not conclusive of the question of obedience."[12] That is, for a man to know that he ought to obey a certain law, policy, or decision of his government it is not sufficient if all he knows (or believes) is that the law, etc., is legally valid. This must be so, since 'I ought to do x' cannot be deduced from 'There is a valid law that applies to me and prescribes the doing of x.' So anyone's obligation to obey any law is pretty clearly contingent on what the law happens to be. . . . If we take the view that legal obligation is radically contingent, there is no problem at all in answering the question, 'How can anyone ever have a right to disobey the law?' The answer is simply, 'Because no one ever ought to do something just because it is the law.' Surely, it is because it is so often easy to see and to approve of what a law is designed to accomplish and to agree that it does, more or less, succeed, that one tends to overlook the heavy burden morality

---

[9] Thus, I tend to agree with those who think that the absence of these legal devices is a necessary condition of any form of justifiable resistance. See Guenter Lewy, "Resistance to Tyranny," *Western Political Quarterly,* **13** (September, 1960): 585, 591 f.

[10] Probably it does, if the government in question professes "democratic" principles and if the civil disobedience is undertaken on behalf of policies implied by those principles. See Spitz, *op. cit.,* pp. 396 f.

[11] *Moral Obligation* (Oxford, 1949), p. 54.

[12] H. L. A. Hart, *The Concept of Law* (Oxford, 1961), p. 206.

places on a law before it yields any authority to the law to guide one's conduct.

9. The problem of justifying one's decision to resist government arises because it is not sufficient to plead either any special defect of the objectionable law or the conscientiousness of one's decision. It may seem that one could not have a better reason for refusing to do what one's government orders than that one conscientiously believes it to be wrong. . . . But we hesitate to allow that a man can know that he ought not to accept a certain policy of his government if all he knows is that he has conscientious scruples against it. It is logically possible that his moral convictions are most unfortunate, so that we would like nothing better than for anyone with his principles to fail in what he thinks he ought to do. His predicament (which is ours, too, of course) is that he cannot support his convictions and his estimate of his circumstances by appeal to some more objective and thus more authoritative appraisal, without also surrendering the opportunity to direct his own conduct. But it does not follow from the fact that a man cannot do more than what he conscientiously thinks he ought to do that he ought to do whatever he thinks he ought to do. The force of saying, 'I ought to disobey this law' cannot be derived from 'Obeying this law is inconsistent with my moral convictions.' To enable the deduction obviously requires begging the question. The most we can say is that one has a right to conscientious disobedience; we need not and we cannot always go on to say that conscientious disobedience is the right thing to do. But being able to say the latter, and not just the former, is surely the main aim of trying to justify an act of disobedience.

Thus, it is possible that a government is sometimes right in having its way against the will of those who conscientiously disobey. So one cannot say, as some have,[13] that a government ought never to force a man to obey a law against his conscience. Perhaps one comes to the contrary view from supposing that no one's conscience could really advise him to disobey except in the name of justice, basic rights, freedom, or the general welfare and that all that could be at issue is the relatively unimportant question of whether he or the government is right about the availability of those benefits under the law in question, since no government worthy of the name would aim at anything other than these ends, and that, in those cases where he is mistaken, the harm involved in forcing his compliance is always greater than the harm of letting him disobey and take the legal consequences. This is a set of amiable but nevertheless false suppositions.

10. Thus, the insufficiency of a law for obedience (and of conscientious scruples for disobedience) forces one to look elsewhere if one is to specify a principle that would identify the sufficient and necessary conditions, applicable in all situations, under which one's obedience (or disobedience) is justified. Unfortunately, I do not see how any such principle could be produced, or that it would be of any use once it was available. Any principle that could do

---

[13] Ewing, *op. cit.,* p. 68, and also, it would appear, Spitz, *op. cit.,* p. 400.

the job required, being a principle of conduct, would itself be open to the very kind of demurrers and controversy it was designed to settle. Second, there is no compelling reason for anyone to adopt any principle in advance of knowing exactly what it will require of him. Since the kind of principle at issue here is likely to be formulated in the chronically open-textured moral concepts of justice, rights, and the like, one cannot know. Thus, anyone who searches for such a principle or who thinks he has one in hand really only disguises from himself the fact that the only way he could use his principle is by tacitly deciding on each occasion either to interpret the principle so as to cover the situation he is in or to describe the situation so as to fit the principle. . . .

11. The difficulties brought forward in the previous two sections do not bear particularly on civil disobedience; they apply to any resistance to government. They signify nothing more and nothing less than the fact that this kind of political behavior is bound to be morally relevant conduct and thus subject to the characteristic potentialities and risks of such conduct.

The question naturally arises whether there is anything special to be said on behalf of civil disobedience which perhaps puts it in a more favorable light than any of its alternatives, viz., violent resistance, obedience under legal public protest, furtive disobedience, or silent acquiescence. Many people evidently think so at present, since they reject these other alternatives out of hand. The first they usually reject because, even if they did not scruple at violence, which they do, they apparently have decided that it would not be successful in persuading their government or their fellow citizens to reexamine the objectionable law. They have also reasoned that violence would tend to excuse violent counter-measures, thereby crushing their capacity to continue the resistance. The other alternatives they dismiss either as ineffective or as something to be pursued only out of diffidence or cowardice in the face of the genuine dangers that active resistance can bring on the head of the dissenter. Their course they explain thus: Events in which the government's laws, policies, decisions, etc., play a decisive role are so distressing that if not soon improved they will lead to disaster. Therefore, directly or indirectly, action must be taken which could be fairly widely practiced (or threatened) and which, if it were, would force the government to change its course. Since one has no path to the seats of authority or to the minds of one's countrymen other than open resistance and since the method of resistance must be consistent, as far as possible, with preserving respect for law and order, the only thing to do is to commit civil disobedience, and the sooner the better.

The major obstacle in the way of granting a privileged status to such acts is that such status would rest on a series of empirical facts whose factuality is still in doubt. Is it true that a government can be brought to reverse its policy through civil disobedience alone? If so, what sort of government and what sort of policies? If not, under what circumstances can civil disobedience be effective? What sort of civil disobedience in general has the most chance of success? Is it false that a relatively bloodless coup is always less effective than civil disobedience? If the availability to the general public of a fairly clear-cut alternative, complete with step-by-step implementation, is necessary to the success of civil disobedience, can this condition always be satisfied in time? Is it really possible to influence the foreign relations of one nation through civil disobedience when there are serious and widespread doubts in the government and the public at large whether the dissenter's politics are acceptable to the other nation? These are a few of the familiar empirical questions that must be raised, and it is not too much to say that there is still responsible disagreement on the answers. The only way to get answers is to conduct actual experiments in civil disobedience. But it is one thing to commit such acts in order to help behavioral scientists get on with their work and another to commit them as though this work had been completed.

There is a regrettable failure on the part of dissenting minorities and those whom government has victimized to explore those situations in which civil disobedience might have some chance of success. Direct nonviolent resistance can often be conducted without interfering with community functions that no sane man would disrupt if he could avoid it. Speaking for myself, I think that, in such cases, civil disobedience would vastly improve the quality of individual participation in public affairs and perhaps accelerate the painfully slow and uncertain advance in the concern of governments for the aspirations of mankind.

TOPICS FOR FURTHER STUDY

1. According to Bedau, one of the defining characteristics of the civil disobedient is that he or she acts conscientiously, which is to say on the basis of an honest, reflective, morally grounded conviction. Historically, most civil disobedients have been religious men and women who believed that there was a higher law than that of the state, a higher voice whose commands took precedence over any earthly injunctions. Obviously, if you truly believe that God has commanded you to act in a certain way, and if your government, any government, issues a contrary command, then you will conclude that you ought to obey God. But Bedau makes no appeal to religion. How can an appeal to conscience be justified when it is *not* backed up by religious faith? What right has the isolated individual to set himself or herself up against the collective will of society?

2. Following most proponents of civil disobedience, Bedau specifies *nonviolence* as one of the essential characteristics of true civil disobedience. What precisely *is* violence? If I physically demolish your restaurant, I am presumably acting violently. But suppose I and my fellow protestors occupy the booths of your restaurant without buying anything, so that you go broke and can't pay your rent. The police will evict you forcibly, if necessary, once you have defaulted on your lease. Have we acted violently or not? Aren't we merely letting someone else do our dirty work?

3. Everything in the political philosophy and political practice of democracy suggests that the burden of proof is on the dissenter, that anyone who wishes to violate the law needs a very strong justification indeed. Why shouldn't the shoe be on the other foot? What right has the state—any state—to issue commands? What obligation have I to obey any law save the moral law that binds all of us? Does a genuine democracy have a special legitimacy not shared by other, non-democratic states? If the answer is yes, then does it follow that no citizen of a true democracy has any right to act in a civilly disobedient manner? How do you think Rousseau would have handled this issue? How would Locke have dealt with it?

SUGGESTIONS FOR FURTHER READING

CARL COHEN, ed., *Communism, Fascism, and Democracy*

G. W. F. HEGEL, *The Philosophy of Right*

THOMAS HOBBES, *Leviathan*

L. T. HOBHOUSE, *The Metaphysical Theory of the State*

V. I. LENIN, *State and Revolution*

KARL MARX, *A Contribution to the Critique of Hegel's Philosophy of Right*

C. B. McPHERSON, *The Political Theory of Possessive Individualism*

JOHN STUART MILL, *On Representative Government*

ROBERT NOZICK, *Anarchy, State, and Utopia*

J. ROLAND PENNOCK and JOHN CHAPMAN, eds., *Anarchism* (NOMOS, Vol. XIX)

PLATO, *Crito*

EUGENE V. ROSTOW, ed., *Is Law Dead?*

HENRY DAVID THOREAU, *On Civil Disobedience*

ROBERT PAUL WOLFF, *In Defense of Anarchism*

PLATO (427?–347 B.C.) is one of the immortal geniuses of philosophy. Born in Athens to a wealthy and politically influential aristocratic family, he was closely associated as a young man with Socrates, who died when Plato was in his late twenties. When the democracy was restored, Plato's family fell out of favor, and his hostility to democratic government is reflected in a number of his works. At some time after Socrates' death, perhaps as much as fifteen years or more, Plato started to write dialogues in which moral, political, religious, cosmological, logical and other subjects were explored. In the early dialogues, Socrates is always the principal

5 PHILOSOPHY OF ART

speaker, and there is some reason to suppose that Plato's picture of Socrates' personality and doctrines bears a close resemblance to the actual historical man who was his teacher. Later on, however, the dialogues clearly come more and more to reflect Plato's own philosophical investigations, and in the works that he composed last, Socrates disappears altogether as a character.

Retreating from public life, Plato founded a school at his home in Athens. The home was called the "Academy," and the word has since then meant a school or university. Many of the most gifted philosophers of the day worked or studied at the Academy, including the other great genius of ancient thought, Aristotle. Eventually, the Academy became an independent institution, and it continued in existence for almost 900 years before it was finally closed by the Roman emperor Justinian in 529 A.D.

Plato's greatest work was the *Republic,* a dialogue on the nature of justice, but much of his work in later life was devoted to mathematics and cosmology, and members of the Academy made significant contributions to formal logic and to such mathematical fields as solid geometry.

I
_____

Here is a short parable: There was a singer with a clear, strong, beautiful voice, whose songs were so lovely that people would come from miles round to hear him sing. The singer was a thoughtful, compassionate man whose heart was troubled by the poverty and misery of the people for whom he sang. After much reflection, he concluded that the people should rise up and change their condition. And he realized that his songs, because of their loveliness, were a distraction to the people, making them forget for the moment the real causes of their misery. He decided to tell the people what he had discovered, but alas, they would only listen to him when he sang. So he wrote a song about the misery of the people and the dangerousness of lovely songs. But because he was a great singer, his song was a lovely song, and the people, listening to it, were soothed and distracted from their misery, and so did nothing.

Plato was just such a singer of philosophical songs, and nothing is more poignant or paradoxical than his attitude toward the great works of art which he himself created. You have several times met Socrates in these pages, always in his role as the principal character in Plato's Dialogues (his "philosophical songs"). But Plato, the artist himself, is not to be confused with the dramatic character who sometimes speaks for him in his dialogues, any more than the real historical Socrates should be confused with that character. Socrates wrote nothing himself, as Plato's own portrait of him tells us; but Plato wrote a great deal, and so he was forced to ask himself, as every artist must, whether artistic creation is good or evil, whether a life spent in the forming of artworks is a life well-spent, what indeed the function of art is in human life and society, and whether there is a place for art in the good society.

"The edges are nice and hard, but your colors aren't icky enough." *

Sometimes meaning, as well as beauty, is in the eye
of the beholder!

Since Plato's Dialogues, at least as we encounter them today, are classified as philosophical works rather than as works of art, it might be worth saying a few words about what sets them off from all the other philosophical works which no one would dream of calling "artistic." A philosophical dialogue is easy enough to write, if all you care about is getting the arguments down on paper. Just put your own theories in the mouth of one character—call her Ms. Wise—and whatever objections you can think of in the mouth of a second character—"The Fool," perhaps—and then write the whole thing down as though it were a play. The result will not exactly be beautiful, but as long as it has two characters in it, you can call it a dialogue. A number of great and not-so-great philosophers have actually written some of their philosophy in roughly this way, including the seventeenth-century Dutch metaphysician Baruch Spinoza, who was no artist at all, and the eighteenth-century Irish cleric George Berkeley, who wasn't either.

But Plato's Dialogues are quite another thing altogether. Their artistic brilliance results from Plato's ability to do three things at the same time, and to do them all superbly. First, his dialogues are not shadowboxing, or put-up jobs. Plato constructs real arguments, in which Socrates' opponents score points and make philosophical moves that are genuinely persuasive. We have already seen how Plato puts into the mouth of Callicles an argument against the practice of philosophy which many readers have considered overpowering. Second, the characters in the dialogues are not cardboard figures, two-dimensional pop-ups with name tags attached. They are fully realized human beings, with feelings, passions, characteristic ways of speaking. Some of them run on in great long speeches; others are mulish, grudging, giving nothing in an argument and resisting even the most obvious implications of their own statements. Some are dignified old men, full of years and self-confident in an awareness that they are nearing the end of life with their honor unsullied; others are eager, ambitious young men, out to score a quick knockout over Socrates and make their reputations. Most of the characters in the dialogues were apparently modeled after real people, and the original readers presumably could judge how skillfully Plato had caught their characters in his portraits. But for those of us who read the dialogues two millennia later, it matters only that they are completely successful artistic creations.

Finally, Plato accomplishes the most difficult creative feat of all—he makes the personalities and speech of his characters actually exemplify, and thereby provide evidence for, the philosophical theories he is trying to expound. His characters are not merely believable; they are just what they ought to be, given the philosophy they are expressing, if Plato's own theories are true. This fit between character and belief is designed by Plato as an expression of the central thesis of his philosophy: the doctrine that the metaphysical order of the universe is mirrored in the inner psychic order of the soul. Plato bases his philosophy upon a distinction between *appearance* and *reality,* a distinction that turns up over and over in many different guises throughout his works (indeed, we can quite accurately say that although the distinction *appears* in many different forms, it is *really* always the same distinction, and that is just one more example, Plato would say, of the distinction between appearance and reality). For example, a straight stick looks bent when half of it is put in water (because of the refraction of light). Sugar may seem good to a diabetic even though it would really make him sick. A tricky argument may look correct, but really be invalid. A devil may appear to be an angel of the Lord, but really be a messenger from Satan. It may seem smart to cheat on an exam, even though it is really wrong. Popular opinion may sound wise, but really be foolish.

In all these cases, and countless others besides, there is an image, a belief, an action, a feeling, which seems to be right, true, good, accurate, veridical, or healthy but is really wrong, false, evil, misleading, fallacious, or harmful. The ability to tell the difference between the two is always, according to Plato, a matter of some sort of knowledge, and the power or part of the soul whose job it is to make that distinction is *reason*. Reason tells us that the stick is really straight, even though it looks bent; reason tells the diabetic not to eat the apparently good sugar; reason finds the flaw in the valid-looking argument; and reason shows us when the easy way—cheating, or going along with popular opinion—is in the end the harmful, destructive way.

As these examples suggest, knowledge of reality, and the ability to distinguish it from misleading appearance, is more than just "book learning." You can study the principles of optics in the classroom, but you need some common sense and the power of observation to tell when to apply the formulae to a real stick in some real water. The diabetic patient can carefully write down his doctor's instructions not to eat candy, but he needs a quite different kind of knowledge and a much stronger power of reason to apply those instructions when temptation appears in the guise of a rich, tasty dessert. Socrates needed more than just a "philosophical" understanding of justice to resist the chance to escape from his punishment by the Athenians and instead remain, calm and resigned, to drink the hemlock.

According to Plato, a woman who has some true opinions but does not really understand what makes them true will *look* wise as long as she doesn't get into morally difficult or complicated situations, but she will not *really be* wise. We are liable to confuse her good habits and her true opinions with real knowledge until we see her come unstuck in a crunch. Then we will realize that we were deceived, and that what we took for real wisdom was only its appearance. So too, a man who mouths current arguments without really having thought them through for himself will sound very knowledgeable until we press him with some hard questions. Then we will discover that his knowledge is only appearance. Worst of all, according to Plato, a person who has no systematic grasp of the true good for humanity will not be able to tell what is going to make him or her truly happy, and so will do what looks pleasant but is ultimately harmful. He will allow himself to be flattered into betraying a trust, or beguiled away from the hard work that brings real satisfaction, or frightened by imagined evils into shameful or dishonorable deeds.

Plato weaves his philosophical theory about appearance and reality together with his psychological insights into human character to produce a series of persuasive and fundamentally true portraits in his Dialogues. (Needless to say, he deliberately intends the dramatic persuasiveness of his characters—their appearance—to reveal, rather than conceal, the truth about their souls—their reality.)

One example may make all this a bit clearer. In the dialogue entitled *Gorgias,* you will remember, there are three characters who argue with Socrates. The first is the title role, a traveling public speaker and teacher named Gorgias; the second is a young disciple named Polus; and the third is the hot-headed, brilliant Callicles. Now Plato sees Gorgias as one of those decent human beings who personally would not do anything shameful or wicked, but who does not really have rational knowledge of the right moral principles. In fact, although in his own life he is an upright person, the philosophy he expounds is totally false. Plato thinks that Gorgias is dangerous, because his pupils tend to do as he says, not as he does. Instead of imitating the decency and honorableness of Gorgias' private life, his pupils listen to his relativistic moral arguments and act on them in the law courts and public life of Athens. Plato presents Gorgias as a man who is stuffily self-confident, easily trapped into logical contradictions, but personally horrified at the thought that anyone would take his philosophy as an excuse for dishonorable behavior. Plato lets him off rather easily in the dialogue, because he respects Gorgias' personal decency as a human being, while nevertheless condemning the confusion of his thought. When Polus, the young disciple, enters the argument in Gorgias' place, the tone changes immediately. Polus is one of those impressionable young men who have been misled by Gorgias' statements and insufficiently impressed by Gorgias' actual character. Polus argues better than Gorgias, because he is not restrained—as Gorgias is—by a well-developed sense of what it is fitting and proper to maintain in a moral argument. Gorgias cannot bring himself to say something he knows to be wrong merely to make a point in a debate, but Polus is not so hesitant. Nevertheless, since he is merely repeating things he has heard in current conversation, without any deep thought, he is easily refuted by Socrates. But Plato permits Socrates to make fun of Polus, thereby expressing his moral evaluation of Polus as compared with Gorgias. When Callicles jumps into the debate to replace Polus, a real tension develops between him and Socrates. Callicles really believes, as he says, that might makes right, that there are no universal rational principles binding the weak and the strong, the ordinary and the extraordinary, to a single standard of conduct. This total confusion (as Plato sees it) is mirrored in the disorder of Callicles' soul. He rants, he shouts, he grows abusive, he loses whatever dignity he may have possessed. In short, his personality exhibits precisely that breakdown of true reason which his philosophy also reveals. The dialogue becomes, at one and the same time, an argument between two philosophies and a contrast between two personalities. The truth of Socrates' position is shown as much by his composure, his ironic self-deprecation, his inner peace, as it is by the forcefulness of his arguments.

Now let me connect up the parable at the beginning of the chapter with Plato's theory of appearance and reality and his long example from the *Gorgias* of Plato's artistic skill. Strange and paradoxical as it may seem, Plato actually believed, on the basis of his theoretical distinction between appearance and reality, that artistic creations were *appearances,* and that as such they led us away from knowledge and away from a proper inner harmony of the soul. And like the singer in the parable, Plato expressed this conviction in a series of artistic works of such beauty that the attention of his audience is turned away from the message rather than toward it!

Our first selection in this chapter is, once again, from the *Republic*. It contains Plato's reasons for believing that art is misleading, harmful, and therefore that it ought not to be permitted a place in the ideal society he is sketching. In much of this selection, Plato seems to be talking about what philosophers call *metaphysics*, or the study of the forms and nature of being, as much as about art. This interconnection of the different branches of philosophy is typical of the work of the great philosophers, and you should not be misled by the organization of this book into supposing that philosophy consists of a number of separate subfields locked away in watertight compartments. Indeed, the distinction between appearance and reality also bears directly on John Stuart Mill's claim, in the last chapter, that some pleasures are higher or truer or better than others. Plato held the same view, and he defended it precisely by saying that some pleasures are *more real* than others.

Plato's objections to art focus on two distinct but related questions: First, does art give us knowledge, or does it mislead us about the nature of reality? and second, does art help us to achieve a proper, harmonious inner psychic order, or does it stir up our emotions and destroy the rule of reason within the personality. Plato convicts art on both counts. Art leads us away from reality rather than toward it, he claims, and it destroys our psychic harmony rather than reinforcing it. These twin issues, of the truthfulness of art and the psychological effect of art on the audience, run through all the philosophies of art that we shall be examining in this chapter.

Can you tell me what is meant by representation in general?

. . . shall we proceed as usual and begin by assuming the existence of a single essential nature or Form for every set of things which we call by the same name? . . .

Then let us take any set of things you choose. For instance there are any number of beds or of tables, but only two Forms, one of Bed and one of Table. . . .

And we are in the habit of saying that the craftsman, when he makes the beds or tables we use or whatever it may be, has before his mind the Form of one or other of these pieces of furniture. The Form itself is, of course, not the work of any craftsman. . . .

Now what name would you give to a craftsman who can produce all the things made by every sort of workman?

He would need to have very remarkable powers!

Wait a moment, and you will have even better reason to say so. For, besides producing any kind of artificial thing, this same craftsman can create all plants and animals, himself included, and earth and sky and gods and the heavenly bodies and all the things under the earth in Hades.

That sounds like a miraculous feat of virtuosity.

Are you incredulous? Tell me, do you think there could be no such craftsman at all, or that there might be someone who could create all these things in one sense, though not in another? Do you not see that you could do it yourself, in a way?

In what way, I should like to know.

There is no difficulty; in fact there are several ways in which the thing can be done quite quickly. The quickest perhaps would be to take a mirror and turn it round in all directions. In a very short time you could produce sun and stars and earth and yourself and all the other animals and plants and lifeless objects which we mentioned just now.

Yes, in appearance, but not the actual things.

Quite so; you are helping out my argument. My notion is that a painter is a craftsman of that kind. You may say that the things he produces are not real; but there is a sense in which he too does produce a bed.

Yes, the appearance of one.

And what of the carpenter? Were you not saying just now that he only makes a particular bed, not what we call the Form or essential nature of Bed?

Yes, I was.

If so, what he makes is not the reality, but only something that resembles it. It would not be right to call the work of a carpenter or of any other handicraftsman a perfectly real thing. . . .

We must not be surprised, then, if even an actual bed is a somewhat shadowy thing as compared with reality.

True.

Now shall we make use of this example to throw light on our question as to the true nature of this artist who represents things? We have here three sorts of bed: one which exists in the nature of things and which, I imagine, we could only describe as a product of divine workmanship; another made by the carpenter; and a third by the painter. So the three kinds of bed belong respectively to the domains of these three: painter, carpenter, and god.

Yes.

Now the god made only one ideal or essential Bed, whether by choice or because he was under some necessity not to make more than one; at any rate two or more were not created, nor could they possibly come into being.

Why not?

Because, if he made even so many as two, then once more a single ideal Bed would make its appearance, whose character those two would share; and that one, not the two, would be the essential Bed. Knowing this, the god, wishing to be the real maker of a real Bed, not a particular manufacturer of one particular bed, created one which is essentially unique.

So it appears.

Shall we call him, then, the author of the true nature of Bed, or something of that sort?

Certainly he deserves the name, since all his works constitute the real nature of things.

And we may call the carpenter the manufacturer of a bed?

Yes.

Can we say the same of the painter?

Certainly not.

Then what is he, with reference to a bed?

I think it would be fairest to describe him as the artist who represents the things which the other two make.

Very well, said I; so the work of the artist is at the third remove from the essential nature of the thing?

Exactly.

The tragic poet, too, is an artist who represents things; so this will apply to him: he and all other artists are, as it were, third in succession from the throne of truth.

Just so.

We are in agreement, then, about the artist. But now tell me about our painter: which do you think he is trying to represent—the reality that exists in the nature of things, or the products of the craftsman?

The products of the craftsman.

As they are, or as they appear? You have still to draw that distinction.

How do you mean?

I mean: you may look at a bed or any other object from straight in front or slantwise or at any angle. Is there then any difference in the bed itself, or does it merely look different?

It only looks different.

Well, that is the point. Does painting aim at reproducing any actual object as it is, or the appearance of it as it looks? In other words, is it a representation of the truth or of a semblance?

Of a semblance.

The art of representation, then, is a long way from reality; and apparently the reason why there is nothing it cannot reproduce is that it grasps only a small part of any object, and that only an image. Your painter, for example, will paint us a shoemaker, a carpenter, or other workman without understanding any one of their crafts; and yet, if he were a good painter, he might deceive a child or a simple-minded person into thinking his picture was a real carpenter, if he showed it them at some distance.

. . . the content of this poetical representation is something at the third remove from reality, is it not?

Yes.

On what part of our human nature, then, does it produce its effect?

What sort of part do you mean?

Let me explain by an analogy. An object seen at a distance does not, of course, look the same size as when it is close at hand; a straight stick looks bent when part of it is under water; and the same thing appears concave or convex to an eye misled by colours. Every sort of confusion like these is to be found in our minds; and it is this weakness in our nature that is exploited, with a quite magical effect, by many tricks of illusion, like scene-painting and conjuring.

. . . Instead of trusting merely to the analogy from painting, let us directly consider that part of the mind to which the dramatic element in poetry appeals, and see how much claim it has to serious worth. We can put the question in this way. Drama, we say, represents the acts and fortunes of human beings. It is wholly concerned with what they do, voluntarily or against their will, and how they fare, with the consequences which they regard as happy or otherwise, and with their feelings of joy and sorrow in all these experiences. That is all, is it not?

Yes.

And in all these experiences has a man an undivided mind? Is there not an internal conflict which sets him at odds with himself in his conduct, much as we were saying that the conflict of visual impressions leads him to make contradictory judgments? However, I need not ask that question; for, now I come to think of it, we have already agreed that innumerable conflicts of this sort are constantly occurring in the mind. But there is a further point to be considered now. We have said that a man of high character will bear any stroke of fortune, such as the loss of a son or of anything else he holds dear, with more equanimity than most people. We may now ask: will he feel no pain, or is that impossible? Will he not rather observe due measure in his grief?

Yes, that is nearer the truth.

Now tell me: will he be more likely to struggle with his grief and resist it when he is under the eyes of his fellows or when he is alone?

He will be far more restrained in the presence of others.

Yes; when he is by himself he will not be ashamed to do and say much that he would not like anyone to see or hear.

Quite so.

What encourages him to resist his grief is the lawful authority of reason, while the impulse to give way comes from the feeling itself; and, as we said, the presence of contradictory impulses proves that two distinct elements in his nature must be involved. One of them is law-abiding, prepared to listen to the authority which declares that it is best to bear misfortune as quietly as possible without resentment, for several reasons: it is never certain that misfortune may not be a blessing; nothing is gained by chafing at it; nothing human is matter for great concern; and, finally, grief hinders us from calling in the help we most urgently need. By this I mean reflection on what has happened, letting reason decide on the best move in the game of life that the fall of the dice permits. Instead of behaving like a child who goes on shrieking after a fall and hugging the wounded part, we should accustom the mind to set itself at once to raise up the fallen and cure the hurt, banishing lamentation with a healing touch.

Certainly that is the right way to deal with misfortune.

And if, as we think, the part of us which is ready to act upon these reflections is the highest, that other part which impels us to dwell upon our sufferings and can never have enough of grieving over them is unreasonable, craven, and faint-hearted.

Yes.

Now this fretful temper gives scope for a great diversity of dramatic representation; whereas the calm and wise character in its unvarying constancy is not easy to represent, nor when represented is it readily understood, especially by a promiscuous gathering in a theatre, since it is foreign to their own habit of mind. Obviously, then, this steadfast disposition does not naturally attract the dramatic poet, and his skill is not designed to find favour with it. If he is to have a popular success, he must address himself to the fretful type with its rich variety of material for representation.

Obviously.

We have, then, a fair case against the poet and we may set him down as the counterpart of the painter, whom he resembles in two ways: his creations are poor things by the standard of truth and reality, and his appeal is not to the highest part of the soul, but to one which is equally inferior. So we shall be justified in not admitting him into a well-ordered commonwealth, because he stimulates and strengthens an element which threatens to undermine the reason. As a country may be given over into the power of its worst citizens while the better sort are ruined, so, we shall say, the dramatic poet sets up a vicious form of government in the individual soul: he gratifies that senseless part which cannot distinguish great and small, but regards the same things as now one, now the other; and he is an image-maker whose images are phantoms far removed from reality.

Quite true.

Plato, *Republic*

One final word on the paradox of the parable of the singer before we move on to the views of other philosophers. Plato feared that art would lead us away from reality, rather than toward it. Considering how famous Plato has become, how widely his works have been read and studied in both the West and the East, it is tempting to dismiss his fears as foolish. But the fact is that in a peculiar way, Plato's own success is evidence that he was right. Through the dramatic power of Plato's art, Socrates has become an immortal figure of Western thought. When we read the Dialogues today, all of us—students and trained philosophers alike—instinctively cast Socrates as the hero and his opponents as the villains of the drama. This encourages us to accept Socrates' (and Plato's) doctrines without properly criticizing them or evaluating them. In other words, we treat Socrates in exactly the way that the ancient Athenians treated Gorgias and the other popular speakers. We are swayed by Plato's art, rather than persuaded by his arguments. Now, Socrates took what we today would call a conservative political position, and his opponents—at least according to some scholars—were the "liberals" of their society. Strange as it may seem, many modern philosophers whose own political opinions are liberal still treat Socrates as the good guy and Gorgias or Protagoras or Thrasymachus or Callicles as the bad guys. In short, they are so beguiled by the beauty of Plato's song that they do not reflect, calmly and rationally, on its words. That is just the danger Plato saw and warned of when he banned the artists from his ideal Republic.

II

Plato was not yet thirty when Socrates died. Later in life, he founded a school or center for mathematical, cosmological, and philosophical investigation called the Academy. Far and away the most distinguished "student" at the Academy, if we can speak of students at all, was a man named Aristotle. There are many students of philosophy who consider Aristotle the greatest philosopher of all. St. Thomas Aquinas, the medieval theologian who figures so prominently in

ARISTOTLE (384–322 B.C.) is the most influential figure in the history of Western philosophy. Born in Stagira, a Greek colony on the Aegean Sea, he came to Athens as a very young man to study with Plato in the school known as the Academy. He remained a student and member of the Academy for twenty years, leaving only in 347 B.C. on Plato's death. Eventually, he founded his own school, where he lectured on a range of subjects so broad that he must have been virtually a one-man faculty. In addition to his major philosophical discoveries in the fields of logic, metaphysics, and the theory of knowledge, Aristotle did an enormous amount of empirical work on problems of astronomy, biology, comparative politics, and anatomy.

Aristotle is remembered today for his philosophy, but during his middle life, after leaving Plato's Academy and before founding his own school, he spent seven years as a tutor to the young prince who was to become Alexander the Great. Alexander, heir to the throne of Macedonia, eventually conquered the entire Greek world, and pushed his military campaigns as far east as India. Aristotle persuaded Alexander to send back biological specimens and other data from his explorations.

Although much of Aristotle's work has been surpassed by later investigators in the 2000 years and more since his death, some of his writings, particularly those in the areas of psychology and the theory of art, remain as suggestive and useful today as they were in ancient times.

the development of Catholic doctrine, had so high an opinion of Aristotle that he referred to him simply as "the philosopher," as if there were no other. When you think about it, the odds must be simply astronomical against such a sequence of teachers and students as Socrates, Plato, and Aristotle.

Aristotle was not at all gifted artistically as Plato was, though in his youth he tried his hand at writing some dialogues. His temperament was rather that of a scientist, and the writings which we have today by him are actually treatises or lecture notes for the teaching he did at the Academy. Because they were written for a specialized audience rather than for the general public, they are very condensed, rather dry, and sometimes hard to follow if you aren't already pretty well up on what Aristotle is talking about. The range of Aristotle's investigations was simply staggering. In addition to his great work in logic, he wrote on systematic comparative political science, moral philosophy, cosmology, psychology, biology, astronomy, and physics, and he even developed several proofs for the existence of a "prime mover," or God. In Athens at that time, the public theater was an important part of the religious and civic as well as cultural life of the people, and the annual performances of the tragedies written by the great Greek playwrights were a focus of public interest. Aristotle wrote a short treatise on the subject of tragedy. We know that little work today as *The Poetics,* and despite its brevity, it is much read and quoted, for it has had a wide and deep influence throughout the ages on philosophical theories about art.

For our purposes, Aristotle's treatise is interesting because of its defense of art against the twofold attack of his teacher, Plato. Recall the charge that Plato had leveled against poetry: it leads us away from truth, and it disorders the soul. Aristotle does not say a great deal about these two criticisms, but he indicates rebuttals to both. First of all, consider the claim that art misleads us by offering nothing more than imperfect copies of the world of the senses, which is itself no better than an imperfect copy or realization of the ideal standards of beauty, goodness, and justice which Plato calls the Forms or Ideas. If I want to know the true nature of a circle, I had better turn my eyes away from physical objects and reflect instead upon the pure definitions of mathematical forms. It is bad enough that my inadequate intelligence sometimes needs the aid of wheels, coins, and other imperfectly round objects which I encounter in life. I will simply stray farther from the truth if I fix my eyes on a picture of a wheel! The same is true for the knowledge of the human soul. True or ideal justice has never been achieved by a living man or woman, so I can learn very little about the eternal standard of justice through an examination of the lives of even the noblest men and women. What can a tragedian do, save conjure up for me on the stage an admittedly imperfect imitation of an admittedly imperfect character! I might as well try to get a feel for fine cowhide by looking at a photograph of imitation leather!

Not so, Aristotle replies. Plato is right in insisting that we should seek a knowledge of the unchanging, universal forms of justice. beauty, and goodness, but he is wrong in supposing that art merely provides us with imperfect copies of particular instances of those universal forms. Great artists have the ability, through their art, to grasp the universal that lies within the particular, and to present it to us in such a way that we achieve a greater knowledge than we would otherwise have. When Shakespeare creates for us the character of Hamlet (needless to say, this is my example, not Aristotle's), he shows us, through the particularities of the vacillations and inner conflicts of one young prince, some universal truths about fathers and sons, sons and mothers, intellect and will, thought and action. Plato to the contrary notwithstanding, we are wiser for seeing a performance of *Hamlet* than we would be were we to travel back in time and meet the real man on whom the play is based.

The dispute between Plato and Aristotle is partly a disagreement about art, of course, but it is, at a deeper level, a disagreement about metaphysics. Plato seems to have held that the universal, eternal, unchanging Forms actually exist independently of the particular, time-bound, changing objects and events which fitfully and inadequately embody them. (I say, "seems to have held," because this is a subject on which scholars differ among themselves.) In other words, Plato believed that there is a reality which transcends the appearances of the senses and the world of space, time, and physical things. True knowledge was for him, therefore, a rational understanding of that transcendent realm of universal Forms. Aristotle, on the other hand, held that the universal Forms were completely embodied in the particular things of the world of space and time. True knowledge did indeed consist of a grasp of those forms, and Plato was certainly right that we must penetrate the changing particularity of this and that moment or event in order to get at the universal truths. But because the universals were embodied in the particulars—because true circularity was to be found within actual circular things, true rationality within actual rational creatures, true beauty within actual works of art, our attention should be focused even more intently on those particular instances, rather than directed entirely away from them toward an independent realm of eternal Forms.

Aristotle's answer to Plato's second charge rests on a point of psychology rather than metaphysics. Plato was afraid that tragedy would arouse uncontrollable passions in the audience and thereby disarrange the proper harmony of the soul. It would weaken the ascendency of the rational forces within the personality and release erotic and aggressive elements that were destructive and deluding. Aristotle argued that just the opposite was the case. Since those harmful passions are present anyway, far better to release them in the controlled setting of the drama than to bottle them up entirely. In art, we experience those terrible feelings vicariously, through our identification with the characters in the play. When they suffer, triumph, love, hate, rage, and mourn, we in the audience do also. When the play ends, we are purged of the pent-up passions without having expressed them in the terrible deeds that the playwright has depicted on the stage. We leave the theater calmed, not aroused.

All this seems thin, bloodless, "academic" until we realize that exactly the same debate now rages in America about violence and sex in our movies and television shows. Does the portrayal of violence make our children more prone to act violently in their real lives, or does it drain away the violence that lies within all of us, giving it a safe, harmless outlet? Does sado-masochistic pornography stimulate its viewers to commit sex crimes, or does it divert passions which otherwise would lead to rape or mutilation?

The following brief selections from Aristotle's *Poetics* will give you some sense of his approach to the analysis and justification of art, but they will hardly settle such a host of difficult and controversial questions. In the remainder of this chapter, we shall take a look at a number of other conceptions of the nature and rationale of art. Perhaps somewhere in this debate you will find your own answer to Plato's question: Does art have a legitimate place in the good society?

From what we have said it will be seen that the poet's function is to describe, not the thing that has happened, but a kind of thing that might happen, i.e. what is possible as being probable or necessary. The distinction between historian and poet is not in the one writing prose and the other verse—you might put the work of Herodotus into verse, and it would still be a species of history; it consists really in this, that the one describes the thing that has been, and the other a kind of thing that might be. Hence poetry is something more philosophic and of graver import than history, since its statements are of the nature rather of universals, whereas those of history are singulars. . . .

. . . A tragedy, then, is the imitation of an action that is serious and also, as having magnitude, complete in itself; in language with pleasurable accessories, each kind brought in separately in the parts of the work; in a *dramatic*, not in a narrative *form;* with incidents arousing pity and fear, wherewith to accomplish its catharsis of such emotions. . . .

We assume that, for the finest form of Tragedy, the Plot must be not simple but complex; and further, that it must imitate actions arousing fear and pity, since that is the distinctive function of this kind of imitation. It follows, therefore, that there are three forms of Plot to be avoided. (1) A good man must not be seen passing from happiness to misery, or (2) a bad man from misery to happiness. The first situation is not fear-inspiring or piteous, but simply odious to us. The second is the most untragic that can be; it has no one of the requisites of Tragedy; it does not appeal either to the human feeling in us, or to our pity, or to our fears. Nor, on the other hand, should (3) an extremely bad man be seen falling from happiness into misery. Such a story may arouse the human feeling in us, but it will not move us to either pity or fear; pity is occasioned by undeserved misfortune, and fear by that of one like ourselves; so that there will be nothing either piteous or fear-inspiring in the situation. There remains, then, the intermediate kind of personage, a man not pre-eminently virtuous and just, whose misfortune, however, is brought upon him not by vice and depravity but by some error of judgement, of the number of those in the enjoyment of great reputation and prosperity; e.g. Oedipus, Thyestes, and the men of note of similar families. The perfect Plot, accordingly, must have a single, and not (as some tell us) a double issue; the change in the hero's fortunes must be not from misery to happiness, but on the contrary from happiness to misery; and the cause of it must lie not in any depravity, but in some great error on his part; the man himself being either such as we have described, or better, not worse, than that . . .

The tragic fear and pity may be aroused by the Spectacle; but they may also be aroused by the very structure and incidents of the play—which is the better way and shows the better poet. The Plot in fact should be so framed that, even without seeing the things take place, he who simply hears the account of them shall be filled with horror and pity at the incidents; which is just the effect that the mere recital of the story in *Oedipus* would have on one. To produce this same effect by means of the Spectacle is less artistic, and requires extraneous aid. Those, however, who make use of the Spectacle to put before us that which is merely monstrous and not productive of fear, are wholly out of touch with Tragedy; not every kind of pleasure should be required of a tragedy, but only its own proper pleasure.

The tragic pleasure is that of pity and fear, and the poet has to produce it by a work of imitation; it is clear, therefore, that the causes should be included in the incidents of his story. Let us see, then, what kinds of incident strike one as horrible, or rather as piteous. In a deed of this description the parties must necessarily be either friends, or enemies, or indifferent to one another. Now when enemy does it on enemy, there is nothing to move us to pity either in his doing or in his meditating the deed, except so far as the actual pain of the sufferer is concerned; and the same is true when the parties are indifferent to one another. Whenever the tragic deed, however, is done within the family—when murder or the like is done or meditated by brother on brother, by son on father, by mother on son, or son on mother—these are the situations the poet should seek after.

ARISTOTLE, *Poetics*

III

Plato claims that art is harmful, both intellectually and emotionally. Aristotle replies that art teaches and purges, that it aids us in acquiring knowledge of universal truths and in maintaining the proper internal order of our psyches. Though they seem to disagree fundamentally, nevertheless they are united in believing that art should be judged according to the positive or negative value of its effects on us. Most philosophers who have reflected on the value of art have judged it in this way, as useful or harmful for some purpose. But one group of defenders of art, repelled by the merely instrumental conception of art, developed the view that art needs no justification outside itself, that art should be encouraged, valued, cherished for itself alone. The slogan of this group, who lived and wrote in the nineteenth century, was "art for art's sake," and before going on to several of the more prominent philosophical defenses of art, it might be interesting to spend a few moments looking at the "art for art's sake" doctrine.

The central notion that we need here is a distinction, long current in philosophy, between what is sometimes called *instrumental value* and *intrinsic value.* Human beings are purposive creatures. They have goals or ends or purposes which they pursue by choosing what seem to them to be appropriate means. (As you know, Michael Oakeshott dissents from this view of human action. There probably isn't any statement ever made, and certainly not an interesting or important statement, which every philosopher would agree to—not even the statement that philosophy is a worthwhile enterprise!) Very often, when we describe something as valuable, or useful, or good, we simply mean that it is especially helpful to us in achieving some purpose or getting to some goal that we have. If I call a car a good car, I probably mean that it runs smoothly, or rarely breaks down, or uses relatively little gas. In short, I mean that it is a useful means or *instrument* for doing what I want to do, which may be to get somewhere fast, or safely, or cheaply, or reliably. If I say that a good education is the most valuable gift that parents can give their child, I probably mean that in the modern world, a good education will be more useful to that child in achieving his or her goals than anything else. Someone who replies that strong character is even more valuable than a good education will probably mean that certain strengths of personality turn out to make more difference in the adult world than formal book learning or credits and degrees.

A good car is good *for* doing something; an education is valuable as a means *to* something; character will be a source of strength *for* some end. All these, and countless other things besides, are valuable as means or instruments, which is to say that they have *instrumental value.* Now, if you stop and think about it for a moment, it should be obvious that you will never consider something valuable *as a means* unless there is something else that you consider just plain valuable in itself. If there is nothing you want for *itself,* nothing you like or desire or consider worthy *in and of itself,* then it would make no sense to value other things simply as "useful." Suppose for example that you are quite happy right where you are, and have no desire whatsoever to go anywhere else. A friend comes along and says, "Now that road there is a really great road. You ought to take a ride down it." You say, "Why should I take a ride down it? I don't want to go where it leads." And she answers, "It doesn't matter! It is such a great road, you ought to take it anyway." Well, your friend is either joking, or she is crazy. As the old saying goes, a bargain isn't a bargain unless it is a bargain for you. And a road isn't a good road for you unless it is a good road to somewhere you want to go.

Or you might go into a hardware store to buy a hammer so that you can hang some pictures. But even if the store has nothing better than a mediocre hammer and a really great sale on saws, the sensible thing to do is to buy the hammer. You don't want "a good tool." You want a tool that is *good for* whatever you want to do, which in this case is to hang some pictures.

By contrast, things which are good in themselves, rather than being good for something else, are said to have *intrinsic value.* That simply means that their merit, value, goodness, or whatever is possessed by them independently of anything else in the world. One way to make this point about something that has intrinsic value is to say that it would be valuable even if nothing else in the world existed. A road has only instrumental value, for if there were nothing in the world but that road—and in particular, if there were noplace at the other end of it—who would value it as a road? Similarly, if there were no nails, no pictures to hang, nothing to hit, who would value a hammer? But when something has intrinsic value, it retains that value even in the absence of other objects, places, events, or states of affairs with regard to which it might be useful.

Is there anything at all that has intrinsic value? Well, we might argue that unless *something* has intrinsic value, then nothing has instrumental value. If one thing is useful for getting another, and that other is not valuable in itself, but simply useful for getting a third thing, and so on and on, we get into what is sometimes called "an infinite regress." It is like the ancient Hindu theory that the world rests on the back of an elephant, which stands on the back of a giant sea turtle, which swims in an enormous ocean. The obvious question is, what is the ocean in? So something must have intrinsic value, if anything is to have any sort of value at all.

OSCAR WILDE (1854–1900) was a brilliant Irish playwright and novelist whose super-aesthetic mannerisms typified the movement known as "art-for-art's sake." He wrote *The Picture of Dorian Gray*, which was made many years later into a truly scary horror film, and the much-revived play *The Importance of Being Earnest*. In Gilbert and Sullivan's delightful light opera, *Patience*, the character of Bunthorne is a take-off on Wilde.

We have already encountered two philosophical candidates for the title of things having intrinsic value, although we didn't use that language when we met them. Immanuel Kant said that humanity is an end in itself, and that is another way of claiming that *humanity* has intrinsic value. And Jeremy Bentham said that the only good thing is *pleasure,* by which he obviously meant that pleasure was the only thing that is intrinsically valuable. In the nineteenth century, Walter Pater, Clive Bell, and Oscar Wilde, all of them British, argued that art has intrinsic value, that it is valuable in and of itself. Wilde carried this view to such lengths that he ended by reversing the usual order of priority between life and art. Instead of saying, as most philosophers have, that art is valuable insofar as it contributes to life, Wilde argued that life acquired value by contributing to art! In this selection from his book, *Intentions,* Wilde summarizes his doctrine. Incidentally, Wilde was a gifted and successful playwright, as well as a thoughtful philosopher of art. You probably know the old joke that those who can, do, and those who can't, teach. Sometimes a third line is added: and those who cannot even teach, philosophize. But in this chapter, most of the philosophers we read are also able practitioners of some form of artistic creation.

CYRIL . . . But in order to avoid making any error I want you to tell me briefly the doctrines of the new aesthetics.

VIVIAN.   Briefly, then, they are these. Art never expresses anything but itself. It has an independent life, just as Thought has, and develops purely on its own lines. It is not necessarily realistic in an age of realism, nor spiritual in an age of faith. So far from being the creation of its time, it is usually in direct opposition to it, and the only history that it preserves for us is the history of its own progress. Sometimes it returns upon its footsteps, and revives some antique form, as happened in the archaistic movement of late Greek Art, and in the pre-Raphaelite movement of our own day. At other times it entirely anticipates its age, and produces in one century work that it takes another century to understand, to appreciate and to enjoy. In no case does it reproduce its age. To pass from the art of a time to the time itself is the great mistake that all historians commit.

The second doctrine is this. All bad art comes from returning to Life and Nature, and elevating them into ideals. Life and Nature may sometimes be used as part of Art's rough material, but before they are of any real service to art they must be translated into artistic conventions. The moment Art surrenders its imaginative medium it surrenders everything. As a method Realism is a complete failure, and the two things that every artist should avoid are modernity of form and modernity of subject-matter. To us, who live in the nineteenth century, any century is a suitable subject for art except our own. The only beautiful things are the things that do not concern us. It is, to have the pleasure of quoting myself, exactly because Hecuba is nothing to us that her sorrows are so suitable a motive for a tragedy. Besides, it is only the modern that ever becomes old-fashioned. M. Zola sits down to give us a picture of the Second Empire. Who cares for the Second Empire now? It is out of date. Life goes faster than Realism, but Romanticism is always in front of Life.

The third doctrine is that Life imitates Art far more than Art imitates Life. This results not merely from Life's imitative instinct, but from the fact that the self-conscious aim of Life is to find expression, and that Art offers it certain beautiful forms through which it may realise that energy. It is a theory that has never been put forward before, but it is extremely fruitful, and throws an entirely new light upon the history of Art.

It follows, as a corollary from this, that external Nature also imitates Art. The only effects that she can show us are effects that we have already seen through poetry, or in paintings. This is the secret of Nature's charm, as well as the explanation of Nature's weakness.

The final revelation is that Lying, the telling of beautiful untrue things, is the proper aim of Art. But of this I think I have spoken at sufficient length. And now let us go out on the terrace, where "droops the milk-white peacock like a ghost," while the evening star "washes the dusk with silver." At twilight nature becomes a wonderfully suggestive effect, and is not without loveliness, though perhaps its chief use is to illustrate quotations from the poets. Come! We have talked long enough.

OSCAR WILDE, *Intentions*

IV

The most powerful and influential aesthetic movement of the past several centuries, both in England and on the continent of Europe, is undoubtedly romanticism. In the late eighteenth century, poets, painters, and philosophers of art rebelled against the style and tenets of the neo-classicism which had until then dominated the theory and practice of art. Neo-classicism exalted order, proportion, reason, and the subordination of the creative artist to objective principles of aesthetic taste. In England especially, neo-classicism looked back to the calm gravity of the art and language of the great period of Roman culture known—after the emperor Caesar Augustus—as the Augustan Age. The English romantic poets overturned all of the entrenched tenets of neo-classical art, and in doing so carried out a revolution whose effects are still being felt today even beyond the confines of the world of art and literature.

The key to the romantic rebellion was two reversals or denials of the traditional doctrine. First, the romantics denied the supremacy of *reason* in art and life. Instead, they insisted that the power of creative *imagination* was the highest human faculty. From Plato on, philosophers and students of art had insisted that reason is our primary organ of knowledge, our source for whatever truth we can attain. The romantics granted the power of reason to accumulate knowledge of the ordinary, or work-a-day sort. But for deep insight into the inner being of humanity and nature, for a grasp of that eternal, unchanging realm beyond the world of the senses, artistic imagination was necessary.

The second reversal was the substitution of the subjective for the objective as the test and source of true knowledge. Philosophers traditionally had dismissed the subjective, the particular, the individual, as lacking in value or cognitive significance. What mathematics or philosophy or science could validate as universally and objectively true, independently of the momentary subjective state of the individual investigator, could be accepted as established. But the intense fleeting feeling of the lone artist could not possibly serve as a conduit of important truth. The romantics turned this traditional view on its head. They insisted that the most intense and momentary emotional states of the most extraordinary individuals were our glimpse of the infinite, our window on eternity.

Plato was suspicious of poets and the poetic impulse, because he believed that the act of artistic creation had more than a touch of madness about it. Poets were, in popular Greek opinion, possessed by the gods, and certainly their moments of inspiration bore little resemblance to the quiet rational progress of dialectical philosophical argument. Art, Plato said, could not put us in touch with the eternal because it was irrational. The romantics turned Plato completely around, and asserted that art *could* put us in touch with the eternal precisely *because* it was ecstatic, subjective, emotionally intense, and in that sense irrational. The great irony of the romantics is that they considered themselves neo-Platonists!

One of the finest statements of the romantic philosophy is, as you might expect, a poem, namely the ode by William Wordsworth entitled "Intimations of Immortality from Recollections of Early Childhood." I would have liked to use it as our selection, but since this is a philosophy text, I have instead selected a portion of the preface which Wordsworth wrote for a book of verse entitled *Lyrical Ballads.* Ask your English teacher to read Wordsworth's ode with you.

. . . All good poetry is the spontaneous overflow of powerful feelings: and though this be true, Poems to which any value can be attached were never produced on any variety of subjects but by a man who, being possessed of more than usual organic sensibility, had also thought long and deeply. For our continued influxes

Frederick Chopin, pianist and composer of the romantic era, painted in the romantic style by Eugene Delacroix.

WILLIAM WORDSWORTH (1770–1850) was one of the leading poets of the English romantic movement. In his youth, he traveled to France, and became an enthusiastic supporter of the revolution. After fathering an illegitimate child by a French woman, Marie Anne Vallen, he returned to England and eventually settled in Somerset, near Samuel Coleridge. During the last years of the old century and the first years of the new, Coleridge and Wordsworth wrote a series of poems, entitled *Lyrical Ballads,* which remain among the classic works of romanticism.

In middle life, Wordsworth turned against the liberal views of his youth, and became increasingly conservative. He continued to write poetry throughout his lifetime, but never achieved the heights of his early work. In 1843, he was named Poet Laureate of England, succeeding Robert Southey.

of feelings are modified and directed by our thoughts, which are indeed the representatives of all our past feelings; and, as by contemplating the relation of these general representatives to each other, we discover what is really important to men, so, by the repetition and continuance of this act, our feelings will be connected with important subjects, till at length, if we be originally possessed of much sensibility, such habits of mind will be produced, that, by obeying blindly and mechanically the impulses of those habits, we shall describe objects, and utter sentiments, of such a nature, and in such connexion with each other, that the understanding of the Reader must necessarily be in some degree enlightened, and his affections strengthened and purified. . . .

However exalted a notion we would wish to cherish of the character of a Poet, it is obvious, that while he describes and imitates passions, his employment is in some degree mechanical, compared with the freedom and power of real and substantial action and suffering. So that it will be the wish of the Poet to bring his feelings near to those of the persons whose feelings he describes, nay for short spaces of time, perhaps, to let himself slip into an entire delusion, and even confound and identify his own feelings with theirs; modifying only the language which is thus suggested to him by a consideration that he describes for a particular purpose, that of giving pleasure. Here, then, he will apply the principle of selection which has been already insisted upon. He will depend upon this for removing what would otherwise be painful or disgusting in the passion; he will feel that there is no necessity to trick out or to elevate nature: and, the more industriously he applies this principle, the deeper will be his faith that no words, which *his* fancy or imagination can suggest, will be to be compared with those which are the emanations of reality and truth.

But it may be said by those who do not object to the general spirit of these remarks, that, as it is impossible for the Poet to produce upon all occasions language as exquisitely fitted for the passion as that which the real passion itself suggests, it is proper that he should consider himself as in the situation of a translator, who does not scruple to substitute excellencies of another kind for those which are unattainable by him; and endeavours occasionally to surpass his original, in order to make some amends for the general inferiority to which he feels that he must submit. But this would be to encourage idleness and unmanly despair. Further, it is the language of men who speak of what they do not understand; who talk of Poetry as of a matter of amusement and idle pleasure; who will converse with us as gravely about a *taste* for Poetry, as they express it, as if it were a thing as indifferent as a taste for rope-dancing, or Frontiniac or Sherry. Aristotle, I have been told, has said, that Poetry is the most philosophic of all writing: it is so: its object is truth, not individual and local, but general, and operative; not standing upon external testimony, but carried alive into the heart by passion; truth which is its own testimony, which gives competence and confidence to the tribunal to which it appeals, and receives them from the same tribunal. Poetry is the image of man and nature. The obstacles which stand in the way of the fidelity of the Biographer and Historian, and of their consequent utility, are incalculably greater than those which are to be encountered by the Poet who comprehends the dignity of his art. The Poet writes under one restriction only, namely, the necessity of giving immediate pleasure to a human Being possessed of that information which may be expected from him, not as a lawyer, a physician, a mariner, an astronomer, or a natural philosopher, but as a Man. Except this one restriction, there is no object standing between the Poet and the image of things; between this, and the Biographer and Historian, there are a thousand.

WILLIAM WORDSWORTH, *Preface to the Lyrical Ballads*

V

The romantics follow Plato, Aristotle, and most other philosophers of art in assigning instrumental value to art, but their conception of its instrumentality leads them to emphasize the unusual rather than the ordinary, the outstanding rather than the commonplace. The characteristic romantic image of the artist is the gifted, tortured genius, alone in his garret, unappreciated by the multitudes but nevertheless tearing great works of art quivering from his breast.

Just about the most completely opposite conception of art and the artist was put forward by another great literary figure, the Russian novelist Leo Tolstoy. You have all heard of Tolstoy's immortal novel, *War and Peace,* though in all likelihood very few of you have plowed your way through that immensely long book. Tolstoy is an extraordinary figure in literature and philosophy. He was born, in 1828, into the Russian aristocracy, and served in the army as a young man. When he was only thirty-eight he published *War and Peace,* his great novel of Russian life and thought during the period of the Napoleonic

Wars. Some time later, he underwent a deep religious conversion, and adopted a life of poverty and peasant simplicity. Out of his conversion emerged a new, simplified Christian faith and a rejection of the cultivated aesthetic sensibilities which he himself had contributed to in his earlier writings. Thirty years after the publication of *War and Peace,* in 1896, Tolstoy gave formal philosophical expression to his new conception of art and life in an essay entitled *What Is Art?*

COUNT LEO TOLSTOY (1828–1910) is one of the immortal geniuses of European literature. He and Feodor Dostoyevsky have, in their novels, given us matchless pictures of Russian life in the nineteenth century. In his youth, Tolstoy served in the Czar's army, seeing action as the commander of a battery in the Crimean War (1854–56). He retired to his family's estates, and began his career as a writer. His masterpiece, *War and Peace,* was published in 1866. It is a panoramic story of Russian life and thought during the great struggle of Russia against Napoleon.

In 1876, Tolstoy underwent a profound spiritual conversion to a form of Russian Orthodox Christianity that emphasized the virtues of the simple life and hard, physical labor. He worked alongside the peasants in the fields of his estates, while continuing to write novels and essays. Among the works of this later period in his life are *Anna Karenina,* which was begun before his conversion and completed in 1877; *The Death of Ivan Ilyich;* and the essay on the nature of art from which the selection in this book is taken.

Tolstoy argues that there are two basic means by which human beings communicate with one another. The first is speech, by which men and women communicate their *thoughts;* the second is art, by which they communicate their *feelings.* Each of us has the capacity to communicate feelings by arousing them in others. We not only tell our listeners that we are sad, we actually arouse feelings of sadness in them, sometimes by reporting what it is that has made us sad, sometimes by the tone of our voice, sometimes by looks, gestures, or other means of expression. Feelings are infectious. When one person laughs, others laugh too. When one cries, others cry. Tolstoy describes art in this way:

> To evoke in oneself a feeling one has experienced, and having evoked it in oneself, then, by means of movements, lines, colors, sounds, or forms expressed in words, so to transmit that feeling that others may experience the same feeling—this is the activity of art.

Art is a human activity consisting in this, that one man consciously, by means of certain external signs, hands on to others feelings he has lived through, and that other people are infected by these feelings and also experience them.

The stronger the degree of infectiousness of art, the better the art is, Tolstoy maintains. And the fundamental source of infectiousness—the quality in the artist which enables him or her to spark a contagion of feeling in the audience— is not reason nor imaginative brilliance, nor metaphysical insight, nor extraordinary creativity, but simply *sincerity*. Honesty of feeling is directly apprehended and responded to by an artist's audience.

Folk art.

So far as the content of the work of art is concerned, Tolstoy—as you might expect—turns the usual canons of aesthetic judgment upside down. Common subjects are best, for they will enable the artist to reach the largest audience. The purpose of art (Tolstoy is an instrumentalist, remember) is to unite humanity through shared feeling. Art that relies on specialized knowledge or highly refined taste will exclude rather than include, divide rather than unite. If a work of art is so specialized that men and women can respond to it emotionally only after long training and cultivation, then it will mark off the few from the many and place obstacles in the way of a union of all humanity.

If sincerity and universality of emotional appeal are the criteria of greatness

High art.

in art, then obviously some so-called artistic "masterpieces" are going to get pretty low marks. Sure enough, Tolstoy downgrades some of the works of music, literature, and painting that had been held up for generations as perfect examples of great art, and in their place offers peasant stories, folk music, and other arts of the common people.

There is one last element in Tolstoy's aesthetic theory which we have not yet mentioned—namely, the *religious* dimension of art. In the following selection from *What Is Art?*, Tolstoy draws upon his analysis of art as a means for the communication of feeling and as an instrument for uniting human beings in a universal community, in order to lay the foundations for a religious justification of art.

In every period of history, and in every human society, there exists an understanding of the meaning of life which represents the highest level to which men of that society have attained, an understanding defining the highest good at which that society aims. And this understanding is the religious perception of the given time and society. And this religious perception is always clearly expressed by some advanced men, and more or less vividly perceived by all the members of the society. Such a religious perception and its corresponding expression exists always in every society. If it appears to us that in our society there is no religious perception, this is not because there really is none, but only because we do not want to see it. And we often wish not to see it because it exposes the fact that our life is inconsistent with that religious perception.

Religious perception in a society is like the direction of a flowing river. If the river flows at all, it must have a direction. If society lives, there must be a religious perception indicating the direction in which, more or less consciously, all its members tend. . . .

I know that according to an opinion current in our times religion is a superstition which humanity has outgrown, and that it is therefore assumed that no such thing exists as a religious perception, common to us all, by which art, in our time, can be evaluated. I know that this is the opinion current in the pseudo-cultured circles of today. People who do not acknowledge Christianity in its true meaning because it undermines all their social privileges, and who, therefore, invent all kinds of philosophic and aesthetic theories to hide from themselves the meaninglessness and wrongness of their lives, cannot think otherwise. These people intentionally, or sometimes unintentionally, confusing the conception of a religious perception think that by denying the cult they get rid of religious perception. But even the very attacks on religion and the attempts to establish a life-conception contrary to the religious perception of our times most clearly demonstrate the existence of a religious perception condemning the lives that are not in harmony with it.

If humanity progresses, i.e., moves forward, there must inevitably be a guide to the direction of that movement. And religions have always furnished that guide. All history shows that the progress of humanity is accomplished not otherwise than under the guidance of religion. But if the race cannot progress without the guidance of religion—and progress is always going on, and consequently also in our own times—then there must be a religion of our times. So that, whether it pleases or displeases the so-called cultured people of today, they must admit the existence of religion—not of a religious cult, Catholic, Protestant, or another, but of religious perception—which, even in our times, is the guide always present where there is any progress. And if a religious perception exists among us, then our art should be appraised on the basis of that religious perception; and, as has always and everywhere been the case, art transmitting feelings flowing from the religious perception of our time should be chosen from all the indifferent art, should be acknowledged, highly esteemed, and encouraged, while art running counter to that perception should be condemned and despised, and all the remaining indifferent art should neither be distinguished nor encouraged. . . .

Christian art, i.e., the art of our time, should be catholic in the original meaning of the word, i.e., universal, and therefore it should unite all men. And only two kinds of feeling do unite all men: first, feelings flowing from the perception of our sonship to God and of the brotherhood of man; and next, the simple feelings of common life, accessible to every one without exception—such as the feeling of merriment, of pity, of cheerfulness, of tranquillity, etc. Only these two kinds of feelings can now supply material for art good in its subject matter. . . .

Beethoven's *Ninth Symphony* is considered a great work of art. To verify its claim to be such, I must first ask myself whether this work transmits the highest religious feeling. I reply in the negative, for music in itself cannot transmit those feelings; and therefore I ask myself next, Since this work does not belong to the highest kind of religious art, has it the other characteristic of the good art of our time—the quality of uniting all men in one common feeling: does it rank as Christian universal art? And again I have no option but to reply in the negative; for not only do I not see how the feelings transmitted by this work could unite people not specially trained to submit themselves to its complex hypnotism, but I am unable to imagine to myself a crowd of normal people who could understand anything of this long, confused, and artificial production, except short snatches which are lost in a sea of what is incomprehensible. And therefore, whether I like it or not, I am compelled to conclude that this work belongs to the rank of bad art. It is curious to note in this connection that attached to the end of this very symphony is a poem of Schiller's which (though somewhat obscurely) expresses this very thought, namely, that feeling (Schiller speaks only of the feeling of gladness) unites people and evokes love in them. But though this poem is sung at the end of the symphony, the music does not accord with the thought expressed in the verses; for the music is exclusive and does not unite all men, but unites only a few, dividing them off from the rest of mankind.

And just in this same way, in all branches of art, many and many works considered great by the upper classes of our society will have to be judged. By this one sure criterion we shall have to judge the celebrated *Divine Comedy* and *Jerusalem Delivered,* and a great part of Shakespeare's and Goethe's works, and in painting every representation of miracles, including Raphael's *Transfiguration,* etc.

Whatever the work may be and however it may have been extolled, we have first to ask whether this work is one of real art or a counterfeit. Having acknowledged, on the basis of the indication of its infectiousness even to a small class of people, that a certain production belongs to the realm of art, it is necessary, on the basis of the indication of its accessibility, to decide the next question. Does this work belong to the category of bad, exclusive art, opposed to religious perception, or to Christian art uniting people? And having acknowledged an article to belong to real Christian art, we must then, according to whether it transmits the feelings flowing from love to God and man, or merely the simple feelings uniting all men, assign it a place in the ranks of religious art or in those of universal art.

Only on the basis of such verification shall we find it possible to select from the whole mass of what in our society claims to be art those works which form real, important, necessary spiritual food, and to separate them from all the harmful and useless art and from the counterfeits of art which surround us. Only on the basis of such verification shall we be able to rid ourselves of the pernicious results of harmful art and to avail ourselves of that beneficent action which is the purpose of true and good art and which is indispensable for the spiritual life of man and of humanity.

LEO TOLSTOY, *What Is Art?*

VI

Plato says that art is negative, disruptive, antirational, and therefore that it ought to be banned from the good society. Aristotle, Wordsworth, and Tolstoy all in their different ways say that good art is positive, constructive, and ought to play an important role in social life. Wilde, Bell, and the art-for-art's-sake movement insist that art is intrinsically rather than instrumentally valuable, and therefore deserves a central place in human life regardless of its consequences.

You might think that we had exhausted the possibilities so far as the function of art is concerned, but our last theory of art puts these elements together in a startling, apparently contradictory way. Herbert Marcuse argues that great art is negative, destructive, irrational, and *therefore* is a valuable element in human life! Why on earth would anyone praise art for having precisely the qualities that other philosophers have considered worthy of condemnation? To put the question in its most paradoxical form, what is positive about being negative?

HERBERT MARCUSE (1889–1979) was born in Berlin. He was one of the original members of the famous Frankfurt School of Social Research which flourished in Germany in the years before World War Two. After fleeing to the United States to escape the Nazis, Marcuse became a major voice on the left. During the 1960s, he was the most widely quoted radical critic of American capitalist society. His best-known books include *Eros and Civilization* and *One-Dimensional Man*.

Marcuse begins his argument with a puzzle that doesn't at first seem to have anything to do with art. Why is it that the most dramatic, outrageous, powerful words and ideas so rapidly become domesticated and acceptable in America today, *without changing anything along the way?* Radicals call America imperialist, and decent people everywhere are horrified. Several years later, Senator J. William Fulbright refers in passing to America's imperialist foreign policy on a television interview program and none of the newsmen thinks it worth commenting on. Black militants shout "Power to the people!" and "nice folks" cringe in their beds. Next season, "Power to the people!" is a liberal Democratic campaign slogan, and soon thereafter a Richard Nixon campaign promise. Avant-garde artists violate every canon of artistic sensibility in a last-ditch effort to repudiate the plastic culture of Madison Avenue capitalism, and Madison Avenue reproduces their most outrageous productions as decorations for its advertisements. Woodstock begins as a cry of protest against middle America, and ends as the name of a bird in *Peanuts.* How can this be? Is nothing sacrilegious? Can modern American society absorb anything into itself without changing? Must every protest turn into this year's fad and next year's ancient history?

To answer these questions, Marcuse draws on the psychological theory of the origins of the ego and of civilization which Sigmund Freud set forth in *Civilization and its Discontents,* and which Marcuse revised and developed in *Eros and Civilization.* Freud argued that the objective, "un-get-over-able" constraints of the real world force each infant to, as he put it, substitute the reality principle for the pleasure principle. Because the physical world just won't always fit itself to our desires, and also because we all inevitably get into interpersonal conflicts, particularly those fueled by sexual desire, we are forced to regulate or deny entirely some of our strongest desires. The psychic means for the regulation, Freud suggested, are repression, sublimation, and fantasy, of which repression is the first and most important. Thus is generated the realm of the "unconscious," populated by wishes, impulses, desires, loves, and hatreds which cannot be expressed and acted out in the real world. Civilization itself, our organized collective life, rests upon a foundation of repression, for not even the most miraculous technical wonders or the most flexible social arrangements can gratify the infantile wishes that lie beneath the conscious surface in every adult man and woman.

Two features of the content and structure of the unconscious are crucial to Marcuse's analysis. First, the unconscious is timeless. The thwarted desires and fears which reside there retain their power across decades of real-world time, returning again and again irrespective of changes in the world which originally thwarted them. A mother who loses her child grieves, mourns, and eventually becomes reconciled to the loss. Time heals her wounds, and the objective passage of events places the loss further and further behind her. The child whose mother dies before he or she can cope with the loss may repress the grief and anger, so that half a century later, the anger at the mother's desertion will recur as strongly, albeit in transmuted forms. In particular, all of us carry with us unrelinquished infantile desires for the sorts of total, immediate, ecstatic satisfaction which as tiny babies we imagined we could, in our omnipotence, command.

Second, the content of the unconscious has a thoroughly ambivalent character. In the unconscious is to be found everything that reality (either natural or social) has decreed to be bad, inefficient, worthless, dirty, ugly, hostile, shameful. But the wishes and desires that fill the unconscious retain their power, even though they have been denied fulfillment. Part of the self—the part that identifies with society, reality, adulthood, and the world—hates, loathes, feels shame for what is repressed. That is the part of the self that cannot acknowledge a fascination with its own feces, or sexual desire for objects deemed socially inappropriate, or laziness, or messiness, or the urge to inflict pain and suffering. But another part of the self secretly delights in the content of the repressed. And what is more, it delights in the repressed *because* it is repressed. So we have the men and women who can only enjoy illicit sex; or, rather less dramatically, we find the familiar folk-character of the perpetual child who refuses to grow up—Pan, Til Eulenspiegel, Peter Pan.

Marcuse accepts Freud's fundamental claim that repression is essential to civilization. But in a brilliant deployment of one of Marx's key notions, he revises Freud's theory of repression by introducing a distinction between necessary repression and surplus repression. Necessary repression is simply that kind and amount of repression that is required at any stage of social development in order to carry on the struggle for existence. It involves, for example, denying ourselves part of the harvest even when we are hungry so that we have seed for the next planting; it involves forcing ourselves to continue laboring at painful tasks because of our rational recognition that hunger, disease, danger, and death may result if we let up too soon. But some repression, Marcuse argues, is not required by the objective constraints of reality. Rather, it is required by the specific system of domination and submission that exists in society at that moment in history. In short, some repression serves only to protect the favored position of the rulers by restraining the subjects from rising up and overthrowing their masters. That repression is "surplus repression," and human progress consists in eliminating surplus repression while simultaneously decreasing the amount of necessary repression through technological advance. Indeed, Marcuse argues, at a time when our technology should permit us considerably to relax the bonds of necessary repression, through the shortening and lightening of the workday, through the relaxation of work discipline, and so forth, surplus repression grows greater and greater so that the total burden of repression suffered in modern industrial society is not appreciably lighter than that suffered in technically less advanced societies. The purpose of that ever-increasing sector of surplus repression is, Marcuse claims, to maintain the ever more manifestly unjustifiable dominance of the ruling sectors of our society.

The concept of surplus repression is one of those brilliant insights which are too often rejected by hard-headed social scientists because they prove difficult to quantify or operationalize. How would we measure the relative proportions of necessary and surplus repression in an individual psyche? Indeed, how could we ever show of a single instance of repression that it was unnecessary, and hence surplus? I don't know the answer to these questions, but I remain convinced that Marcuse has his finger on a fundamental fact here, and that to the extent that it is fuzzy or imprecise, we should struggle to clarify it rather than use the unclarity as an excuse for rejecting it.

Now, with the notion of surplus repression, and the theory of the unconscious, we can sketch Marcuse's theory of the function of negative thinking and thereby approach his analysis of the function of art. Briefly, his position is this: The repressed content of the unconscious in all of us exists as a permanent psychic pool or source of opposition to the established order of society. We all construct powerful defenses against this repressed content within ourselves, using such familiar mechanisms as denial, projection, and transference. When a rebellious member of society violates some taboo, by uncovering a part of the body that is supposed to be concealed, or by using, in public, language that is supposed only to be used in private, or by defying canons of dress, decorum, or deference, he or she provokes a response that is exaggerated all out of proportion. The rest of us recoil from the temporary and perhaps insignificant breach of the rules of repression because it provokes the ever-present desire within us to liberate ourselves from the same rules, and we can control that desire only by clamping down on the transgressor. A struggle over bare nipples or long hair or even an insolent, slouching way of standing becomes a struggle between the repressed content and the forces of civilization.

If all the actual repression were necessary repression, then it would be clear that the rebel should be contained, however sympathetically we might acknowledge that he or she speaks for a part of each of us. Marcuse's claim, however, is precisely that not all of the repression is necessary, that some of it is surplus, unnecessary, and that in the interest of human happiness it ought to be eliminated. But—and this is the key to his entire theory, so far as I can see—in order to generate sufficient emotional energy in enough people to conquer the surplus repression inflicted by our society, it is necessary to tap the ubiquitous, irrational, infantile desire for a release from all repression. To put it bluntly, you must promise people an impossible liberation from necessary repression in order to get them to struggle for the elimination of the merely surplus repression. To get us to the barricades, it is not enough to say, "Workers of the world, unite! After the revolution you shall suffer only necessary repression." Instead, you must say, "Workers of the world, unite! After the revolution you shall be free." And each projects his or her own fantasy of absolute freedom, a daydream both inevitable and unfulfillable.

The revolutionary role of negative, oppositional styles of artistic expression is precisely to tap the reservoir of repressed desires, to draw on the permanent opposition within us to necessary repression, and thereby to fuel the fight against surplus repression. The artist's image of liberation is necessary, and illusory. The particular content of the rebellion against the established order of aesthetic canons is not crucial. In one social setting, the expletive "damn" will have as much effect as total nudity in another. The point is that no matter what is permitted, there remains both a repressed content that is denied and a longing to express it that can be tapped. The fight always appears to be about the particular artistic rule that has been broken, but it is always really about the existence of repression itself. If the rebellion is successful, surplus repression is reduced, but that success is always perceived as a failure by the participants themselves, because they must sooner or later relinquish their fantasy of total liberation.

The social function of art is thus to keep alive the possibility of what Marcuse calls "transcendence." By transcendence, he does not mean, as Plato or Wordsworth might, the passing from this world of space, time, and objects to a higher, eternal realm of forms or ideal entities. Rather, he means the imaginative leap beyond the given social world, with its repressions, oppressions, and reality-oriented sacrifices, to the conception of possible future social orders in which some of the repressed libidinal energy has been liberated. In thus adding a second "dimension" to our existence, Marcuse claims, art helps us to escape the one-dimensionality of present society. But it is not art's job to draw us blueprints of the future. It must simply keep alive those repressed dreams of liberation and gratification whose energies, blocked but not diminished, will fuel the revolutions that reduce surplus repression and bring us closer to conditions of genuine human happiness.

In this last selection of the chapter, we listen to Marcuse talking about the "negative" function of great art. Despite the difficulty of his philosophical language, I think you will be able to see here some of the themes I have been discussing in the last few pages.

> The achievements and the failures of this society invalidate its higher culture. The celebration of the autonomous personality, of humanism, of tragic and romantic love appears to be the ideal of a backward stage of the development. What is happening now is not the deterioration of higher culture into mass culture but the refutation of this culture by the reality. The reality surpasses its culture. Man today can do *more* than the culture heros and half-gods; he has solved many insoluble problems. But he has also betrayed the hope and destroyed the truth which were perserved in the sublimations of higher culture. To be sure, the higher culture was always in contradiction with social reality, and only a privileged minority enjoyed its blessings and represented its ideals. The two antagonistic spears of society have always coexisted; the higher culture has always been accommodating, while the reality was rarely disturbed by its ideals and its truth.
>
> Today's novel feature is the flattening out of the antagonism between culture and social reality through the obliteration of the oppositional, alien, and transcendent elements in the higher culture by virtue of which it constituted *another dimension* of reality. This liquidation of *two-dimensional* culture takes place not through the denial and rejection of the "cultural values," but through their wholesale incorporation into the established order, through their reproduction and display on a massive scale.
>
> In contrast to the Marxian concept, which denotes man's relation to himself and to his work in capitalist society, the *artistic alienation* is the conscious transcendence of the alienated existence—a "higher level" or mediated alienation. The conflict with the world of progress, the negation of the order of business, the anti-bourgeois elements in bourgeois literature and art are neither due to the aesthetic lowliness of this order nor to romantic reaction—nostalgic consecration of a disappearing stage of civilization. "Romantic" is a term of condescending defamation which is easily applied to disparaging avant-garde positions, just as the term "decadent" far more often denounces the genuinely progressive traits of a dying culture than the real factors of decay. The traditional images of artistic alienation are indeed

romantic in as much as they are in aesthetic incompatibility with the developing society. This incompatibility is the token of their truth. What they recall and preserve in memory pertains to the future: images of a gratification that would dissolve the society which suppresses it.

The tension between the actual and the possible is transfigured into an insoluble conflict, in which reconciliation is by grace of the oeuvre as *form:* beauty as the "promesse de bonheur." In the form of the oeuvre, the actual circumstances are placed in another dimension where the given reality shows itself as that which it is. Thus it tells the truth about itself; its language ceases to be that of deception, ignorance, and submission. Fiction calls the facts by their name and their reign collapses; fiction subverts everyday experience and shows it to be mutilated and false. But art has this magic power only as the power of negation. It can speak its own language only as long as the images are alive which refuse and refute the established order.

Whether ritualized or not, art contains the rationality of negation. In its advanced positions, it is the Great Refusal—the protest against that which is. The modes in which man and things are made to appear, to sing and sound and speak, are modes of refuting, breaking, and recreating their factual existence. But these modes of negation pay tribute to the antagonistic society to which they are linked. Separated from the sphere of labor where society reproduces itself and its misery, the world of art which they create remains, with all its truth, a privilege and an illusion.

In this form it continues, in spite of all democratization and popularization, through the nineteenth and into the twentieth century. The "high culture" in which this alienation is celebrated has its own rites and its own style. The salon, the concert, opera, theater are designed to create and invoke another dimension of reality. Their attendance requires festive-like preparation; they cut off and transcend everyday experience.

Now this essential gap between the arts and the order of the day, kept open in the artistic alienation, is progressively closed by the advancing technological society. And with its closing, the Great Refusal is in turn refused; the "other dimension" is absorbed into the prevailing state of affairs. The works of alienation are themselves incorporated into this society and circulate as part and parcel of the equipment which adorns and psychoanalyzes the prevailing state of affairs. Thus they become commercials—they sell, comfort, or excite.

HERBERT MARCUSE, *One-Dimensional Man*

Philosophers through the ages have adopted oddly contradictory attitudes toward art and artistic creation. Most of the great philosophers have had something to say about the nature of art, about its relation to knowledge, to religious experience, to sense perception, about the role of feelings or emotions in the creation and experience of art. Most of the great philosophers, in short, have taken art seriously. But Western philosophers have exalted logic, mathematics, and the physical sciences above all other branches of human effort (save, perhaps, theology), and then have tended to downgrade art, by comparison, to the status of "mere" subjective expression. Indeed, some philosophers, as we have just seen, actually view art as dangerous to the emotional and social well-being of humanity.

It may not have been obvious to you, as you read this chapter, but the central issue underlying the widely divergent philosophical evaluations of art is the *cognitive status* of artistic experience. Is the experience of art a form of knowledge? Do we *learn* something from art, and if so, what sort of thing do we learn? If the answer is *yes,* as Wordsworth and Tolstoy, for example, believe, then we can go on to ask whether the knowledge art gives us is dangerous knowledge or beneficial knowledge. But if the answer is *no*—if art leads us away from true knowledge, as Plato argued—then it will be very difficult indeed to justify either the activity of the artist or the experience of the artistic audience.

Clearly, art arouses strong emotions in us, and that arousal may be good for us (as Aristotle held), or bad for us (as Plato thought), or it may even be an instrument of fundamental and social change (as Marcuse claimed). But strong feeling is not, by itself, knowledge, though it may possibly be a condition for knowledge, or an element in knowledge. Knowledge requires reason, concepts, judgments—it requires *form.* Whatever we know of a thing, whether it be a physical object like a horse or an abstract object like a triangle, must be some aspect of its *form.*

Susanne Langer, whose philosophical interests ranged from logic to aesthetics, advances the thesis that art is a means of capturing and communicating what she calls *expressive form.* In order to grasp what she has in mind, let us consider an extended example. This is not her example, but I think it may help you to understand her argument.

Let us suppose that I have been raised in a devoutly religious Roman Catholic home. As a boy, I was taken to Sunday mass, studied my catechism, made my first Communion, served as an altar boy, and in general received what would be called a good Catholic upbringing. Obviously, the dogmas, the rituals, the words, the music, the very smells of a Catholic church will have enormous emotional significance for me. They will be bound up in my mind with a host of personal memories— the funeral service for my grandmother, a particularly embarrassing confession, the time when my attention strayed to my friends across the aisle and my father brought me back to my prayers with a sharp rap on the knuckles, the cheerful priest whose instruction was always filled with jokes, the sour-faced priest who put the fear of God into me.

Let us suppose, further, that after a searing crisis of conscience as a young man, I rejected the Catholic faith, concluding that I could not honestly submit myself to a church and a religion in which I did not fully believe. Now imagine that I am some years older, still not practicing any formal religion, a lapsed Catholic. Nevertheless, I am by no means quits with the faith of my childhood. I feel a certain supersti-tious awe when I enter a Catholic church; I half cross myself when an ambulance goes by; as I contemplate the prospect of becoming a father, I find myself beginning to worry about whether my children ought, perhaps, to be christened and given at least the rudiments of a religious upbringing, "just in case."

Now, this is obviously an extremely complex psychological, social, and intellectual state of affairs. For those of you who have been raised in some formal religion or other, it will be obvious that the few descriptive remarks I have made cannot begin to capture the subtle interplay of thoughts and feelings that constitute the condition of being a "lapsed Catholic." Indeed, I would argue that *no* purely descriptive itemiza-tion can exhaust the richness of such a situation. What is more, despite the extreme specificity of the scenario I have sketched, there is something about the condition of a lapsed Catholic that bears a formal, or structural, similarity to the condition of a once-Orthodox Jew who no longer obeys the old laws, or a Fundamentalist Protes-tant who has fallen away from the faith of the old generation.

Susanne Langer argues very persuasively that art can capture, and communicate, complex experiences whose *expressive form* is not amenable to other modes of formal communication, such as discursive language, mathematics, or logic. As with all communication, it is *form* or structure which is articulated in art. In the case of art, however, what would otherwise be ephemeral, shifting, subjective, is given an objective form which freezes or captures it so that many generations may reexperi-ence the particular complex that the artist seeks to communicate. As Langer says at the very end of her essay, a work of art "is a developed metaphor, a non-discursive symbol that articulates what is verbally ineffable—the logic of consciousness itself." If we think of the artist as capturing the expressive form of experiences too complex for the cruder, less modulated communication of discursive prose or mathematics, we will perhaps understand the sense in which art, like science, gives us *knowledge*.

SUSANNE K. LANGER: *Problems of Art*

When we talk about "Art" with a capital "A"—that is, about any or all of the arts: painting, sculpture, architecture, the potter's and goldsmith's and other designers' arts, music, dance, poetry, and prose fiction, drama and film—it is a constant temptation to say things about "Art" in this general sense that are true only in one special domain, or to assume that what holds for one art must hold for another. For instance, the fact that music is made for performance, for presentation to the ear, and is simply not the same thing when it is given only to the tonal imagination of a reader silently perusing the score, has made some aestheticians pass straight to the conclusion that literature, too, must be physically heard to be fully experienced, because words are originally spoken, not written; an obvious parallel, but a careless and, I think, invalid one. It is dangerous to set up principles by analogy, and generalize from a single consider-ation.

But it is natural, and safe enough, to ask analogous questions: "What is the function of sound in music? What is the function of sound in poetry? What is the function of sound in prose composition? What is the function of sound in drama?" The answers may be quite heterogeneous; and that is itself an important fact, a guide to something more than a simple and sweeping theory. Such findings guide us to exact relations and abstract, variously exemplified basic principles.

At present, however, we are dealing with principles that have proven to be the same in all the arts, when each kind of art—plastic, musical, balletic, poetic, and each major mode, such as literary and dramatic writing, or painting, sculpturing, building plastic shapes—has been studied in its own terms. Such candid study is more rewarding than the usual passionate declaration that all the arts are alike, only their materials differ, their principles are all the same, their techniques all analogous, etc. That is not only unsafe, but untrue. It is in pursuing the differences among them that one arrives, finally, at a point where no more differences appear; then one has found, not postulated, their unity. At that deep level there is only one concept exemplified in all the different arts, and that is the concept of Art.

The principles that obtain wholly and fundamentally in every kind of art are few, but decisive; they determine what is art, and what is not. Expressiveness, in one definite and appropriate sense, is the same in all art works of any kind. What is created is not the same in any two distinct arts—that is, in fact, what makes them distinct—but the principle of creation is the same. And "living form" means the same in all of them.

A work of art is an expressive form created for our perception through sense or imagination, and what it expresses is human feeling. The word "feeling" must be taken here in its broadest sense, meaning *everything that can be felt,* from physical sensation, pain and comfort, excitement and repose, to the most complex emotions, intellectual tensions, or the steady feeling-tones of a conscious human life. In stating what a work of art is, I have just used the words "form," "expressive," and "created"; these are key words. One at a time, they will keep us engaged.

Let us consider first what is meant, in this context, by a *form.* The word has many meanings, all equally legitimate for various purposes; even in connection with art it has several. It may, for instance—and often does—denote the familiar, characteristic structures known as the sonnet form, the sestina, or the ballad form in poetry, the sonata form, the madrigal, or the symphony in music, the contredance or the classical ballet in choreography, and so on. This is not what I mean; or rather, it is only a very small part of what I mean. There is another sense in which artists speak of "form" when they say, for instance, "form follows function," or declare that the one quality shared by all good works of art is "significant form," or entitle a book *The Problem of Form in Painting and Sculpture,* or *The Life of Forms in Art,* or *Search for Form.* They are using "form" in a wider sense, which on the one hand is close to the commonest, popular meaning, namely just the *shape* of a thing, and on the other hand to the quite unpopular meaning it has in science and philosophy, where it designates something more abstract; "form" in its most abstract sense means structure, articulation, a whole resulting from the relation of mutually dependent factors, or more precisely, the way that whole is put together.

The abstract sense, which is sometimes called "logical form," is involved in the notion of expression, at least the kind of expression that characterizes art. That is why artists, when they speak of achieving "form," use the word with something of an abstract connotation, even when they are talking about a visible and tangible art object in which that form is embodied.

The more recondite concept of form is derived, of course, from the naive one, that is, material shape. Perhaps the easiest way to grasp the idea of "logical form" is to trace its derivation.

Let us consider the most obvious sort of form, the shape of an object, say a lampshade. In any department store you will find a wide choice of lampshades, mostly monstrosities, and what is monstrous is usually their shape. You select the least offensive one, maybe even a good one, but realize that the color, say violet, will not fit into your room; so you look about for another shade of the same shape but a different color, perhaps green. In recognizing this same shape in another object, possibly of another material as well as another color, you have quite naturally and easily abstracted the concept of this shape from your actual impression of the first lampshade. Presently it may occur to you that this shade is too big for your lamp; you ask whether they have *this same shade* (meaning another one of this shape) in a smaller size. The clerk understands you.

But what is *the same* in the big violet shade and the little green one? Nothing but the interrelations among their respective various dimensions. They are not "the same" even in their spatial properties, for none of their actual measures are alike; but their shapes are congruent. Their respective spatial factors are put together in the same way, so they exemplify the same form.

It is really astounding what complicated abstractions we make in our ordinary dealing with forms—that is to say, through what twists and transformations we recognize the same logical form. Consider the similarity of your two hands. Put one on the table, palm down, superimpose the other, palm down, as you may have superimposed cut-out geometric shapes in school—they are not alike at all. But their shapes are *exact opposites.* Their respective shapes fit the same description, provided that the description is modified by a principle of application whereby the measures are read one way for one hand and the other way for the other—like a timetable in which the list of stations is marked: "Eastbound, read down; Westbound, read up."

As the two hands exemplify the same form with a principle of reversal understood, so the list of stations describes two ways of moving, indicated by the advice to "read down" for one and "read up" for the other. We can all abstract the common element in these two respective trips, which is called the *route.* With a return ticket we may return only by the same route. The same principle relates a mold to the form of the thing that is cast in it, and establishes their formal correspondence, or common logical form.

So far we have considered only objects—lampshades, hands, or regions of the earth—as having forms. These have fixed shapes; their parts remain in fairly stable relations to each other. But there are also substances that have no definite shapes, such as gases, mist, and water, which take the shape of any bounded space that contains them. The interesting thing about such amorphous fluids is that when they are put into violent motion they do exhibit visible forms, not bounded by any container. Think of the momentary efflorescence of a bursting rocket, the mushroom cloud of an atomic bomb, the funnel of water or dust screwing upward in a whirlwind. The instant the motion stops, or even slows beyond a certain degree, those shapes collapse and the apparent "thing" disappears. They are not shapes of things at all, but forms of motions, or dynamic forms.

Some dynamic forms, however, have more permanent manifestations, because the stuff that moves and makes them visible is constantly replenished. A waterfall seems to hang from the cliff, waving streamers of foam. Actually, of course, nothing stays there in mid-air; the water is always passing; but there is more and more water taking the same paths, so we have a lasting shape made and maintained by its passage—a permanent dynamic form. A quiet river, too, has dynamic form; if it stopped flowing it would either go dry or become a lake. Some twenty-five hundred years ago, Heracleitos was struck by the fact that you cannot step twice into the same river at the same place—at least, if the river means the water, not its dynamic form, the flow.

When a river ceases to flow because the water is deflected or dried up, there remains the river bed, sometimes cut deeply in solid stone. That bed is shaped by the flow, and records as graven lines the currents that have ceased to exist. Its shape is static, but it *expresses* the dynamic form of the river. Again, we have two congruent forms, like a cast and its mold, but this time the congruence is more remarkable because it holds between a dynamic form and a static one. That relation is important; we shall be dealing with it again when we come to consider the meaning of "living form" in art.

The congruence of two given perceptible forms is not always evident upon simple inspection. The common *logical* form they both exhibit may become apparent only when you know the principle whereby to relate them, as you compare the shapes of your hands not by direct correspondence, but by correspondence of opposite parts. Where the two exemplifications of the single logical form are unlike in most other respects one needs a rule for matching up the relevant factors of one with the relevant factors of the other; that is to say, a *rule of translation,* whereby one instance of the logical form is shown to correspond formally to the other.

The logical form itself is not another thing, but an abstract concept, or better an *abstractable* concept. We usually don't abstract it deliberately, but only use it, as we use our vocal cords in speech without first learning all about their operation and then applying our knowledge. Most people perceive intuitively the similarity of their two hands without thinking of them as conversely related; they can guess at the shape of the hollow inside a wooden shoe from the shape of a human foot, without any abstract study of topology. But the first time they see a map in the Mercator projection—with parallel lines of longitude, not meeting at the poles—they find it hard to believe that this corresponds logically to the circular map they used in school, where the meridians bulged apart toward the equator and met at both poles. The visible shapes of the continents are different on the two maps, and it takes abstract thinking to match up the two representations of the same earth. If, however, they have grown up with both maps, they will probably see the geographical relationships either way with equal ease, because these relationships are not *copied* by either map, but *expressed,* and expressed equally well by both; for the two maps are different *projections* of the same logical form, which the spherical earth exhibits in still another—that is, a spherical—projection.

An expressive form is any perceptible or imaginable whole that exhibits relationships of parts, or points, or even qualities or aspects within the whole, so that it may be taken to represent some other whole whose elements have analogous relations. The reason for using such a form as a symbol is usually that the thing it represents is not perceivable or readily imaginable. We cannot see the earth as an object. We let a map or a little globe express the relationships of places on the earth, and think about the earth by means of it. The understanding of one thing through another seems to be a deeply intuitive process in the human brain; it is so natural that we often have difficulty in distinguishing the symbolic expressive form from what it conveys. The symbol seems to be the thing itself, or contain it, or be contained in it. A child interested in a globe will not say: "This means the earth," but: "Look, this is the earth." A similar identification of symbol and meaning underlies the widespread conception of holy names, of the physical efficacy of rites, and many other primitive but culturally persistent phenomena. It has a bearing on our perception of artistic import; that is why I mention it here.

The most astounding and developed symbolic device humanity has evolved is language. By means of language we can conceive the intangible, incorporeal things we call our *ideas,* and the equally inostensible elements of our perceptual world that we call *facts.* It is by virtue of language that we can think, remember, imagine, and finally conceive a universe of facts. We can describe things and represent their relations, express rules of their interactions, speculate and predict and carry on a long symbolizing process known as reasoning. And above all, we can communicate, by producing a serried array of audible or visible words, in a pattern commonly known, and readily understood to reflect our multifarious concepts and percepts and their interconnections. This use of language is *discourse;* and the pattern of discourse is known as *discursive form.* It is a highly versatile, amazingly powerful pattern. It has impressed itself on our tacit thinking, so that we call all systematic reflection "discursive thought." It has made, far more than most people know, the very frame of our sensory experience—the frame of objective facts in which we carry on the practical business of life.

Yet even the discursive pattern has its limits of usefulness. An expressive form can express any complex of conceptions that, via some rule of projection, appears congruent with it, that is, appears to be of that form. Whatever there is in experience that will not take the impress—directly or indirectly—of discursive form, is not discursively communicable or, in the strictest sense, logically thinkable. It is unspeakable, ineffable; according to practically all serious philosophical theories today, it is unknowable.

Yet there is a great deal of experience that is knowable, not only as immediate, formless, meaningless impact, but as one aspect of the intricate web of life, yet defies discursive formulation, and therefore verbal expression: that is what we sometimes call the *subjective aspect* of experience, the direct feeling of it—what it is like to be waking and moving, to be drowsy, slowing down, or to be sociable, or to feel self-sufficient but alone; what it feels like to pursue an elusive thought or to have a big idea. All such directly felt experiences usually have no names—they are named, if at all, for the outward conditions that normally accompany their occurrence. Only the most striking ones have names like "anger," "hate," "love," "fear," and are collectively called "emotion." But we feel many things that never develop into any designable emotion. The ways we are moved are as various as the lights in a forest; and they may intersect, sometimes without cancelling each other, take shape and dissolve, conflict, explode into passion, or be transfigured. All these inseparable elements of subjective reality compose what we call the "inward life" of human beings. The usual factoring of that life-stream into mental, emotional, and sensory units is an arbitrary scheme of simplification that makes scientific treatment possible to a considerable extent; but we may already be close to the limit of its usefulness, that is, close to the point where its simplicity becomes an obstacle to further questioning and discovery instead of the revealing, ever-suitable logical projection it was expected to be.

Whatever resists projection into the discursive form of language is, indeed, hard to hold in conception, and perhaps impossible to communicate, in the proper and strict sense of the word "communicate." But fortunately our logical intuition, or form-perception, is really much more powerful than we commonly believe, and our knowledge—genuine knowledge, understanding—is considerably wider than our discourse. Even in the use of language, if we want to name something that is too new to have a name (e.g., a newly invented gadget or a newly discovered creature), or want to express a relationship for which there is no verb or other connective word, we resort to metaphor; we mention it or describe it as something else, something analogous. The principle of metaphor is simply the principle of saying one thing and meaning another, and expecting to be understood to mean the other. A metaphor is not language, it is an idea expressed by language, an idea that in its turn functions as a symbol to express something. It is not discursive and therefore does not really make a statement of the idea it conveys; but it formulates a new conception for our direct imaginative grasp.

Sometimes our comprehension of a total experience is mediated by a metaphorical symbol because the experience is new, and language has words and phrases only for familiar notions. Then an extension of language will gradually follow the wordless insight, and discursive expression will supersede the nondiscursive pristine symbol. This is, I think, the normal advance of human thought and language in that whole realm of knowledge where discourse is possible at all.

But the symbolic presentation of subjective reality for contemplation is not only tentatively beyond the reach of language—that is, not merely beyond the words we have; it is impossible in the essential frame of language. That is why those semanticists who recognize only discourse as a symbolic form must regard the whole life of feeling as formless, chaotic, capable only of symptomatic expression, typified in exclamations like "Ah!" "Ouch!" "My sainted aunt!" They usually do believe that art is an expression of feeling, but that "expression" in art is of this sort, indicating that the speaker has an emotion, a pain, or other personal experience, perhaps also giving us a clue to the general kind of experience it is—pleasant or unpleasant, violent or mild—but not setting that piece of inward life objectively before us so we may understand its intricacy, its rhythms and shifts of total appearance. The differences in feeling-tones or other elements of subjective experience are regarded as differences in quality, which must be felt to be appreciated. Furthermore, since we have no intellectual access to pure subjectivity, the only way to study it is to study the symptoms of the person who is having subjective experiences. This leads to physiological psychology—a very important and interesting field. But it tells us nothing about the phenomena of subjective life, and sometimes simplifies the problem by saying they don't exist.

Now, I believe the expression of feeling in a work of art—the function that makes the work an expressive form—is not symptomatic at all. An artist working on a tragedy need not be in personal despair or violent upheaval; nobody, indeed, could work in such a state of mind. His mind would be occupied with the causes of his emotional upset. Self-expression does not require composition and lucidity; a screaming baby gives his feeling far more release than any musician, but we don't go into a concert hall to hear a baby scream; in fact, if that baby is brought in we are likely to go out. We don't want self-expression.

A work of art presents feeling (in the broad sense I mentioned before, as everything that can be felt) for our contemplation, making it visible or audible or in some way perceivable through a symbol, not inferable from a symptom. Artistic form is congruent with the dynamic forms of our direct sensuous, mental, and emotional life; works of art are projections of "felt life," as Henry James called it, into spatial, temporal, and poetic structures. They are images of feeling, that formulate it for our cognition. What is artistically good is whatever articulates and presents feeling to our understanding.

Artistic forms are more complex than any other symbolic forms we know. They are, indeed, not abstractable from the works that exhibit them. We may abstract a shape from an object that has this shape, by disregarding color, weight and texture, even size; but to the total effect that is an artistic form, the color matters, the thickness of lines matters, and the appearance of texture and weight. A given triangle is the same in any position, but to an artistic form its location, balance, and surroundings are not indifferent. Form, in the sense in which artists speak of "significant form" or "expressive form," is not an abstracted structure, but an apparition; and the vital process of sense and emotion that a good work of art expresses seem to the beholder to be directly contained in it, not symbolized but really presented. The congruence is so striking that symbol and meaning appear as one reality. Actually, as one psychologist who is also a musician has written, "Music sounds as feelings feel." And likewise, in good painting, sculpture, or building, balanced shapes and colors, lines and masses look as emotions, vital tensions and their resolutions feel.

An artist, then, expresses feeling, but not in the way a politician blows off steam or a baby laughs and cries. He formulates that elusive aspect of reality that is commonly taken to be amorphous and chaotic; that is, he objectifies the subjective realm. What he expresses is, therefore, not his own actual feelings, but what he knows about human feeling. Once he is in possession of a rich symbolism, that knowledge may actually exceed his entire personal experience. A work of art expresses a conception of life, emotion, inward reality. But it is neither a confessional nor a frozen tantrum; it is a developed metaphor, a nondiscursive symbol that articulates what is verbally ineffable—the logic of consciousness itself.

TOPICS FOR FURTHER STUDY

1. According to Langer, the expressive form of artworks permits us to communicate aspects of our experience that cannot be captured by the discursive form of language. But what cannot be said, cannot be known, or so it would seem. How does Langer avoid retreating to the view that art communicates nothing at all?

2. Langer tells us that art expresses certain immediate elements of our inner life. Does art also capture any aspects of nature, or of the social life of human beings, that cannot otherwise or as well be communicated?

3. Does Langer's theory of expressive form work better for the so-called plastic arts, such as sculpture, or for such linguistic arts as poetry and drama? Is there any reason to suppose that *one* analysis of art will fit all of the varied objects, activities, and performances that we call "art"?

4. Art critics frequently describe works in one art medium with language that seems more suitable for a quite different medium. They will speak of the "lyrical" quality of a statue, the "movement" in a painting, the "tonal coloring" of a poem. Can Langer's theory of expressive form give us any insight into why it seems to make sense to speak this way about works of art? Is there something common to artworks in different media, something that transcends the differences of their specific genres?

5. Drawing on the arguments of Plato, Aristotle, Marcuse, and the other philosophers discussed in this chapter, explore the question whether there is any social or moral utility in the creation of an artwork that permits the communication of expressive form. Ought society as a whole to support artists whose creative efforts are devoted to the communicating of expressive form? Why?

SUGGESTIONS FOR FURTHER READING

MONROE BEARDSLEY, *Aesthetics*

CLIVE BELL, *Art*

R. G. COLLINGWOOD, *The Principles of Art*

JOHN DEWEY, *Art as Experience*

G. W. F. HEGEL, Introduction to *Philosophy of Fine Art*

JOHN HOSPERS, *Meaning and Truth in the Arts*

IMMANUEL KANT, *Critique of Judgment*

SUSANNE LANGER, *Philosophy in a New Key*

KARL MARX, *Economic-Philosophic Manuscripts of 1844*

PLATO, *Symposium*

G. PLEKHANOV, *Art and Social Life*

I. A. RICHARDS, *The Principles of Literary Criticism*

MORRIS WEITZ, *Philosophy of the Arts*

RICHARD WOLLHEIM, *Art and Its Objects*

SØREN KIERKEGAARD (1813–1855) was the founder and most brilliant spokesman of the style of philosophizing known as "existentialism." His life was devoted to an unending inward reflection on human existence and the terror and uncertainty which each of us experiences in the face of his own death. Kierkegaard was deeply religious, though he rejected what he felt to be the superficial self-satisfied Lutheranism of his native Denmark. In a series of books, some on philosophical topics others more directly religious in their focus, he redefined the nature of faith, making it radically subjective and totally alien to the processes of ordinary systematic reason.

6 PHILOSOPHY OF RELIGION

Kierkegaard was a witty, brilliantly provocative writer. His works abound in complex ironies which are challenges to the reader. He seems always to seek to unsettle his readers, to put us off balance and thereby force us to examine our lives as Kierkegaard had examined his own. One of his many literary devices to achieve this was the practice of publishing his books under pseudonyms. The *Philosophical Fragments,* for example, was published with its author listed as "Johannes Climacus." Further down on the page, there appeared the statement, "Responsible for publication: S. Kierkegaard." By this and other devices, Kierkegaard hoped to block any attempt by his readers to classify his position and pigeon-hole him, for Kierkegaard was convinced that such techniques of systematic professional philosophy were merely ways of defusing a book and making it safe.

As he himself pessimistically predicted, Kierkegaard has fallen into the hands of professors and systematizers, and even his challenge to established philosophy has itself come to be treated merely as one more philosophy, namely Existentialism. Kierkegaard would have laughed, or perhaps he would have wept, to see his struggle with death and eternity reduced to an "ism."

I

Søren Kierkegaard was born in 1813 to a father fifty-six and a mother forty-four. His early life and education were very closely supervised by his father, who demanded both a scholarly mastery of classical languages and a highly charged imaginative appreciation of the literature his young son read. The young Søren had laid upon him the full weight of the guilt which extreme Pietist Protestantism so often inflicted upon its communicants. Although Kant and Kierkegaard thus had roughly the same sort of religious upbringing, Kierkegaard completely lacked Kant's quiet inner confidence and peace. He reacted first against the torment of his religious training by plunging himself into a life of physical self-indulgence, eating, drinking, dressing the dandy. But these distractions could not free him from the black gloom which hung over him, and he decided finally to return to his studies and become a pastor.

The dramatic turning point in Kierkegaard's private life was his engagement, and then the breaking of it, to seventeen-year-old Regine Olson. Kierkegaard wrote endlessly of his feelings for Regine, of the philosophical significance of marriage, love, and the problems of such a life commitment, but one cannot help thinking that she was more important to him as a subject for meditation than as a real, live woman. After pouring out a series of essays and books on aesthetic, moral, and religious topics, Kierkegaard died at the relatively early age of forty-two.

Kierkegaard's inner emotional life, his lifelong struggle with religious faith, and his reaction to the dominant Hegelian philosophy of his day are all so intimately intertwined that it is very difficult to speak of any one without immediately bringing in all three. There is hardly space in an introductory text of this sort to explore the subject fully, but a few systematic remarks may be helpful to you. I especially want you to develop an interest in Kierkegaard, because in my opinion, he is, after the immortal Plato, the most gifted artist among all the important philosophers who have come down to us in the Western tradition. If you pick up one of his books, many of which are easily available in paperback editions, you will find him profound, troubling, witty, touching, and in the end deeply rewarding.

The passionate center of Kierkegaard's thought and life is his confrontation with the ever-present terror of existential dread—the obsessive, unavoidable fact of my own impending death, the infinity of the universe and the meaninglessness of my own brief life in comparison. Every man, woman, and child faces these terrible, fundamental facts of the human condition. We may deny them, flee from them, repress them, distract ourselves to escape from them, but always they are there, at the edge of consciousness, waiting to return in the darkness of night. The first lesson Kierkegaard teaches us, both in his books and by his life, is that this dread of death and meaninglessness must be faced, confronted, not shoved aside again and again. If I may speak personally—and the greatest honor we can pay to Kierkegaard is precisely to be honest, each one of us, about our own encounter with the fear of death—I first came face to face with this dread as a teenager. I was obsessed with fears of death, and the more I thrust them from my mind, the more intensely they returned. In my case, the fear was not of pain, or age, or sickness, but simply of nonbeing. The more I turned the thought over in my mind, the closer my own eventual death seemed to come, until finally I would seize any distraction to divert my attention from what was, and of course still is, an unavoidable fate.

For Kierkegaard, the dread of death was both heightened and complicated by the hope of eternal life which the religion of his fathers held out to him. All of you have heard the expression, "Trust in the Lord." But how many of you have actually asked yourselves what it means to "trust in the Lord"? What does it mean to "believe in" God, to have faith in Him?

Well, what it *doesn't* mean is believing *that* God exists! In our increasingly nonreligious society, when a person says that she "believes in God," we automatically assume that she means that she believes there is such a thing as God.

But in the Judeo-Christian religious tradition, particularly in the extreme individualistic Protestant sort of Christianity that was Kierkegaard's heritage, the phrase "belief in God" has quite a different meaning. To believe in God, to trust in Him, to have faith in Him, means to believe that He will keep His promise to humanity; it is to have faith that He will keep the pact, or covenant, that He made with the beings He created. That pact is testified to first in what we call the Old Testament, and then again in a renewed form in the New Testament.

The promise, of course, is the promise of salvation, of a life after death, of true happiness, of fruitfulness, of a union of the soul with God. (Needless to say, long books could be written on the various interpretations that Jews, Christians, and Muslims have placed upon this notion of a covenant with God. The version I am summarizing here is something like what Kierkegaard would have learned and brooded upon.) According to the Old Testament, God made a promise to Noah, He repeated it to Abraham, He renewed it again and again, despite the failure of the Hebrews to keep His Law and follow His commands. Finally, God embodied that Law (or Word or Logos) in the Person of Jesus Christ, in order that His offer of salvation might be made once more. With the birth, suffering, and death of Jesus, God sealed His free gift of eternal life. As the price of that blessedness, He asked only faith, an unstinting, unconditioned, unqualified belief by us that He would keep His promise of this free gift.

Other Christian traditions had emphasized the role of right behavior, or "good works," either as part of the price of salvation or else as worldly evidence of one's true belief. But the Pietist strain of Protestantism placed a very heavy

The Old Testament doctrine of God's promise to humanity.

emphasis upon the pure possession of that unconditioned faith in God. So it was that for Kierkegaard, the central religious problem quite naturally became the problem of *faith.*

You might think, on first reflection, that the Christian message would be a very welcome message indeed! After all, life is short, bedeviled by suffering, terminated by the absolute finality of unavoidable death. It was good enough news to be told, in the Old Testament, that God would grant life everlasting to those who kept His commandments. But we are weak, imperfect creatures, and it soon became clear that doing God's bidding was a task too hard for us, even with the promise of salvation to lead us on. He took upon Himself, in the Person of His Son, the atonement for *our* sins, and offered to us the priceless pearl of salvation for the merest asking. All we needed do was believe that we would receive it. What could possibly be better news than that? Small wonder that this message was called the Gospel, which means "good news." Small wonder too that those who spread the message were called Evangelists, which means "bringers of good news."

But strange to tell, the glad tidings of God's free gift have brought fear, dread, doubt, torment, and tortured self-examination to countless hearers, among them Søren Kierkegaard. The gift is so great, the price so small—and yet, the price of faith must be paid freely, unhesitatingly, without doubts or second thoughts. Therein lie the seeds of terror. Do I truly believe? Is my faith pure? Can I trust in the Lord, or is there lurking deep within my heart a doubt that so great a gift will be conferred on so undeserving a creature as myself? Out of this inner hell Kierkegaard tore the writings by which we remember him. His doubts and fears concerned his very *existence* as an individual, mortal creature longing to believe in God's promise, not the abstract, impersonal logical relationships among disembodied forms, or "essences." Hence, Kierkegaard's way of thinking has come to be called *existentialist.* Indeed, Kierkegaard is universally acknowledged to be the first true existentialist philosopher. Whether he would have appreciated such a categorization and sterilization of his inner torment is of course not so clear.

In his lifelong struggle with the problem of faith, Kierkegaard did battle with three enemies, against whom he turned not only his considerable philosophical and theological gifts, but also a brilliant, convoluted, ironic wit. The first of his enemies was the established Christianity of his own day, the solid, comfortable, Sunday-sermon Lutheranism of nineteenth-century Denmark. Like so many passionate prophets before him, Kierkegaard accused the established church of mouthing empty formulae which were neither lived nor understood. Sin, redemption, damnation, salvation, all were the subjects of elegant sermons and pious attitudes which did not for a moment interfere with the secular, weekday activities of this world. Kierkegaard once observed that just as it is hard to jump up in the air and land exactly on the spot from which one began, so too it is harder to become a Christian when one has been born a Christian. He meant that those who were born into Christianity, who were baptized, confirmed, and raised in the official emptiness of its dogmas and rituals, might actually find it more difficult to take the message of Christianity seriously than would a pagan to whom the divine promise came as wonderful, terrible, astonishing news. Kierkegaard devoted many of his books to a sustained effort to breathe new existential significance into the familiar phrases and concepts of Christian theology.

His second enemy was the complacent middle-class culture of his society, the "bourgeois" culture of solid tradesmen and lawyers—sound, self-confident people who disdained anyone so odd, so passionate, so disruptive as Kierkegaard. The word "bourgeois" has drifted into our vocabulary these days as a catch-all term for what we in America call "middle-class" life, but in the nineteenth century in Europe, it had a much richer, more resonant set of associations. Historically, a "bourgeois," or a "burgher," is simply a resident of a "bourg" or "burg," which in the late Middle Ages was a walled city. By extension, the word came to mean a member of the urban merchant class, and also a "freeman" or citizen of one of the cities whose charter came from the king rather than from the feudal aristocracy. The burghers of the European cities were men of substance, solid citizens, true to their word in business deals, extremely conservative in their family relationships, jealous of their rights as city leaders, forward-looking in commerce, and quite often supporters of a strong

A bourgeois couple in nineteenth-century France as the painter Toulouse-Lautrec saw them.

monarchy against the ancient and dispersed powers of the landed aristocracy. For the burghers of Copenhagen, religion was first of all a matter of propriety, of respectability, and only then a matter of conscience or salvation. One dressed in one's finest clothes on Sunday and went with one's family to church; one sat in a front pew, purchased at great expense, where one was seen by one's neighbors. One listened piously to the sermon, which, though heavy on damnation, was conveniently light on social responsibility, and then one returned to one's substantial townhouse for a good Sunday dinner.

As you can imagine, the unthinking religiosity, the self-satisfied complacency of the solid citizens of Denmark made Kierkegaard furious. Many of his most spectacular literary tricks and devices, and particularly his extremely heavy irony, are aimed at puncturing that complacency and somehow reaching the real human beings behind those masks.

The final enemy was the official philosophy of Kierkegaard's day, the vast, pompous, elaborate philosophical systems constructed by the disciples and followers of the great German philosopher Georg Hegel. The Hegelian philosophy, as it was expounded by the professors of Europe, put itself forward as the

"You seem troubled, Brother Timothy. Is anything worrying you? I mean besides the sins of the world, the vanities of man-kind, and that sort of thing."*

* Drawing by Stevenson; © 1960 The New Yorker Magazine, Inc.

objective, impersonal, purely rational, totally systematic, absolutely final truth about just about everything. It was turgid, jargon-filled, and completely self-confident. It claimed to wrap up space, time, eternity, being, history, man, the state, and God in one vast metaphysical synthesis that simultaneously answered all our questions about the universe and also—rather conveniently—demonstrated the superiority of precisely the social and religious system then dominant in European society.

In short, Kierkegaard's three enemies were really one and the same enemy in different disguises. The Christianity of his day was bourgeois Christianity, buttressed and justified by the official philosophical system. The burghers were Establishment Christians, who—though they knew precious little philosophy—were justified and rationalized by that same philosophy. And the philosophy, though it claimed to be the purest product of reason, was a thoroughgoing justification of the reign of the burghers and the ascendency of their religion.

Karl Marx, facing this very same union of religion, philosophy, and the ascendent bourgeoisie, turned his attack on the social and economic consequences, for Marx was a secular man, concerned with this-worldly issues of justice, poverty, and work. Kierkegaard, before all else a man of God, attacked the same union of forces on its religious front. He cared nothing at all for worldly happiness or misery. Rather, he brushed all secular considerations aside and instead demanded that the good Christians of Denmark begin to pay to eternal life as much attention as they regularly gave to a daily profit.

Kierkegaard's onslaught was complex and subtle, and hence is impossible to summarize in a few paragraphs. Two ideas lie at the heart of his religio-philosophical message, and we can at least take a first step toward understanding them. These notions are the inwardness, or subjectivity, of truth, and the irrational, unarguable "leap of faith." Now, that sounds more like a Hegelian mouthful than a bit of biting wit, so let us take a look at each.

The Hegelian philosophers put their doctrines forward as *rational* and *objective*. They were, in a way, like today's scientists. All of you have noticed, I imagine, that there is a very big difference in the teaching style and approach of science professors as compared with professors of literature or philosophy. In a literature class, you are encouraged to express your own "interpretation" of Dickens or Mailer or Shakespeare. In a philosophy class—I hope!—you are prompted to think out your own position, to develop your own arguments, and to defend whatever point of view you think closest to the truth. But nobody teaches calculus or physics that way! Can you imagine a physics quiz with questions like "Write a ten-minute essay on your impressions of Boyle's Law," or "Take a position for or against relativity and defend it—in your answer, make reference to the text." Hardly! Scientists quite confidently assume that their knowledge is objective, and that what they teach is a matter neither of "opinion" nor of personality. In the same way, the Hegelian philosophers represented themselves as objective, rational discoverers of the truth. Their private fears, hopes, terrors, and joys were no more a part of their philosophy, they thought, than would a modern biochemist's neuroses be a part of her theory of DNA. To be sure, readers might be curious, in a gossipy way, about the personal lives of the great philosophers, just as we today like to read stories about Albert Einstein. But no one would suppose for a moment that there was any important scientific connection between those delightful or depressing glimpses into the scientist's private life and the scientific truth of his theories.

In a total reversal of the received philosophical-scientific opinion of his day, Kierkegaard argued that Truth is Subjectivity. In other words, he denied the objective impersonality of truth, and insisted instead that all truth must be inward, dependent upon the subject, particular rather than universal, personal rather than interpersonal or impersonal.

When Kierkegaard says that Truth is Subjectivity, he is denying the ancient philosophical doctrine that the truth of an idea or a statement consists in its conformity to an independent object. When I say, "That is a very good picture of Jim," I mean that the picture looks like Jim, that it resembles, or copies, or conforms to the objective nature of Jim's body. When I say, "It is true that Sacramento is the capital of California," I mean that the real world—California, in this case—actually has the characteristics that my statement says it has. In other words, truth is conformity to the objective state of things in the world. Or, Truth is Objectivity. If this familiar conception of truth is correct, then the truth of a statement or belief depends only on the relationship between the statement or belief and the world, *not* on the relationship between the statement or belief and the person who thinks it. If Truth is Objectivity, then it doesn't matter, so far as truth is concerned, whether I believe Sacramento to be the capital of California passionately, calmly, tentatively, with all my heart, or simply because a friend told me so.

Kierkegaard doesn't care about the capitals of states or nations, of course. He cares about salvation, the Christian message. And when it comes to salvation, *how* you believe is as important as *what* you believe, he thought. The Hegelian system-builders wanted to treat the Christian message as though it were merely one subpart of their grand structure of objective knowledge. So "Jesus died for my sins" would be treated by them as more or less on a par with "Space is three-dimensional and homogeneous." Each statement would be true if it corresponded correctly to the objective state of things, false otherwise. But that treatment of the promise of salvation as "objective" was precisely wrong, Kierkegaard insisted. Truth does not consist in the proper relationship between the belief and the *object;* rather, it consists in the proper relationship between the belief and the *subject,* the individual human being who holds that belief. *How* he or she holds it is the criterion of its truth. In order for the belief to be true, it must be held passionately, unconditionally, absolutely without inner reservation or doubt.

But—and here we come to the second of Kierkegaard's great ideas, the "leap of faith." That belief in God's promise of eternal life can have no rational justification, no evidence, no proof. Theologians since the time of Aristotle had sought to *prove* the existence of God, to prove the truth of this or that religious doctrine. Sometimes they used evidence of their senses—what they could see, hear, and touch. At other times, they erected abstract arguments of pure logic, deducing the absolute, objective truth of Christianity (or Islam, or Judaism). But Kierkegaard believed that all such attempts at rational justification were doomed to total failure. The absolute gap between finite man and infinite God made any rational bridge-building between the two on man's part futile. God might reach down to man, though how He could manage that was beyond our comprehension. But man could no more reason his way into the presence of God than a mathematician, by doggedly adding unit to unit, could calculate his way to infinity.

Because reason was inadequate to the task of supporting our belief in God's promise, Kierkegaard said, our only hope was an absolutely irrational, totally unjustifiable leap of faith. I must take the plunge and say, with all my heart, *Credo*—I believe.

Couldn't we perhaps look for a little bit of support from reason? Mightn't reason at least show that God's promise is probable? That the weight of the evidence inclines us toward God's promise? That a reasonable person could tend to believe God's promise?

Not a bit of it! That is just what a fat, solid, smug merchant or a pompous, self-important professor would say. Can't you just imagine the two of them sitting in front of the fire, the burgher after a long day at the counting house, the professor after a day of serious, important lectures. The burgher leans back in his comfortable chair, puffs a bit on his pipe (one wouldn't want to speak too quickly on such matters—it might show a lack of seriousness), and then asks, "Is it your opinion that the weight of the evidence, objectively and impartially considered, inclines us to the view that God has promised us eternal life rather than eternal death?" The professor takes a sip of beer, strokes his beard thoughtfully, and answers, "Well, on the one hand, Hegel, in the *Phenomenology of Mind,* seems to suggest that God does make such a promise; but on the other hand, Kant, in the *Critique of Pure Reason,* argues that we cannot know with certainty that such a promise has been made. In the light of recent research which I understand has been reported in the latest issue of the Berlin *Journal of Metaphysics,* I would judge professionally that the answer is a qualified yes."

Both the subjectivity of truth and the leap of faith are central to the writings of Kierkegaard. The *Concluding Unscientific Postscript to the Philosophical Fragments* is Kierkegaard's major systematic exposition of his philosophical theology. The title, in typical Kierkegaardian fashion, is an elaborate joke. The *Philosophical Fragments* was short—not quite one hundred pages. The *Postscript,* on the other hand, ran to more than five hundred pages. By calling his most important work a mere "postscript" to the *Fragments,* a lengthy p.s. to a short letter, so to speak, Kierkegaard was laughing at the self-important philosophers of his day. The word "unscientific," of course, is another dig at the Hegelian systematiz-ers, who called everything they did "scientific."

The *Philosophical Fragments* deals with the contrast between secular truth and religious truth, between the objective and the subjective, between reason and faith, between wisdom and salvation. Kierkegaard imagines all these con-trasts as gathered together into the person of Socrates, who is the greatest of all teachers, and Jesus, who is not a teacher in the rational sense, but the Saviour. Kierkegaard's argument goes like this (yes indeed, Kierkegaard uses arguments to show us that arguments cannot be used in matters of faith! I leave it to you to determine whether there is a contradiction in his mode of procedure). Secular knowledge of morality is something that can be learned through rational self-reflection. Teachers like Socrates help us to bring our moral knowledge to consciousness by probing questions that force us to justify our beliefs. But since in some sense this moral knowledge already lies within each of us, a teacher—even so great a teacher as Socrates—is merely helpful; if we had to, we could get along without one. As philosophers say, a teacher is "acci-dental" rather than "essential." But salvation is a matter of the fate of my soul. It is a matter of my *existence,* not merely of my state of knowledge. And salvation is not something I can acquire on my own if I am forced to do so. Salvation requires that God reach down and lift me up to His Kingdom. Somehow, the gulf between myself and God must be crossed. Thus salvation is totally different from the acquisition of wisdom, for there is no gulf to be crossed on the road to wisdom. I need only look carefully and critically enough inside myself.

Jesus is God's instrument for bridging the gulf between Himself and myself. Jesus is the Saviour. And since salvation concerns my *existence,* the actual, historical reality of Jesus is all-important. You see, it doesn't really matter to me whether Socrates ever actually lived. Once I have learned from Plato's Dia-logues how to engage in Socratic questioning, it would make no difference if I were to discover that the Dialogues were a hoax, and that there never had been any Socrates. But if God never actually became Man in the form of Jesus Christ; if Christ never died for my sins; then I am damned rather than saved. The mere Idea of the Saviour isn't enough. I need to be absolutely certain that God did actually become Man, that He really died for my sins, that God did renew His free gift to me through His only begotten Son.

But just because I need so desperately to know that Jesus really lived, I am hopelessly at a loss for evidence or argument sufficient to my need. Can I rest comfortably in the belief that I have been promised eternal life, when the evidence for my belief is merely probable, merely the sort of evidence that an historian or a philosopher can produce? No, too much is at stake: salvation is everything, it is eternity of life rather than death. I am reduced by my terror and my need to infinite concern for something that defies rational grounding. In short, I am reduced to an absolute *leap of faith.*

This passage comes from a portion of the *Postscript* entitled "The Subjective

Thinker." The focus of Kierkegaard's argument is the contrast between my relationship to some other human thinker, such as Socrates, and my relationship to the divine Saviour, Jesus.

The mode of apprehension of the truth is precisely the truth. It is therefore untrue to answer a question in a medium in which the question cannot arise. So for example, to explain reality within the medium of the possible, or to distinguish between possibility and reality within possibility. By refraining from raising the question of reality from the aesthetic or intellectual point of view, but asking this question only ethically, and here again only in the interest of one's own reality, each individual will be isolated and compelled to exist for himself. Irony and hypocrisy as opposite forms, but both expressing the contradiction that the internal is not the external, irony by seeming to be bad, hypocrisy by seeming to be good, emphasize the principle anent the contemplative inquiry concerning ethical inwardness, that reality and deceit are equally possible, and that deceit can clothe itself in the same appearance as reality. It is unethical even to ask at all about another person's ethical inwardness, in so far as such inquiry constitutes a diversion of attention. But if the question is asked nevertheless, the difficulty remains that I can lay hold of the other's reality only by conceiving it, and hence by translating it into a possibility; and in this sphere the possibility of a deception is equally conceivable. This is profitable preliminary training for an ethical mode of existence: to learn that the individual stands alone.

It is a misunderstanding to be concerned about reality from the aesthetic or intellectual point of view. And to be concerned ethically about another's reality is also a misunderstanding, since the only question of reality that is ethically pertinent, is the question of one's own reality. Here we may clearly note the difference that exists between faith *sensu strictissimo* on the one hand (referring as it does to the historical, and the realms of the aesthetic, the intellectual) and the ethical on the other. To ask with infinite interest about a reality which is not one's own, is faith, and this constitutes a paradoxical relationship to the paradoxical. Aesthetically it is impossible to raise such a question except in thoughtlessness, since possibility is aesthetically higher than reality. Nor is it possible to raise such a question ethically, since the sole ethical interest is the interest in one's own reality. The analogy between faith and the ethical is found in the infinite interest, which suffices to distinguish the believer absolutely from an aesthetician or a thinker. But the believer differs from the ethicist in being infinitely interested in the reality of another (in the fact, for example, that God has existed in time). . . .

Precisely in the degree to which I understand a thinker I become indifferent to his reality; that is, to his existence as a particular individual, to his having really understood this or that so and so, to his actually having realized his teaching, and so forth. Aesthetic and speculative thought is quite justified in insisting on this point, and it is important not to lose sight of it. But this does not suffice for a defense of pure thought as a medium of communication between man and man. Because the reality of the teacher is properly indifferent to me as his pupil, and my reality conversely to him, it does not by any means follow that the teacher is justified in being indifferent to his own reality. His communication should bear the stamp of this consciousness, but not directly, since the ethical reality of an individual is not directly communicable (such a direct relationship is exemplified in the paradoxical relation of a believer to the object of his faith), and cannot be understood immediately, but must be understood indirectly through indirect signs.

When the different spheres are not decisively distinguished from one another, confusion reigns everywhere. When people are curious about a thinker's reality and find it interesting to know something about it, and so forth, this interest is intellectually reprehensible. The maximum of attainment in the sphere of the intellectual is to become altogether indifferent to the thinker's reality. But by being thus muddle-headed in the intellectual sphere, one acquires a certain resemblance to a believer. A believer is one who is infinitely interested in another's reality. This is a decisive criterion for faith, and the interest in question is not just a little curiosity, but an absolute dependence upon faith's object.

The object of faith is the reality of another, and the relationship is one of infinite interest. The object of faith is not a doctrine, for then the relationship would be intellectual, and it would be of importance not to botch it, but to realize the maximum intellectual relationship. The object of faith is not a teacher with a doctrine; for when a teacher has a doctrine, the doctrine is *eo ipso* more important than the teacher, and the relationship is again intellectual, and it again becomes important not to botch it, but to realize the maximum intellectual relationship. The object of faith is the reality of the teacher, that the teacher really exists. The answer of faith is therefore unconditionally yes or no. For it does not concern a doctrine, as to whether the doctrine is true or not; it is the answer to a question concerning a fact: "Do you or do you not suppose that he has really existed?" And the answer, it must be noted, is with infinite passion. In the case of a human being, it is thoughtlessness to lay so great and infinite a stress on the question whether he has existed or not. If the object of faith is a human being, therefore, the whole proposal is the vagary of a stupid person, who had not even understood the spirit of the intellectual and the aesthetic. The object of faith is hence the reality of the God-man in the sense of his existence. But existence involves first and foremost particularity, and this is why thought must abstract from existence, because the particular cannot be thought, but only the universal. The object of faith is thus God's reality in existence as a particular individual, the fact that God has existed as an individual human being.

Christianity is no doctrine concerning the unity of the divine and the human, or concerning the identity of subject and object; nor is it any other of the logical transcriptions of Christianity. If Christianity were a doctrine, the relationship to it would not be one of faith, for only an intellectual type of relationship can correspond to a doctrine. Christianity is therefore not a doctrine, but the fact that God has existed.

The realm of faith is thus not a class for numskulls in the sphere of the intellectual, or an asylum for the feeble-minded. Faith constitues a sphere all by itself, and every misunderstanding of Christianity may at once be recognized by its transforming it into a doctrine, transferring it to the sphere of the intellectual. The maximum of attainment within the sphere of the intellectual, namely, to realize an entire indifference as to the reality of the teacher, is in the sphere of faith at the opposite end of the scale. The maximum of attainment within the sphere of faith is to become infinitely interested in the reality of the teacher.

SØREN KIERKEGAARD,
Concluding Unscientific Postscript to the Philosophical Fragments

When students are introduced to the study of philosophy, one of the standard moves is to go through what are usually referred to as the "proofs of the existence of God." This is a set of arguments, developed over the past 2000 years by many different philosophers, which purport to demonstrate that there is, or exists, an infinite, omnipotent, omniscient, benevolent creator of the universe who goes by the name of God. When I teach an introduction to philosophy, I try to slip the proofs for the existence of God in just before Christmas in the fall semester, and just before Easter in the spring semester. It seems fitting, somehow.

Is anyone ever convinced by the proofs? Well you may ask! I have, from time to time, started off my presentation of them by asking how many members of the class believe in God. I mean by that, of course, how many believe that there is a God, not how many believe that He will keep His promise of eternal life. Anyway, I count the hands, and then I present one of the proofs. Usually, I try out what is called the Cosmological Argument, and sometimes I go right into the real number one proof, which is called the Ontological Argument. (We'll get to these in a minute. Don't despair!) After running through the proof, I ask whether there are any objections or criticisms. Usually there aren't any (how many students are going to tell their professor that they think he is crazy?). Then I ask for another show of hands on those who believe in God. Now, it is the most peculiar thing, but even though no one ever objects to my proofs or raises any doubts, not a single person is ever converted to the faith by them! I don't think I have convinced a single, solitary nonbeliever in all the years I have been proving the existence of God. Next I run through the standard refutations for the proofs. (In philosophy, there is an argument against just about everything that there is an argument for.) Same result. I never make agnostics out of the believers, any more than I have made believers out of the agnostics.

When you stop and think about it, there is really something wonderful and mad about a finite, mortal man or woman undertaking to *prove* that God exists. It is as though the philosopher rears up on his hind legs and says, "God! You may be out there, You may exist, but unless You fit into my syllogisms, unless You follow from premises, unless You are a theorem in my system, I won't acknowledge Your existence!" When it comes to sheer effrontery, to what the Greeks called *hubris* and the Jews call *chutzpah,* there just isn't anything to match it.

Philosophers have never been known for their humility, and a fair number of the great ones have had a shot at proving the existence of God. Aristotle tried it, and so did St. Thomas Aquinas. Occam had a proof, Descartes had several, Spinoza came up with some, and even William James, the American pragmatist, offered his own rather odd version of reasons for believing in the existence of God. In this section, we are going to take a close look at the three most famous proofs. These aren't all the proofs, by any means, but they will give you a good idea of some of the different tactics that philosophers have used over the ages. The three proofs are called the *Argument from Design,* the *Cosmological Proof,* and the *Ontological Proof.* We will examine the version of the Argument from Design offered by the eighteenth-century English philosopher William Paley, the Cosmological Argument as it was set forth by the great medieval theologian St. Thomas, and the Ontological Argument in its original version as stated by the man who thought it up, the eleventh-century logician St. Anselm. Since David Hume and Immanuel Kant are the two best proof-for-existence-of-God-refuters who have ever lived, we will look at their refutations together with the proofs. Here we go. Don't be surprised if you hear Kierkegaard laughing at us along the way!

William Paley: The Argument from Design

Our first proof for the existence of God is at once the most obvious, the most natural, the most ancient, the most persuasive, the easiest to understand, and— alas—the philosophically weakest! The *Argument from Design* is quite simple. We observe that certain man-made objects exhibit an internal purposive organization, a fitting of parts to the function of the whole. In a watch, to take the example that Paley himself uses, the various springs and pins and hands are all made precisely to serve the purpose of keeping and telling time. This rational, purposive order in the watch is the direct result of the conscious, rational, purposive activity of its creator, the watchmaker. From the character of the watch, we naturally infer the existence of a watchmaker, whether we actually know him or not. If you show me a watch (or a chair or a painting or even a simple stone axe) and say, It is so old that no one can remember who made it, I would never dream of saying, Perhaps no one made it. The intelligence of its creation inheres in its internal organization. The watch is, if you will permit a bad pun, intelligently produced on the face of it. Well, Paley argues (and so have countless other theologians and philosophers over the ages), nature is more wonderfully organized than the most subtle human contrivance. The human eye far exceeds a camera in sensitivity and fidelity of reproduction; the human brain cannot be duplicated by the most sophisticated computer; the merest one-celled microscopic organism exhibits a biochemical complexity and adaptation that taxes the analytic powers of all science. Who can doubt for a moment that nature has its Creator, an intelligent, purposeful, all-powerful Maker, who in His infinite wisdom has adjusted means to ends, part to whole, organ to organism, throughout the whole of space and time?

The technical name for this is an *argument from analogy.* You have probably encountered ratios or proportions in high school math—problems like: "Eight is to four as six is to *x.* Solve for *x.*" When I was in school, the way to state that mathematically was either like this: $8:4::6:x$, or else like this: $\frac{8}{4} = \frac{6}{x}$. The solution, of course, is $x = 3$. The same sort of "analogy" turns up in

WILLIAM PALEY (1743–1805) was an English churchman whose writings in defense of Christianity were widely read and much admired in the eighteenth and nineteenth centuries. Paley was a defender of utilitarianism in moral philosophy and of the truths of revelation in theology (a position known as *theism*). His book, *Natural Theology,* was a systematic presentation of the so-called "argument from design" for the existence of God, an argument which David Hume had vigorously attacked in his *Dialogues Concerning Natural Religion.*

aptitude tests. "Fire engine is to fire department as _____ is to police department." The answer is "police car." The point is that if we already know the relationship between one pair of things (such as the numbers 8 and 4, or a fire engine and the fire department), then when we are presented with only one member of another pair, we may be able to figure out what the other member of the pair is (3 in the math example, or a police car in the other case). Now all this may seem like baby talk to you, but philosophers frequently build powerful arguments from what look like very simple pieces.

Paley and the other arguers from design draw up two sorts of analogies. The first is between a man-made object and its human maker on the one hand, and a particular organism or bit of natural organization and its divine Creator on the other. So we get:

Watch is to watchmaker as the human eye is to *x.*   *x* = God.

The other analogy is between a man-made object and its human maker on the one hand, and the whole universe and its divine Creator on the other. So this time we get:

Watch is to watchmaker as the universe is to *x.*   *x* = God.

Here is Paley's own statement of the argument. Because he tends to be rather wordy, I have edited it down to the bare bones.

In crossing a heath, suppose I pitched my foot against a *stone,* and were asked how the stone came to be there, I might possibly answer, that for any thing I knew to the contrary it had lain there for ever; nor would it, perhaps, be very easy to show the absurdity of this answer. But suppose I had found a *watch* upon the ground, and it should be inquired how the watch happened to be in that place, I should hardly think of the answer which I had before given, that for any thing I knew the watch might have always been there. Yet why should not this answer serve for the watch as well as for the stone; why is it not as admissible in the second case as in the first? For this reason, and for no other, namely, that when we come to inspect the watch, we perceive—what we could not discover in the stone—that its several parts are framed and put together for a purpose, *e.g.* that they are so formed and adjusted as to produce motion, and that motion so regulated as to point out the hour of the day; that if the different parts had been differently shaped from what they are, or placed after any other manner or in any other order than that in which they are placed, either no motion at all would have been carried on in the machine, or none which would have answered the use that is now served by it. . . .

. . . This mechanism being observed—it requires indeed an examination of the instrument, and perhaps some previous knowledge of the subject, to perceive and understand it; but being once, as we have said, observed and understood, the inference we think is inevitable, that the watch must have had a maker—that there must have existed, at some time and at some place or other, an artificer or artificers who formed it for the purpose which, we find it actually to answer, who comprehended its construction and designed its use. . . .

Were there no example in the world of contrivance except that of the *eye,* it would be alone sufficient to support the conclusion which we draw from it, as to the necessity of an intelligent Creator. It could never be got rid of, because it could not be accounted for by any other supposition which did not contradict all the principles we possess of knowledge—the principles according to which things do, as often as they can be brought to the test of experience, turn out to be true or false. . . .

. . . If other parts of nature were inaccessible to our inquiries, or even if other parts of nature presented nothing to our examination but disorder and confusion, the validity of this example would remain the same. If there were but one watch in the world, it would not be less certain that it had a maker. If we had never in our lives seen any but one single kind of hydraulic machine, yet if of that one kind we understood the mechanism and use, we should be as perfectly assured that it proceeded from the hand and thought and skill of a workman, as if we visited a museum of the arts, and saw collected there twenty different kinds of machines for drawing water, or a thousand different kinds for other purposes. Of this point each machine is a proof independently of all the rest. So it is with the evidences of a divine agency. The proof is not a conclusion which lies at the end of a chain of reasoning, of which chain each instance of contrivance is only a link, and of which, if one link fail, the whole falls; but it is an argument separately supplied by every separate example. An error in stating an example affects only that example. The argument is cumulative, in the fullest sense of that term. The eye proves it without the ear; the ear without the eye. The proof in each example is complete; for when the design of the part, and the conduciveness of its structure to that design is shown, the mind may set itself at rest; no future consideration can detract any thing from the force of the example.

WILLIAM PALEY, *Natural Theology*

This argument has an antique sound, of course. It was written 175 years ago, after all. But the principle underlying it is one we use today in interplanetary exploration. When men first walked on the moon, they looked of course for evidences of intelligent life, though they didn't really expect to find such evidences on an atmosphereless body. Now how on earth (or elsewhere) could they possibly tell what would *be* evidence of intelligent life? Having no advance knowledge of the sorts of creatures that might inhabit other parts of the universe, by what signs could the astronauts infer their existence and presence? The answer is obvious. Any sort of device, or instrument, or machine, that exhibited some purposive internal organization, and that seemed not to grow naturally in that environment, would permit them to infer by analogy the existence of some (presumably) nonhuman intelligent maker.

Anyone who has been enraptured, bemused, or awestruck by the wonder of nature will appreciate the psychological force of the Argument from Design. Can the order of planets, stars, and galaxies, the underlying simplicity and regularity of natural forces, the exquisitely delicate adjustment of part to part in living things really just *be?* Must there not be some intelligence directing, organizing, creating this vast interconnected universe?

Well, maybe so, but the Argument from Design won't prove it! There are basically two things wrong with the Argument from Design. First of all, even if it is correct, it doesn't prove what Paley and most other Christian, Jewish, or Muslim theologians want it to prove. And second, it doesn't really prove much of anything at all. The first point is liable to slip by us because we are so mesmerized by the word "God." In the great Western religions, God is conceived as an infinite, eternal, omnipotent (infinitely powerful), omniscient (all-knowing) creator of the universe. But the most that the Argument from Design can prove, even if it is sound, is that there is a *very* long-lived (not eternal), very powerful (not omnipotent), very wise (not omniscient) world-or-ganizer who has worked up the raw materials of space, time, and matter into a reasonably well-integrated machinelike universe. After all, the watchmaker does not create his materials, he merely fashions them to his purposes. And the human eye is not infinitely complex, it is just a good deal more complex than a camera. So if the analogy is taken strictly, we can at best demonstrate the existence of a conscious, purposeful, powerful, very knowledgeable, very old world-maker. But if we label that world-maker "God," then we may mistak-enly slip into identifying him or it with the God of the Old and New Testaments, the God of the great Western religions, the God who lays down commandments, punishes the wicked, offers the free gift of eternal life, and so forth. And absolutely nothing in the analogy justifies any of those conclusions!

But the argument isn't even very sound, as David Hume pointed out in one of his most brilliant works, the *Dialogues Concerning Natural Religion.* Hume actually wrote the dialogues in the 1750s, twenty years before his death in 1776, but he was prevailed upon by his friends (including the economist and philosopher Adam Smith) to withhold them from publication, because the forcefulness of their attack on received religious opinions would open Hume to condemnation. Eventually, they were brought out posthumously in 1779 by his nephew. The work is a three-person discussion of all the principal arguments for the existence of God, in which first one character and then another comes to the fore. In the subtlety of their development and pacing, the *Dialogues* have something of the quality of a Baroque trio, and I think it may fairly be said that Hume is the only great philosopher after Plato to use the dialogue form to its full literary effect. The work is in twelve parts, and this selection comes from Part Two. The speaker is the skeptic, Philo:

In reality, CLEANTHES, continued he, there is no need of having recourse to that affected scepticism, so displeasing to you, in order to come at this determination. Our ideas reach no farther than our experience: We have no experience of divine attributes and operations: I need not conclude my syllogism: You can draw the inference yourself. And it is a pleasure to me (and I hope to you too) that just reasoning and sound piety here concur in the same conclusion, and both of them establish the adorably mysterious and incomprehensible nature of the supreme Being. . . .

What I chiefly scruple in this subject, said PHILO, is not so much, that all religious arguments are by CLEANTHES reduced to experience, as that they appear not to be even the most certain and irrefragable of that inferior kind. That a stone will fall, that fire will burn, that the earth has solidity, we have observed a thousand and a thousand times; and when any new instance of this nature is presented, we draw without hesitation the accustomed inference. The exact similarity of the cases gives us a perfect assurance of a similar event; and a stronger evidence is never desired nor sought after. But wherever you depart, in the least, from the similarity of the cases, you diminish proportionably the evidence; and may at last bring it to a very weak *analogy,* which is confessedly liable to error and uncertainty. After having experienced the circulation of the blood in human creatures, we make no doubt that it takes place in Titius and Maevius: But from its circulation in frogs and fishes, it is only a presumption, though a strong one, from analogy, that it takes place in men and other animals. The analogical reasoning is much weaker, when we infer the circulation of the sap in vegetables from our experience that the blood circulates in animals; and those, who hastily followed that imperfect analogy, are found, by more accurate experiments, to have been mistaken.

If we see a house, CLEANTHES, we conclude, with the greatest certainty, that it had an architect or builder; because this is precisely that species of effect, which we have experienced to proceed from that species of cause. But surely you will not affirm, that the universe bears such a resemblance to a house, that we can with the same certainty infer a similar cause, or that the analogy is here entire and perfect. The dissimilitude is so striking, that the utmost you can here pretend to is a guess, a conjecture, a presumption concerning a similar cause; and how that pretension will be received in the world, I leave you to consider. . . .

Were a man to abstract from every thing which he knows or has seen, he would be altogether incapable, merely from his own ideas, to determine what kind of scene the universe must be, or to give the preference to one state or situation of things above another. For as nothing, which he clearly conceives, could be esteemed impossible or implying a contradiction, every chimera of his fancy would be upon an equal footing; nor could he assign any just reason, why he adheres to one idea or system, and rejects the others, which are equally possible.

Again; after he opens his eyes, and contemplates the world, as it really is, it would be impossible for him, at first, to assign the cause of any one event; much less, of the whole of things or of the universe. He might set his fancy a rambling; and she might bring him in an infinite variety of reports and representations. These would all be possible; but being all equally possible, he would never, of himself, give a satisfactory account for his preferring one of them to the rest. Experience alone can point out to him the true cause of any phenomenon.

DAVID HUME, *Dialogues Concerning Natural Religion*

Although Hume's refutation stands pretty well on its own feet, it also draws upon the more fundamental criticisms which Hume developed of causal reasoning of all sorts. In Chapter Seven, we will have another opportunity to examine the reasons for his skepticism concerning any attempt to infer causes from effects or effects from causes.

St. Thomas Aquinas: The Cosmological Argument

Christian theologians derive their beliefs about God from two sources. The first is *revelation,* consisting of those truths which God has revealed to us through the holy writings of the Old and New Testaments or through His miraculous appearance to particular individuals. Revelation must of course be interpreted, and therein lies the origin of many learned disputes and bloody wars. But everyone agrees that the *fact* of revelation is simply a miracle, to be taken on faith. The second source is *reason,* our natural human power of analysis, argument, observation, and inference. We must wait for revelation. We cannot make it happen, and we cannot predict when or where God will reveal Himself. But reason is our own instrument, and we can deploy it at will to seek out the origins of the universe and the existence and nature of a Creator. The greatest of all the rational theologians, by universal agreement, is the thirteenth-century Christian philosopher St. Thomas Aquinas. His elaboration and codification of the rational metaphysical basis for Christian theology remains to this day the dominant intellectual influence in the Roman Catholic Church. The philosophy known as Thomism is an enduring monument of medieval intellectual architecture, as impressive in its way as the great Cathedral of Notre Dame in Paris.

Aquinas actually offers five separate proofs for the existence of God in his most important work, the *Summa Theologica.* The first three of these are variations of the same argument, and we shall examine them all together. In each case, Aquinas begins with some fact about the world: The first argument takes off from the fact that things *move* in the world around us; the second

ST. THOMAS AQUINAS (1225–1274) is the greatest intellectual figure of the high medieval culture that flourished in Europe during the thirteenth century. Aquinas was an Italian theologian and philosopher who spent his life in the Dominican Order, teaching and writing. His writings, which run to many volumes, set forth in extremely systematic form a full-scale theory of God, man, and the universe. The official dogma of the Church, as established by revelation and interpretation of holy scriptures, was combined by Aquinas with the secular metaphysical doctrines of Aristotle and the post-Aristotelian Greek and Roman philosophers.

Aquinas' philosophical synthesis of philosophy and theology became the accepted teaching of the Roman Catholic Church. It is known today as Thomism, and in various forms continues to exercise a profound intellectual influence both on Church doctrine and on the philosophical work of Catholic and non-Catholic thinkers.

from the fact that every event that is observed to take place is made to happen, or caused, by something else that precedes it; the third from the fact that there are at least some things in the world whose existence is not necessary, which are, in metaphysical language, "possible." Aquinas then reasons that the observed motion, or event, or possible thing, is the last in a chain of motions or causes or possible things, and he asserts that such a chain cannot reach back endlessly to prior motions, to earlier causes, to other possible things on which this thing depends for its existence. Somewhere, the chain must end, with a mover that is not itself also moved by something else, with a cause which is not itself caused by yet another cause, with a being whose existence is not merely possible but necessary. That first mover, first cause, or necessary being, is God.

If the task of proving the existence of God weren't such a serious business, we might say that the cosmological argument is a very sophisticated answer to the four-year-old's question, "Where did I come from, Mommy?" Now a straight answer would be, "You came from inside mommy's womb." And after a few more details have been added, that answer usually satisfies a four-year-old. Eventually, the obvious follow-up question will occur to a six- or seven-year-old, namely, "Where did you come from, mommy?" A somewhat longer story about grandma and grandpa should handle that one. But sooner or later, a bright child is going to start brooding on the *real* problem. Maybe I came from Mom and Dad, each of whom came in turn from a mother and father; maybe the earliest human mothers and fathers evolved through a combination and mutation and selection from prehuman mammals, who in turn evolved from reptiles, or what have you; and maybe life itself sprang up spontaneously through chance rearrangements of amino-acid-like compounds, which in turn emerged from the stuff of which the earth was formed, but *damn it,* somewhere the buck has got to stop! If there isn't anything that was *first,* then how can there be anything at all? If the existence of each particular thing is to be explained by saying that it came from some preceding thing, then we have no explanation at all. We just have a chain that leads so far back into the misty past that finally we get tired of asking, and mistake our fatigue for an answer. In short, an "infinite regress" is no answer at all. We might just as well have answered the very first question by saying, "Shut up and don't ask silly questions!"

So we might summarize Aquinas' proofs by saying that if the universe makes any sense at all, if it is through and through rational, then there must be a necessary being, a first mover, a first cause. Here are the three proofs as Aquinas stated them. Notice that he doesn't waste any words! He proves the existence of God three times in the space it takes Plato to introduce one of the characters in a dialogue.

. . . The existence of God can be proved in five ways.

The first and more manifest way is the argument from motion. It is certain, and evident to our senses, that in the world some things are in motion. Now whatever is moved is moved by another, for nothing can be moved except it is in potentiality to that towards which it is moved; whereas a thing moves inasmuch as it is in act. For motion is nothing else than the reduction of something from potentiality to actuality. But nothing can be reduced from potentiality to actuality, except by something in a state of actuality. Thus that which is actually hot, as fire, makes wood, which is potentially hot, to be actually hot, and thereby moves and changes it. Now it is not possible that the same thing should be at once in actuality and potentiality in the same respect but only in different respects. For what is actually hot cannot simultaneously be potentially hot; but it is simultaneously potentially cold. It is therefore impossible that in the same respect and in the same way a thing should be both mover and moved, *i.e.,* that it should move itself. Therefore, whatever is moved must be moved by another. If that by which it is moved be itself moved, then this also must needs be moved by another, and that by another again. But this cannot go on to infinity, because then there would be no first mover, and, consequently, no other mover, seeing that subsequent movers move only inasmuch as they are moved by the first mover; as the staff moves only because it is moved by the hand. Therefore it is necessary to arrive at a first mover, moved by no other; and this everyone understands to be God.

The second way is from the nature of efficient cause. In the world of sensible things we find there is an order of efficient causes. There is no case known (neither is it, indeed, possible) in which a thing is found to be the efficient cause of itself; for so it would be prior to itself, which is impossible. Now in efficient causes it is not possible to go on to infinity, because in all efficient causes following in order, the first is the cause of the intermediate cause, and the intermediate is the cause of the ultimate cause, whether the intermediate cause be several, or one only. Now to take away the cause is to take away the effect. Therefore, if there be no first cause among efficient causes, there will be no ultimate, nor any intermediate, cause. But if in efficient causes it is possible to go on to infinity, there will be no first efficient cause, neither will there be an ultimate effect, nor any intermediate efficient causes; all of which is plainly false. Therefore it is necessary to admit a first efficient cause, to which everyone gives the name of God.

The third way is taken from possibility and necessity, and runs thus. We find in nature things that are possible to be and not to be, since they are found to be generated, and to be corrupted, and consequently, it is possible for them to be and not to be. But it is impossible for these always to exist, for that which can not-be at some time is not. Therefore, if everything can not-be, then at one time there was nothing in existence. Now if this were true, even now there would be nothing in existence, because that which does not exist begins to exist only through something already existing. Therefore, if at one time nothing was in existence, it would have been impossible for anything to have begun to exist; and thus even now nothing would be in existence—which is absurd. Therefore, not all beings are merely possible, but there must exist something the existence of which is necessary. But every necessary thing either has its necessity caused by another, or not. Now it is impossible to go on to infinity in necessary things which have their necessity caused by another, as has been already proved in regard to efficient causes. Therefore we cannot but admit the existence of some being having of itself its own necessity, and not receiving it from another, but rather causing in others their necessity. This all men speak of as God.

ST. THOMAS AQUINAS, *Summa Theologica*

Hume has an answer to these arguments as well as to the argument from design. In Part IX of his *Dialogues,* he considers a version which reasons from cause and effect to the existence of a first cause, whose existence must therefore be necessary. It is thus a combination of the second and third of Aquinas' proofs. Hume's refutation, put this time into the mouth of the character named

Cleanthes, begins with a paragraph that is also a refutation of the third great proof, the ontological argument. More of that a little later.

I shall begin with observing, that there is an evident absurdity in pretending to demonstrate a matter of fact, or to prove it by any arguments a *priori*. Nothing is demonstrable, unless the contrary implies a contradiction. Nothing, that is distinctly conceivable, implies a contradiction. Whatever we conceive as existent, we can also conceive as non-existent. There is no Being, therefore, whose non-existence implies a contradiction. Consequently there is no Being, whose existence is demonstrable. I propose this argument as entirely decisive, and am willing to rest the whole controversy upon it.

It is pretended that the Deity is a necessarily existent Being; and this necessity of his existence is attempted to be explained by asserting that, if we knew his whole essence or nature, we should perceive it to be as impossible for him not to exist as for twice two not to be four. But it is evident, that this can never happen, while our faculties remain the same as at present. It will still be possible for us, at any time, to conceive the non-existence of what we formerly conceived to exist; nor can the mind ever lie under a necessity of supposing any object to remain always in being: in the same manner as we lie under a necessity of always conceiving twice two to be four. The words, therefore, *necessary existence,* have no meaning; or, which is the same thing, none that is consistent.

But farther; why may not the material universe be the necessarily existent Being, according to this pretended explication of necessity? We dare not affirm that we know all the qualities of matter; and for aught we can determine, it may contain some qualities, which, were they known, would make its non-existence appear as great a contradiction as that twice two is five. I find only one argument employed to prove, that the material world is not the necessarily existent Being; and this argument is derived from the contingency both of the matter and the form of the world. "Any particle of matter," it is said, "may be *conceived* to be annihilated; and any form may be *conceived* to be altered. Such an annihilation or alteration, therefore, is not impossible." But it seems a great partiality not to perceive, that the same argument extends equally to the Deity, so far as we have any conception of him; and that the mind can at least imagine him to be nonexistent, or his attributes to be altered. It must be some unknown, inconceivable qualities, which can make non-existence appear impossible, or his attributes unalterable: And no reason can be assigned, why these qualities may not belong to matter. As they are altogether unknown and inconceivable, they can never be proved incompatible with it.

Add to this, that in tracing an eternal succession of objects, it seems absurd to inquire for a general cause or first Author. How can any thing, that exists from eternity, have a cause, since that relation implies a priority in time and a beginning of existence?

In such a chain too, or succession of objects, each part is caused by that which preceded it, and causes that which succeeds it. Where then is the difficulty? But the WHOLE, you say, wants a cause. I answer, that the uniting of these parts into a whole, like the uniting of several distinct counties into one kingdom, or several distinct members into one body, is performed merely by an arbitrary act of the mind, and has no influence on the nature of things. Did I show you the particular causes of each individual in a collection of twenty particles of matter, I should think it very unreasonable, should you afterwards ask me, what was the cause of the whole twenty. This is sufficiently explained in explaining the cause of the parts.

DAVID HUME, *Dialogues Concerning Natural Religion*

St. Anselm: The Ontological Argument

Here it is, the most famous, the most mystifying, the most outrageous and irritating philosophical argument of all time! Read it carefully and see what you think.

Truly there is a God, although the fool hath said in his heart, There is no God.

And so, Lord, do thou, who dost give understanding to faith, give me, so far as thou knowest it to be profitable, to understand that thou art as we believe; and that thou art that which we believe. And, indeed, we believe that thou art a being than which nothing greater can be conceived. Or is there no such nature, since the fool hath said in his heart, there is no God? (Psalms xiv. 1). But, at any rate, this very fool, when he hears of this being of which I speak—a being than which nothing greater can be conceived—understands what he hears, and what he understands is in his understanding; although he does not understand it to exist.

For, it is one thing for an object to be in the understanding, and another to understand that the object exists. When a painter first conceives of what he will afterwards perform, he has it in his understanding, but he does not yet understand it to be, because he has not yet performed it. But after he has made the painting,

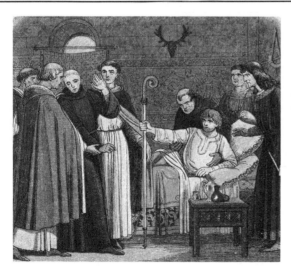

SAINT ANSELM (1033–1109) was born in Italy, and was trained there for the priesthood. In 1093, he was appointed Archbishop of Canterbury in England by the Norman king William Rufus. His most important philosophical work is the *Proslogion,* in which he set forth a startling and radically new proof for the existence of God. The proof, known now as the "ontological argument," has been defended over the past nine centuries by Descartes, Spinoza, and others. St. Thomas Aquinas, on the other hand, claimed that it was not a valid proof, and he rejected it.

This drawing shows the ceremony in which Anselm (standing, with hand raised) was appointed Archbishop of Canterbury by the king.

he both has it in his understanding, and he understands that it exists, because he has made it.

Hence, even the fool is convinced that something exists in the understanding, at least, than which nothing greater can be conceived. For, when he hears of this, he understands it. And whatever is understood, exists in the understanding. And, assuredly that, than which nothing greater can be conceived, cannot exist in the understanding alone. For, suppose it exists in the understanding alone: then it can be conceived to exist in reality; which is greater.

Therefore, if that, than which nothing greater can be conceived, exists in the understanding alone, the very being, than which nothing greater can be conceived, is one, than which a greater can be conceived. But obviously this is impossible. Hence, there is no doubt that there exists a being, than which nothing greater can be conceived, and it exists both in the understanding and in reality.

And it assuredly exists so truly, that it cannot be conceived not to exist. For, it is possible to conceive of a being which cannot be conceived not to exist; and this is greater than one which can be conceived not to exist. Hence, if that, than which nothing greater can be conceived, can be conceived not to exist, it is not that, than which nothing is greater can be conceived. But this is an irreconcilable contradiction. There is, then, so truly a being than which nothing greater can be conceived to exist, that it cannot even be conceived not to exist; and this being thou art, O Lord, our God.

So truly, therefore, dost thou exist, O Lord, my God, that thou canst not be conceived not to exist; and rightly. For, if a mind could conceive of a being better than thee, the creature would rise above the Creator; and this is most absurd. And, indeed, whatever else there is, except thee alone, can be conceived not to exist. To thee alone, therefore, it belongs to exist more truly than all other beings, and hence in a higher degree than all others. For, whatever else exists does not exist so truly, and hence in a less degree it belongs to it to exist. Why, then, has the fool said in his heart, there is no God (Psalms xiv. 1), since it is so evident, to a rational mind, that thou dost exist in the highest degree of all? Why, except that he is dull and a fool?

ST. ANSELM, *Proslogion*

Whenever I read the Ontological Argument, I have the same feeling that comes over me when I watch a really good magician. Nothing up this sleeve; nothing up the other sleeve; nothing in the hat; presto! A big, fat rabbit. How can Anselm pull God out of an idea? At least the Argument from Design and Cosmological Arguments start from some actual fact about the world, whether it is the apparently purposeful organization of living things, or the motion of bodies in space, or whatever. But the Ontological Argument starts from a mere idea in the mind of the philosopher and undertakes to prove, from that idea alone, that there must actually be something corresponding to the idea. The argument makes no use at all of facts that might be gathered by observation or analysis of the world. Philosophers call an argument of this sort an *a priori* argument. Propositions that can be known to be true without consideration of factual support, merely from an analysis of the concepts involved in the judgments, are called propositions *knowable a priori,* or simply "*a priori* propositions."

Now, philosophers have for a long time held that there are *a priori* propositions, or propositions whose truth can be known merely from a consideration of their meaning. For example, consider the proposition, "If an aardvark is a mammal, then it bears its young live." Is that true? Well, your first reaction might be to ask yourself whether you know what an aardvark is, or maybe to look it up in the encyclopedia. But stop and think about it for a moment. A mammal is an animal that bears its young live rather than laying eggs. That is what we *mean* when we call something a mammal. This is part of the definition of the word "mammal." So if anything is to be classified as a mammal, it will have to be the sort of thing that bears its young live. Otherwise, we wouldn't call it a mammal; we would call it something else, or even just say that we don't have a word for it. If you think about it, you will realize that you can decide about the truth of my proposition without knowing anything about aardvarks, indeed without ever having heard the word "aardvark" before. Whatever aardvarks are, "If an aardvark is a mammal, then it bears its young live." In short, you can know the truth of the proposition *a priori,* or even more briefly, it is an *a priori* proposition.

But are there any aardvarks? Ah well, that is quite another question. My *a priori* proposition only tells me that if there are any, and if they are mammals, then they bear their young live. It doesn't tell me whether there are any. Indeed, it doesn't even tell me whether aardvarks are mammals. It just says, *if* there are aardvarks and they are mammals, then they bear their young live. Propositions that can be known to be true merely on the basis of the meanings of the words used in them are called *tautologies,* and you can make up tautologies all day long, with no more material to work with than the English language.

The Ontological Argument seems to depend on a tautology too. First Anselm *defines* the word "God" as meaning "a being than which nothing greater can be conceived." Then he argues that this concept, of a greatest being, must include the notion that the being cannot be conceived not to exist. In other words, he argues that when we spell out the definition of "God" as "a being than which nothing greater can be conceived," we will find that the definition includes the characteristic "necessarily existing," just as when we spell out the definition of "mammal," we find that it includes the notion "bearing its young live."

Well, "Mammals bear their young live" is a tautology; it is true by definition; we can know it to be true merely by understanding the words used in the statement. It follows from the definition. So too, Anselm claims, "God necessarily exists" is a tautology; it too is true by definition; it too can be known merely through an understanding of the words used in the statement. But there is one enormous difference. The statement about mammals, and all the other ordinary tautologies that have ever been thought up, say nothing about whether something *exists*. Ordinary tautologies just tell us that *if* there are any things fitting a certain definition, *then* they have the following characteristics. If there are mammals, then they bear their young live; if there are any bachelors, then they are unmarried (because "bachelor" means "unmarried man"); if there are any triangles, then they have three angles; and so forth. The Ontological Argument is the only case in which a tautology is used to prove that something—namely, God—exists.

Now, of course philosophers who use the Ontological Argument are perfectly well aware that this is a very special and peculiar sort of tautology. If they can prove the existence of God this way, why can't I use the same trick to prove the existence of a perfect horse, or a necessarily existent ox, or a mosquito than which none greater can be conceived? Their answer is that God is different from all the other beings in or out of the universe, and that God's existence is a different sort of existence from the existence of every created thing. God is infinite, all other things are finite; God's existence is necessary, the existence of every other thing is merely contingent; God is perfect, all else is imperfect; and God's existence follows *a priori* from His definition, whereas the existence of every other thing, since it depends ultimately on God and not on itself alone, follows *not* from its own definition but only from God's act of creation.

The Ontological Argument remains to this day one of the most controversial arguments in all of philosophy. Some very devout theologians, including St. Thomas Aquinas, have believed that it was wrong, invalid, a confusion. Several of the greatest philosophers of the seventeenth century, including Descartes and Spinoza, thought it was valid, and developed their own versions of it. In his great *Critique of Pure Reason*, Immanuel Kant offered an elaborate refutation of the argument which for more than a hundred years was thought to have permanently laid it to rest. Just recently, however, there has been a revival of philosophical interest in the Ontological Argument, and philosophers like myself, who grew up thinking that Kant had once and for all finished it off, now find the technical journals full of new versions of the Ontological Argument, in which the latest tools of formal logic are used to give the old warhorse some new life.

Let us wind up this discussion of proofs for the existence of God with Kant's refutation of the Ontological Argument. This is a difficult passage, harder even than the argument itself, which was no breeze. Please don't expect to understand everything Kant is saying. I have been studying Kant for twenty-five years, and I am not sure what he means sometimes. But read through this selection two or three times, with the aid of your professor. Kant always repays hard work, and his treatment of the Ontological Argument is one of his most brilliant efforts.

One bit of explanation before you begin. Kant asks whether the proposition "God exists" is an *analytic* or a *synthetic* proposition. An *analytic* proposition, according to Kant, is a statement which merely spells out, or *analyzes,* what is already contained in the subject of the statement. For example, the proposition,

"Triangles have three angles," tells us nothing new about triangles. All it does is repeat what is already contained in the idea of a triangle. *Synthetic* propositions, on the other hand, add something to what is contained in the idea of the subject of the proposition. "Bachelors are unhappy" is synthetic (whether or not it is true!), because being unhappy is *not* part of what we mean by being a bachelor. "Bachelors are unmarried" is analytic, however, for being unmarried *is* part of what we mean by being a bachelor. Kant argues, as you will see, that any proposition which asserts the existence of something must be a synthetic proposition. He thinks that this claim successfully undermines the Ontological Argument.

Notwithstanding all these general considerations, in which every one must concur, we may be challenged with a case which is brought forward as proof that in actual fact the contrary holds, namely, that there is one concept, and indeed only one, in reference to which the not-being or rejection of its object is in itself contradictory, namely, the concept of the *ens realissimum*. It is declared that it possesses all reality, and that we are justified in assuming that such a being is possible (the fact that a concept does not contradict itself by no means proves the possibility of its object: but the contrary assertion I am for the moment willing to allow). Now 'all reality' includes existence; existence is therefore contained in the concept of a thing that is possible. If, then, this thing is rejected, the internal possibility of the thing is rejected—which is self-contradictory.

My answer is as follows. There is already a contradiction in introducing the concept of existence—no matter under what title it may be disguised—into the concept of a thing which we profess to be thinking solely in reference to its possibility. If that be allowed as legitimate, a seeming victory has been won: but in actual fact nothing at all is said: the assertion is a mere tautology. We must ask: Is the proposition that *this* or *that thing* (which, whatever it may be, is allowed as possible) *exists,* an analytic or a synthetic proposition? If it is analytic, the assertion of the existence of the thing adds nothing to the thought of the thing; but in that case either the thought, which is in us, is the thing itself, or we have presupposed an existence as belonging to the realm of the possible, and have then, on that pretext, inferred its existence from its internal possibility—which is nothing but a miserable tautology. The word "reality," which in the concept of the thing sounds other than the word "existence" in the concept of the predicate, is of no avail in meeting this objection. For if all positing (no matter what it may be that is posited) is entitled reality, the thing with all its predicates is already posited in the concept of the subject, and is assumed as actual; and in the predicate this is merely repeated. But if, on the other hand, we admit, as every reasonable person must, that all existential propositions are synthetic, how can we profess to maintain that the predicate of existence cannot be rejected without contradiction? This is a feature which is found only in analytic propositions, and is indeed precisely what constitutes their analytic character.

I should have hoped to put an end to these idle and fruitless disputations in a direct manner, by an accurate determination of the concept of existence, had I not found that the illusion which is caused by the confusion of a logical with a real predicate (that is, with a predicate which determines a thing) is almost beyond correction. Anything we please can be made to serve as a logical predicate; the subject can even be predicated of itself; for logic abstracts from all content. But a *determining* predicate is a predicate which is added to the concept of the subject and enlarges it. Consequently, it must not be already contained in the concept.

"*Being*" is obviously not a real predicate; that is, it is not a concept of something which could be added to the concept of a thing. It is merely the positing of a thing, or of certain determinations, as existing in themselves. Logically, it is merely the copula of a judgment. The proposition, "God is omnipotent," contains two concepts, each of which has its object—God is omnipotent," contains two concepts, each of which has its object—God and omnipotence. The small word "is" adds no new predicate, but only serves to posit the predicate *in its relation* to the subject. If, now, we take the subject (God) with all its predicates (among which is omnipotence), and say "God is," or "There is a God," we attach no new predicate to the concept of God, but only posit the subject in itself with all its predicates, and indeed posit it as being an *object* that stands in relation to my *concept*. The content of both must be one and the same; nothing can have been added to the concept, which expresses merely what is possible, by my thinking its object (through the expression "it is") as given absolutely. Otherwise stated, the real contains no more than the merely possible. A hundred real thalers do not contain the least coin more than a hundred possible thalers. For as the latter signify the concept, and the former the object and the positing of the object, should the former contain more than the latter, my concept would not, in that case, express the whole object, and would not therefore be an adequate concept of it. My financial position is, however, affected very differently by a hundred real thalers than it is by the mere concept of them (that is, of their possibility). For the object, as it actually exists, is not analytically contained in my concept, but is added to my concept (which is a determination of my state) synthetically; and yet the conceived hundred thalers are not themselves in the least increased through thus acquiring existence outside my concept.

IMMANUEL KANT, *Critique of Pure Reason*

III
___

Kierkegaard concentrated entirely on *faith,* on the inner passionate concern with the truth of the Christian message. He scorned all rational evidences and arguments as radically inadequate to his religious needs. Anselm, Aquinas, and Paley, together with thousands of other rational theologians and religious philosophers, have looked to *reason* to support their faith, either through *a priori* arguments for the existence of God, or through *a posteriori* arguments founded upon His effects in the world He created. But for Kierkegaard, Anselm, Aquinas, Paley and all the rest, there can be no real human doubt about the truth and centrality of religion. Even Kant was, in his personal life, a devoted, practicing Christian.

To some men and women, however, religion has seemed to be a fraud, a sham, a delusion foisted by humanity upon itself, or else foisted by priests and holy men on the common people. Karl Marx believed that the proletarian revolution would eliminate established religious institutions along with all the other instruments by which ruling classes have oppressed mankind. Eventually, religion, like the state, would wither away, leaving a society thoroughly secular and thoroughly rational.

Quite apart from formal attacks on religion by philosophers or social reformers, there has been a dramatic decline in the religiosity of Western society during the last century and a half. Even in such countries as Italy, which maintains official ties with the Roman Catholic Church, the influence of religious belief on the everyday lives of men and women has declined. In the United States, religion plays virtually no part in the public affairs of the nation, and despite a fair amount of Sunday church-going, only a small portion of the American people place their religious beliefs at the center of their private lives in the way that almost all people did two centuries ago. This progressive secularization of Western society seems to be related to industrialization, to urbanization, to the gradual rise to dominance of scientific modes of dealing with the world, rather than to changes in philosophical arguments. Periodically, religious revivals sweep the country, apparently reversing the tide of secularization. But when the waves recede, the level of religiosity settles at a new low, and the process continues.

One of the most powerful attacks on religious belief comes not from a philosopher but from the father of modern psychoanalytic theory, Sigmund Freud. Freud is famous for the discovery of the unconscious, for his theory of infant sexuality, and for his invention of the method of psychoanalysis. "Lying on the couch" and "going to the shrink" have entered into our language as slang for receiving the treatment which Freud developed for emotional problems. Because of his emphasis on the irrational components in the human personality, Freud is sometimes thought of as an enemy of rationalism. Certainly, he was an enemy of the facile and comfortable belief that man is a rational animal, and that reason can without much trouble establish control over the nonrational forces in the soul. But in a deeper sense, Freud was a rationalist through and through. He believed, as Plato did, that human beings suffer great unhappiness when the irrational elements in the soul control and manipulate the rational elements. He believed too, as Plato did, that self-knowledge was the cure for that unnecessary unhappiness. But Freud parted company with Plato, and with many other students of the human condition as well, in his pessimistic conviction that even a healthy personality would necessarily suffer pain and misery. The problem, as Freud saw it, was that the human condition is fundamentally compromised by disease, by death, and by the unbridgeable gap between the deep desires we all have for erotic gratification and the limited opportunities we have in the real world for the satisfaction of those desires.

Faced with frustration and death, Freud argued, we systematically fool

SIGMUND FREUD (1856–1939) was the founder of the branch of medicine and psychological theory known as psychoanalysis. Freud was born in Austria, where he was trained as a neurologist. Through his clinical work on problems of hysterical paralysis, he became interested in the possibility of unconscious mental processes. Working first with the techniques of hypnosis and later with techniques of dream interpretation and word association which he invented, Freud made major discoveries about the workings of the mind. His studies of the unconscious and his emphasis on the central importance of sexuality in the mental life of adults and of children aroused great controversy and brought down on Freud considerable criticism both from the medical community and from the general public. Freud had many pupils and disciples who carried on his research and developed the therapeutic techniques he had devised. Though only a portion of modern-day psychiatrists and psychoanalysts describe themselves as "Freudians," virtually every branch of psychiatry is deeply indebted to Freud's work. In the last years of his life Freud was forced to leave Austria to escape persecution by the Nazis. He died in England.

ourselves with fairy tales, dreams, fantasies, and illusions. The greatest of those illusions is religion, and its hold on us is so strong that we persist in believing even in the face of the most powerful negative evidence. We believe in heaven, in God, in a life after death, in reward for virtue and punishment for sin, not because there is the slightest evidence for our beliefs, but because we *want* so much to believe. Religion is indeed an opiate, as Marx had said, but for all humanity, not merely for the working class. To those who ask Freud what he offers in place of religion, he can only answer, the hard truth, however painful it is to face.

Here is Freud's statement of his conception of religion. Notice that even if Freud is right, the issue is not settled, for though we believe because we want to believe rather than because evidence or reasoning justifies our belief, our belief might still be true!

> Religious ideas . . . which are given out as teachings, are not precipitates of experience or end-results of thinking: they are illusions, fulfilments of the oldest, strongest and most urgent wishes of mankind. The secret of their strength lies in the strength of those wishes. As we already know, the terrifying impression of helplessness in childhood aroused the need for protection—for protection through love—which was provided by the father; and the recognition that this helplessness lasts throughout life made it necessary to cling to the existence of a father, but this time a more powerful one. Thus the benevolent rule of a divine Providence allays our fear of the dangers of life; the establishment of a moral world-order ensures the fulfilment of the demands of justice, which have so often remained unfulfilled in human civilization; and the prolongation of earthly existence in a future life provides the local and temporal framework in which these wish-fulfilments shall take place. Answers to the riddles that tempt the curiosity of man, such as how the universe began or what the relation is between body and mind, are developed in conformity with the underlying assumptions of this system. It is an enormous relief to the individual psyche if the conflicts of its childhood arising from the father-complex—conflicts which it has never wholly overcome—are removed from it and brought to a solution which is universally accepted.
>
> When I say that these things are all illusions, I must define the meaning of the word. An illusion is not the same thing as an error; nor is it necessarily an error. Aristotle's belief that vermin are developed out of dung (a belief to which ignorant people still cling) was an error; so was the belief of a former generation of doctors that *tabes dorsalis* is the result of sexual excess. It would be incorrect to call these errors illusions. On the other hand, it was an illusion of Columbus's that he had discovered a new sea-route to the Indies. The part played by his wish in this error is very clear. One may describe as an illusion the assertion made by certain nationalists that the Indo-Germanic race is the only one capable of civilization; or the belief, which was only destroyed by psycho-analysis, that children are creatures without sexuality. What is characteristic of illusions is that they are derived from human wishes. In this respect they come near to psychiatric delusions. But they differ from them, too, apart from the more complicated structure of delusions. In the case of delusions, we emphasize as essential their being in contradiction with reality. Illusions need not necessarily be false—that is to say, unrealizable or in contradiction to reality. For instance, a middle-class girl may have the illusion that a prince will come and marry her. This is possible; and a few such cases have occurred. That the Messiah will come and found a golden age is much less likely. Whether one classifies this belief as an illusion or as something analogous to a delusion will depend on one's personal attitude. Examples of illusions which have proved true are not easy to find, but the illusion of the alchemists that all metals can be turned into gold might be one of them. The wish to have a great deal of gold, as much gold as possible, has, it is true, been a good deal damped by our present-day knowledge of the determinants of wealth, but chemistry no longer regards

the transmutation of metals into gold as impossible. Thus we call a belief an illusion when a wish-fulfilment is a prominent factor in its motivation, and in doing so we disregard its relations to reality, just as the illusion itself sets no store by verification.

Having thus taken our bearings, let us return once more to the question of religious doctrines. We can now repeat that all of them are illusions and insusceptible of proof. No one can be compelled to think them true, to believe in them. Some of them are so improbable, so incompatible with everything we have laboriously discovered about the reality of the world, that we may compare them—if we pay proper regard to the psychological differences—to delusions. Of the reality value of most of them we cannot judge; just as they cannot be proved, so they cannot be refuted. We still know too little to make a critical approach to them. The riddles of the universe reveal themselves only slowly to our investigation; there are many questions to which science to-day can give no answer. But scientific work is the only road which can lead us to a knowledge of reality outside ourselves.

SIGMUND FREUD, *The Future of an Illusion*

In every age, logic has been the backbone of philosophy. The distinctive mark of philosophy, one might say, is the attempt to gain insight into some realm of nature or the human condition by means of an analysis of the formal structure of the thought processes by which we grasp our world. The ancient cosmologists, for example, puzzled about the fundamental building blocks of the universe, and they sought to solve that puzzle by a reflection upon the very grammar of their language, as well as by observations of the heavens. The great seventeenth-century thinker, Gottfried Leibniz, thought that he could penetrate to the inner nature of space, time, matter, and mind through a logical analysis of the formal relations among the basic concepts with which we seek to understand the universe. In our own century, countless philosophers have attempted to overcome their uncertainties about substantive moral issues by a close logical analysis of the concepts of right, obligation, and value. It is hardly surprising, therefore, that during the Middle Ages, that great age of religious faith in the history of Western civilization, philosophers should have sought to know God through the instrumentalities of logical analysis.

In this chapter, we have taken a preliminary look at the Ontological Argument of St. Anselm—probably the boldest attempt ever made to wrest truth from logic. As we saw, Anselm thought that he could actually demonstrate the existence of God purely *a priori*—merely from concepts, without the slightest bit of scientific or other evidence to back up his deductions! We also saw that subsequent philosophers had called Anselm's arguments into question, and that the greatest of the eighteenth-century theorists of knowledge, Immanuel Kant, presented what he, and most other philosophers, considered a decisive refutation of Anselm's Ontological Argument.

If the Middle Ages was an age of faith, the twentieth century is an age of doubt, of skepticism, of secularism. How astonishing it was, therefore, only twenty years ago, when one of the best-known American philosophers published an article in an extremely prestigious philosophical journal reviving and defending Anselm's discredited argument! Norman Malcolm was in 1960, and is today, a tough-minded, no-nonsense analytic philosopher—a member of the Philosophy Department at Cornell University, which is known as a leading center of modern philosophical thought. The ontological argument was an old chestnut—one of those arguments that no one took seriously, even though everyone taught it in introductory philosophy courses for its shock value. There was just about universal agreement that David Hume and Immanuel Kant had made mincemeat of the argument. Even St. Thomas Aquinas, the great medieval theologian, writing a century after Anselm, had not accepted the ontological argument.

What Malcolm did was to take a fresh look at Anselm's argument, bringing to his task some of the most modern notions of logical analysis derived from a general study of language and formal reasoning. Philosophers had been looking more closely at a group of concepts called "modal concepts"—notions such as "necessary," "possible," "impossible," and so forth, which we use in making claims about certain sorts of knowledge or certain sorts of arguments. Everyone agrees, for example, that the sun is larger than the moon; everyone agrees, as well, that if the sun is larger than the earth, and the earth is larger than the moon, then the sun is larger than the moon. But there is a fundamental difference between these two bits of knowledge—or, more precisely, between these two propositions. The first is simply a statement of fact—the sun is larger than the moon—and presumably there is nothing written into the laws of the universe that says that the sun *must* be larger than the moon, that it is literally impossible for the moon to be larger than the sun. Indeed, science fiction writers make their living by thinking up imaginary worlds in which things are different from the way they are in the real world, and in some sense, if we can *imagine* something, then it can't be *impossible*. But matters are rather different with regard to the second bit of knowledge. Surely, we wish to say, if the sun is larger than the earth and the earth is larger than the moon, then the sun *must* be larger than the moon. Indeed, in general, if A is larger than B, and B is larger than C, then A *must* be larger than C. That follows from the very meaning of "larger than."

Now, according to Kant, Anselm and the later defenders of the Ontological Argument such as René Descartes and Baruch Spinoza made a rather subtle logical mistake. The got all tangled up in a confusion between the statement, "Necessarily, God exists," and the totally different statement, "God has [some very special sort of existence called] necessary existence." The trouble, Kant showed, was that "Necessarily, God exists" makes sense, but cannot be shown to be true; whereas "God has necessary existence" doesn't really make any sense because we can't explain what we mean by "necessary existence."

All this sounds like a terrible quibble, but actually a very great deal hangs on it. The crux of the matter is this: in the Judeo-Christian tradition of Western civilization, God has come to be thought of as absolutely different from anything in the world. Theologians have many different ways of expressing this difference, this otherness. They say that we are finite, and God is infinite; or they say that we live in time, and God is eternal; or they say that we are material, and God is utterly nonmaterial. But the central thought is always the same: that there is a gulf between God and His universe. Now, if God is totally different from anything in His creation, then it must be that he exists in a different way from the things He created. They are dependent things, having come into existence only because He willed them to; but His existence is not of that sort. God was not Himself created. The things of this world exist, but it is at least possible that they should *not* exist. God, however, *must* exist, for nothing has created Him, and nothing could destroy Him.

What Malcolm does in this essay is to take up the concept of *necessary existence* and defend it against the attacks of Kant and other philosophers. As you will notice when you read the essay, Malcolm stops short of endorsing Anselm's proof. He is more concerned to refute the refutations than to defend the original argument. In a sense, therefore, this essay merely puts us back at square one with the original proof itself. But by clearing away two centuries and more of standard objections to this most paradoxical of all the proofs for the existence of God, Malcolm has posed a serious challenge to his analytically inclined fellow philosophers. If we do not, in our hearts, believe that one can prove the existence of God by means of Anselm's argument, then we can no longer lean on the counter-arguments put forward by Hume and Kant in the eighteenth century. Instead, we must rethink the issue from the very start, and come up with new and better answers to Anselm.

Then again, there is always the possibility that we may see the error of our ways, and accept the proof as valid!

I believe that in Anselm's *Proslogion* and *Responsio editoris* there are two different pieces of reasoning which he did not distinguish from one another, and that a good deal of light may be shed on the philosophical problem of "the ontological argument" if we do distinguish them.

I take up now the consideration of the second ontological proof, which Anselm presents in the very next chapter of the *Proslogion*. (There is no evidence that he thought of himself as offering two different proofs.) Speaking of the being a greater than which cannot be conceived, he says:

> And it so truly exists that it cannot be conceived not to exist. For it is possible to conceive of a being which cannot be conceived not to exist; and this is greater than one which can be conceived not to exist. Hence, if that, than which nothing greater can be conceived, can be conceived not to exist, it is not that than which nothing greater can be conceived. But this is a contradiction. So truly, therefore, is there something than which nothing greater can be conceived, that it cannot even be conceived not to exist. And this being thou art, O Lord, our God.[1]

Anselm is saying two things: first, that a being whose nonexistence is logically impossible is "greater" than a being whose non-existence is logically possible (and therefore that a being a greater than which cannot be conceived must be one whose nonexistence is logically impossible); second, that *God* is a being than which a greater cannot be conceived.

In regard to the second of these assertions, there certainly is a use of the word "God," and I think far the more common use, in accordance with which the statements "God is the greatest of all beings," "God is the most perfect being," "God is the supreme being," are *logically* necessary truths, in the same sense that the statement "A square has four sides" is a logically necessary truth. If there is a man named "Jones" who is the tallest man in the world, the statement "Jones is the tallest man in the world" is merely true and is not a logically necessary truth. It is a virtue of Anselm's unusual phrase, "a being a greater than which cannot be conceived," to make it explicit that the sentence "God is the greatest of all beings" expresses a logically necessary truth and not a mere matter of fact such as the one we imagined about Jones.

With regard to Anselm's first assertion (namely, that a being whose nonexistence is logically impossible is greater than a being whose nonexistence is logically possible) perhaps the most puzzling thing about it is the use of the word "greater." It appears to mean exactly the same as "superior," "more excellent," "more perfect." This equivalence by itself is of no help to us, however, since the latter expressions would be equally puzzling here. What is required is some explanation of their use.

---

[1] *Proslogion* 3; S. N. Deane: *St. Anselm* (La Salle, Illinois, 1948), pp. 8–9.

We do think of *knowledge,* say, as an excellence, a good thing. If A has more knowledge of algebra than B we express this in common language by saying that A has a *better* knowledge of algebra than B, or that A's knowledge of algebra is *superior* to B's, whereas we should not say that B has a better or superior *ignorance* of algebra than A. We do say "greater ignorance," but here the word "greater" is used purely quantitatively.

Previously I rejected *existence* as a perfection. Anselm is maintaining in the remarks last quoted, not that existence is a perfection, but that *the logical impossibility of nonexistence is a perfection.* In other words, *necessary existence* is a perfection. His first ontological proof uses the principle that a thing is greater if it exists than if it does not exist. His second proof employs the different principle that a thing is greater if it necessarily exists than if it does not necessarily exist.

Some remarks about the notion of *dependence* may help to make this latter principle intellibible. Many things depend for their existence on other things and events. My house was built by a carpenter: its coming into existence was dependent on a certain creative activity. Its continued existence is dependent on many things: that a tree does not crush it, that it is not consumed by fire, and so on. If we reflect on the common meaning of the word "God" (no matter how vague and confused this is), we realize that it is incompatible with this meaning that God's existence should *depend* on anything. Whether we believe in Him or not we must admit that the "almighty and everlasting God" (as several ancient prayers begin), the "Maker of heaven and earth, and of all things visible and invisible" (as is said in the Nicene Creed), cannot be thought of as being brought into existence by anything or as depending for His continued existence on anything. To conceive of anything as dependent upon something else for its existence is to conceive of it as a lesser being than God.

If a housewife has a set of extremely fragile dishes, then as dishes they are *inferior* to those of another set like them in all respects except that they are *not* fragile. Those of the first set are *dependent* for their continued existence on gentle handling; those of the second set are not. There is a definite connection in common language between the notions of dependency and inferiority, and independence and superiority. To say that something which was dependent on nothing whatever was superior to ("greater than") anything that was dependent in any way upon anything is quite in keeping with the everyday use of the terms "superior" and "greater." Correlative with the notions of dependence and independence are the notions of *limited* and *unlimited.* An engine requires fuel and this is a limitation. It is the same thing to say that an engine's operation is *dependent* on as that it is *limited* by its fuel supply. An engine that could accomplish the same work in the same time and was in other respects satisfactory, but did not require fuel, would be a *superior* engine.

God is usually conceived of as an *unlimited* being. He is conceived of as a being who *could not* be limited, that is, as an absolutely unlimited being. This is no less than to conceive of Him as *something a greater than which cannot be conceived.* If God is conceived to be an absolutely unlimited being

He must be conceived to be unlimited in regard to His existence as well as His operation. In this conception it will not make sense to say that He depends on anything for coming into or continuing in existence. Nor, as Spinoza observed, will it make sense to say that something could *prevent* Him from existing.[2] Lack of moisture can prevent trees from existing in a certain region of the earth. But it would be contrary to the concept of God as an unlimited being to suppose that anything other than God Himself could prevent Him from existing, and it would be self-contradictory to suppose that He Himself could do it.

Some may be inclined to object that although nothing could prevent God's existence, still it might just *happen* that He did not exist. And if He did exist that too would be by chance. I think, however, that from the supposition that it could happen that God did not exist it would follow that, if He existed, He would have mere duration and not eternity. It would make sense to ask, "How long has He existed?," "Will He still exist next week?," "He was in existence yesterday but how about today?," and so on. It seems absurd to make God the subject of such questions. According to our ordinary conception of Him, He is an eternal being. And eternity does not mean endless duration, as Spinoza noted. To ascribe eternity to something is to exclude as senseless all sentences that imply that it has duration. If a thing has duration then it would be merely a *contingent* fact, if it was a fact, that its duration was endless. The moon could have endless duration but not eternity. If something has endless duration it will *make sense* (although it will be false) to say that it will cease to exist, and it will make sense (although it will be false) to say that something will *cause* it to cease to exist. A being with endless duration is not, therefore, an absolutely unlimited being. That God is conceived to be eternal follows from the fact that He is conceived to be an absolutely unlimited being.

I have been trying to expand the argument of *Proslogion* 3. In *Responsio* 1 Anselm adds the following acute point: if you can conceive of a certain thing and this thing does not exist then if it *were* to exist its nonexistence would be *possible*. It follows, I believe, that if the thing were to exist it would depend on other things both for coming into and continuing in existence, and also that it would have duration and not eternity. Therefore it would not be, either in reality or in conception, an unlimited being, *aliquid quo nihil maius cogitari possit.*

Anselm states his argument as follows:

> If it [the thing a greater than which cannot be conceived] can be conceived at all it must exist. For no one who denies or doubts the existence of a being a greater than which is inconceivable, denies or doubts that if it did exist its non-existence, either in reality or in the understanding, would be impossible. For otherwise it would not be a being a greater than which cannot be conceived. But as to whatever can be conceived but does not exist: if it were to exist its non-existence either in

---

[2] *Ethics,* pt. I, prop. 11.

reality or in the understanding would be possible. Therefore, if a being a greater than which cannot be conceived, can even be conceived, it must exist.[3]

What Anselm has proved is that the notion of contingent existence or of contingent nonexistence cannot have any application to God. His existence must either be logically necessary or logically impossible. The only intelligible way of rejecting Anselm's claim that God's existence is necessary is to maintain that the concept of God, as a being a greater than which cannot be conceived, is self-contradictory or nonsensical. Supposing that this is false, Anselm is right to deduce God's necessary existence from his characterization of Him as a being a greater than which cannot be conceived.

Let me summarize the proof. If God, a being a greater than which cannot be conceived, does not exist then he cannot *come* into existence. For if He did He would either have been *caused* to come into existence or have *happened* to come into existence, and in either case He would be a limited being, which by our conception of Him He is not. Since He cannot come into existence, if He does not exist His existence is impossible. If He does exist He cannot have come into existence (for the reasons given), nor can He cease to exist, for nothing could cause Him to cease to exist nor could it just happen that He ceased to exist. So if God exists His existence is necessary. Thus God's existence is either impossible or necessary. It can be the former only if the concept of such a being is self-contradictory or in some way logically absurd. Assuming that this is not so, it follows that He necessarily exists.

It may be helpful to express ourselves in the following way: to say, not that *omnipotence* is a property of God, but rather that *necessary omnipotence* is; and to say, not that omniscience is a property of God, but rather that *necessary omniscience* is. We have criteria for determining that a man knows this and that and can do this and that, and for determining that one man has greater knowledge and abilities in a certain subject than another. We could think of various tests to give them. But there is nothing we should wish to describe, seriously and literally, as "testing" God's knowledge and powers. That God is omniscient and omnipotent has not been determined by the application of criteria: rather these are requirements of our conception of Him. They are internal properties of the concept, although they are also rightly said to be properties of God. *Necessary existence* is a property of God in the *same sense* that *necessary omnipotence* and *necessary omniscience* are His properties. And we are not to think that "God necessarily exists" means that it follows necessarily from something that God exists *contingently*. The a priori proposition "God necessarily exists" entails the proposition "God exists," if and only if the latter also is understood as an a priori proposition: in which case the two propositions are equivalent. In this sense Anselm's proof is a proof of God's existence. . . .

I wish to consider now a part of Kant's criticism of the ontological argument which I believe to be wrong. He says:

---

[3] *Responsio* 1; Deane, pp. 154–155.

If, in an identical proposition, I reject the predicate while retaining the subject, contradiction results; and I therefore say that the former belongs necessarily to the latter. But if we reject subject and predicate alike, there is no contradiction; for nothing is then left that can be contradicted. To posit a triangle, and yet to reject its three angles, is self-contradictory; but there is no contradiction in rejecting the triangle together with its three angles. The same holds true of the concept of an absolutely necessary being. If its existence is rejected, we reject the thing itself with all its predicates; and no question of contradiction can then arise. There is nothing outside it that would then be contradicted, since the necessity of the thing is not supposed to be derived from anything external; nor is there anything internal that would be contradicted, since in rejecting the thing itself we have at the same time rejected all its internal properties. "God is omnipotent" is a necessary judgment. The omnipotence cannot be rejected if we posit a Deity, that is, an infinite being; for the two concepts are identical. But if we say, "There is no God," neither the omnipotence nor any other of its predicates is given; they are one and all rejected together with the subject, and there is therefore not the least contradiction in such a judgment.[4]

To these remarks the reply is that when the concept of God is correctly understood one sees that one cannot "reject the subject." "There is no God" is seen to be a necessarily false statement. Anselm's demonstration proves that the proposition "God exists" has the same a priori footing as the proposition "God is omnipotent."

Many present-day philosophers, in agreement with Kant, declare that existence is not a property and think that this overthrows the ontological argument. Although it is an error to regard existence as a property of things that have contingent existence, it does not follow that it is an error to regard necessary existence as a property of God. A recent writer says, against Anselm, that a proof of God's existence "based on the necessities of thought" is "universally regarded as fallacious: it is not thought possible to build bridges between mere abstractions and concrete existence."[5] But this way of putting the matter obscures the distinction we need to make. Does "concrete existence" mean contingent existence? Then to build bridges between concrete existence and mere abstractions would be like inferring the existence of an island from the concept of a perfect island, which both Anselm and Descartes regarded as absurd. What Anselm did was to give a demonstration that the proposition "God necessarily exists" is entailed by the proposition "God is a being a greater than which cannot be conceived" (which is equivalent to "God is an absolutely unlimited being"). Kant declares that when "I think a being as the supreme reality, without any defect, the question still remains whether it exists or not."[6] But once one

[4] *The Critique of Pure Reason*, tr. by Norman Kemp Smith (London, 1929), p. 502.

[5] J. N. Findlay, "Can God's Existence Be Disproved?," *New Essays in Philosophical Theology*, ed. by A. N. Flew and A. MacIntyre (London, 1955), p. 47.

[6] *Op. cit.*, pp. 505–506.

has grasped Anselm's proof of the necessary existence of a being a greater than which cannot be conceived, no question remains as to whether it exists or not, just as Euclid's demonstration of the existence of an infinity of prime numbers leaves no question on that issue.

Kant says that "every reasonable person" must admit that "all existential propositions are synthetic."[7] Part of the perplexity one has about the ontological argument is in deciding whether or not the proposition "God necessarily exists" is or is not an "existential proposition." But let us look around. Is the Euclidean theorem in number theory, "There exists an infinite number of prime numbers," an "existential proposition"? Do we not want to say that *in some sense* it asserts the existence of something? Cannot we say, with equal justification, that the proposition "God necessarily exists" asserts the existence of something, *in some sense?* What we need to understand, in each case, is the particular sense of the assertion. Neither proposition has the same sort of sense as do the propositions, "A low pressure area exists over the Great Lakes," "There still exists some possibility that he will survive," "The pain continues to exist in his abdomen." One good way of seeing the difference in sense of these various propositions is to see the variously different ways in which they are proved or supported. It is wrong to think that all assertions of existence have the same kind of meaning. There are as many kinds of existential propositions as there are kinds of subjects of discourse. . . .

Professor J. N. Findlay ingeniously constructs an ontological *dis*proof of God's existence based on a "modern" view of the nature of "necessity in propositions": the view, namely, that necessity in proportions "merely reflects our use of words, the arbitrary conventions of our language."[8] Findlay undertakes to characterize what he calls "religious attitude," and here there is a striking agreement between his observations and some of the things I have said in expounding Anselm's proof. Religious attitude, he says, presumes *superiority* in its object and superiority so great that the worshiper is in comparison as nothing. Religious attitude finds it "anomalous to worship anything *limited* in any thinkable manner. . . . And hence we are led on irresistibly to demand that our religious object should have an *unsurpassable* supremacy along all avenues, that it should tower *infinitely* above all other objects" (p. 51). We cannot help feeling that "the worthy object of our worship can never be a thing that merely *happens* to exist, nor one on which all other objects merely *happen* to depend. The true object of religious reverence must not be one, merely, to which no *actual* independent realities stand opposed: it must be one to which such opposition is totally *inconceivable.* . . . And not only must the existence of *other* things be unthinkable without him, but his own non-existence must be wholly unthinkable in any circumstances" (p. 52). And now, says Findlay, when we add up these various requirements, what they entail is "not only that there isn't a God,

---

[7] *Ibid.,* p. 504.

[8] Findlay, *op. cit.,* p. 154.

but that the Divine Existence is either senseless or impossible" (p. 54). For on the one hand, "if God is to satisfy religious claims and needs, He must be a being in every way inescapable, One whose existence and whose possession of certain excellences we cannot possibly conceive away." On the other hand, "modern views make it self-evidently absurd (if they don't make it ungrammatical) to speak of such a Being and attribute existence to Him. It was indeed an ill day for Anselm when he hit upon his famous proof. For on that day he not only laid bare something that is of the essence of an adequate religious object, but also something that entails its necessary non-existence" (p. 55).

Now I am inclined to hold the "modern" view that logically necessary truth "merely reflects our use of words" (although I do not believe that the conventions of language are always *arbitrary*). But I confess that I am unable to see how that view is supposed to lead to the conclusion that "the Divine existence is either senseless or impossible." Findlay does not explain how this result comes about. Surely he cannot mean that this view entails that nothing can have necessary properties: for this would imply that mathematics is "senseless or impossible," which no one wants to hold. Trying to fill in the argument that is missing from his article, the most plausible conjecture I can make is the following: Findlay thinks that the view that logical necessity "reflects the use of words" implies, not that nothing has necessary properties, but that *existence* cannot be a necessary property of anything. That is to say, every proposition of the form "*x* exists," including the proposition "God exists," must be *contingent*. At the same time, our concept of God requires that His existence be *necessary*, that is, that "God exists" be a necessary truth. Therefore, the modern view of necessity proves that what the concept of God requires *cannot* be fulfilled. It proves that God *cannot* exist.

The correct reply is that the view that logical necessity merely reflects the use of words cannot possibly have the implication that every existential proposition must be contingent. That view requires us to *look at* the use of words and not manufacture a priori theses about it. In the Ninetieth Psalm it is said: "Before the mountains were brought forth, or ever thou hadst formed the earth and the world, even from everlasting to everlasting, thou art God." Here is expressed the idea of the necessary existence and eternity of God, an idea that is essential to the Jewish and Christian religions. In those complex systems of thought, those "languages-games," God has the status of a necessary being. Who can doubt that? Here we must say with Wittgenstein, "This language-game is played!"[9] I believe we may rightly take the existence of those religious systems of thought in which God figures as a necessary being to be a disproof of the dogma, affirmed by Hume and others, that no existential proposition can be necessary.

Another way of criticizing the ontological argument is the following. "Granted that the concept of necessary existence follows from the concept of a being a greater than which cannot be conceived, this amounts to no more

---

[9] *Philosophical Investigations* (New York, 1953), sec. 654.

than granting the *a priori* truth of the *conditional* proposition, 'If such a being exists then it necessarily exists.' This proposition, however, does not entail the *existence of anything,* and one can deny its antecedent without contradiction." Kant, for example, compares the proposition (or "judgment," as he calls it) "A triangle has three angles" with the proposition "God is a necessary being." He allows that the former is "absolutely necessary" and goes on to say:

> The absolute necessity of the judgment is only a conditional necessity of the thing, or of the predicate in the judgment. The above proposition does not declare that three angles are absolutely necessary, but that, under the condition that there is a triangle (that is, that a triangle is given), three angles will necessarily be found in it.[10]

He is saying, quite correctly, that the proposition about triangles is equivalent to the conditional proposition, "If a triangle exists, it has three angles." He then makes the comment that there is no contradiction "in rejecting the triangle together with its three angles." He proceeds to draw the alleged parallel: "The same holds true of the concept of an absolutely necessary being. If its existence is rejected, we reject the thing itself with all its predicates; and no question of contradiction can then arise. . . ."[11] I think that Caterus, Kant, and numerous other philosophers have been mistaken in supposing that the proposition "God is a necessary being" (or "God necessarily exists") is equivalent to the conditional proposition. "If God exists then He necessarily exists."[12] For how do they want the antecedent clause, "*If* God exists," to be understood? Clearly they want it to imply that it is *possible* that God does *not* exist.[13] The whole point of Kant's

[10] *Op. cit.,* pp. 501–502.

[11] *Ibid.,* p. 502.

[12] I have heard it said by more than one person in discussion that Kant's view was that it is really a misuse of language to speak of a "necessary being," on the grounds that necessity is properly predicated only of propositions (judgments) not of *things.* This is not a correct account of Kant. (See his discussion of "The Postulates of Empirical Thought in General," *op. cit.,* pp. 239–256, esp. p. 239 and pp. 247–248.) But if he had held this, as perhaps the above philosophers think he should have, then presumably his view would not have been that the pseudo-proposition "God is a necessary being" is equivalent to the conditional "If God exists then He necessarily exists." Rather his view would have been that the genuine proposition " 'God exists' is necessarily true" is equivalent to the conditional "If God exists then He exists" (*not* "If God exists then He *necessarily* exists," which would be an illegitimate formulation, on the view imaginatively attributed to Kant).

"If God exists then He exists" is a foolish tautology which says nothing different from the tautology "If a new earth satellite exists then it exists." If "If God exists then He exists" were a correct analysis of " 'God exists' is necessarily true," then "If a new earth satellite exists then it exists" would be a correct analysis of " 'A new earth satellite exists' is necessarily true." If the *analysans* is necessarily true then the *analysandum* must be necessarily true, provided the analysis is correct. If this proposed Kantian analysis of " 'God exists' is necessarily true" were correct, we should be presented with the consequence that not only is it necessarily true that God exists, but also it is necessarily true that a new earth satellite exists: which is absurd.

[13] When summarizing Anselm's proof (in part II, *supra*) I said: "If God exists He necessarily exists." But there I was merely stating an entailment. "If God exists" did not have the implication that it is possible He does not exist. And of course I was not regarding the conditional as *equivalent* to "God necessarily exists."

analysis is to try to show that it is possible to "reject the subject." Let us make this implication explicit in the conditional proposition, so that it reads: "If God exists (and it is possible that He does not) then He necessarily exists." But now it is apparent, I think, that these philosophers have arrived at a self-contradictory position. I do not mean that this conditional proposition, taken alone, is self-contradictory. Their position is self-contradictory in the following way. On the one hand, they agree that the proposition "God necessarily exists" is an a priori truth; Kant implies that it is "absolutely necessary." On the other hand, they think that it is correct to analyze this proposition in such a way that it will entail the proposition "It is possible that God does not exist." But so far from its being the case that the proposition "God necessarily exists" entails the proposition "It is possible that God does not exist," it is rather the case that they are *incompatible* with one another! Can anything be clearer than that the conjunction "God necessarily exists but it is possible that He does not exist" is self-contradictory? Is it not just as plainly self-contradictory as the conjunction "A square necessarily has four sides but it is possible for a square not to have four sides"? In short, this familiar criticism of the ontological argument is self-contradictory, because it accepts *both* of two incompatible propositions.

One conclusion we may draw from our examination of this criticism is that (contrary to Kant) there is a lack of symmetry, in an important respect, between the propositions "A triangle has three angles" and "God has necessary existence," although both are a priori. The former can be expressed in the conditional assertion "If a triangle exists (and it is possible that none does) it has three angles." The latter cannot be expressed in the corresponding conditional assertion without contradiction. . . .

TOPICS FOR FURTHER STUDY

1. Malcolm's essay raises *four* questions, each one of which requires an answer if we are to determine the significance of his discussion for *religion* in the usual sense of the term. The four questions are these: *First,* is Malcolm's refutation of the refutations correct? Has he succeeded in answering Anselm's most powerful critics? *Second,* assuming that Malcolm has succeeded, where does that leave the original proof? Is Anselm's argument sound, or are there other, unanswerable objections to it? *Third,* if Anselm's argument is sound (and that is a very big "if" indeed!), is the Being whose existence he thereby proves recognizable as the God of the Judeo-Christian-Islamic tradition? In short, does the Ontological Argument prove the existence of the God of the Old and New Testaments and the Koran? *Fourth,* even if St. Anselm *has* succeeded in proving the existence of the God of Abraham, the God of the Bible and the Koran, can that or any other rational proof create in me the *faith* which all of the great religions say is the foundation of the religious life? Even the great theologian St. Thomas Aquinas denied that reason could produce faith, although he claimed, as you have seen in this chapter, to be able to prove the existence of God in a number of different ways.

2. Plato argued that we have and use many concepts, such as the idea of a perfectly straight line, which we could never have obtained from our sense experience. Descartes suggested that our concept of God is just such a concept and on that fact he based his own proof of God's existence. Is the notion of necessary existence a legitimate, coherent idea? If it is, could we derive it from observations of nature or from reflections upon our own mental processes? How could we have formed so strange an idea?

3. The Argument from Design remains the most humanly persuasive of the proofs for the existence of God, even though philosophers tend to treat it with disdain. Can Anselm's ontological argument give us any insight into order and purpose in the universe? Could a Being possessing necessary existence create a purposeless world? Now that analytic philosophers seem to be taking a serious second look at the Ontological Argument, do you see any way in which the Argument from Design might also be dusted off and strengthened, so as to become once again a subject of philosophical investigation?

4. In recent years, astronomers and physicists have done a good deal of speculating about the origins of the physical universe. One of the most widely discussed theories tells us that many billions of years ago, the universe as we now know it began with a "big bang," an explosion of a small but unimaginably dense mass containing all the matter in what is now the universe. Do explanations like this make any sense without some reference to a force—call it God, if you will—that gets the bang going? Can any explanation of the existence and nature of the universe stand on its own feet without some support from an essentially religious theory of creation?

SUGGESTIONS FOR FURTHER READING

A. J. AYER, *Language, Truth, and Logic,* Chapter VI

J. BAILLIE, *The Sense of the Presence of God*

LUDWIG FEUERBACH, *The Essence of Christianity*

H. M. GARELICK, *The Anti-Christianity of Kierkegaard*

CHARLES HARTSHORNE, *The Logic of Perfection*

J. HICK (ed.), *The Existence of God*

WILLIAM JAMES, *The Will to Believe*

A. KENNY, *Aquinas: A Collection of Critical Essays*

SØREN KIERKEGAARD, *Fear and Trembling*

A. C. MACINTYRE, *Difficulties in Christian Belief*

A. PLANTINGA (ed.), *The Ontological Argument*

————, *God and Other Minds*

BERTRAND RUSSELL, *Why I Am Not A Christian, and Other Essays*

RENÉ DESCARTES (1596–1650) is universally recognized among philosophers as the first great figure of the modern age. Born in a small town in Touraine, France, Descartes was educated by the Jesuits, and he remained throughout his life a devoted Catholic. His early interest was principally in mathematics and physics, two fields in which exciting new work was being done by many continental and English thinkers. In his early twenties, perhaps as the result of a dramatic trio of dreams, Descartes conceived the grandiose plan of formulating an entirely new system of science founded upon mathematics. Though he never accomplished this impossible task, his many contributions to mathematics and

7 THEORY OF KNOWLEDGE

physics place him in the forefront of seventeenth-century science.

Descartes' primary concern throughout his life was with problems of methodology, justification, and certainty. His first work was entitled *Rules for the Direction of the Mind,* and in it he sought to establish the proper procedures by which a question could be investigated without danger of error or confusion. His most famous work, *Meditations on First Philosophy,* was immediately recognized as a dramatic challenge to all established philosophy and science. It was circulated widely throughout Europe, and provoked a series of objections, to which Descartes wrote extended replies. In these objections and replies we can see a number of profound and dramatic debates unfolding, in which such famous thinkers as Hobbes, Gassendi, and Arnauld locked horns with Descartes.

Although Descartes was deeply influenced by the scholastic philosophy which had preceded him, the problems he posed, the questions he raised, and the demands he made for absolute subjective certainty in knowledge served to undermine the influence of the 2000-year-old tradition of Aristotelian philosophizing. Virtually all the great philosophy written during the 150 years following Descartes' death can be seen as an attempt to answer the questions raised by the brilliant, iconoclastic Frenchman.

I
_____

If you have been working your way through this book carefully, reading and thinking, discussing the problems it raises with your teacher and your fellow students, you should by now be getting some feel for what philosophy is and how philosophers think. And if I have been at all successful, then philosophy ought to seem a fairly sensible sort of business to you. Perhaps philosophical questions aren't exactly what your mind would turn to if you had a few spare moments caught in a traffic jam or if you couldn't sleep late at night, but at least it is easy enough to understand how reasonable men and women might get genuinely worked up about them. What rules should I use to decide the hard moral choices that life poses for me? How should the wealth of a society be divided up among its members? Do I have an obligation to obey the state, even when I believe that its laws are unjust? What place should painting and poetry, music and fiction play in a good society? Is there a God? Can I trust

Him to keep His promise of eternal life? These may not be everyone's questions, but they are surely questions worth asking. Some of them even get asked in political campaigns, in hospital emergency wards, in law courts, or in the front lines of a war.

In this chapter, the situation changes dramatically. We are going to take a look at philosophical attempts to deal with questions that some of you may think are just plain crazy. Suppose a friend of yours asks whether you and he really did go to the movies last night or whether he just dreamed it. A little odd, perhaps, but people do have very lifelike dreams; I have myself on a couple of occasions had dreams so real that afterwards I wasn't entirely sure whether they had actually happened or not. You wouldn't think your friend was being *philosophical,* but on the other hand you wouldn't think he was crazy either. Suppose he went on to wonder, in absolute seriousness, whether everything that had ever happened to him was a dream, whether his childhood, his adolescence, his school days, his fights with his parents, his first romance, his first trip away from home, his coming to college, and his standing right there in front of you were *all just dreams.* If he was really dead serious, not just kidding around or trying to get a rise out of you, then about now you would start edging toward the phone, trying to figure out how you could call the school psychiatrist without getting your friend too upset. People who really aren't sure whether their whole lives have been dreams "need help," as the saying goes.

Suppose another friend said, as the two of you were waiting for an elevator, that she couldn't really be sure that she needed an elevator to get back down to the first floor. Maybe if she stepped out of the window, she would be able simply to fly down. Suppose, indeed, that she expressed doubt about whether she could ever tell what would happen next—whether she would drown if she held her head under water, whether her finger would burn if she held it in a flame, whether her books would fall down or up if she let go of them. She might even admit that she wasn't sure there was anyone else in the whole world besides herself, though of course there might be a lot of human-looking bodies that made speechlike noises and acted in peoplelike ways. Well, once again, you would probably think that either the whole act was a put-on, or your friend was in the midst of a bad trip, or else that it was time for the shrink. You certainly wouldn't think that she was simply doing philosophy!

From the beginning of the seventeenth century until the present day, some of the most brilliant thinkers ever to grace the cultural and intellectual life of Western civilization have devoted their best philosophical efforts to just such questions as the ones we have been imagining your friends to be asking. And though I would be the first to admit that philosophers have suffered their share of mental illness, there is no reason at all to suspect that any of these great thinkers was mentally unsound when he wrote his philosophy. (Rousseau, as we have seen, was more than a little odd, but we won't be talking about him in this chapter.) The greatest challenge any teacher of philosophy faces is to present the epistemological theories of the seventeenth- and eighteenth-century theorists of knowledge in such a way that students not only understand the arguments but also understand why in heaven's name sane people worried about such peculiar problems.

Why not just leave the theory of knowledge out of an introductory course—or book—altogether? After all, physicists don't try to teach the most sophisticated wrinkles of particle physics or quantum theory to beginning students. Mathematicians save ring topology for math majors. Couldn't we just sort of skip over the theory of knowledge? The answer is no, for two reasons. First of all, the theory of knowledge is the heart and soul of the philosophy that has been written since the beginning of the seventeenth century. All of the most important philosophers—Descartes, Leibniz, Locke, Berkeley, Hume, Kant—set epistemological investigations at the center of their work. If we cannot understand what made them take so seriously the questions that seem odd to us today, then we cannot really understand philosophy as it has been done during the past four centuries. In the second place, the strange-seeming problems of the modern theory of knowledge (in philosophy, anything since 1600 is called "modern") connect up directly with one of the dominant cultural and intellectual developments of the post-medieval world—namely, the steady movement toward a radical individualism in religion, in politics, in art, and in literature, as well as in philosophy. Though the epistemological puzzles of seventeenth- and eighteenth-century philosophy seem bizarre or unintuitive on first inspection, they have deeply influenced the way painters painted, the way poets wrote, the way theologians reinterpreted the Word of God, and even the way economists, political scientists, and sociologists have explained our collective social life. So like it or not, we are in for some complicated philosophy in this chapter.

By common agreement, the man who started the new theory of knowledge on its way in philosophy was a Frenchman, born in 1596, named René Descartes. Indeed, though Descartes wrote a number of important works during his fifty-four years, in which mathematics, physics, and other subjects as well as philosophy were discussed, we can even name the precise piece of philosophy that marks the beginning of modern philosophy as we study it today. That honor clearly belongs to a seventy-page work entitled *Meditations on First Philosophy,* published by Descartes in 1641.

The seventeenth century was an age of scientific giants, and among the truly great thinkers whose efforts created what we know today as modern science, only the German Gottfried Leibniz and the Englishman Isaac Newton can stand with Descartes. You have probably already met Descartes, or at least spent some time working with one of his contributions to knowledge, for it was he who invented what is called analytic geometry. (That is why, when you draw a graph and plot points on it, you are said to be using "Cartesian" coordinates.) In Chapter Eight, we will be talking about some of the metaphysical problems which were raised by the new science, but now we shall concentrate on Descartes' revolutionary transformation of our understanding of knowledge itself. In short, we shall look at Descartes' *theory of knowledge.*

Descartes was born in 1596, three-quarters of a century after Martin Luther had begun the Protestant Reformation by nailing his famous theses to the church door in Wittenberg. Descartes himself was, and remained throughout his life, a Roman Catholic, and his early education was received from the Jesuits. Nevertheless, if the essence of the Protestant Reformation was the rejection of the religious authority of the institution of the Church and the emphasis on the primacy of individual conscience, then it is clear that Descartes was, intellectually and emotionally, an extreme protestant. The keynote of his life work was a thoroughgoing rejection of received opinion, established doctrine, and the authority of the ancients, and a thoroughly individualistic insistence upon accepting only those truths which his own reason could certify to be correct.

In his early twenties, Descartes' interest turned to mathematics and physics, fields which at that time were dominated by concepts and methods almost 2000 years old. Exciting new work was being done in both areas, and Descartes, like many young scientific geniuses, moved immediately to the scientific frontier. On the night of November 10, 1619, the 23-year-old Descartes had a series of three dreams which seem to have transformed his life. He spoke and wrote of them ever after as the turning point in his career. I am not going to try my hand at armchair dream interpretation. As Freud made very clear when he first described the psychoanalytic method of interpreting dreams, you cannot figure out what a dream meant to the person who had it unless you can get that person actually to talk to you about the dream. There isn't any code book of dream symbols in which you can look up the meaning of falling, or a mirror, or whatever. But Descartes himself interpreted his dreams as a sign that he was to spend his life establishing a new, unified theory of the universe based upon mathematics—what we today would call mathematical physics.

The important part of Descartes' plan, for our purposes, is not the new science he developed, but his conception of the *method* by which he was to proceed. Descartes devoted a great deal of thought to problems of intellectual and scientific method, and his contributions in this field are, if anything, more revolutionary than his actual mathematical and scientific work itself. Descartes published nothing while he was young, despite the fact that he had made a number of important discoveries in his twenties and thirties. In 1637, when he was past forty, he brought out his first published work, appropriately titled "Discourse on the Method of Rightly Conducting the Reason and Seeking for Truth in the Sciences." In this partly autobiographical, partly philosophical work, he lays down a set of four rules which he claims are sufficient to guide the mind in whatever inquiry it may undertake. Here are the rules, as Descartes stated them:

> The first of these was to accept nothing as true which I did not clearly recognize to be so: that is to say, carefully to avoid precipitation and prejudice in judgements, and to accept in them nothing more than what was presented to my mind so clearly and distinctly that I could have no occasion to doubt it.
>
> The second was to divide up each of the difficulties which I examined into as many parts as possible, and as seemed requisite in order that it might be resolved in the best manner possible.
>
> The third was to carry on my reflections in due order, commencing with objects that were the most simple and easy to understand, in order to rise little by little, or by degrees, to knowledge of the most complex, assuming an order, even if a fictitious one, among those which do not follow a natural sequence relatively to one another.
>
> The last was in all cases to make enumerations so complete and reviews so general that I should be certain of having omitted nothing.
>
> RENÉ DESCARTES, *Discourse on Method*

They don't seem like much when you first read them, do they? Avoid prejudice, don't take anything on faith, be careful, tackle questions a step at a time, be orderly, and so forth. It sounds more like instructions to an army filing clerk or the directions for assembling an outdoor barbecue grill than a great revolution in philosophy. Indeed, Leibniz once remarked rather sarcastically that Descartes' famous "method" boiled down to saying, "Take what you need, and do what you should, and you will get what you want." But first impressions are often wrong (as Descartes himself pointed out), and in this case Leibniz was being more clever than wise.

The real importance of Descartes' method lies in *two* of its features, and a consequence that follows from those two. Since what follows may be easier to understand if you have some labels to attach to it, let me start by telling you that Descartes' method is both a *method of inquiry* and a *method of doubt,* and that the combined consequence of these two methods is to set in motion a philosophical transformation known as the *epistemological turn.* Now, if you have carefully underlined these three terms in red or yellow or blue, we can try to make some sense out of them.

First of all, Descartes' method is a *method of inquiry.* In other words, it is a method for finding things out and making sure that you get them right; it is not a method for proving what you already know, or for setting forth your knowledge in the most systematic way. Think for a moment about traditional Euclidean geometry. On the first page of a geometry book (at least this was so when I went to school) you find definitions, axioms, and postulates. These are the simplest, or the most fundamental part of the geometric theory, but they are hardly the first things that a real mathematician would think up if she were doing geometry. Then come the theorems, each one neatly set forth, step by step, from the axioms or previously proved theorems down to what is to be proved, Q.E.D. That may be the way Euclid rearranged his proofs once he had thought them up, but it surely isn't the way he discovered them! Most likely, when he wanted to prove something (say, the theorem that the line bisecting the apex of an isosceles triangle is perpendicular to the base), he drew a diagram, fiddled around with the lines, looked to see whether there was anything that was equal to anything else, worked his way up from the conclusion and down from the premises, until the proof finally fell into place. So his *method of inquiry*—his way of finding something out—was very different from his method of proof or exposition. Descartes' rules for the mind are obviously intended as guides for someone who is trying to solve a problem or analyze a phenomenon. In other words (and this is going to turn out to be very important indeed), he adopts the point of view of someone who does not yet know anything, but is trying by the use of his or her intelligence to discover something, rather than the point of view of a teacher or expert who is quite sure he or she knows something, and is simply trying to explain it to someone else.

Second, Descartes' method is a *method of doubt.* His first rule is "to accept nothing as true which I do not clearly recognize to be so." Just how radical this rule will be depends on how we interpret the phrase "clearly recognize." If Descartes merely wants us to stop and think before we say we are sure, as a quiz show contestant might pause before answering the jackpot question, then obviously that rule is not going to produce any great intellectual revolution. But as you shall see in a few pages, when you read part of the *Meditations on First Philosophy,* Descartes had much more in mind. When he tells us not to accept anything unless we can "clearly recognize" it as true, he means that we should refuse to accept anything, however sure we once were of it, however many people believe it, however obvious it seems, unless we can be *absolutely certain that it is one hundred percent right.* If there is the slightest, the wildest, the farthest-out chance that it just might be false, then we are not to accept it. Now that opens up quite a can of worms! For example, I am quite sure that Washington, D.C. is the capital of the United States of America. If you ask me how I can be so sure, I will tell you that I have read it in history and government books, that I have heard Washington referred to a thousand times on television as "our nation's capital," that I have visited Washington and actually sat for a day in the visitors' gallery of the Senate, and so forth. But does that make it absolutely, one hundred percent certain? Couldn't I be wrong? It isn't likely that I am wrong, but is it logically possible? Maybe the books were wrong; maybe the television commentators were wrong; maybe I was actually in Philadelphia when I thought I was in Washington; indeed, maybe there is a giant conspiracy afoot to fool me into thinking that Washington is the capital. I can't imagine why anyone would go to all that trouble, but it *is* possible. Put it this way: I could write a science fiction story about such a conspiracy, and although you might say it wasn't very plausible, you couldn't say that the story was a total impossibility.

Well, you protest, if Descartes is going to interpret "clearly recognize" like that, then just about everything anyone has ever believed will go out the window! I might as well doubt that there is even a United States, or an earth, or a human race, or space and time and the universe. If I am going to refuse to accept things like that, then maybe I ought to start doubting that two plus two is four. After all, if a giant conspiracy might be underway to trick me into believing that Washington is the capital of the United States, then maybe some mysterious, evil, powerful demon is reaching into my mind and tricking me into thinking that two plus two is four when really it is five. Maybe every time I take two objects and place them next to two more, that demon sneaks one of them away, so that as I count them up, I get only four instead of five, which is the right number!

Strange as it may sound, this is just what Descartes has in mind. When he says accept *nothing* that isn't certain, he means *nothing*. But, you object, that is madness! We have to start somewhere. Why, if I am going to doubt everything that has even the most minute bit of possible uncertainty attached to it, then I might even have to doubt my own existence! Perhaps I don't exist either; maybe that evil demon is fooling me about myself as well as about simple arithmetic! No, says Descartes, with one of the most dramatic reversals in all philosophical literature. Doubt all else, but you cannot doubt your own existence. That, and nothing but that, is the true foundation, the unshakable first principle, the rock on which all the rest of your knowledge shall be raised up. How does he manage to prove that I cannot rationally doubt my own existence, when he has erected a standard of certainty so strict that literally everything else that I have ever believed fails to meet it? You shall see when you read the *Meditations.* I do not want to spoil the effect of the argument by giving it away. Descartes' proof of his own existence is one of the high points in the history of philosophy. It is also, in a way, the high point of unbridled individualism in Western civilization. Imagine a philosopher who proposes to base the entire edifice of scientific, mathematical, and religious knowledge *not* on the collective learning and wisdom of humanity, *not* on the evidence of the laboratory, *not* on the existence of God, *not even* on the first principles of logic, *but simply on the fact of his own existence!*

When the method of inquiry is combined with the method of doubt, a transformation in the central nature of philosophy is begun. That transformation, which I am calling the *epistemological turn,* took a century and a half to complete. Not until Kant's *Critique of Pure Reason* was the epistemological turn brought to its end; thereafter, all philosophy was so changed that the very questions philosophers asked, as well as the answers they gave, looked little like what was written before the *Meditations.* The epistemological turn is a very simple, but tricky, notion. Even after you have it, you find it slipping away from you. Like Einstein's notion of relativity, or a Picasso painting, it makes you see familiar things in an entirely new way.

The heart of the E.T. (philosophers these days like to abbreviate things, so let's use E.T. for *epistemological turn*) is a simple reversal in order of two basic questions. From the ancient pre-Socratic cosmologists up to the time of Descartes, philosophers put questions about what exists, about the nature of the universe, before questions about what I can know to exist, about what I can know the nature of the universe to be. That is to say, philosophers considered questions of *being* to take precedence over questions of *knowing.* Aristotle, for example, called the essays in which he discussed questions of being "essays on first philosophy." He didn't mean that these very difficult, very abstract essays were the first sorts of philosophy a student should read. He meant that questions about the nature of being were the logically first, or most fundamental, or most basic questions to be dealt with.

To be sure, Aristotle and many of his predecessors and followers discussed the nature of knowledge. They talked about the nature of the mind, the role of the senses (sight, hearing, touch, and so forth) in knowledge, the role of reasoning, the limits of human knowledge, and countless other topics. But they considered these *epistemological* questions to be secondary, less important than questions about the nature of God, the reality of space and time, and all the other topics dealt with in "first philosophy," or as we call it today, metaphysics. So we can sum up philosophy prior to Descartes by saying that in it, *metaphysics took precedence over epistemology.*

Descartes' two methods—the method of inquiry and the method of doubt—had the effect of reversing this order of precedence. Properly understood and carried out with a consistency and rigor which Descartes himself never achieved, these two methods forced philosophers to set aside questions of being until they had dealt with the questions of knowing. And that fact in turn changed the meaning of the questions about being, so that by the time the revolution begun by Descartes had run its course, old-style metaphysics was finished, and new-style epistemology had taken its place as "first philosophy." Let us see how Descartes' two methods began this transformation.

First, as we have noted, the method of inquiry tells us to adopt the point of view of someone who is ignorant but is trying to learn, rather than the point of view of someone who knows something and is trying to explain. What is more, it teaches us to take questions in an orderly manner, not moving on to the next until we have settled the first. There is an old case in the English common law, going back to the Middle Ages, which illustrates the hidden force of Descartes' rule. Jones sued Smith for damages, claiming that Smith had borrowed a water jug from him and had returned it broken. Smith's defense was a classic of what we now call "stonewalling." First of all, he argued, the jug does not exist; second, I didn't borrow it; third, it was whole when I returned it; and fourth, it was cracked when I borrowed it. Smith wasn't out of his mind. He was simply saying to Jones, Before I am going to pay you any money, you are going to have to prove every single item in your story. You must prove that the jug even exists; then you must prove that I borrowed it; then you must prove that I didn't return it whole; and then you must prove that it wasn't cracked when I borrowed it, but was cracked when I returned it. Now the legal point of this story is that proving one of these points might be a good deal harder than proving another, and Jones must prove them all in order to collect damages. If he threw the jug away after it was returned broken, then he may have trouble proving that it ever existed. Even if he kept the pieces, he may have trouble proving that it wasn't already cracked when he lent it to Smith. And so on. When the defense in a court case agrees not to dispute some assertion by the prosecution about the facts of the case, it is called "stipulating." Descartes' first rule tells us not to stipulate anything!

For example, at the beginning of his book entitled *Physics,* Aristotle says that the subject matter of physics is motion, or rather things in motion. If anyone wants to deny that there is motion in the world (as some philosophers in fact had denied), then a book on physics is not the right place to argue with him or her. "We physicists," Aristotle writes, "must take for granted that the things that exist by nature are, either all or some of them, in motion. . . . No man of science is bound to solve every kind of difficulty that may be raised, but only as many as are drawn falsely from the principles of the science." But Descartes adopts the opposite view. Before we can do physics, we must prove that there are bodies in motion in space. Once we have established that, we can appeal to the experiments and observations, deductions and proofs, which scientists have developed in their study of nature. But until we have shown that nature exists—until we have, like Jones, proved that there is a jug—we must set aside such investigations. We shall not stipulate the universe.

The second half of Descartes' method—the method of doubt—makes things ten times worse, of course. Having refused to stipulate anything, even the existence of the world, Descartes now insists that the standard of proof be absolute certainty. In a court of law, the jury is asked whether the case has been proved "beyond a reasonable doubt." There is a whole lot of difference between absolute certainty and beyond a reasonable doubt. I am pretty sure that my car won't turn into a boa constrictor and squeeze me to death while I am putting on my seat belt. I am sure enough of it to bet my life on it every day when I drive somewhere. My conviction goes way beyond any reasonable doubt. But if Descartes asks me whether I can be *certain* that my car won't turn into a boa, I must answer that of course I cannot rule it out as absolutely impossible. I can, after all, imagine some weird planet across the galaxy in which cars turn into boa constrictors. In a way, that isn't much stranger than the fact that caterpillars turn into butterflies!

Combining the two methods seems to drive us into the corner which philosophers call "skepticism." If we can't move on to point B until we have proved point A, and if in order to prove point A, we must establish it with absolute certainty, then it looks as though we will have a very hard time proving any point at all. Instead of wandering all over the universe, studying the stars, the planets, the origins of life, the workings of the human body, the laws of society, or the movement of the tides, we are going to be huddled in a corner, trying to figure out how to take step A, so that we can take step B. Now, if your car is working, you go on trips and look at the scenery. But if your car won't run, you open the hood and inspect the motor. So too, if your logical engine is in good working order, then you cruise through the world of knowledge, looking at one interesting field after another; but if your logical engine breaks down—if your rules of inquiry and proof don't permit you to move with ease from one truth to another—then you stop, raise the lid on your mind (which is, after all, your logical engine), and take a good hard look to see what is wrong. In short, you start analyzing and examining the process by which you come to know anything. Epistemology is the study of the way in which we know, the rules by which we reason, the limits of what we can know, and the criteria or standards we use for judging whether a supposed piece of knowledge really is knowledge. If we follow Descartes' rules, we cannot take a scientific or metaphysical trip through the universe until we have checked out our means of transportation—our knowing process itself—and made sure that it will take us where we want to go.

Descartes himself never realized the full magnitude of the revolution that his two methods were to produce. He thought of himself as laying the basis for a new, unified system of scientific knowledge free of all reliance on tradition, the wisdom of the ancients, or the old concepts of Aristotelian metaphysics. But he seems still to have supposed that questions of being would take precedence over questions of knowing. In the *Meditations,* after the section which you are about to read, he went on to offer "proofs" for the existence of God, of the physical universe, and of all the other things he had so carefully doubted at the beginning of the essay. It remained for later philosophers, both on the continent of Europe and in Great Britain, to draw out the deeper implications of the process which Descartes started.

Here now are selections from the First and Second Meditation.

MEDITATION I

It is now some years since I detected how many were the false beliefs that I had from my earliest youth admitted as true and how doubtful was everything I had since constructed on this basis; and from that time I was convinced that I must once for all seriously undertake to rid myself of all the opinions which I had formerly accepted, and commence to build anew from the foundation, if I wanted to establish any firm and permanent structure in the sciences.

Now for this object it is not necessary that I should show that all of these are false—I shall perhaps never arrive at this end. But inasmuch as reason already persuades me that I ought no less carefully to withhold my assent from matters which are not entirely certain and indubitable than from those which appear to me manifestly to be false, if I am able to find in each one some reason to doubt, this will suffice to justify my rejecting the whole. And for that end it will not be requisite that I should examine each in particular, which would be an endless undertaking; for owing to the fact that the destruction of the foundations of necessity brings with it the downfall of the rest of the edifice, I shall only in the first place attack those principles upon which all my former opinions rested.

All that up to the present time I have accepted as most true and certain I have learned either from the senses or through the senses; but it is sometimes proved to me that these senses are deceptive, and it is wiser not to trust entirely to any thing by which we have once been deceived.

But it may be that although the senses sometimes deceive us concerning things which are hardly perceptible, or very far away, there are yet many others to be met with as to which we cannot reasonably have any doubt, although we recognise them by their means. For example, there is the fact that I am here, seated by the fire, attired in a dressing gown, having this paper in my hands and other similar matters. And how could I deny that these hands and this body are mine, were it not perhaps that I compare myself to certain persons, devoid of sense, whose cerebella are so troubled and clouded by the violent vapours of black bile, that they constantly assure us that they think they are kings when they are really quite poor, or that they are clothed in purple when they are really without covering, or who imagine that they have an earthenware head or are nothing but pumpkins or are made of glass. But they are mad, and I should not be any the less insane were I to follow examples so extravagant.

At the same time I must remember that I am a man, and that consequently I am in the habit of sleeping, and in my dreams representing to myself the same things or sometimes even less probable things, than do those who are insane in their waking moments. How often has it happened to me that in the night I dreamt that I found myself in this particular place, that I was dressed and seated near the fire, whilst in reality I was lying undressed in bed! At this moment it does indeed seem to me that it is with eyes awake that I am looking at this paper; that this head which I move is not asleep, that it is deliberately and of set purpose that I extend my hand and perceive it; what happens in sleep does not appear so clear nor so distinct as does all this. But in thinking over this I remind myself that on many occasions I have in sleep been deceived by similar illusions, and in dwelling carefully on this reflection I see so manifestly that there are no certain indications by which we may clearly distinguish wakefulness from sleep that I am lost in astonishment. And my astonishment is such that it is almost capable of persuading me that I now dream.

Now let us assume that we are asleep and that all these particulars, e.g. that we open our eyes, shake our head, extend our hands, and so on, are but false delusions; and let us reflect that possibly neither our hands nor our whole body are such as they appear to us to be. At the same time we must at least confess that the things which are represented to us in sleep are like painted representations which can only have been formed as the counterparts of something real and true, and that in this way those general things at least, i.e. eyes, a head, hands, and a whole body, are not imaginary things, but things really existent. For, as a matter of fact, painters, even when they study with the greatest skill to represent sirens and satyrs by forms the most strange and extraordinary, cannot give them natures which are entirely new, but merely make a certain medley of the members of different animals; or if their imagination is extravagant enough to invent something so novel that nothing similar has ever before been seen, and that then their work represents a thing purely fictitious and absolutely false, it is certain all the same that the colours of which this is composed are necessarily real. And for the same reason, although these general things, to wit, [a body], eyes, a head, hands, and such like, may be imaginary, we are bound at the same time to confess that there are at least some other objects yet more simple and more universal, which are real and true; and of these just in the same way as with certain real colours, all these images of things which dwell in our thoughts, whether true and real or false and fantastic, are formed.

To such a class of things pertains corporeal nature in general, and its extension, the figure of extended things, their quantity or magnitude and number, as also the place in which they are, the time which measures their duration, and so on.

That is possibly why our reasoning is not unjust when we conclude from this that Physics, Astronomy, Medicine and all other sciences which have as their end the consideration of composite things, are very dubious and uncertain; but that Arithmetic, Geometry and other sciences of that kind which only treat of things that are very simple and very general, without taking great trouble to ascertain whether they are actually existent or not contain some measure of certainty and an element of the indubitable. For whether I am awake or asleep, two and three together always form five, and the square can never have more than four sides, and it does not seem possible that truths so clear and apparent can be suspected of any falsity [or uncertainty].

Nevertheless I have long had fixed in my mind the belief that an all-powerful God existed by whom I have been created such as I am. But how do I know that He has not brought it to pass that there is no earth, no heaven, no extended body, no magnitude, no place, and that nevertheless [I possess the perceptions of all these things and that] they seem to me to exist just exactly as I now see them? And, besides, as I sometimes imagine that others deceive themselves in the things which they think they know best, how do I know that I am not deceived every time that I add two and three, or count the sides of a square, or judge of things yet simpler, if anything simpler can be imagined? But possibly God has not desired that I should be thus deceived, for He is said to be supremely good. If, however, it is contrary to His goodness to have made me such that I constantly deceive myself, it would also appear to be contrary to His goodness to permit me to be sometimes deceived, and nevertheless I cannot doubt that He does permit this.

I shall then suppose, not that God who is supremely good and the fountain of truth, but some evil genius not less powerful than deceitful, has employed his whole energies in deceiving me; I shall consider that the heavens, the earth, colours, figures, sound, and all other external things are nought but the illusions and dreams of which this genius has availed himself in order to lay traps for my credulity; I shall consider myself as having no hands, no eyes, no flesh, no blood, nor any senses, yet falsely believing myself to possess all these things; I shall remain obstinately attached to this idea, and if by this means it is not in my power to arrive at the knowledge of any truth, I may at least do what is in my power [i.e. suspend my judgment], and with firm purpose avoid giving credence to any false thing, or being imposed upon by this arch deceiver, however powerful and deceptive he may be. . . .

MEDITATION II

The Meditation of yesterday filled my mind with so many doubts that it is no longer in my power to forget them. And yet I do not see in what manner I can resolve them; and, just as if I had all of a sudden fallen into very deep water, I am so disconcerted that I can neither make certain of setting my feet on the bottom, nor can I swim and so support myself on the surface. I shall nevertheless make an effort and follow anew the same path as that on which I yesterday entered, i.e. I shall proceed by setting aside all that in which the least doubt could be supposed to exist, just as if I had discovered that it was absolutely false; and I shall ever follow in this road until I have met with something which is certain, or at least, if I can do nothing else, until I have learned for certain that there is nothing in the world that is certain. Archimedes, in order that he might draw the terrestrial globe out of its place, and transport it elsewhere, demanded only that one point should be fixed and immoveable; in the same way I shall have the right to conceive high hopes if I am happy enough to discover one thing only which is certain and indubitable.

I suppose, then, that all the things that I see are false; I persuade myself that nothing has ever existed of all that my fallacious memory represents to me. I consider that I possess no senses; I imagine that body, figure, extension, movement and place are but the fictions of my mind. What, then, can be esteemed as true? Perhaps nothing at all, unless that there is nothing in the world that is certain.

But how can I know there is not something different from those things that I have just considered, of which one cannot have the slightest doubt? Is there not some God, or some other being by whatever name we call it, who puts these reflections into my mind? That is not necessary, for is it not possible that I am capable of producing them myself? I myself, am I not at least something? But I have already denied that I had senses and body. Yet I hesitate, for what follows from that? Am I so dependent on body and senses that I cannot exist without these? But I was persuaded that there was nothing in all the world, that there was no heaven, no earth, that there were no minds, nor any bodies: was I not then likewise persuaded that I did not exist? Not at all; of a surety I myself did exist since I persuaded myself of something [or merely because I thought of something]. But there is some deceiver or other, very powerful and very cunning, who ever employs his ingenuity in deceiving me. Then without doubt I exist also if he deceives me, and let him deceive me as much as he will, he can never cause me to be nothing so long as I think that I am something. So that after having reflected well and carefully examined all things, we must come to the definite conclusion that this proposition: I am, I exist, is necessarily true each time that I pronounce it, or that I mentally conceive it.

But I do not yet know clearly enough what I am, I who am certain that I am; and hence I must be careful to see that I do not imprudently take some other object in place of myself, and thus that I do not go astray in respect of this knowledge that I hold to be the most certain and most evident of all that I have formerly learned. That is why I shall now consider anew what I believed myself to be before I embarked upon these last reflections; and of my former opinions I shall withdraw all that might even in a small degree be invalidated by the reasons which I have just brought forward, in order that there may be nothing at all left beyond what is absolutely certain and indubitable.

RENÉ DESCARTES, *Meditations on First Philosophy*

II

When Descartes summarized his proof for his own existence in Latin, he used the phrase *Cogito, ergo sum,* which means "I think, therefore I am." So his proof has come to be known in philosophical shorthand as the Cogito argument. Now, if you read the selection from the *Meditations* carefully, you will realize that "I think, therefore I am" is not exactly what Descartes says. Instead, he says something slightly but very significantly different, namely, "The proposition, I exist, is necessarily true each time I pronounce it." Pronouncing or asserting the proposition is crucial, because it is the asserting that guarantees its truth. The point is that if the proposition is being *asserted,* then someone must be doing the asserting, and if I am asserting it, then that someone must be me. Needless to say, I cannot use this proof to establish the existence of anyone else. Suppose, for example, that I try to prove my wife's existence by saying, "The proposition, She exists, is necessarily true each time I pronounce it." Well, that just won't work. The fact that I pronounce or assert that she exists in no way guarantees that she does. But it does guarantee that I exist! In fact, my asserting any proposition, true or false, about myself or about anything else, guarantees that *I* exist, because I am the subject, the asserter, the conscious thinker of the proposition. And—this is the key point—propositions or assertions or statements cannot simply hang in midair with no one asserting them. A proposition is an assertion, and therefore it must be asserted *by* someone.

Incidentally, I hope you realize that Descartes' Cogito argument only proves his existence to him; it doesn't prove his existence to you or to me. "The proposition, Descartes exists, is necessarily true everytime I pronounce it" doesn't hold water at all. Descartes can use his new argument to prove his existence to himself, I can use his argument to prove my existence to myself, and each of you can use his argument to prove your own existence to yourself. But no one can use the argument to prove someone else's existence. This fact about the Cogito argument has two important consequences for subsequent epistemology. First, it drives each philosopher into the position called *solipsism:* that is, the individual subject knows its own existence prior to, and better than, anything else, and perhaps knows the existence of nothing but itself. Second, it turns the attention of philosophers away from the *objects* of knowledge, the things that we know about, and toward the *subject* of knowledge, the mind that does the knowing. Later in this chapter, we shall see that this pair of implications of the Cogito argument is used by Kant in his effort to find a way out of the skepticism and solipsism of the Cartesian position.

Descartes got himself, and us, into the skeptical solipsist box in the First Meditation by doubting everything that was not known with certainty. He proceeded, you will recall, by adopting a criterion of certainty so strict that in the end, nothing save the assertion of his own existence could meet its requirements. In surveying the multitude of his beliefs, furthermore, Descartes divided them into two major groups: those which he thought he knew on the basis of the evidence of his own senses, and those which he thought he knew on the basis of reasoning with general concepts. In this way, two central problems are raised by the argument in the First Meditation. The first is the problem of *certainty.* What criterion of truth should we adopt as the standard against which to measure our various knowledge claims? The second is the problem of the sources of knowledge. Insofar as we know anything, is our knowledge based upon the evidence of the senses, upon abstract reasoning, or upon some combination of the two? The philosophy of the 150 years following the publication of the *Meditations* was very largely a series of variations on these two themes.

Descartes himself offered preliminary answers to the questions of certainty and the sources of knowledge in the latter part of the Second Meditation. Before taking our leave of him, and moving on to survey the attempts of his successors to deal with the problems he raised, perhaps we ought to see what he had to say about them. On the problem of certainty, he offered two criteria, two tests of the certainty of an assertion. Here is what he says:

> . . . I am certain that I am a thing which thinks; but do I not then likewise know what is requisite to render me certain of a truth? Certainly in this first knowledge there is nothing that assures me of its truth, excepting the clear and distinct perception of that which I state, which would not indeed suffice to assure me that what I say is true, if it could ever happen that a thing which I conceived so clearly and

distinctly could be false; and accordingly it seems to me that already I can establish as a general rule that all things which I perceive very clearly and very distinctly are true.

Clearness and distinctness aren't much as a hedge against the far-reaching skepticism fostered by the method of doubt. How can I be sure that I really perceive a proposition clearly or distinctly? It is no good saying that it really, truly *seems* clear and distinct to me. After all, it really, truly seems to me that I am awake, but as Descartes himself pointed out, I might nonetheless be mistaken. Later on, after using the clearness and distinctness test to prove the existence of God, Descartes turns around and uses the goodness of God as a proof that clearness and distinctness are adequate criteria of certainty. A good God, he argues, would not deceive me! Well, that is about as obvious a case of arguing in a circle as you will find in the writings of great philosophers, and I think we can agree that having posed the problem of certainty, Descartes didn't really have a solution to it.

As for the sources of our knowledge, Descartes came down foursquare on the side of reason rather than the senses. That is what you would expect from someone whose dream it was to create a mathematical physics. In place of observation and the collecting of data from sight, smell, hearing, and touch, Descartes wanted a universal system of science derived from logical and mathematical premises and proved by rigorous deduction. In order to persuade his readers of the primacy of reason in our acquiring of knowledge, Descartes uses what is called a "thought experiment." That is, he asks us to imagine with him a situation—in this case, that he is sitting near his fire with a piece of wax in his hand—and then he tries to get us to see, through an analysis of the situation, that our methods of reasoning or of acquiring knowledge must have a certain character. Philosophers frequently argue in this way when they are trying to establish some general proposition rather than to prove a particular fact. The thought experiment isn't supposed to be evidence, in the modern scientific sense. Rather, it is merely a device for exploring the logical or conceptual relationships between different ideas. Here is Descartes' thought experiment to show that our knowledge comes from understanding or reason or the mind, rather than through the senses.

Let us begin by considering the commonest matters, those which we believe to be the most distinctly comprehended, to wit, the bodies which we touch and see; not indeed bodies in general, for these general ideas are usually a little more confused, but let us consider one body in particular. Let us take, for example, this piece of wax: it has been taken quite freshly from the hive, and it has not yet lost the sweetness of the honey which it contains; it still retains somewhat of the odour of the flowers from which it has been culled; its colour, its figure, its size are apparent; it is hard, cold, easily handled, and if you strike it with the finger, it will emit a sound. Finally all the things which are requisite to cause us distinctly to recognise a body, are met with in it. But notice that while I speak and approach the fire what remained of the taste is exhaled, the smell evaporates, the colour alters, the figure is destroyed, the size increases, it becomes liquid, it heats, scarcely can one handle it, and when one strikes it, no sound is emitted. Does the same wax remain after this change? We must confess that it remains; none would judge otherwise. What then did I know so distinctly in this piece of wax? It could certainly be nothing of all that the senses brought to my notice, since all these things which fall under taste, smell, sight, touch, and hearing, are found to be changed, and yet the same wax remains.

Perhaps it was what I now think, viz. that this wax was not that sweetness of honey, nor that agreeable scent of flowers, nor that particular whiteness, nor that figure, nor that sound, but simply a body which a little while before appeared to me as perceptible under these forms, and which is now perceptible under others. But what, precisely, is it that I imagine when I form such conceptions? Let us attentively consider this, and, abstracting from all that does not belong to the wax, let us see what remains. Certainly nothing remains excepting a certain extended thing which is flexible and movable. But what is the meaning of flexible and movable? Is it not that I imagine that this piece of wax being round is capable of becoming square and of passing from a square to a triangular figure? No, certainly it is not that, since I imagine it admits of an infinitude of similar changes, and I nevertheless do not know how to compass the infinitude by my imagination, and consequently this conception which I have of the wax is not brought about by the faculty of imagination. What now is this extension? Is it not also unknown? For it becomes greater when the wax is melted, greater when it is boiled, and greater still when the heat increases, and I should not conceive [clearly] according to truth what wax is, if I did not think that even this piece that we are considering is capable of receiving more variations in extension than I have ever imagined. We must then grant that I could not even understand through the imagination what this piece of wax is, and that it is my mind alone which perceives it. I say this piece of wax in particular, for as to wax in general it is yet clearer. But what is this piece of wax which cannot be understood excepting by the [understanding or] mind? It is certainly the same that I see, touch, imagine, and finally it is the same which I have always believed it to be from the beginning. But what must particularly be observed is that its perception is neither an act of vision, nor of touch, nor of imagination, and has never been such although it may have appeared formerly to be so, but only an intuition of the mind, which may be imperfect and confused as it was formerly, or clear and distinct as it is at present according as my attention is more or less directed to the elements which are found in it, and of which it is composed.

RENÉ DESCARTES, *Meditations on First Philosophy*

The debate over Descartes' problems soon resolved itself into a conflict between two more or less unified schools of thought, the continental rationalists and the British empiricists. (Since this makes it sound a bit like an international soccer match, let me explain that those are labels we put on the two groups today; they themselves did not go about wearing T-shirts saying "Continental Rationalist" or "British Empiricist.") The rationalists accepted Descartes' demand for certainty, agreed with his view that logic and mathematics were the model for all true knowledge, and sought to discover ways of establishing the principal propositions of science and metaphysics with as much certainty as the truths of the syllogism or geometry possessed. They sought proofs for the existence of God (using some that had been around for quite a while, such as the cosmological and ontological proofs that we have already examined); they offered demonstrations of the fundamental principles of the new physics; and they pursued Descartes' dream of a universal system of knowledge. Like Descartes, they downgraded the senses as a source of knowledge, and instead claimed that all valid knowledge-claims must rest upon the operations of reason.

The empiricists also accepted Descartes' demand for certainty, but in progressively more sweeping attacks on the knowledge-claims of the rationalists, they argued that nothing could meet that demand. David Hume, the most brilliant and thoroughgoing of the empiricists, produced devastating proofs that neither the theorems of science nor the beliefs of common sense could possibly qualify as knowledge when measured against Descartes' own standard of certainty.

The empiricists also challenged the rationalists' reliance upon reason as the sole source of knowledge. First John Locke, in his *Essay Concerning the Human Understanding,* and then Hume, in the *Treatise of Human Nature,* insisted that all the ideas in the human mind must ultimately be derived from the sights, sounds, smells, feels, and tastes of our sense organs. Reason, they argued, could do no more than rearrange and sort the materials provided to the mind by sensation. This subordination of reason to the senses was one of the most powerful weapons in the empiricists' assault on the systems of science and metaphysics erected by the rationalist philosophers.

If you have managed to follow our discussion of epistemology thus far, it should be obvious to you that there is much more to be discussed in the theory of knowledge than we can hope to touch on in the remainder of this chapter. Rather than mentioning everyone and everything without explaining anything, therefore, I shall limit myself to *three* areas. First, we shall take a brief look at Gottfried Leibniz's attempt to deal with the criteria of certainty, and his very important distinction between what he calls truths of reasoning and truths of fact. Then we shall examine David Hume's attempt to reduce all the contents of the mind to data of the senses, and his analysis of the criterion of certainty, so that we can understand the full force of his skeptical attack on the claims of science and common sense. And finally, I will try to explain how Immanuel Kant sought to overcome the division between the rationalists and the empiricists by compromising their dispute over the sources of knowledge and the criteria of certainty. If you can get all that under your belts, then you will have had quite enough philosophy for one chapter!

Descartes' tests of certainty were clearness and distinctness. These essentially psychological criteria tell us very little about the structure of knowledge, about the kinds of knowledge claims that can meet the test of certainty and the kinds that cannot. After all, any belief might, upon inspection, turn out to be conceived clearly and distinctly, or at least it might seem to be. I think I clearly and distinctly apprehend that two things added to two things make a total of four things; but I also think I clearly and distinctly apprehend that I am seated now at a desk in my office, with a typewriter in front of me and a chair under me.

In place of Descartes' psychological tests, Leibniz offered logical criteria of truth and certainty. All truths, he proposed, could be divided into two sorts. The first are truths that can be known merely by application of a fundamental principle of logic called the *law of contradiction*. When we state some truth, we do so by making an assertion. "Two plus two equals four" is an assertion; "Washington, D.C. is the capital of the United States" is an assertion; "$E = mc^2$" is an assertion. Any declarative statement in its ordinary usage makes an assertion. If I have one assertion, I can make another, opposite assertion simply by denying the first. So from "Two plus two equals four" I can make "It is not the case that two plus two equals four." From "Washington, D.C. is the capital of the United States" I can make "It is not the case that Washington, D.C. is the capital of the United States." The denial of an assertion is called its *negation,* and since "It is not the case that" is a little clumsy to keep repeating, philosophers and logicians shorten it to "not." The negation of "Two plus two equals four" would thus be "Not two plus two equals four," and so on.

If you think about it for a moment, you will see that an assertion and its negation cannot both be true. Maybe Washington is our capital, maybe it isn't, but there is just no way that it can both be and not be our capital. Logicians express this in very general form by saying that for any assertion, it cannot be the case that both the assertion and its negation are true. Because two assertions are said to "contradict" one another if they cannot both be true, this general principle about assertions and their negations is called the law of contradiction. There is another law of logic which usually goes along with the law of contradiction, according to which for any assertion, either it is true or else its negation is true. There is no third possibility, no middle ground. This law is called the *law of the excluded middle.* So logic teaches us that no matter what assertion we are thinking about, either it is true or its negation is true, but not both.

According to Leibniz, truths of reasoning are those assertions which we can know to be true merely by using the law of contradiction (and the law of the excluded middle, although he doesn't mention it). For example, suppose a fast-talking door-to-door salesman tries to push a fifteen-volume encyclopedia on you. "This encyclopedia is absolutely free," he says. "You only pay ten dollars per volume." Now you don't have to know anything about encyclopedias to be certain that he isn't telling you the truth. All you have to do is whip out your trusty law of contradiction, and perform the following process of reasoning:

Number one, you say this encyclopedia is absolutely free.

Number two, you say I must pay ten dollars per volume for it.

But "free" means "I don't have to pay."

So you are saying that I don't have to pay, and I do have to pay.

Or, as we logicians put it,

I do have to pay and not I do have to pay.

And that violates the law of contradiction, so it must be false. What is more, with a quick application of the law of the excluded middle, I can draw the absolutely certain conclusion that

Either I have to pay or I do not have to pay, so stop the fast talk and tell me which it is.

Truths of reasoning are nice, because we can know them to be certain merely by application of these two simple laws, but they leave a good deal to be desired. Thus, my bit of reasoning doesn't tell me whether I have to pay. It just tells me that either I have to or I don't, but not both. Truths that cannot be certified by appeal to the laws of logic are called *truths of fact* by Leibniz. They include most of what we ordinarily call *knowledge,* and to establish their truth, we must appeal to a quite different principle, which Liebniz labeled the *principle of sufficient reason.* Here is the passage from his short summary work, *The Monadology,* in which he defined and distinguished the two sorts of truths.

Our reasoning is based upon two great principles: first, that of Contradiction, by means of which we decide that to be false which involves contradiction and that to be true which contradicts or is opposed to the false.

And second, the principle of Sufficient Reason, in virtue of which we believe that no fact can be real or existing and no statement true unless it has a sufficient reason why it should be thus and not otherwise. Most frequently, however, these reasons cannot be known by us.

There are also two kinds of Truths: those of Reasoning and those of Fact. The Truths of Reasoning are necessary, and their opposite is impossible. Those of Fact, however, are contingent, and their opposite is possible. When a truth is necessary, the reason can be found by analysis in resolving it into simpler ideas and into simpler truths until we reach those which are primary. . . .

There are finally simple ideas of which no definition can be given. There are also the Axioms and Postulates or, in a word, the primary principles which cannot be proved and, indeed, have no need of proof. These are identical propositions whose opposites involve express contradictions.

But there must be also a sufficient reason for contingent truths or truths of fact; that is to say, for the sequence of the things which extend throughout the universe of created beings, where the analysis into more particular reasons can be continued into greater detail without limit because of the immense variety of the things in nature and because of the infinite division of bodies. There is an infinity of figures and of movements, present and past, which enter into the efficient cause of my present writing, and in its final cause there are an infinity of slight tendencies and dispositions of my soul, present and past.

And as all this detail again involves other and more detailed contingencies, each of which again has need of a similar analysis in order to find its explanation, no real advance has been made. Therefore, the sufficient or ultimate reason must needs be outside of the sequence or series of these details of contingencies, however infinite they may be.

It is thus that the ultimate reason for things must be a necessary substance, in which the detail of the changes shall be present merely potentially, as in the fountain-head, and this substance we call God.

GOTTRIED LEIBNIZ, *The Monadology*

As you can see, Leibniz thought that when it came to truths of fact, such as the laws of physics or the facts of history, we could only certify them by an indirect appeal to God. The skeptical opponents of the rationalists had very little faith in the proofs for the existence of God, so you can imagine that they were not much impressed by this sort of justification for scientific theories. (Take a look back at Chapter Six for Hume's objections to some of those proofs.)

IV

The first major assault on the continental rationalists was launched by the Englishman John Locke, whose theory of the social contract you have already encountered. Locke hit upon a simple but very powerful strategy for attacking the claims by Descartes and others that reason alone could provide us with knowledge. Instead of examining our knowledge claims directly, Locke suggested, let us instead ask from what source we derive the ideas which we use in stating these knowledge claims. Scientists and metaphysicians had been accustomed to express their theories by statements using terms like "matter," "space," "time," "substance," "cause," "necessary," "possible," "object," and "self." In addition, of course, they used more familiar terms like "red," "hard," "round," and "sweet." If our knowledge claims make any sense at all, Locke argued, then these words must correspond to ideas in our minds. Otherwise, we will simply seem to be saying something, but really we won't be asserting anything at all. (That is what humorists do when they write nonsense verse. Lewis Carroll, the author of *Alice in Wonderland,* wrote a poem that begins, "Twas brillig, and the slithy toves did gyre and gimbel in the wabe." That sounds as though it ought to mean something, but it doesn't, because "words" like "brillig" and "toves" don't correspond to any ideas in our minds.)

According to Locke, the mind is a blank when we are born. He compares it to a piece of white paper on which experience writes. Here, from his *Essay Concerning the Human Understanding* (Book II, Chapter 1), is his statement of this famous doctrine:

> Let us then suppose the mind to be, as we say, white paper, void of all characters, without any ideas:—How comes it to be furnished? Whence comes it by that wide store which the busy and boundless fancy of man has painted on it with almost endless variety? Whence has it all the *materials* of reason and knowledge? To this I answer, in one word, EXPERIENCE. In that all our knowledge is founded; and from it ultimately derives itself.

That doesn't sound like such a brilliant philosophical strategy when you first hear it. Indeed, it sounds positively obvious. But in the hands of Locke, of George Berkeley, and especially of David Hume, it turned out to be a crusher. To see why this is so, think for a moment about all the assertions that philosophers and theologians have made over the ages about God. Every one of those assertions uses the idea of God somehow. For example, one assertion is that God exists; a second is that God is omnipotent; a third is that God has promised us eternal life if only we will obey His laws; and so forth. If we follow Locke's suggestion, instead of asking directly what evidence there is for these assertions, we will instead ask, Is there an *idea* of God in our minds corresponding to the word "God" which is used in each of the assertions? And following Locke's theory of the blank white paper, we will ask whether the idea of God has come to us through our eyes, our ears, our fingertips, our noses, or our other sense organs. As soon as you put the question that way, it is obvious that we couldn't have derived the idea of God from any sensory sources. God is supposed to be infinite, but we can only see, hear, feel, and taste finite things. God is supposed to be eternal, but we cannot see or hear or feel something that exists outside time, or even something that exists in time forever and ever. God is supposed to be omnipotent, but the most our senses could ever show us is something very powerful, not something infinitely powerful. So it would seem to follow simply and directly from Locke's strategy that *we do not really have an idea of God at all!* We have the word "God," and we make up what we think are meaningful assertions using it, but all that talk about God turns out

GEORGE BERKELEY (1685–1753) was an Irish philosopher and cleric who is remembered as the defender of a philosophical position known as "idealism." Berkeley's most important philosophical works, including his *Treatise Concerning the Principles of Human Knowledge* and *Three Dialogues Between Hylas and Philonus,* were all written before his thirtieth birthday. Berkeley defended the view that the only things that could be known to exist are human minds, the ideas in these minds, and God. This doctrine is opposed to the view, defended by Hobbes and others, that physical bodies are the only things that exist ("materialism").

Berkeley spent three years in the New World, seeking to found a college in the Bermudas. Though his plans never were carried out, he did leave his philosophical library to the then recently founded Yale College in New Haven, Connecticut.

to have no more meaning than Lewis Carroll's poem about slithy toves. (Incidentally, Locke himself did not draw his antireligious conclusion from his theory of ideas, and he would have been horrified by it!)

Since that last paragraph may have whipped by a bit fast, let's stop a moment and be sure that we understand what the argument is really saying. Lewis Carroll's poem isn't *false;* it is *meaningless,* because it uses "words" which don't correspond to ideas in our minds, and hence have no meaning. An assertion has to mean something before we can ask whether it is true or false. Philosophical books are full of arguments about the truth or falsehood of various theological, metaphysical, and scientific theories. But Locke's attack cuts these arguments off at the knees. Before two philosophers can even begin to argue about the existence of God, they must show that their words have meaning, and according to Locke, that means showing that the words correspond to ideas in our minds which have been derived from the senses. So by his strategy of looking to the sources of our ideas, together with his doctrine of the mind as a blank sheet of paper written on by experience, Locke shifted the whole debate into a new channel.

Locke's weapon, incidentally, is a double-edged sword. If the theory proves that we do not even have a coherent idea of God, then one possible conclusion is that all our talk about God is nonsense, and all our theories of religion meaningless. But another possible conclusion is that since his theory implies such a ridiculous notion, it must itself be false! It comes down to deciding which is harder to believe. If I do have an idea of God, then it cannot have come through my senses, so I am going to have to explain how the mind can acquire ideas which it does not derive from sense experience; on the other hand, if all my ideas are derived from sense experience, then I cannot have an idea of God, so I am going to have to explain why so many apparently reasonable people firmly believe that they have such an idea, and why people who talk about God think they are making sense and not nonsense.

The empiricist who carried Locke's strategy to its logical conclusion was David Hume. As you will recall from Chapter One, Hume conceived the plan, when still a very young man, of writing a full-scale theory of the human mind along the lines of Isaac Newton's enormously successful theory of the physical universe. In the very opening pages of the *Treatise of Human Nature,* Hume adopts Locke's strategy and stakes out his own version of the "white paper" principle. In the following selection, remember that Hume uses the word "perception" to mean any content of the mind. He then divides perceptions into those which come directly from our senses and those which we form from our impressions by copying, rearranging, and otherwise altering them.

All the perceptions of the human mind resolve themselves into two distinct kinds, which I shall call IMPRESSIONS and IDEAS. The difference betwixt these consists in the degrees of force and liveliness with which they strike upon the mind, and make their way into our thought or consciousness. Those perceptions, which enter with most force and violence, we may name *impressions;* and under this name I comprehend all our sensations, passions and emotions, as they make their first appearance in the soul. By *ideas* I mean the faint images of these in thinking and reasoning; such as, for instance, are all the perceptions excited by the present discourse, excepting only, those which arise from the sight and touch, and excepting the immediate pleasure or uneasiness it may occasion. I believe it will not be very necessary to employ many words in explaining this distinction. Every one of himself will readily perceive the difference betwixt feeling and thinking. The common degrees of these are easily distinguished; tho' it is not impossible but in particular instances they may very nearly approach to each other. Thus in sleep, in a fever, in madness, or in any very violent emotions of soul, our ideas may approach to our impressions: As on the other hand it sometimes happens, that our impressions are so faint and low, that we cannot distinguish them from our ideas. But notwithstanding this near resemblance in a few instances, they are in general so very different, that no-one can make a scruple to rank them under distinct heads, and assign to each a peculiar name to mark the difference.

There is another division of our perceptions, which it will be convenient to observe, and which extends itself both to our impressions and ideas. This division is into SIMPLE and COMPLEX. Simple perceptions or impressions and ideas are such as admit of no distinction nor separation. The complex are the contrary to these, and may be distinguished into parts. Tho' a particular colour, taste, and smell are qualities all united together in this apple, 'tis easy to perceive they are not the same, but are at least distinguishable from each other.

Having by these divisions given an order and arrangement to our objects, we may now apply ourselves to consider with the more accuracy their qualities and relations. The first circumstance, that strikes my eye, is the great resemblance betwixt our impressions and ideas in every other particular, except their degree of force and vivacity. The one seem to be in a manner the reflexion of the other; so that all the perceptions of the mind are double, and appear both as impressions and ideas. When I shut my eyes and think of my chamber, the ideas I form are exact representations of the impressions I felt; nor is there any circumstance of the one, which is not to be found in the other. In running over my other perceptions, I find still the same resemblance and representation. Ideas and impressions appear always to correspond to each other. This circumstance seems to me remarkable, and engages my attention for a moment.

Upon a more accurate survey I find I have been carried away too far by the first appearance, and that I must make use of the distinction of perceptions into *simple and complex,* to limit this general decision, *that all our ideas and impressions are resembling.* I observe, that many of our complex ideas never had impressions, that corresponded to them, and that many of our complex impressions never are exactly copied in ideas. I can imagine to myself such a city as the *New Jerusalem,* whose pavement is gold and walls are rubies, tho' I never saw any such. I have seen *Paris;* but shall I affirm I can form such an idea of that city, as will perfectly represent all its streets and houses in their real and just proportions?

I perceive, therefore, that tho' there is in general a great resemblance betwixt our *complex* impressions and ideas, yet the rule is not universally true, that they are exact copies of each other. We may next consider how the case stands with our *simple* perceptions. After the most accurate examination, of which I am capable, I venture to affirm, that the rule here holds without any exception, and that every simple idea has a simple impression, which resembles it; and every simple impression a correspondent idea. That idea of red, which we form in the dark, and that impression, which strikes our eyes in sun-shine, differ only in degree, not in nature. That the case is the same with all our simple impressions and ideas, 'tis impossible to prove by a particular enumeration of them. Every one may satisfy himself in this point by running over as many as he pleases. But if any one should deny this universal resemblance, I know no way of convincing him, but by desiring him to shew a simple impression that has not a correspondent idea, or a simple idea, that has not a correspondent impression. If he does not answer this challenge, as 'tis certain he cannot, we may from his silence and our own observation establish our conclusion.

Thus we find, that all simple ideas and impressions resemble each other; and as the complex are formed from them, we may affirm in general, that these two species of perception are exactly correspondent. Having discover'd this relation, which requires no farther examination, I am curious to find some other of their qualities. Let us consider how they stand with regard to their existence, and which of the impressions and ideas are causes, and which effects.

The *full* examination of this question is the subject of the present treatise; and therefore we shall here content ourselves with establishing one general proposition. *That all our simple ideas in their first appearance are deriv'd from simple impressions, which are correspondent to them, and which they exactly represent.*

DAVID HUME, *A Treatise of Human Nature*

Hume's style is not nearly as technical or forbidding as that of Aristotle, Descartes, Leibniz, or Kant, but you mustn't be misled into supposing that his arguments are therefore less powerful. The few simple principles which he lays down in the opening pages of the *Treatise* turn out to be more than enough to destroy some of the most impressive systems built up by his philosophical predecessors. There are three key points to notice in the passage you have just read. The first, of course, is Hume's adoption of the "white paper" theory. The second is what is sometimes called the *copy theory* of ideas. According to Hume, all our ideas are either straight copies of sense impressions or combinations and rearrangements of copies of sense impressions. When we are confronted with some metaphysical assertion, therefore, we need not ask immediately whether it is true or false. Instead, we may simply examine the words in which it is expressed and ask whether they correspond to ideas in our minds. If we do have such ideas, then either they will be copies of sense impressions or they will be constructed out of copies of sense impressions by combinations and rearrangements. We have already seen what a blow this doctrine can be to the claim that we have an idea of God. The third important point is that Hume has an "atomic" theory of the contents of the mind. That is to say, he conceives of the mind as containing little indivisible "atomic" bits of sensation, plus indivisible copies of those bits of sensation, plus what we might call "molecular" combinations of atomic sensations. But unlike chemical molecules, the combinations of atomic sensations don't have any properties that the atomic components lack.

Since all the contents of the mind can be divided into atomic units, it follows that we can always distinguish one unit from another. In addition, Hume says, the mind has the power to "separate" two units of sensation from

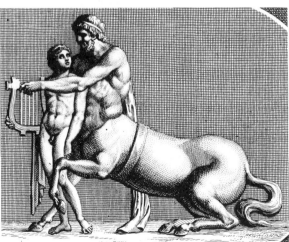

The mind combines the head and torso of a man with the body of a horse, to form an image of something it has never seen.

one another by imagining one away while keeping the other in mind. For example, when I look at a horse, I can distinguish my visual perception of its head from my visual perception of its body. Therefore, I can at least *imagine* the head without the body, or the body without the head. That power of "separating" impressions in imagination, and then recombining the parts in new ways, is of course what we all do when we imagine giants, or unicorns, or little green men, or anything else we have not actually seen. Hume summarizes this third point, a bit later on in the *Treatise,* in two principles:

1. Whatever objects are different are distinguishable.
2. Whatever objects are distinguishable are separable by thought and imagination.

By means of these two principles, which follow directly from his copy theory of ideas and his atomic theory of the contents of the mind, Hume constructs an argument which at one blow wipes out all metaphysics, all natural science, and just about all our common-sense beliefs about the world. Here is the entire argument, as it appears in the *Treatise.*

'Tis a general maxim in philosophy, that *whatever begins to exist, must have a cause of existence.* This is commonly taken for granted in all reasonings, without any proof given or demanded. 'Tis suppos'd to be founded on intuition, and to be one of those maxims, which tho' they may be deny'd with the lips, 'tis impossible for men in their hearts really to doubt of. But if we examine this maxim by the idea of knowledge above-explain'd, we shall discover in it no mark of any such intuitive certainty; but on the contrary shall find, that 'tis of a nature quite foreign to that species of conviction.

All certainty arises from the comparison of ideas, and from the discovery of such relations as are unalterable, so long as the ideas continue the same. These relations are *resemblance, proportions in quantity and number, degrees of any quality, and contrariety;* none of which are imply'd in this proposition, *Whatever has a beginning has also a cause of existence.* That proposition therefore is not intuitively certain. At least any one, who wou'd assert it to be intuitively certain, must deny these to be the only infallible relations, and must find some other relation of that kind to be imply'd in it; which it will then be time enough to examine.

But here is an argument, which proves at once, that the foregoing proposition is neither intuitively nor demonstrably certain. We can never demonstrate the necessity of a cause to every new existence, or new modification of existence, without shewing at the same time the impossibility there is, that any thing can ever begin to exist without some productive principle; and where the latter proposition cannot be prov'd, we must despair of ever being able to prove the former. Now that the latter proposition is utterly incapable of a demonstrative proof, we may satisfy ourselves by considering, that as all distinct ideas are separable from each other, and as the ideas of cause and effect are evidently distinct, 'twill be easy for us to conceive any object to be non-existent this moment, and existent the next, without conjoining to it the distinct idea of a cause or productive principle. The separation, therefore, of the idea of a cause from that of a beginning of existence, is plainly possible for the imagination; and consequently the actual separation of these objects is so far possible, that it implies no contradiction nor absurdity; and is therefore incapable of being refuted by any reasoning from mere ideas; without which 'tis impossible to demonstrate the necessity of a cause.

Accordingly we shall find upon examination, that every demonstration, which has been produc'd for the necessity of cause, is fallacious and sophistical. All the points of time and place, say some philosophers, in which we can suppose any object to begin to exist, are in themselves equal; and unless there be some cause, which is peculiar to one time and to one place, and which by that means determines and fixes the existence, it must remain in eternal suspense; and the object can never begin to be, for want of something to fix its beginning. But I ask; Is there any more difficulty in supposing the time and place to be fix'd without a cause, than to suppose the existence to be determin'd in that manner? The first question that occurs on this subject is always, *whether* the object shall exist or not: The next, *when* and *where* it shall begin to exist. If the removal of a cause be intuitively absurd in the one case, it must be so in the other: And if that absurdity be not clear without a proof in the one case, it will equally require one in the other. The absurdity, then, of the one supposition can never be a proof of that of the other; since they are both upon the same footing, and must stand or fall by the same reasoning.

The second argument, which I find us'd on this head, labours under an equal difficulty. Every thing, 'tis said, must have a cause; for if any thing wanted a cause, *it* wou'd produce *itself;* that is, exist before it existed; which is impossible. But this reasoning is plainly unconclusive; because it supposes, that in our denial of a cause we still grant what we expressly deny, *viz.* that there must be a cause; which therefore is taken to be the object itself; and *that,* no doubt, is an evident contradiction. But to say that any thing is produc'd, or to express myself more properly, comes into existence, without a cause, is not to affirm, that 'tis itself its own cause; but on the contrary in excluding all external causes, excludes *a fortiori* the thing itself which is created. An object, that exists absolutely without any cause, certainly is not its own cause; and when you assert, that the one follows from the other, you suppose the very point in question, and take it for granted, that 'tis utterly impossible any thing can ever begin to exist without a cause, but that upon the exclusion of one productive principle, we must still have recourse to another.

'Tis exactly the same case with the third argument, which has been employ'd to demonstrate the necessity of a cause. Whatever is produc'd without any cause, is produc'd by *nothing;* or in other words, has nothing for its cause. But nothing can never be a cause, no more than it can be something, or equal to two right angles. By the same intuition, that we perceive nothing not to be equal to two right angles, or not to be something, we perceive, that it can never be a cause; and consequently must perceive, that every object has a real cause of its existence.

I believe it will not be necessary to employ many words in shewing the weakness of this argument, after what I have said of the foregoing. They are all of them founded on the same fallacy, and are deriv'd from the same turn of thought. 'Tis sufficient only to observe, that when we exclude all causes we really do exclude them, and neither suppose nothing nor the object itself to be the causes of the existence; and consequently can draw no argument from the absurdity of these suppositions to prove the absurdity of that exclusion. If every thing must have a cause, it follows, that upon the exclusion of other causes we must accept of the object itself or of nothing as causes. But 'tis the very point in question, whether every thing must have a cause or not; and therefore, according to all just reasoning, it ought never to be taken for granted.

They are still more frivolous, who say, that every effect must have a cause, because 'tis imply'd in the very idea of effect. Every effect necessarily pre-supposes a cause; effect being a relative term, of which cause is the correlative. But this does not prove, that every being must be preceded by a cause; no more than it follows, because every husband must have a wife, that therefore every man must be marry'd. The true state of the question is, whether every object, which begins to exist, must owe its existence to a cause; and this I assert neither to be intuitively nor demonstratively certain, and hope to have prov'd it sufficiently by the foregoing arguments.

DAVID HUME, *A Treatise of Human Nature*

It doesn't take much imagination to see how deeply Hume's argument cuts. We can hardly get out of bed in the morning without implicitly relying on a host of causal beliefs. I believe that when I swing my legs over the side of the bed, they will naturally fall down toward the floor. (As astronauts have discovered, that is a belief which turns out to be false once we get away from the gravitational pull of the earth.) I believe that when I take a drink of water, it will cause my thirst to be abated. I believe that when I push the light switch, it will cause the lights to go on. The simplest propositions of physics, chemistry, and biology either are, or else depend upon, causal judgments. Needless to say, the proofs for the existence of God are invalid if we cannot infer causes from effects or effects from causes.

Hume himself did not believe that it was psychologically possible for human beings to suspend their belief in causal judgments for very long. Although he was absolutely convinced that no adequate justification could ever be found for our beliefs, he also thought that we were naturally so constituted that we believed anyway. In a much-quoted passage from the end of the First Book of the *Treatise,* Hume tells us how he disperses the clouds of gloom and doubt that settle over him when he follows out the logical conclusions of his powerful arguments.

Most fortunately it happens, that since reason is incapable of dispelling these clouds, nature herself suffices to that purpose, and cures me of this philosophical melancholy and delirium, either by relaxing this bent of mind, or by some avocation, and lively impression of my senses, which obliterate all these chimeras. I dine, I play a game of back-gammon, I converse, and am merry with my friends; and when after three or four hours' amusement, I wou'd return to these speculations, they appear so cold, and strain'd, and ridiculous, that I cannot find in my heart to enter into them any farther.

V

But Immanuel Kant was not content to flee from the skepticism into which Hume had plunged philosophy by his wholesale destruction of causal beliefs. If Hume's arguments were accepted, then I could not even be sure that anything at all existed outside my own mind. Descartes' fanciful notion that his whole life was a mere dream might be true, as far as philosophers could prove. It was, Kant said, a "scandal to philosophy and to human reason in general that the existence of things outside us . . . must be accepted merely on *faith,* and that if anyone thinks good to doubt their existence, we are unable to counter his doubts by any satisfactory proof." So Kant decided to return to Descartes' starting point, the Cogito, or "I think." He wanted to see whether he could derive directly from that fundamental premise an argument that would avoid the skepticism and solipsism that seemed to be implied by the powerful attacks of the British empiricists.

As we have seen, Descartes' philosophical investigations raised two basic problems: the problem of certainty and the problem of the sources of knowledge. But Kant realized that the Cogito argument raised an even more fundamental issue which both the rationalists and the empiricists had tended to ignore. The conclusion of Descartes' argument, you will recall, was the following:

> This proposition: I am, I exist, is necessarily true each time that I pronounce it, or that I mentally conceive it.

On the basis of this conclusion, Descartes went on to argue that he was essentially a "thing that thinks." Descartes' successors concentrated on the criteria to be used in judging the truth of what the mind thinks, and they concentrated on the sources of the ideas with which the mind thinks, but they paid much less attention to the central fact that the mind, in thinking, is *conscious.* Trees are not conscious, rocks are not conscious, even calculating machines (which Descartes and the others did not know about) are not conscious, but the mind is. It occurred to Kant that perhaps a proof of our scientific beliefs in the existence of physical objects and in causal connections between them could be based on the mere fact of consciousness. Such a proof would certainly be very hard to find, for the mere fact of consciousness isn't much to go on in proving anything as large-scale as the truth of science. But if he could find such a proof, Kant would have an answer to anyone who wanted to challenge the claims of reason, even someone prepared to go as far in the direction of skepticism as David Hume.

Descartes had simply accepted consciousness as an indisputable, directly observable, inexplicable fact. I know that I am conscious because I can think about my own thoughts and become aware of myself thinking about them. This self-awareness or self-consciousness is clearly central to the mind's operation; what is more, it is directly self-confirming. Even an evil demon could not trick me into thinking I was conscious when I wasn't, because if I thought anything at all, it would have to be the case that I was conscious. So instead of the premise "I think" as the starting point of all philosophy, Kant instead adopted the slightly different premise "I am conscious." But introspection reveals, and logical analysis confirms, that my consciousness has a certain basic structure or characteristic: it is unified into a *single* consciousness. All the thoughts, impressions, beliefs, expectations, hopes, and doubts that I have are *my* thoughts, etc. They occur in *my* consciousness, and that consciousness is a single consciousness, or—to put it somewhat differently—the consciousness of a single subject, a single center of thought. Kant described this fundamental fact as the *unity of consciousness.* In order to show the connection between what he was doing and what Descartes had done, Kant invoked Descartes' language when he stated his own basic premise. In the central section of the *Critique of Pure Reason,* as he started the argument which he hoped would refute the skeptics and reinstate science as objectively justified, Kant stated his premise in the following way:

It must be possible for the "I think" to accompany all my representations.

This was his way of saying that all the contents of my consciousness are bound up in a unity of consciousness.

Kant argued that the *unity* of my thoughts and perceptions could not be a given fact of my experience. The individual thoughts and impressions might just be brute facts of consciousness, but their unity could only be explained by some unifying act of the mind itself. Kant claimed that when my mind unifies its various thoughts and perceptions, when it holds them all together in a single consciousness and thinks of them all as *my* thoughts, it follows a certain set of *rules.* These rules are rules for holding thoughts together in the mind, and he gave them the technical name "categories." The only way in which I can think all of my thoughts as unified in a single consciousness is by following the rules or categories for holding thoughts together. Kant claimed that the categories were innate in the human mind; we are all born with them, he said, and we cannot change them.

What are these rules, or categories? Well, it turns out—if Kant is right—that they are just exactly those crucial concepts which play so large a role in the metaphysics, mathematics, and physics that Hume and the skeptics were attacking. Among the categories are such central concepts as substance, cause and effect, unity, plurality, possibility, necessity, and reality.

It may not look as though Kant moved very far toward an answer to Hume, but stop and reflect for a moment on what he is saying. Descartes claimed I could be conscious of my own thoughts, and even conscious of their unity *as* my thoughts, without knowing whether they were really accurate or truthful thoughts about substances, causation, and a world independent of my mind. In other words, Descartes admitted that my subjective knowledge of my own thoughts was better established than any claims I might make about a world of objects. Locke, Hume, and other critics of the rationalists accepted Descartes' starting point—they agreed that I could know the contents of my own mind—but they threw doubt on all Descartes' attempts to move from that purely subjective knowledge to anything further.

Kant turned the whole argument around by denying Descartes' first premise. I cannot know the contents of my own mind unless I first unify them into a single consciousness, he said. And that means that I must first have applied the categories to them, for those categories are the rules for unifying contents of consciousness. Now the categories are precisely the concepts (substance, cause, etc.) which we use in making objective judgments about the world outside the mind. So Kant concluded that I could not even be subjectively conscious, à la Descartes, unless I had first put my thoughts and perceptions together in ways that would allow me to make objective judgments about them. Descartes' nightmare of life as an endless dream is an epistemological impossibility, Kant argued.

But Kant paid a price for his solution to the problem of skepticism. It might very well be that my objective concepts were guaranteed to apply to my experiences—it might, in short, be a sure thing that I would encounter substances related to one another causally—but such knowledge as I obtained through the use of the categories would not and could not be knowledge of the world as it really is in itself. Rather, my knowledge must be merely of a world of things as they appear to me.

We have already encountered the distinction between appearance and reality in the philosophy of Plato, you will recall. But Plato claimed that we could, by the use of our reason, gain knowledge of true reality. Kant, by contrast, insists that we can only obtain knowledge of appearance, even though such knowledge is real knowledge, and not—as the skeptics claimed—error or unfounded belief.

The dispute between the rationalists and the empiricists was changed by Kant's new theory of the unity of consciousness. Even though many subsequent philosophers rejected his distinction between appearance and reality, they continued to ponder the problem of the nature of consciousness, a problem that Descartes had discovered and that Kant had substantially deepened by his arguments.

What can I know with certainty? This question, as we have seen, is the starting point of modern philosophical investigations. With his dramatic posing of the problem of skepticism and certainty, René Descartes initiated two centuries of intense analysis of the nature, foundations, origins, and limits of human knowledge. In this chapter, we have traced the debate through the thought and writings of some of the great philosophers of the seventeenth and eighteenth centuries, from Descartes himself to Immanuel Kant.

But the debate did not end with Kant, central though his contributions to it were. The nature and status of science and mathematics, the role of sense perception and of reason in our knowing, the very possibility of any but the most trivial knowledge of mere verbal identities—these and other issues continue to be debated today.

Nevertheless, as you will by now have come to expect, the great issues of epistemology have taken on a somewhat different look in the present century. As in other branches of philosophy, the study of logic and of language has altered epistemology. The discussions have become more refined, more precise—and, on occasion, rather farther from our ordinary understanding than they were in their original seventeenth- or eighteenth-century formulations.

The pivotal issue for that school of epistemologists whom we have called the *empiricists* remains the role of sense-experience in our knowledge of the world. The empiricists begin with the conviction that direct sense experience—the testimony of our eyes, our ears, of all our sense organs—must be the foundation of all non-trivial claims to knowledge. If the mind is to go beyond the mere combining and recombining of its concepts in empty identities (such as "All triangles are triangles," or "All circles are round"), then it must do so by way of its contact with a world of independent objects. And sense-perception is the mind's only access to that world of objects.

There is a fundamental problem with this view, as we have already seen. It might appear that we have direct awareness of physical objects in the world around us—of tables and chairs, of books, cars, buildings, of other persons. But even a little reflection seems to show us that we cannot possibly be *directly* aware of such things. Consider the following quite simple and straightforward argument:

Step 1. When I am *directly* aware of something, when I *immediately* grasp or apprehend it, there is no way at all that I can be mistaken about what it is that I apprehend.

Step 2. Experience has long since made me aware that I *can* be wrong about what I think to be my apprehension of physical objects or other persons. I can think myself to be seeing a sunset when it is only a movie set; I can (at Disney World) believe that I am listening to a living person when I am actually hearing a recording issuing from an animated dummy; and so forth.

Step 3. Therefore, I cannot possibly be directly aware of physical objects and persons. If I do immediately apprehend something, it must be something other than independent objects in the world about me.

This is essentially Descartes' argument in slightly altered form, and it remains a powerful argument three centuries after Descartes first advanced it. The rationalist response, as we have seen, is to move away from knowledge-claims concerning individual objects (about which we could perfectly well be mistaken) and towards universal or general knowledge-claims (about *all* material things, or *all* triangles, or *all* human beings), about which, they believe, we cannot be mistaken. The empiricist response is to move in precisely the opposite direction, away from knowledge-claims concerning individual objects and towards limited or reduced claims about nothing more than the direct sense-experience of which we can be immediately, self-consciously aware.

The empiricist move is attractive, of course, because it is cautious and hence less open to objection. But, as Hume taught us so persuasively, it threatens to lead us directly into a debilitating and self-defeating skepticism. If the direct presentations of sense are all that we can know with certainty, then how can we ever move from them to a knowledge of nature, of mathematics, of society? In short, how can we get from the empiricist starting-point to any of the end-points we wish to reach?

In the twentieth century, one of the central figures in the empiricist attempts to answer this question is the great British philosopher Bertrand Russell. Russell began his long and distinguished philosophical career as a logician. After making major contributions to our understanding of the logical foundations of mathematics, he turned his attention to the epistemological problem of the foundations of our knowledge of nature. Russell's logical investigations had led him to puzzle over a rather peculiar problem which had been bothering philosophers for some time. Although the problem appears at first sight to be an oddity—almost a joke—Russell had the wit to see that it was really a gateway to a much larger problem, one which lay at the very roots of the empiricist attempt to ground knowledge in sense-perception. His solution to the puzzle advanced the empiricist program considerably, and in this selection, we shall take a look at his classic treatment of it.

The puzzle is this: let us suppose that I say that the King of the United States is Episcopalian. Is what I am saying true or false? Well, it obviously isn't true! But it hardly seems that it can be false either. Because if I say, "It is false that the King of the United States is Episcopalian," I appear to leave myself open to the obvious next question: Well, if he isn't Episcopalian, what *is* his religion? And that is not a question to which there is a sensible answer, *because there is no king of the United States.* In general, then, what sense am I to make of statements about things that do not exist? If they cannot be true, and cannot be false, how can they *mean* anything at all?

Not a particularly pressing problem, you may think. Puzzling, perhaps; interesting even. But not something about which philosophers ought to get agitated. But now suppose that we set aside silly examples about kings of the United States, and consider instead a perfectly ordinary, sensible knowledge-claim, such as that the sun is roughly ninety-three million miles from the earth. Descartes and Hume and the others have taught us that any beliefs about objects such as the sun are open to question; indeed, as Descartes argued quite powerfully in the opening Meditation, it is even open to question whether there *is* such a thing as the sun or not. But if it should happen to be that there is no sun, then *both* the statement that it is ninety-three million miles from the earth *and* the statement that it is *not* ninety-three million miles from the earth will be cast into the same sort of peculiar limbo as the statements that the King of the United States *is* and *is not* Episcopalian.

Generally speaking, if we can make sense only of those knowledge-claims which say something about objects which we can be certain to exist, then we will find ourselves in the utterly unacceptable position of not knowing whether most of what we want to say is even meaningful. We won't know, to put it bluntly, whether we are making sense or talking gibberish.

Clearly, something has gone very wrong here, and Russell figured out what the trouble was. By means of his distinction between knowledge by acquaintance and knowledge by description, and his analysis of what he calls definite descriptions, Russell is able to get us out of the paradoxical trap we have fallen into. He clears the way for an empiricist theory of knowledge which does not collapse when confronted with knowledge-claims about objects whose existence is a matter of possible dispute.

This essay is an example of the best sort of analytic philosophy. It takes up a genuine, major philosophical problem, brings to bear on it certain techniques of logical analysis, focusses closely on the key conceptual issue, and advances a solution which leaves us clearer about the original problem, and better able therefore to search for a solution to it.

BERTRAND RUSSELL: *Knowledge by Acquaintance and Knowledge by Description*

In the preceding chapter we saw that there are two sorts of knowledge: knowledge of things, and knowledge of truths. In this chapter we shall be concerned exclusively with knowledge of things, of which in turn we shall have to distinguish two kinds. Knowledge of things, when it is of the kind we call knowledge by *acquaintance,* is essentially simpler than any knowledge of truths, and logically independent of knowledge of truths, though it would be rash to assume that human beings ever, in fact, have acquaintance with things without at the same time knowing some truth about them. Knowledge of things by *description,* on the contrary, always involves . . . some knowledge of truths as its source and ground. But first of all we must make clear what we mean by 'acquaintance' and what we mean by 'description.'

We shall say that we have *acquaintance* with anything of which we are directly aware, without the intermediary of any process of inference or any knowledge of truths. Thus in the presence of my table I am acquainted with the sense-data that make up the appearance of my table—its colour, shape, hardness, smoothness, etc.; all these are things of which I am immediately conscious when I am seeing and touching my table. The particular shade of colour that I am seeing may have many things said about it—I may say that it is brown, that it is rather dark, and so on. But such statements, though they make me know truths *about* the colour, do not make me know the colour itself any better than I did before: so far as concerns knowledge of the colour itself, as opposed to knowledge of truths about it, I know the colour perfectly and completely when I see it, and no further knowledge of it itself is even theoretically possible. Thus the sense-data which make up the appearance of my table are things with which I have acquaintance, things immediately known to me just as they are.

My knowledge of the table as a physical object, on the contrary, is not direct knowledge. Such as it is, it is obtained through acquaintance with the sense-data that make up the appearance of the table. . . . My knowledge of the table is of the kind which we shall call 'knowledge by description.' The table is 'the physical object which causes such-and-such sense-data.' This *describes* the table by means of the sense-data. In order to know anything at all about the table, we must know truths connecting it with things with which we have acquaintance: we must know that 'such-and-such sense-data are caused by a physical object.' There is no state of mind in which we are directly aware of the table; all our knowledge of the table is really knowledge of *truths,* and the actual thing which is the table is not, strictly speaking, known to us at all. We know a description, and we know that there is just one object to which this description applies, though the object itself is not directly known to us. In such a case, we say that our knowledge of the object is knowledge by description.

All our knowledge, both knowledge of things and knowledge of truths, rests upon acquaintance as its foundation. It is therefore important to consider what kinds of things there are with which we have acquaintance.

Sense-data, as we have already seen, are among the things with which we are acquainted; in fact, they supply the most obvious and striking example of knowledge by acquaintance. But if they were the sole example, our knowledge would be very much more restricted than it is. We should only know what is now present to our senses: we could not know anything about the past—not even that there was a past—nor could we know any truths about our sense-data, for all knowledge of truths, as we shall show, demands acquaintance with things which are of an essentially different character from sense-data, the things which are sometimes called 'abstract ideas,' but which we shall call 'universals.' We have therefore to consider acquaintance with other things besides sense-data if we are to obtain any tolerably adequate analysis of our knowledge.

The first extension beyond sense-data to be considered is acquaintance by *memory.* It is obvious that we often remember what we have seen or heard or had otherwise present to our senses, and that in such cases we are still immediately aware of what we remember, in spite of the fact that it appears as past and not as present. This immediate knowledge by memory is the source of all our knowledge concerning the past: without it, there could be no knowledge of the past by inference, since we should never know that there was anything past to be inferred.

The next extension to be considered is acquaintance by *introspection.* We are not only aware of things, but we are often aware of being aware of them. When I see the sun, I am often aware of my seeing the sun; thus 'my seeing the sun' is an object with which I have acquaintance. When I desire food, I may be aware of my desire for food; thus 'my desiring food' is an object with which I am acquainted. Similarly we may be aware of our feeling pleasure or pain, and generally of the events which happen in our minds. This kind of acquaintance, which may be called self-consciousness, is the source of all our knowledge of mental things. It is obvious that it is only what goes on in our own minds that can be thus known immediately. What goes on in the minds of others is known to us through our perception of their bodies, that is, through the sense-data in us which are associated with their bodies. But for our acquaintance with the contents of our own minds, we should be unable to imagine the minds of others, and therefore we could never arrive at the knowledge that they have minds. It seems natural to suppose that self-consciousness is one of the things that distinguish men from animals: animals, we may suppose, though they have acquaintance with sense-data, never become aware of this acquaintance. I do not mean that they *doubt* whether they exist, but that they have never become conscious of the fact that they have sensations and feelings, nor therefore of the fact that they, the subjects of their sensations and feelings, exist.

We have spoken of acquaintance with the contents of our minds as *self-consciousness*, but it is not, of course, consciousness of our *self:* it is consciousness of particular thoughts and feelings. The question whether we are also acquainted with our bare selves, as opposed to particular thoughts and feelings, is a very difficult one, upon which it would be rash to speak positively. When we try to look into ourselves we always seem to come upon some particular thought or feeling, and not upon the 'I' which has the thought or feeling. Nevertheless there are some reasons for thinking that we are acquainted with the 'I,' though the acquaintance is hard to disentangle from other things. To make clear what sort of reason there is, let us consider for a moment what our acquaintance with particular thoughts really involves.

When I am acquainted with 'my seeing the sun,' it seems plain that I am acquainted with two different things in relation to each other. On the one hand there is the sense-datum which represents the sun to me, on the other hand there is that which sees this sense-datum. All acquaintance, such as my acquaintance with the sense-datum which represents the sun, seems obviously a relation between the person acquainted and the object with which the person is acquainted. When a case of acquaintance is one with which I can be acquainted (as I am acquainted with my acquaintance with the sense-datum representing the sun), it is plain that the person acquainted is myself. Thus, when I am acquainted with my seeing the sun, the whole fact with which I am acquainted is 'Self-acquainted-with-sense-datum.'

Further, we know the truth 'I am acquainted with this sense-datum.' It is hard to see how we could know this truth, or even understand what is meant by it, unless we were acquainted with something which we call 'I.' It does not seem necessary to suppose that we are acquainted with a more or less permanent person, the same to-day as yesterday, but it does seem as though we must be acquainted with that thing, whatever its nature, which sees the sun and has acquaintance with sense-data. Thus, in some sense it would seem we must be acquainted with our Selves as opposed to our particular experiences. But the question is difficult, and complicated arguments can be adduced on either side. Hence, although acquaintance with ourselves seems *probably* to occur, it is not wise to assert that it undoubtedly does occur.

We may therefore sum up as follows what has been said concerning acquaintance with things that exist. We have acquaintance in sensation with the data of the outer senses, and in introspection with the data of what may be called the inner sense—thoughts, feelings, desires, etc.; we have acquaintance in memory with things which have been data either of the outer senses or of the inner sense. Further, it is probable, though not certain, that we have acquaintance with Self, as that which is aware of things or has desires towards things.

In addition to our acquaintance with particular existing things, we also have acquaintance with what we shall call *universals,* that is to say, general ideas, such as *whiteness, diversity, brotherhood,* and so on. Every complete sentence must contain at least one word which stands for a universal, since all verbs have a meaning which is universal. . . . Awareness of universals is called *conceiving,* and a universal of which we are aware is called a *concept.*

It will be seen that among the objects with which we are acquainted are not included physical objects (as opposed to sense-data), nor other people's minds. These things are known to us by what I call 'knowledge by description,' which we must now consider.

By a 'description' I mean any phrase of the form 'a so-and-so' or 'the so-and-so.' A phrase of the form 'a so-and-so' I shall call an 'ambiguous' description; a phrase of the form 'the so-and-so' (in the singular) I shall call a 'definite' description. Thus 'a man' is an ambiguous description, and 'the man with the iron mask' is a definite description. There are various problems connected with ambiguous descriptions, but I pass them by, since they do not directly concern the matter we are discussing, which is the nature of our knowledge concerning objects in cases where we know that there is an object answering to a definite description, though we are not *acquainted* with any such object. This is a matter which is concerned exclusively with *definite* descriptions. I shall therefore, in the sequel, speak simply of 'descriptions' when I mean 'definite descriptions.' Thus a description will mean any phrase of the form 'the so-and-so' in the singular.

We shall say that an object is 'known by description' when we know that it is 'the so-and-so,' i.e. when we know that there is one object, and no more, having a certain property; and it will generally be implied that we do not have knowledge of the same object by acquaintance. We know that the man with the iron mask existed, and many propositions are known about him; but we do not know who he was. We know that the candidate who gets the most votes will be elected, and in this case we are very likely also acquainted (in the only sense in which one can be acquainted with some one else) with the man who is, in fact, the candidate who will get most votes; but we do not know which of the candidates he is, i.e. we do not know any proposition of the form 'A is the candidate who will get most votes' where A is one of the candidates by name. We shall say that we have 'merely descriptive knowledge' of the so-and-so when, although we know that the so-and-so exists, and although we may possibly be acquainted with the object which is, in fact, the so-and-so, yet we do not know any proposition '*a* is the so-and-so,' where *a* is something with which we are acquainted.

When we say 'the so-and-so exists,' we mean that there is just one object which is the so-and-so. The proposition '*a* is the so-and-so' means that *a* has the property so-and-so, and nothing else has. 'Mr. A. is the Unionist candidate for this constituency' means 'Mr. A. is a Unionist candidate for this constituency, and no one else is.' 'The Unionist candidate for this constituency exists' means 'some one is a Unionist candidate for this constituency, and no one else is.' Thus, when we are acquainted with an object which is the so-and-so, we know that the so-and-so exists; but we may know that the so-and-so exists when we are not acquainted with any object which we know to be the so-and-so, and even when we are not acquainted with any object which, in fact, is the so-and-so.

Common words, even proper names, are usually really descriptions. That is to say, the thought in the mind of a person using a proper name correctly can generally only be expressed explicitly if we replace the proper name by a description. Moreover, the description required to express the thought will vary for different people, or for the same person at different times. The only thing constant (so long as the name is rightly used) is the object to which the name applies. But so long as this remains constant, the particular description involved usually makes no difference to the truth or falsehood of the proposition in which the name appears.

Let us take some illustrations. Suppose some statement made about Bismarck. Assuming that there is such a thing as direct acquaintance with oneself, Bismarck himself might have used his name directly to designate the particular person with whom he was acquainted. In this case, if he made a judgement about himself, he himself might be a constituent of the judgement. Here the proper name has the direct use which it always wishes to have, as simply standing for a certain object, and not for a description of the object. But if a person who knew Bismarck made a judgement about him, the case is different. What this person was acquainted with were certain sense-data which he connected (rightly, we will suppose) with Bismarck's body. His body, as a physical object, and still more his mind, were only known as the body and the mind connected with these sense-data. That is, they were known by description. It is, of course, very much a matter of chance which characteristics of a man's appearance will come into a friend's mind when he thinks of him; thus the description actually in the friend's mind is accidental. The essential point is that he knows that the various descriptions all apply to the same entity, in spite of not being acquainted with the entity in question.

When we, who did not know Bismarck, make a judgement about him, the description in our minds will probably be some more or less vague mass of historical knowledge—far more, in most cases, than is required to identify him. But, for the sake of illustration, let us assume that we think of him as 'the first Chancellor of the German Empire.' Here all the words are abstract except 'German.' The word 'German' will, again, have different meanings for different people. To some it will recall travels in Germany, to some the look of Germany on the map, and so on. But if we are to obtain a description which we know to be applicable, we shall be compelled, at some point, to bring in a reference to a particular with which we are acquainted. Such reference is involved in any mention of past, present, and future (as opposed to definite dates), or of here and there, or of what others have told us. Thus it would seem that, in some way or other, a description known to be applicable to a particular must involve some reference to a particular with which we are acquainted, if our knowledge about the thing described is not to be merely what follows *logically* from the description. For example, 'the most long-lived of men' is a description involving only universals, which must apply to some man, but we can make no judgements concerning this man which involve knowledge about him beyond what the description gives. If, however, we say, 'The first Chancellor of the German Empire was an astute diplomatist,' we can only be assured of the truth of our judgement in virtue of something with which we are acquainted—usually a testimony heard or read. Apart from the information we convey to others, apart from the fact about the actual Bismarck, which gives importance to our judgement, the thought we really have contains the one or more particulars involved, and otherwise consists wholly of concepts.

All names of places—London, England, Europe, the Earth, the Solar System—similarly involve, when used, descriptions which start from some one or more particulars with which we are acquainted. I suspect that even the Universe, as considered by metaphysics, involves such a connexion with particulars. In logic, on the contrary, where we are concerned not merely with what does exist, but with whatever might or could exist or be, no reference to actual particulars is involved.

It would seem that, when we make a statement about something only known by description, we often *intend* to make our statement, not in the form involving the description, but about the actual thing described. That is to say, when we say anything about Bismarck, we should like, if we could, to make the judgement which Bismarck alone can make, namely, the judgement of which he himself is a constituent. In this we are necessarily defeated, since the actual Bismarck is unknown to us. But we know that there is an object B, called Bismarck, and that B was an astute diplomatist. We can thus *describe* the proposition we should like to affirm, namely, 'B was an astute diplomatist,' where B is the object which was Bismarck. If we are describing Bismarck as 'the first Chancellor of the German Empire,' the proposition we should like to affirm may be described as 'the proposition asserting, concerning the actual object which was the first Chancellor of the German Empire, that this object was an astute diplomatist.' What enables us to communicate in spite of the varying descriptions we employ is that we know there is a true proposition concerning the actual Bismarck, and that however we may vary the description (so long as the description is correct) the proposition described is still the same. This proposition, which is described and is known to be true, is what interests us; but we are not acquainted with the proposition itself, and do not know *it*, though we know it is true.

It will be seen that there are various stages in the removal from acquaintance with particulars: there is Bismarck to people who knew him; Bismarck to those who only know of him through history; the man with the iron mask; the longest-lived of men. These are progressively further removed from acquaintance with particulars; the first comes as near to acquaintance as is possible in regard to another person; in the second, we shall still be said to know 'who Bismarck was'; in the third, we do not know who was the man with the iron mask, though we can know many propositions about him which are not logically deducible from the fact that he wore an iron mask; in the fourth, finally, we know nothing beyond what is logically deducible from the definition of the man. There is a similar hierarchy in the region of universals. Many universals, like many particulars, are only known to us by description. But here, as in the case of particulars, knowledge concerning what is known by description is ultimately reducible to knowledge concerning what is known by acquaintance.

The fundamental principle in the analysis of propositions containing descriptions is this: *Every proposition which we can understand must be composed wholly of constituents with which we are acquainted.*

We shall not at this stage attempt to answer all the objections which may be urged against this fundamental principle. For the present, we shall merely point out that, in some way or other, it must be possible to meet these objections, for it is scarcely conceivable that we can make a judgement or entertain a supposition without knowing what it is that we are judging or supposing about. We must attach *some* meaning to the words we use, if we are to speak significantly and not utter mere noise; and the meaning we attach to our words must be something with which we are acquainted. Thus when, for example, we make a statement about Julius Caesar, it is plain that Julius Caesar himself is not before our minds, since we are not acquainted with him. We have in mind some *description* of Julius Caesar: 'the man who was assassinated on the Ides of March,' 'the founder of the Roman Empire,' or, perhaps, merely 'the man whose name was *Julius Caesar*.' (In this last description, *Julius Caesar* is a noise or shape with which we are acquainted.) Thus our statement does not mean quite what it seems to mean, but means something involving, instead of Julius Caesar, some description of him which is composed wholly of particulars and universals with which we are acquainted.

The chief importance of knowledge by description is that it enables us to pass beyond the limits of our private experience. In spite of the fact that we can only know truths which are wholly composed of terms which we have experienced in acquaintance, we can yet have knowledge by description of things which we have never experienced. In view of the very narrow range of our immediate experience, this result is vital, and until it is understood, much of our knowledge must remain mysterious and therefore doubtful.

TOPICS FOR FURTHER STUDY

1. According to Russell, we obtain our knowledge of physical objects by making inferences from our knowledge of what he calls sense-data. We are *acquainted* with sense-data, he says, but we have only knowledge by description of physical objects. Russell does not tell us how we are to perform the inferences that take us from sense-experience to a knowledge of objects. Nor does he tell us what logical warrant, or justification, we have for those inferences. This problem, of deriving judgments about physical objects from direct acquaintance with sense-data, has taxed the intellectual gifts of some of the brightest philosophers of the twentieth century, and the results of their efforts have been mixed, to say the least. Do I come to know about physical objects in the way Russell says?

2. Our knowledge of the historical past rests upon the direct evidence of present remains, such as documents, artifacts, buried ruins, and so forth. So it would certainly seem that we have knowledge by description of the past, based upon knowledge by acquaintance of things in the present. But in this case, what we are acquainted with in the present are also physical objects; they are not sense-data. Can an analysis of the logical structure of our knowledge of the historical past be extended to explain our knowledge of all independent reality in general?

3. There is something extremely odd about saying that I am not directly acquainted with the physical objects immediately in front of me, such as my typewriter, my desk, or my own two hands. Russell's colleague at Cambridge University, G. E. Moore, insisted that we could be as certain of the existence of such commonplace objects as we could be of the truths of logic or mathematics. How reasonable is the rationalist's demand for proofs of our fundamental knowledge claims, or the empiricist's skeptical doubts about the possibility of such proofs?

4. Russell says that our knowledge of other persons (his example is the Prussian statesman, Bismarck) is always knowledge by description. Are there any situations in which it makes sense to say that I am immediately *acquainted* with another person, in Russell's sense of the term? If you think the answer is yes, how would you answer Russell's objection that you only have sense-experience of that person's body, and never direct acquaintance of the person as an independent being?

SUGGESTIONS FOR FURTHER READING

J. L. AUSTIN, *Sense and Sensibilia*

A. J. AYER, *The Foundations of Empirical Knowledge*

GEORGE BERKELEY, *Three Dialogues Between Hylas and Philonus*

V. C. CHAPPELL (ed.), *Hume: A Collection of Critical Essays*

R. M. CHISHOLM, *Perceiving—A Philosophical Study*

H. G. FRANKFURT, *Demons, Dreamers, and Madmen*

C. A. FRITZ, *Bertrand Russell's Construction of the External World*

A. KENNY, *Descartes: A Study of His Philosophy*

C. I. LEWIS, *An Analysis of Knowledge and Valuation*

G. E. MOORE, "The Refutation of Idealism," in A. C. Ewing (ed.), *The Idealist Tradition From Berkeley to Blanshard*

H. H. PRICE, *Perception*

BERTRAND RUSSELL, *Human Knowledge*

PETER STRAWSON, *The Bounds of Sense*

R. J. SWARTZ (ed.), *Perceiving, Sensing, and Knowing*

ROBERT PAUL WOLFF, *Kant's Theory of Mental Activity*

GOTTFRIED LEIBNIZ (1646–1716) was the most
original and brilliant rationalist metaphysician of the
modern era. Born in Germany, he was very early
recognized as an enormously gifted thinker. His
efforts to work out a coherent metaphysical
foundation for the new science of the seventeenth
century led him to the discovery of a form of the
differential calculus. This discovery occurred at
roughly the same time that Isaac Newton in
England was developing a different form of the
same branch of mathematics. For years thereafter,
a dispute raged between the Leibnizeans and the
Newtonians over which thinker deserved to take

8 METAPHYSICS AND PHILOSOPHY OF SCIENCE

credit for having made the discovery first.

Leibniz chose to affiliate himself with the courts of the elector of Mainz and the Duke of Brunswick, rather than to hold the position of professor which he was offered. His mathematical, scientific, and philosophical theories were set forth in essays, treatises, and letters which to this day have not been adequately edited and collected. Leibniz's theories of space, time, substance, force, motion, and causation were a subtle interweaving of traditional philosophical concepts with radically new scientific and mathematical ideas.

Although he is remembered now for his work in metaphysics, mathematics, and science, Leibniz was also deeply concerned with problems of religious doctrine. In his book on *Theodicy,* he sought to make the absolute goodness of God compatible with the apparent existence in the world of various evils. Leibniz's conclusion, that the actually existing world is, contrary to appearances, the best of all possible worlds, provoked a brilliant satirical attack from the French philosopher Voltaire. In *Candide,* Voltaire painted a hilarious portrait of a Leibnizean pundit whose repeated catchphrase of mindless optimism was, "All is for the best in this best of all possible worlds."

I

Some years ago, there appeared a listing in the Yellow Pages of the Manhattan telephone book, between "Metals" and "Meteorologists," for "Metaphysician." A gentleman who shall remain nameless had hung out his shingle in Greenwich Village, and was apparently prepared to offer his metaphysical services for a fee to all comers. The listing has disappeared from subsequent editions of the Yellow Pages, but I continue to wonder just what services he offered, and what his clients imagined they were going to get when they sought him out.

What *is* metaphysics? Or should we ask, What *are* metaphysics? The term itself is a sheer historical accident. As you already know, Aristotle wrote a set of essays on fundamental problems concerning the most basic classifications or categories of being, and the most general concepts by means of which we can think about what is. He called his discussions *First Philosophy,* not because they were about things most easily understood, but because they were about fundamentals. Several centuries after Aristotle's death, when other philosophers commented on Aristotle's arguments, they found that the essays on *first philosophy* came after the book on physics in the edition or manuscript with which they worked. Because the essays had no name, they were referred to in Greek as *"ta meta ta physika biblia,"* which is to say "the books which come after the physics." Eventually this was shortened to *The Metaphysics,* and the topics dealt with under this title were dubbed "metaphysics." Unfortunately, over the centuries the prefix "meta" has acquired the bogus sense of "super" or "going beyond" or "transcending sense perception." So metaphysics is thought somehow to deal with what transcends physics, with what is supernatural, occult, mysterious. Perhaps that is what our Greenwich Village metaphysician's clients expected—a touch of the beyond.

In philosophy, metaphysics is not really a single field or discipline, but rather a catch-all for a number of problems whose scope and significance are so broad that they seem to have implications for virtually every other field of philosophy. Let me mention just a few of the questions that are dealt with by philosophers under the heading of "metaphysics." You will very quickly see why this branch of philosophy is considered truly fundamental.

First, there is the basic question, What sorts of things are there? What are the categories into which whatever is can be sorted? Physical bodies in space? Minds? Properties of things, such as size, shape, color, smell, hardness, and taste? Events, such as the moving of a body from one place to another, or the growth of a tree from a seed, or the change in color of a leaf as it dies and browns? Ideas in a mind, thoughts, feelings, sense perceptions? How many different categories are there? Can some of these sorts of things be reduced to instances of other sorts? Is there one correct set of general categories for classifying things? What shall we say of peculiar things, like the number three, which doesn't seem to *exist,* in any ordinary sense, but on the other hand can hardly be said not to exist? (It would certainly sound odd to say there is no such thing as the number three!)

Then there are more particular questions: What is space, and what is time? Are they dimensions? containers in which things exist and happen? relations among things? forms of our perception of things? Can there be space in which nothing exists—a void, as it is called by philosophers and scientists? Can there be a stretch of time in which absolutely nothing happens? Could there be totally empty time, in which nothing happens and nothing even exists? What sense does it make to speak of "empty" time and "empty" space, as though they were huge boxes waiting to be filled up?

Is there such a thing as a soul? Is it made out of physical matter, and if not, what then is it? Is the soul the same as the mind? Can a soul exist without relation to a body? How? Do souls continue to exist after the body dies? Did they exist before they were associated with, or planted in, bodies? What *is* the relationship of the soul to the body? Is the mind the same as the brain? Is the body just an idea in the mind?

Does the past exist? If not, then does nothing exist save whatever there is right now at this very moment? If the past does exist, then where is it? Is there some other universe of past things? What about future things as well? Is there a whole assortment of possible worlds alongside this actual one that we live in? Does it make any sense at all to say that something has *possible* existence?

Are all my actions absolutely causally determined by what has gone before, or am I free in some sense to choose among a variety of alternative actions available to me? If I am determined to act as I do, then can I also consider myself responsible for what I do? If I am free, what is the nature of my freedom? What sort of thing am I, that I should have this strange capacity to act freely?

Why is there anything at all in the universe? Why is there in general something and not nothing? Is the universe fundamentally absurd, or does it make some sort of rational sense? Was it created? Has it existed from all eternity? Can I even imagine a satisfactory *reason* for the universe? Does the universe stretch infinitely away from me in space? Will it go on existing forever?

And last, but of course hardly least, the question we have already examined: Is there an infinite, omnipotent, omniscient creator of all that is—a God?

Well, no one can accuse metaphysics of wasting its time on trivia! But how are we to get a handle on a field this vast in the confines of a single chapter? I propose to adopt a three-stage strategy for imposing some manageable order on the field of metaphysics. Following the practice of previous chapters, we shall begin by focussing on the life and thought of a single great philosopher, Gottfried Leibniz, whose philosophical writings constitute one of the enduring monuments to systematic metaphysical investigation. Our primary concern will be the connections between Leibniz's metaphysical theories of space, time, substance, and God on the one hand, and his interpretation of the new science of the seventeenth century on the other. At one point, we shall look at a famous debate which Leibniz carried on with Samuel Clarke, a follower and defender of the foremost scientist of the century, Sir Isaac Newton. Through the medium of this debate, we shall see how theological questions, metaphysical questions, epistemological questions, mathematical questions, and questions of the latest experimental data got bound up together in a complex dispute going to the foundations of modern science and philosophy.

In the second part of the chapter, we shall choose a single metaphysical topic, the vexing issue of the relationship between the mind and the body, and examine some of the ways philosophers have attempted to deal with it. Since the issue is not settled yet, we shall have the opportunity to look at some contemporary work in metaphysics as well as at some of the theories from the past several centuries.

Finally, we shall bring our story up to date by examining a number of attempts by twentieth-century philosophers to understand the enterprise we call science. Science today is very different from the science of Leibniz's time, and we shall find that while some modern philosophers share Leibniz's enthusiastic confidence in the endless advance of scientific knowledge, others have a much more complex view of what happens when we give up one theory and adopt another. As you might guess, a discussion of the philosophy of science will lead us back into epistemology as well as taking us further into metaphysics.

II

Gottfried Wilhelm Leibniz was born in 1646 in the city of Leipzig, in what is now Germany. He was a precocious child, the son of a professor and the grandson, through his mother, of another professor. (In Germany, the title of "professor" is reserved for a very small number of the most distinguished members of a university faculty. Professors in a German university are treated roughly in the way four-star generals are treated in the army.) Very early, Leibniz distinguished himself in his studies, first at the University of Leipzig and then at Altdorf, where he was actually offered a professorship. Rather than taking up the vocation of professor, Leibniz chose instead to affiliate himself with, or enter the service of, a series of rulers in the various principalities, duchies, and electorates of the area now unified as Germany. It was quite common for artists, composers, and men of learning to join the courts of these little independent territories, serving sometimes as performers at court, sometimes as tutors to the royal children, sometimes simply as confidantes or wise men in residence. Some of you may have heard a series of six concerti for orchestra called the "Brandenburg Concerti." These were written by Johann Sebastian Bach at the request of the Elector of Brandenburg (though never played in Bach's lifetime!). Until the nineteenth century, much of the financial support for artistic and intellectual work took the form of aristocratic or royal patronage. It is a bit difficult to image some man or woman being named "philosopher in residence to the governor of Kansas," but it was not at all odd for Leibniz to serve in effect as resident philosopher to the Duke of Hanover.

Leibniz was a man of the most extraordinarily broad interests. You can get some idea of his brilliance and his breadth if I tell you that he invented a version of the calculus, conceived the idea of a universal encyclopedia of human knowledge, worked out a philosophical explanation for the apparent existence of evil in a world created by an infinitely powerful, infinitely good God, and developed a scheme for sending Jesuits to convert the Chinese!

Today, learned men and women communicate their discoveries to one another by publishing articles in scholarly journals. In Leibniz's day, however, it was much more common for such communication to take the form of long letters. These were not your "Having wonderful time, wish you were here" sorts of things. The writer, after a few courtesies at the beginning, would launch into page after page of technical mathematics, physics, philosophy, or theology. Much of Leibniz's important work was "published" in this form, and it was therefore extremely difficult for several centuries to get a systematic overview of his theories. Only in recent years has anything like a complete edition of the works of Leibniz become available. A bit later on in this section, we shall read excerpts from a series of letters exchanged by Leibniz and Samuel Clarke. The exchange began with a letter from Liebniz to Caroline, Princess of Wales! Can you imagine Albert Einstein setting forth his most important work on the theory of relativity in a letter to the king of England?

Leibniz's metaphysical theory revolves around his conception of the nature of what philosophers call *substance*. This is a technical term that was introduced by Aristotle and has since become one of the key terms in metaphysical disputes. In order to explain what it means, let me do what Aristotle himself did, and take a detour through some facts about language. In English, and many other languages as well, sentences can be put together by combining a subject-term and a predicate-term, using the connector or copula "is." For example, I can make the sentence "Iron is hard" by using "iron" as the subject, "hard" as the predicate, and "is" as the copula or connector. Sometimes, instead of using "is," I just use a verb, as in the sentence "Ice melts." Now, in English and other languages, I can frequently turn a word that has been used as a predicate into a word usable as a subject, simply by adding an ending or altering its form a bit. I can turn the predicate "hard" into a subject by adding -ness to get "hardness." Then I can make the sentence "Hardness is a property of iron." I can also turn the verb "melt" into a subject by adding -ing. Then I can make the sentence, "Melting is what ice does."

It occurred to Aristotle that although many words can be used as both subject and predicate, with appropriate grammatical shifting around, there are some words which can be the subjects of sentences, but cannot also serve as predicates, no matter how they are altered grammatically. For example, I can say, "The earth is round," but there is no way I can change "The earth" into a predicate. Of course, there is the adjective "earthy," but that doesn't do the trick; and there is the rather fancy term "terrestrial," but that means "having to do with, or pertaining to, or existing on, the earth." "Earthness" and "earth-ing" just don't mean anything.

In short, some terms are ultimate subjects, in the sense that they can be the subjects of predication but cannot themselves be predicated of anything else. The things these terms name or refer to, Aristotle said, are *substances.* The characteristics, states, activities, or features which predicates name or refer to are called *attributes* by Aristotle. So a substance is anything that can have attributes predicated of it, but which itself cannot be predicated as an attribute of any other thing. The most obvious examples of substances, of course, are just ordinary physical objects. A tree is a substance, and the word "tree" is an ultimate grammatical subject. Tallness is an attribute, and so are greenness and leafiness and life. So I can say of a tree that it is green, leafy, and alive. In short, I can attribute greenness, leafiness, and life to a tree. But I cannot "attribute" treeness to anything else. So a tree is a bearer of attributes which is not itself an attribute of any other thing, which is to say that it is a *substance*.

Attributes are characteristics *of* substances, so they cannot exist unless the substance exists. Even though the famous Cheshire cat in *Alice in Wonderland* is supposed to have faded slowly away until nothing was left of it but the smile, in real life you cannot have a smile without a face, nor can you have intelligence without a mind, or color without a body. Philosophers express this by saying that attributes must *inhere* in a substance, which is said to "support" them. But substances, Aristotle said, do not inhere in anything, nor do they require the existence of anything other than themselves. A substance can exist without this or that particular property (though it obviously cannot exist without any properties at all), but there are no properties that can exist without being the properties of some substance.

The fundamental idea of Aristotle's theory of "first philosophy"—an idea that peristed into the seventeenth century and beyond, influencing Leibniz and many other philosophers—was that we could get a systematic grasp of the universe by conceiving it in terms of the *substances* that make it up, together with a classification of all the properties or attributes that characterize those substances. Because substances are the sorts of things that can exist without depending on something else, they must be the most real, the most basic things. Aristotle used the linguistic insight which we sketched a few pages ago as a way of linking his theory of the universe with his theory of the way we know the universe. Put simply, the idea was that there is a parallelism of language, thought, and being. In the world, there are substances and their attributes; in our minds, there are concepts of substances and concepts of attributes; and in our language, corresponding to our concepts, there are subject terms that cannot serve as predicates (i.e., the names of substances) and predicate terms (the names of the attributes). So the universe is through and through rational, because its structure is mirrored in the structure of our thought and the structure of our language. A good deal of philosophy since Aristotle has devoted itself either to defending this view of a rational universe mirrored in the human mind or to attacking it by arguing that the mind is not rational, or that the universe is not rational, or that we cannot ever *know* whether our concepts adequately mirror reality.

What sorts of substances is the universe made up of? Philosophers have given many answers to this fundamental question of metaphysics, but they have tended to focus on one or more of three candidates. The ancient cosmologists known as "atomists" argued that tiny, indivisible, simple bits of matter called *atoms* are the building blocks of the universe. They pointed out that complex or composite bodies, because they are made up out of atoms, are in a sense dependent upon their component parts. But the component parts are not dependent upon the whole of which they are parts. A piece of rock cannot exist unless its atomic parts exist, but the individual parts can perfectly well exist even though the rock, as a rock, does not (the atoms go on existing after the rock is broken up or worn away). So the atoms must be the substances of the universe, and any larger bodies, or properties of those larger bodies, are merely dependent complexes or attributes.

A number of philosophers, including Descartes, claimed that minds are substances. This raises all sorts of questions, some of which we shall try to explore in the next section. Minds, Descartes held, are not material—they do not occupy space, they do not have shape, or size, or density. They are "immaterial substances," which just means that they are "not matter," and still leaves us trying to figure out what they are. Philosophers have found two important reasons for insisting on the substantiality of minds, even though such a view is hard to explain. First, Christian doctrine teaches that the soul continues to exist after the death and breakup of the material body, so the soul must be a substance. It seems natural to identify the soul with the mind, and to conclude that the mind is a nonmaterial substance. Second (this is Descartes' reason), consciousness is an absolutely undeniable fact, and consciousness is apparently a feature or characteristic or attribute of minds rather than of bodies. Now if consciousness is an attribute, then it must inhere in some substance, and if it doesn't seem to be the sort of attribute that could inhere in bodies, then the mind must be a different sort of substance.

Finally, many philosophers from Aristotle onward have claimed that God is a special, one-of-a-kind substance. Obviously God meets the requirements for "substance-hood." He can exist independently of other things, and attributes can be predicated of Him. But if God is a substance, and if God created the universe of nondivine substances, then it would seem that He is the *only* substance, for everything else depends for its existence on Him. Some philosophers handled this difficulty by distinguishing *created substances* from *uncreated substance* (God), but at least one philosopher—the seventeenth-century Jewish metaphysician Baruch Spinoza—drew the natural conclusion from the definition of substance and asserted that God is the only substance. Everything else, he said, is merely an attribute of God. Believe it or not, this doctrine led people to accuse Spinoza of being an atheist!

The dispute over the nature and categories of substance has been shaped by different philosophical motivations in different ages. Sometimes, the problems philosophers wanted to deal with by means of a theory of substance were religious or theological; at other times, the problems were mainly logical. But in the seventeenth century, when Leibniz developed his metaphysical theory, the primary motivation was a desire to find an adequate theoretical foundation for the new science, in particular for the physical theories of motion which Galileo, Kepler, Newton, and others were advancing. Four questions at least had to be answered by any philosophical theory adequate to the new science:

First: What is the nature of the substances whose behavior is described by scientific laws of motion?

Second: What is the nature of the space and time in which substances exist, interact, and change in accordance with scientific laws?

Third: What is the nature of the interactions between substances? What forces, or causal influences, connect the behavior of one substance with the behavior of another?

Fourth: What is the relationship, if any, between the universe of spatially located substances governed by the laws of motion, and the God who—at least in the seventeenth century—was agreed on all sides to be the Creator of that universe?

Leibniz's unique and startling theory of *monads* was designed to answer all four of these questions in a manner that permitted the latest scientific discoveries, the most advanced developments in mathematics, and orthodox Christian doctrine all to fit together into a consistent metaphysics.

In 1714, only two years before his death, Leibniz wrote out a short, systematic statement of his metaphysical theory. *The Monadology,* as it is called, remains the best introduction to his philosophy, and in the selection that follows, you will find his answers to several of the four questions we have just articulated. Since this is a summary rather than a full-scale defense, Leibniz's arguments are rather sketchy, but you should be able to form a preliminary notion of his theory from what is presented here.

The Monad, of which we will speak here, is nothing else than a simple substance, which goes to make up composites; by simple, we mean without parts.

There must be simple substances because there are composites; for a composite is nothing else than a collection or *aggregatum* of simple substances.

Now, where there are no constituent parts there is possible neither extension, nor form, nor divisibility. These Monads are the true Atoms of nature, and, in fact, the Elements of things.

Their dissolution, therefore, is not to be feared and there is no way conceivable by which a simple substance can perish through natural means.

For the same reason there is no way conceivable by which a simple substance might, through natural means, come into existence, since it can not be formed by composition.

We may say then, that the existence of Monads can begin or end only all at once, that is to say, the Monad can begin only through creation and end only through annihilation. Composites, however, begin or end gradually.

There is also no way of explaining how a Monad can be altered or changed in its inner being by any other created thing, since there is no possibility of transposition within it, nor can we conceive of any internal movement which can be produced, directed, increased or diminished there within the substance, such as can take place in the case of composites where a change can occur among the parts. The Monads have no windows through which anything may come in or go out. The Attributes are not liable to detach themselves and make an excursion outside the substance, as could *sensible species* of the Schoolmen. In the same way neither substance nor attribute can enter from without into a Monad.

Still Monads must needs have some qualities, otherwise they would not even be existences. And if simple substances did not differ at all in their qualities, there would be no means of perceiving any change in things. Whatever is in a composite can come into it only through its simple elements and the Monads, if they were without qualities, since they do not differ at all in quantity, would be indistinguishable one from another. For instance, if we imagine *a plenum* or completely filled space, where each part receives only the equivalent of its own previous motion, one state of things would not be distinguishable from another.

Each Monad, indeed, must be different from every other. For there are never in nature two beings which are exactly alike, and in which it is not possible to find a difference either internal or based on an intrinsic property.

I assume it as admitted that every created being, and consequently the created Monad, is subject to change, and indeed that this change is continuous in each.

It follows from what has just been said, that the natural changes of the Monad come from an internal principle, because an external cause can have no influence upon its inner being.

Now besides this principle of change there must also be in the Monad a manifoldness which changes. This manifoldness constitutes, so to speak, the specific nature and the variety of the simple substances.

This manifoldness must involve a multiplicity in the unity or in that which is simple. For since every natural change takes place by degrees, there must be something which changes and something which remains unchanged, and consequently there must be in the simple substance a plurality of conditions and relations, even though it has no parts.

GOTTFRIED LEIBNIZ, *The Monadology*

Let us consider in turn each of our four questions, and see how Leibniz's theory of monads answers them. First of all, the created universe consists of an infinity of simple, nonmaterial spiritual substances, or minds. Each of these minds is conscious, and its attributes or states are the thoughts and perceptions, desires and feelings in its consciousness. Monads, as Leibniz calls his simple substances, are created by God, who has—as we shall see—arranged their inner natures according to a rather complex divine plan.

The monad I am best acquainted with, of course, is my self, my own mind. I am not only conscious; I am also self-conscious, as Descartes pointed out. But Leibniz does not think that self-consciousness is necessarily a characteristic of every monad in the universe. Indeed, there is a sort of hierarchy of monads, rising from those monads whose consciousness is so feeble as barely to occur at all, through clear consciousness not combined with self-consciousness, on through the sort of self-aware or reflexive consciousness human beings have, up to the consciousness of angels (if there are any), and finally to God's consciousness, which we mortals can hardly imagine.

What then is a body? Well, bodies are not substances, for substances are simple and bodies are divisible into parts, hence complex. Substances are conscious and bodies are not. Bodies are, as Leibniz puts it, "colonies" of monads. We can think of a body as a set of monads that bear certain relationships to one another. But if this set of monads is broken up, divided, or redistributed, so that the body as such ceases to exist, the monads go right on existing. Each monad can be thought of as occupying a dimensionless point in space (a point has no length, breadth, or depth; it is merely a location, mathematically speaking). So monads, as nonmaterial substances, have no spatial extension, no size or shape. This sounds odd, of course, but it sounds even odder to suggest that the human mind is triangular, or six feet long, or two inches thick. Minds simply aren't the sorts of things to take up space, and monads are fundamentally minds.

Monads have two sorts of properties, internal and external. The internal properties of a monad are all the contents or states of its own consciousness, all the things that happen inside it. The external properties of a monad are its relationships to other monads. For example, if I see a squirrel run across a branch outside my window, and then feel a twinge of pain where I bumped myself yesterday, that visual perception and that twinge are events in my mind (according to Leibniz); they are internal to me, and as such are part of the life of the monad which is my self or soul. On the other hand, my physical distance from the squirrel is a fact about the relationships between two monads—namely, my self or mind or soul and the self or the mind of the squirrel (assuming, for the moment, that there is some consciousness associated with the body I call a squirrel) that is an external relationship or property both of myself and of the squirrel.

Space, according to Leibniz, is the totality or system of the external relations of monads to one another at a single moment of time. Because this is an extremely important part of Leibniz's philosophy, and also a very confusing notion, we had better linger over it a while. There seem to be two basically opposed ways of conceiving of space. Either we can think of it as an independently existing container, or volume, or thereness, *into which* things can move or be placed, and out of which they can be taken again; or else we can think of space as some property or characteristic of independently existing things, such that without them, there is no space. Most of us probably think of space more in the first way than the second, insofar as we think about the subject at all, but the more you try to figure out how there can be empty space that is independent of what is in it, the stranger the notion becomes. Is space something? Presumably it isn't any sort of substance, because if it were, there wouldn't be any room *in* it for things. Well, if it isn't something, then it must be nothing, right? But if it is nothing, then how can I put something in it? The very idea of totally empty space boggles the mind, once you really start puzzling over it.

On the other hand, if there isn't any empty space—what philosophers since ancient times have called *the void*—then how does anything move around? We intuitively understand physical movement as a body's going from some place that it is in to some other place that is either empty or else is made empty by the arrival of the body (as when a billiard ball pushes another ball out of the way to make room for itself). Do you know those pocket puzzles which consist of fifteen little numbered squares in a bigger square that has room for sixteen?

Mathematical pocket puzzle.

The problem is to use the one empty square to move the others around until you get them in the right order. There is no way to do the puzzle unless one of the squares is empty. Well, the world would seem to be in the same fix. Unless there are some empty spaces, it is hard to see how anything can move at all.

Nevertheless, Leibniz claimed that space is simply a characteristic of things that exist (namely monads), not an independently existing place or volume or something into which monads can move. This helped him to explain the nature of space, but it left him with the conclusion that there is no void.

The two opposed theories of space which we have been discussing are sometimes called the *absolute theory* and the *relational theory*. The key difference between them is that according to the absolute theory, it makes sense to talk about the absolute position or location or dimensions of a body in space, whereas according to the relational theory it only makes sense to talk about the position or location or dimensions or size of a body relative to the rest of the system of other bodies. An example from horse-racing may make this a bit clearer. Suppose you have gone to the racetrack with a friend, and have gotten yourself stuck behind a pillar where you can't see the track; so you must rely on your friend's reports of the progress of the horses. In the fifth race, there are six horses, and you bet on number four. As the race begins, you hear a roar, and ask your friend where number four is. She says, "Number four is roughly two hundred yards from the starting gate." She has given you number four's absolute position on the track. But you want to know number four's *relative* position—is he first, second, third, fourth, fifth, or last? Now the peculiar thing about relative, as opposed to absolute, position is that while your friend can perfectly well tell you your horse's absolute position without mentioning the other horses or even knowing where they are, she cannot give you its relative position unless she also knows the relative positions of all six horses. What is more, the absolute position of your horse wouldn't be altered by the sudden, mysterious disappearance of the other five horses from the track; but its relative position might go from sixth to first by virtue of such a disappearance. That is why a disqualification by the judges can't change the time in which your horse ran the race, but can change whether he won or lost.

Time presents many of the same problems as space, and both Leibniz and his philosophical opponents tended to develop analyses of time that followed all the main points of their theories of space. Again, there are absolute and relative conceptions of time. The absolute conception characterizes time as an independently existing dimension, stretching from creation to the end of eternity, within which events take place. The relative conception, which Leibniz held, characterizes time as the relationship among a set of things—in this case, the relationship among all the internal events of consciousness. As in the case of space, so in the case of time, the absolute theory implies the possibility of empty time and the relational theory implies the impossibility of empty time. The absolute theory seems to say that an event has a time location—a date—independently of the occurrences or locations of any other events. The relational theory asserts that the date of an event is determined entirely by its relative occurrence before or after or at the same time as other events. The defenders of the theory of absolute time have the same problem explaining what time is that they have explaining what space is. It can't be a substance, but it can't be nothing either. And if it is an attribute of substance, then the relational theory must be right.

Leibniz and Isaac Newton were absolutely at loggerheads about the nature of space and time. Leibniz was committed to the relational theory, while Newton was equally committed to a theory of absolute space and time. Since the absolute theory seems to commit you to such a peculiar conception of space and time, as neither something nor nothing, why on earth would a man as brilliant as Newton defend that point of view?

The answer can be found in a fascinating argument and counter-argument appearing in the Leibniz-Clarke correspondence. Leibniz, in arguing for his relational theory of space, pointed out that the absolute theory of space had certain peculiar implications over and above its inability to explain exactly what space is. If space is absolute, then as we have seen there can be empty space. And if there can be empty space, then it must make sense to ask whether the entire physical universe could be moved (by God, presumably) three feet to the left, or half a mile up, or whether perhaps the universe as a whole could be rotated a quarter-turn clockwise. Now these questions are sheerly meaningless,

The effect of acceleration.

Weightlessness shows the relative motion of astronaut and space ship.

Leibniz said, because there is no conceivable way that any of us inside the universe could tell that such a change in position or orientation had taken place. In a passage that anticipates what came to be known in the twentieth century as the "verification theory of meaning," Leibniz claimed that a statement has meaning only if there is some possible observation or evidence by means of which we could determine whether it was true or false.

But Clarke was ready for this argument, and in his reply, he appealed to the Newtonian notions of inertia and acceleration to refute Leibniz. On straight scientific grounds, Clarke argued that the relational theory of space must be wrong, and that Newton's absolute theory, however difficult to understand, was the right one. Here is the exchange, as it appears in the letters between Leibniz and Clarke.

Clarke: If the world be finite in dimensions, it is moveable by the power of God and therefore my argument drawn from that moveableness is conclusive. Two places, though exactly alike, are not the same place. Nor is the motion or rest of the universe, the same state; any more than the motion or rest of a ship, is the same state, because a man shut up in the cabin cannot perceive whether the ship sails or not, so long as it moves uniformly. The motion of the ship, though the man perceives it not, is a real different state, and has real different effects; and, upon a sudden stop, it would have other real effects; and so likewise would an indiscernible motion of the universe. To this argument, no answer has ever been given. It is largely insisted on by Sir Isaac Newton in his *Mathematical Principles,* (Definit. 8.) where, from the consideration of the properties, causes, and effects of motion, he shows the difference between real motion, or a body's being carried from one part of space to another; and relative motion, which is merely a change of the order or situation of bodies with respect to each other. This argument is a mathematical one; showing, from real effects, that there may be real motion where there is none relative; and relative motion, where there is none real: and is not to be answered, by barely asserting the contrary.

Leibniz: In order to prove that space, without bodies, is an absolute reality; the author objected, that a finite material universe might move forward in space. I answered, it does not appear reasonable that the material universe should be finite; and, though we should suppose it to be finite; yet 'tis unreasonable it should have motion any otherwise, than as its parts change their situation among themselves; because such a motion would produce no change that could be observed, and would be without design. 'Tis another thing, when its parts change their situation among themselves; for then there is a motion in space; but it consists in the order of relations which are changed. The author replies now, that the reality of motion does not depend upon being observed; and that a ship may go forward, and yet a man, who is in the ship, may not perceive it. I answer, motion does not indeed depend upon being observed; but it does depend upon being possible to be observed. There is no motion, when there is no change that can be observed. And when there is no change that can be observed, there is no change at all. The contrary opinion is grounded upon the supposition of a real absolute space, which I have demonstratively confuted by the principle of the want of a sufficient reason of things.

Clarke: My argument here, for the motion of space being really independent upon body, is founded on the possibility of the material universe being finite and moveable: 'tis not enough therefore for this learned writer to reply, that he thinks it would not have been wise and reasonable for God to have made the material universe finite and moveable. He must either affirm, that 'twas impossible for God to make the material world finite and moveable; or else he must of necessity allow the strength of my argument, drawn from the possiblity of the world's being finite and moveable. Neither is it sufficient barely to repeat his assertion, that the motion of a finite material universe would be nothing, and (for want of other bodies to compare it with) would produce no discoverable change: unless he could disprove the instance which I gave of a very great change that would happen; viz. that the parts would be sensibly shocked by a sudden acceleration, or stopping of the motion of the whole: to which instance, he has not attempted to give any answer.

The Leibniz-Clarke Correspondence

So we have before us now Leibniz's answers to the first two questions. What is the nature of substances? They are nonmaterial, conscious monads. What is the nature of space and time? Space is the order of the external relations among monads and time is the order of the internal relations or attributes of monads. Let us turn to the third question: What is the nature of the interactions between monads? What forces or causal influences connect the behavior of one substance with the behavior of others?

Leibniz's answer to this central question of science and metaphysics is strange, unexpected, and quite astonishing. Indeed, it ranks as one of the oddest views ever expressed on a major philosophical question by a great philosopher. Before telling you what that view is, however, I want you to reflect for a moment on just how peculiar Newton's view was on this subject of the nature of causal connections between substances. Newton is of course famous for making the force of *gravity* central to his system. According to classical physics, those of you who have taken some physics will remember, each body in the universe, each star, planet, comet, or cloud of intergalactic dust exerts a force on each other body, no matter where the two are located. This force of gravity, as we call it, pulls the two bodies together, and according to the Newtonian formula, the force pulling them together is directly proportional to the product of their masses and inversely proportional to the square of the distance between them.

We don't care, here, about the precise formula, which no one but a physicist or astronomer need remember. The crucial thing about this theory of gravity is that, according to Newton, each body exerts such a pull on each other body, no matter how far apart they are from one another! Have you ever stopped to wonder how on earth (or in the heavens) such a long-distance pull could possibly occur? Philosophers traditionally call this sort of thing "action at a distance," and they usually consider it nonsense. We can understand easily enough how one body can move another when they are touching. It pushes it. And we can also understand how one body can indirectly move another when there is a series of bodies in between the two, connecting one to the other. The first body moves the one just next to it, which in turn moves the one next to it, and so forth, until the next-to-last body moves its neighbor. But Newton claimed that one body could move another at a distance, with nothing whatsoever in between them but empty space!

Newton had no idea how this could be. Indeed, he explicitly refused to speculate on the question. "I make no hypotheses," he said, meaning that he offered no metaphysical guesses as to how action at a distance might be possible. But the theory of universal gravitation fit the facts, he claimed, and it fit with the rest of his physical theory as well, so it could be adopted by scientists even though it was philosophically incomprehensible. In other words, Newton took the same line on gravity that he took on the absolute nature of space and time.

What was Leibniz's view of the interactions between substances in nature? Early in his life, he devoted some effort to working out a version of the theory that Descartes had offered. Briefly, Descartes held that there was no void, that the physical universe was completely filled with matter, and that whirlpools or "vortices" of this stuff communicated motion from one heavenly body to another. This hypothesis was extremely complicated to work out in any scientific detail, as compared with the elegant simplicity of Newton's universal gravitation, but it had the philosophical virtue of basing physical interactions on direct contact, rather than on any sort of action at a distance.

Eventually, however, Leibniz came to the extraordinary conclusion that substances do *not* interact with one another at all, despite what would seem to be overwhelming evidence to the contrary. It was his view that each monad, each simple immaterial substance, was complete and self-sufficient unto itself. None of the inner perceptions or states of consciousness of one monad were actually *caused* by the action of any other monad. As he put it in the selection from the *Monadology* which you read earlier, "The Monads have no windows through which anything may come in or go out."

But something is very wrong here! Leibniz is not a skeptic. He does not say that he can have no knowledge of anything save the inner states of his own mind at any given moment. He claims that his thoughts and perceptions accurately represent the world around him, just as they purport to do. Now, if my visual perception of the typewriter in front of me is *caused* by the typewriter, by the light coming from the typewriter into my eyes and affecting the retina, etc., then I can perhaps understand how that perception might accurately represent some aspect of the typewriter. But if nothing outside my mind can affect my mind in any way; if no other substance can cause thoughts or perceptions in my mind; if, in Leibniz's colorful phrase, my mind has no windows; then what conceivable grounds can I possess for supposing that the thoughts in my mind bear any regular relationship at all to the characteristics, events, states, or relations of other substances?

Leibniz's answer provides us at the same time with his reply to the fourth question, concerning the relationship between God and the universe of created substances. According to Leibniz, there is no *secular* ground for supposing that my thoughts adequately reflect the world beyond the walls of my mind. If there were no God, or if God did not see fit to arrange things in a special way, my internal thoughts would give me no clue at all as to things outside of my own inner consciousness. But God is good, and he is all-powerful, and so, Leibniz claims, he has systematically fitted the internal nature of each monad to the totality of the rest, so that the thoughts in any single monad correspond in some way, more or less perfectly, to the universe they purport to represent. This systematic fitting is described by Leibniz as a "pre-established harmony." It is *pre*-established because God builds into each monad, when He creates it, the whole succession of thoughts and perceptions which shall pass through that monad's consciousness as time goes on. It is a *harmony* because the subjective thoughts of each monad are, by divine arrangement, fitted to or harmonized with the rest of the monads.

In order to get a notion of what Leibniz means by this odd doctrine, imagine that you have been locked up in a dark room and strapped to a chair facing a wall. Suddenly, a window *seems* to open in the wall, and you see the people, the cars, the trucks on the street outside. But in fact there is no window! Instead, your mysterious captor is using the wall as a screen, and projecting onto it a *movie* of the street beyond the wall. Now, this mysterious captor is very rich and rather eccentric, so he hires actors to drive and walk on the street at exactly the moment, and in exactly the way, that perfectly similar characters are walking or driving in the movie he is showing on the wall of your cell. There is no direct causal connection, of course, between the pictures in the movie and the people outside. The movie was made before you were ever thrown into the room, and the "cause" of the pictures on the wall is simply the passing of light through the film in the projector behind you. But thanks to the careful planning of your captor, there is a pre-established harmony between the movie and the events on the street.

Roughly speaking, this peculiar arrangement is what Leibniz claims to be the actual relationship between my perceptions and the rest of the universe.

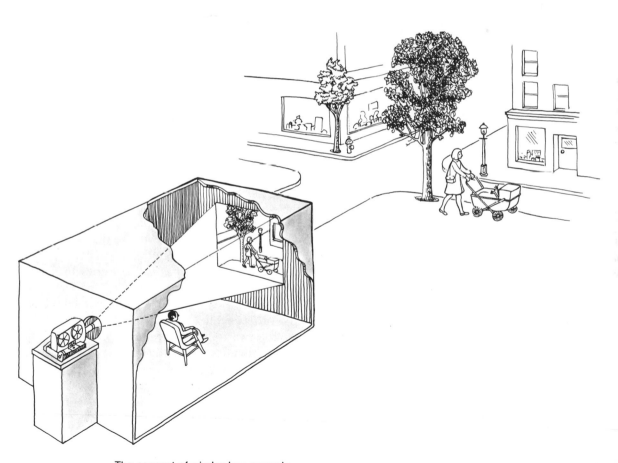

The concept of windowless monads.

They correspond to one another because of God's infinitely careful plan, but there is no actual causal connection between them. In philosophical language, the correspondence is *virtual* rather than *actual*.

Why would God go to all this trouble? God's ways are traditionally said to be mysterious, but this does seem to be carrying mystery a bit far! The truth, I think, is that Leibniz has got himself into a metaphysical box with his theory of simple monads, and he just doesn't know how to get out. The theory of monads is useful for some purposes, including an explanation of the nature of space and time and an account of the nature of force in physics (we haven't talked about this last point). But it compels Leibniz to put forward the implausible notion of a preestablished harmony, and to that extent is clearly an inadequate basis for either metaphysics or science.

Lest you think that Leibniz was just being needlessly silly, let me assure you that the problem he was dealing with—namely, the relationship between the subjective contents of the mind and the physical objects they supposedly represent—was a problem as well for virtually all of the metaphysicians of the seventeenth and eighteenth centuries. Indeed, in the next section, we shall see that it continues to stir up philosophical disagreement today.

III

One of the characteristic symptoms of the mental illness known as schizophrenia is a sense on the part of the patient of being divorced from his or her own body. The patient's foot, or hand, or torso seems to be an alien or independent entity. One patient may say that he doesn't know whether he really has a body; another may wonder whether she can move her hand should she choose to do so; a third may speak of his body as not being *his*. Psychiatrists aren't sure just how to treat schizophrenia, but they have no doubt that it *is* a form of mental disorder or disease. We may perhaps be forgiven for wondering, therefore, whether philosophers for the past three and a half centuries have been suffering from some weird intellectual form of schizophrenia, for Descartes, Berkeley, Hume, and others say some pretty strange things about minds and bodies. In this section, in addition to sketching several theories of the relation of mind to body that have been put forward in the literature of modern philosophy, I shall try to suggest what legitimate concerns have led philosophers to focus so much attention on the so-called mind-body problem.

The physical theories developed by Aristotle, and refined by countless philosophers during the many centuries following, placed great emphasis upon the purposive order of nature. Aristotle himself conceived of nature as exhibiting an inherent purpose that need not be traced to the conscious intentions of a divine creator. Later philosophers in the Christian tradition tended to appeal, at some point in their arguments, to such a divine purpose. But whether religiously based or not, physical theories relied heavily upon notions of goal, end, purpose, and rational order usually associated with the operations of conscious agents. As we saw in the last chapter, Descartes focused his attention entirely on the self-conscious self or mind at the outset of his philosophical deliberations. But when he came to develop his theory of the physical universe, he rejected entirely any appeal to properties, concepts, or modes of explanation associated with the mental or the conscious. The material universe, he argued, was characterized by such properties as extension and motion. All explanation in science must be couched in terms of size, shape, density, velocity, and the like.

This exclusion of the mental from the sphere of physical explanation was prompted by the fact that extension and motion could be quantified and treated mathematically whereas purpose, end, goal, intention, or rational order could not be. The tools of arithmetic and analytic geometry were inapplicable to the notions that Aristotle and his followers had employed in their physical explanations. So it was the search for a mathematical science which led Descartes to exclude all "mentalistic" characteristics from his physical theories. But having thus shunted aside the mental, Descartes was forced to ask himself what relationship there was between the physical realm of extension and motion to which the new science applied, and the realm of thought, purpose, and reason. For Descartes, the problem was especially pressing because his method of doubt had focused attention as never before on the sphere of consciousness.

Drawing on metaphysical theories already in circulation, Descartes put forward a relatively simple but ultimately unworkable theory of the relationship between the realms of consciousness and physics. He argued that there are two kinds of created substances, minds and bodies. Minds are immaterial, unextended, simple conscious substances, and bodies are material, extended, composite, nonconscious substances. A human being is thus a combination of a material substance—the body—and a spiritual substance—the mind.

In the traditional theory of substance, a substance (or "essence") of one sort can only interact with or influence another substance of the same sort. A mind can interact with a mind, a body can intereact with a body. But minds cannot interact with bodies, because there is no way in which a nonmaterial, unextended substance can be touched, moved, altered, or affected by a material, extended substance. And there is no way in which a simple, unextended, conscious substance can touch, move, alter, or affect an extended, material substance. So having excluded the mind from the arena of mathematical physics, Descartes finds himself with no satisfactory way to reintroduce mind back into the world.

The problem is compounded, of course, by Descartes' search for inner subjective certainty. Beginning as he did with the self's conscious awareness of its own existence, he was forced to ask how such a self-aware self could ever come to know the existence and nature of nonconscious bodies external to it. So for some of Descartes' contemporaries and successors, the "mind-body" problem consisted in finding a place in physical, mathematically describable nature for a nonphysical, nonquantitative mind; while for others, the problem

consisted in showing that a mind could acquire well-established knowledge of bodies in space. These two forms of the problem intermingled with one another as philosophers puzzled over them, so that sometimes the scientific-metaphysical aspect was dominant, and at other times the epistemological aspect took precedence.

There are countless metaphysical solutions to the problem of the nature and relationship of mind and body, some of which are enormously subtle and suggestive, but in an introductory text of this sort, it would be madness to try to lay them all out for you. *Three* positions have dominated the history of this debate, and you have actually encountered two of them in this chapter already. The three major theories of the relation of mind to body are the *two-substance theory,* which asserts that minds and bodies are fundamentally different sorts of beings or substances; the *one-substance theory* which states that everything in the universe is a mind, and that bodies are to be analyzed as collections of, or aspects of, or thoughts in, minds; and the *one-substance theory* which states that everything in the universe is a body, and minds are to be analyzed as collections of, or aspects of, or configurations of, bodies. The two-substance theory is called *dualism,* the everything-is-a-mind theory is called *idealism* (not to be confused with a belief in high principles or the flag), and the everything-is-a-body theory is called *materialism* (also not to be confused with an excessive desire for money).

Descartes was a *dualist,* as you know. Leibniz was an *idealist* of a certain sort. He held that there were many minds in the universe, and that bodies were collections or colonies of those minds. Other idealists, such as George Berkeley, developed their theory of mind and body out of epistemological considerations. They argued that bodies could only be collections of perceptions or ideas in the mind of a conscious self, for such perceptions and ideas are the only things that we, as minds, can know anything about. To suggest that there are things outside our minds about which we can know nothing is simply to use words without meaning anything. How, after all, could we even imagine a way of testing such an assertion?

The materialist position is one of the oldest in philosophy, and also one of the most current. The ancient atomists whom you met in the first chapter—

Democritus, Epicurus, Lucretius—were materialists. They explicitly stated that the mind is made up of very small, very fine atoms, rather like the atoms which make up air. They saw no problem in explaining the relationship of mind to body, for the mind on their view *is* body, and the interaction of mind-atoms with other atoms was just like the interaction between any atoms at all.

In Descartes' own day, the most famous defenders of the materialist position were the witty French philosopher Pierre Gassendi and the Englishman Thomas Hobbes. You may have encountered Hobbes in other courses, for he is the author of a book called *Leviathan*, which is one of the classics of political philosophy. Hobbes claimed that sense perception, ideas, imagination, deliberation, reasoning, desire, love, hatred, and all the other "mental" events, activities, and traits were really just motions of the physical matter that made up the sense organs or the nervous system. For him, as for the ancient Greek atomists, there was no difficulty in explaining the interaction of "mind" and "body." Bodies strike the sense organs and set up vibrations in our nervous system, which of course also consists of bodies. The internal motions of the nervous system constitute perception, imagination, memory, and deliberation. Desire is merely the tendency of the body to move physically toward some external object, while aversion is the tendency to move away from such an object. When the internal motions in the nervous system build up to such a point that the muscles and bones are moved one way or the other, Hobbes said, then "thought"

THOMAS HOBBES (1588–1679) is one of the major figures in what has come to be called the "social contract" school of political theory. Deeply moved by the social chaos of the English civil war (1640–1660), and persuaded of the necessity for a strong, authoritative central government as the only defense against humanity's natural *destructive* tendencies, Hobbes argued in his most famous book, *Leviathan,* for a state founded upon an agreement among all persons to give up their natural liberty and submit to the commands of the sovereign.

Hobbes was a materialist; he believed that matter in motion is the only real thing. He combined this metaphysical doctrine with a psychological theory that each human being acts always to satisfy his or her desires and increase his or her power. In *Leviathan,* he attempted to deduce his theory of the social contract from these two fundamental propositions. Hobbes was both an acute observer of human behavior and an elegant stylist of English prose. *Leviathan* is the single most impressive piece of political philosophy written in English.

produces "action," and we say that the mind has caused the body to do something. But actually, of course, all that has happened is that the motion imparted to the nervous system by bodies striking on it from elsewhere has been transmitted through a chain of internal collisions to other bodies once more external to what we call "the" body—i.e., the human body. Here are some selections from the opening chapters of *Leviathan* in which Hobbes lays out some of the basic definitions and theses of his one-substance materialism.

Concerning the thoughts of man, I will consider them first singly, and afterwards in train, or dependence upon one another. Singly, they are every one a *representation* or *appearance,* of some quality, or other accident of a body without us, which is commonly called an *object.* Which object worketh on the eyes, ears, and other parts of a man's body; and by diversity of working, produceth diversity of appearances.

The original of them all, is that which we call SENSE, for there is no conception in a man's mind, which hath not at first, totally, or by parts, been begotten upon the organs of sense. The rest are derived from that original. . . .

The cause of sense, is the external body, or object, which presseth the organ proper to each sense, either immediately, as in the taste and touch; or mediately, as in seeing, hearing, and smelling; which pressure, by the mediation of the nerves, and other strings and membranes of the body, continued inwards to the brain and heart, causeth there a resistance, or counter-pressure, or endeavour of the heart to deliver itself, which endeavour, because *outward,* seemeth to be some matter without. And this *seeming,* or *fancy,* is that which men call *sense;* and consisteth, as to the eye, in a *light,* or *colour figured;* to the ear, in a *sound;* to the nostril, in an *odour;* to the tongue and palate, in a *savour;* and to the rest of the body, in *heat, cold, hardness, softness,* and such other qualities as we discern by *feeling.* All which qualities, called *sensible,* are in the object, that causeth them, but so many several motions of the matter by which it presseth our organs diversely. Neither in us that are pressed, are they any thing else, but divers motions; for motion produceth nothing but motion. But their appearance to us is fancy, the same waking, that dreaming. And as pressing, rubbing, or striking the eye, makes us fancy a light; and pressing the ear, produceth a din; so do the bodies also we see, or hear, produce the same by their strong, though unobserved action. For if those colours and sounds were in the bodies, or objects that cause them, they could not be severed from them, as by glasses, and in echoes by reflection, we see they are; where we know the thing we see is in one place, the appearance in another. And though at some certain distance, the real and very object seem invested with the fancy it begets in us; yet still the object is one thing, the image or fancy is another. So that sense, in all cases, is nothing else but original fancy, caused, as I have said, by the pressure, that is, by the motion, of external things upon our eyes, ears, and other organs thereunto ordained. . . .

That when a thing lies still, unless somewhat else stirs it, it will lie still for ever, is a truth that no man doubts of. But that when a thing is in motion, it will eternally be in motion, unless somewhat else stay it, though the reason be the same, namely, that nothing can change itself, is not so easily assented to. For men measure, not only other men, but all other things, by themselves; and because they find themselves subject after motion to pain, and lassitude, think every thing else grows weary of motion, and seeks repose of its own accord; little considering whether it be not some other motion, wherein that desire of rest they find in themselves consisteth. From hence it is, that the schools say, heavy bodies fall downwards, out of an appetite to rest, and to conserve their nature in that place which is most proper for them; ascribing appetite, and knowledge of what is good for their conservation, which is more than man has, to things inanimate, absurdly.

When a body is once in motion, it moveth, unless something else hinder it, eternally; and whatsoever hindreth it, cannot in an instant, but in time, and by degrees, quite extinguish it; and as we see in the water, though the wind cease, the waves give not over rolling for a long time after: so also it happeneth in that motion, which is made in the internal parts of a man, then, when he sees, dreams, &c. For after the object is removed, or the eye shut, we still retain an image of the thing seen, though more obscure than when we see it. And this is it, the Latins call *imagination,* from the image made in seeing; and apply the same, though improperly, to all the other senses. But the Greeks call it *fancy;* which signifies *appearance,* and is as proper to one sense, as to another. *Imagination* therefore is nothing but *decaying sense;* and is found in men, and many other living creatures, as well sleeping as waking. . . .

There be in animals, two sorts of *motions* peculiar to them: one called *vital;* begun in generation, and continued without interruption through their whole life; such as are the *course* of the *blood,* the *pulse,* the *breathing,* the *concoction, nutrition, excretion,* &c., to which motions there needs no help of imagination: the other is *animal motion,* otherwise called *voluntary motion;* as to *go,* to *speak,* to *move* any of our limbs, in such manner as is first fancied in our minds. That sense is motion in the organs and interior parts of man's body, caused by the action of the things we see, hear, &c.; and that fancy is but the relics of the same motion, remaining after sense, has been already said in the first and second chapters. And because *going, speaking,* and the like voluntary motions, depend always upon a precedent thought of *whither, which way,* and *what;* it is evident, that the imagination is the first internal beginning of all voluntary motion. And although unstudied men do not conceive any motion at all to be there, where the thing moved is invisible; or the space it is moved in is, for the shortness of it, insensible; yet that doth not hinder, but that such motions are. For let a space be never so little, that which is moved over a greater space, whereof that little one is part, must first be moved over that. These small beginnings of motion, within the body of man, before they appear in walking, speaking, striking, and other visible actions, are commonly called ENDEAVOR.

This endeavour, when it is toward something which causes it, is called APPETITE, or DESIRE; the latter being the general name; and the other oftentimes restrained to signify the desire of food, namely *hunger* and *thirst.* And when the endeavour is fromward something, it is generally called AVERSION. These words, *appetite* and *aversion,* we have from the Latins; and they both of them signify the motions, one of approaching, the other of retiring. . . .

That which men desire, they are also said to LOVE: and to HATE those things for which they have aversion. So that desire and love are the same thing; save that by desire, we always signify the absence of the object; by love, most commonly the presence of the same. So also by aversion, we signify the absence; and by hate, the presence of the object. . . .

And because the constitution of a man's body is in continual mutation, it is impossible that all the same things should always cause in him the same appetites, and aversions: much less can all men consent, in the desire of almost any one and the same object.

But whatsoever is the object of any man's appetite or desire, that is it which he for his part calleth *good:* and the object of his hate and aversion, *evil;* and of his contempt, *vile* and *inconsiderable.* for these words of good, evil, and contemptible, are ever used with relation to the person that useth them: there being nothing simply and absolutely so; nor any common rule of good and evil, to be taken from the nature of the objects themselves. . . .

When in the mind of man, appetites, and aversions, hopes, and fears, concerning one and the same thing, arise alternately; and divers good and evil consequences of the doing, or omitting the thing propounded, come successively into our thoughts; so that sometimes we have an appetite to it; sometimes an aversion from it; sometimes hope to be able to do it; sometimes despair, or fear to attempt it; the whole sum of desires, aversions, hopes and fears continued till the thing be either done, or thought impossible, is that we call DELIBERATION.

Therefore of things past, there is no *deliberation;* because manifestly impossible to be changed: nor of things known to be impossible, or thought so; because men know, or think such deliberation vain. But of things impossible, which we think possible, we may deliberate; not knowing it is in vain. And it is called *deliberation;* because it is a putting an end to the *liberty* we had of doing, or omitting, according to our own appetite, or aversion.

This alternate succession of appetites, aversions, hopes and fears, is no less in other living creatures than in man: and therefore beasts also deliberate.

Every *deliberation* is then said to *end,* when that whereof they deliberate, is either done, or thought impossible; because till then we retain the liberty of doing, or omitting; according to our appetite, or aversion.

THOMAS HOBBES, *Leviathan*

Materialism handles the problem of mind-body interaction easily enough, and it also explains quite clearly what place there is for minds in a physical universe of bodies. Minds *are* bodies, so there is no reason why the two should not interact, and as bodies they have a natural place in the physical world. But materialists have a really tough time accounting for the existence and nature of *consciousness.* You remember that Descartes considered consciouness to be *the* distinctive characteristic of the mind. What is more, self-consciousness served as the logical starting point for his search for certainty. There was no conceivable way, he said, in which a self-conscious mind could doubt its own existence. But if the mind is a collection of atoms, if perception is one movement of those atoms, reasoning another movement of those atoms, and desire, aversion, love, hatred, deliberation, and choice yet other movements, then what becomes of consciousness?

My thoughts may be associated in some way with the motions of the atoms of my body, to be sure. There may be some close causal connection which modern techniques of brain surgery, neurophysiology, and the like can discover. But the most that a brain surgeon can prove, surely, is that when she puts an electrode in my brain and sends a little current through it, then I feel or hear or see or taste something. Does that show that my feeling, hearing, seeing, or tasting *is* the movement of the electricity along my nerve paths?

A number of very shrewd and sophisticated philosophers have argued quite recently that the answer is yes. The arguments are complex, as you might imagine, but you get some sense of them from the selections with which we shall close this section. The principal selection is a portion of a 1963 article by the Australian philosopher J. J. C. Smart (1920–), who has taken the lead in defending the modern version of materialism. The brief criticism that follows is by the well-known American philosopher Norman Malcolm (1911–), who teaches at Cornell University.

Smart: First of all let me try to explain what I mean by "materialism." I shall then go on to try to defend the doctrine. By "materialism" I mean the theory that there is nothing in the world over and above those entities which are postulated by physics (or, of course, those entities which will be postulated by future and more adequate physical theories). Thus I do not hold materialism to be wedded to the billiard-ball physics of the nineteenth century. The less visualizable particles of modern physics count as matter. Note that energy counts as matter for my purposes: indeed in modern physics energy and matter are not sharply distinguishable. Nor do I hold that materialism implies determinism. If physics is indeterministic on the micro-level, so must be the materialist's theory. I regard materialism as compatible with a wide range of conceptions of the nature of matter and energy. For example, if matter and energy consist of regions of special curvature of an absolute space-time, with "worm holes" and what not, this is still compatible with materialism: we can still argue that in the last resort the world is made up entirely of the ultimate entities of physics, namely space-time points. . . . [M]y definition will in some respects be narrower than those of some who have called themselves "materialists." I wish to lay down that it is incompatible with materialism that there should be any irreducibly "emergent" laws or properties, say in biology or psychology. According to the view I propose to defend, there are no irreducible laws or properties in biology, any more than there are in electronics. Given the "natural history" of a superheterodyne (its wiring diagram), a physicist is able to explain, using only laws of physics, its mode of behavior and its properties (for example, the property of being able to receive such and such a radio station which broadcasts on 25 megacycles). Just as electronics gives the physical explanation of the workings of superheterodynes, etc., so biology gives (or approximates to giving) physical and chemical explanations of the workings of organisms or parts of organisms. The biologist needs natural history just as the engineer needs wiring diagrams, but neither needs nonphysical laws.

It will now become clear why I define materialism in the way I have done above. I am concerned to deny that in the world there are nonphysical entities and nonphysical laws. In particular I wish to deny the doctrine of psychophysical dualism. (I also want to deny any theory of "emergent properties," since irreducibly nonphysical properties are just about as repugnant to me as are irreducibly nonphysical entities.)

Popular theologians sometimes argue against materialism by saying that "you can't put love in a test tube." Well you can't put a gravitational field in a test tube (except in some rather strained sense of these words), but there is nothing incompatible with materialism, as I have defined it, in the notion of a gravitational field.

Similarly, even though love may elude test tubes, it does not elude materialistic metaphysics, since it can be analyzed as a pattern of bodily behavior or, perhaps better, as the internal state of the human organism that accounts for this behavior. (A dualist who analyzes love as an internal state will perhaps say that it is a soul state, whereas the materialist will say that it is a brain state. It seems to me that much of our ordinary language about the mental is neither dualistic nor materialist but is neutral between the two. Thus, to say that a locution is not materialistic is not to say that it is immaterialistic.)

But what about consciousness? Can we interpret the having of an after-image or of a painful sensation as something material, namely, a brain state or brain process? We seem to be immediately aware of pains and after-images, and we seem to be immediately aware of them as something different from a neurophysiological state or process. For example, the after-image may be green speckled with red, whereas the neurophysiologist looking into our brains would be unlikely to see something green speckled with red. However, if we object to materialism in this way we are victims of a confusion which U. T. Place has called "the phenomenological fallacy." To say that an image or sense datum is green is not to say that the conscious experience of having the image or sense datum is green. It is to say that it is the sort of experience we have when in normal conditions we look at a green apple, for example. Apples and unripe bananas can be green, but not the experiences of seeing them. An image or a sense datum can be green in a derivative sense, but this need not cause any worry, because, on the view I am defending, images and sense data are not constituents of the world, though the processes of having an image or a sense datum are actual processes in the world. The experience of having a green sense datum is not itself green; it is a process occurring in grey matter. The world contains plumbers, but does not contain the average plumber; it also contains the having of a sense datum, but does not contain the sense datum. . . .

It may be asked why I should demand of a tenable philosophy of mind that it should be compatible with materialism, in the sense in which I have defined it. One reason is as follows. How could a nonphysical property or entity suddenly arise in the course of animal evolution? A change in a gene is a change in a complex molecule which causes a change in the biochemistry of the cell. This may lead to changes in the shape or organization of the developing embryo. But what sort of chemical process could lead to the springing into existence of something nonphysical? No enzyme can catalyze the production of a spook! Perhaps it will be said that the nonphysical comes into existence as a by-product: that whenever there is a certain complex physical structure, then, by an irreducible extraphysical law, there is also a nonphysical entity. Such laws would be quite outside normal scientific conceptions and quite inexplicable: they would be, in Herbert Feigl's phrase, "nomological danglers." To say the very least, we can vastly simplify our cosmological outlook if we can defend a materialistic philosophy of mind. . . .

J. J. C. SMART, *Materialism*

Malcolm: I wish to go into Smart's theory that there is a contingent identity between mental phenomena and brain phenomena. If such an identity exists, then brain phenomena must have all the properties that mental phenomena have, with the exception of intentional and modal properties. I shall argue that this condition cannot be fulfilled.

a. First, it is not meaningful to assign spatial locations to some kinds of mental phenomena, e.g., thoughts. Brain phenomena have spatial location. Thus, brain phenomena have a property that thoughts do not have. Therefore, thoughts are not identical with any brain phenomena.

b. Second, any thought requires a background of circumstances ("surroundings"), e.g., practices, agreements, assumptions. If a brain event were identical with a thought, it would require the same. The circumstances necessary for a thought cannot be described in terms of the entities and laws of physics. According to Smart's scientific materialism, everything in the world is "explicable in terms of physics." But if the identity theory were true, not even those brain events which are identical with thoughts would be "explicable in terms of physics." Therefore, the identity theory and scientific materialism are incompatible.

3. According to the identity theory, the identity between a thought and a brain event is contingent. If there is a contingent identity between A and B, the identity ought to be empirically verifiable. It does not appear that it would be empirically verifiable that a thought was identical with a brain event. Therefore, if a thought and a brain event are claimed to be identical, it is not plausible to hold that the identity is contingent.

NORMAN MALCOLM, *Scientific Materialism and the Identity Theory*

Let me give a brief explanation of one point that underlies the position Smart is defending. Smart's key claim, of course, is that states of consciousness just identically *are* states of the brain. You might think that you could test a claim like that immediately and conclusively, merely by examining the meanings of the words used in making it. After all, when I say "John Smith identically is John Smith," I can tell that that is true merely from the logical fact that in general anything is identical to itself. By the same token, when I say "Bachelors just identically are unmarried men," I can tell that that is true by examining the words used and realizing that "bachelor" means "unmarried man." So if states of consciousness really are just identically brain states, then I should be able to tell that that is true forthwith. But although this seems natural enough, it turns out not to be true. The reason is that two words or phrases may refer to one and the same thing, even though that fact is not revealed by their meanings. Let me give you a simple example that has become famous in recent philosophy. It is originally from the influential German mathematician and philosopher Gottlob Frege. As some of you may have noticed, it is sometimes possible to see what looks like a very bright star in the heavens just before sunset. From ancient times, that body has been referred to as "the evening star." It is also sometimes possible to see what looks like a very bright star in the heavens just after sunrise. That has long been called "the morning star." The ancients did not know exactly what those two visible bodies were, and because they appeared in different parts of the skies (one in the east, the other in the west), it was assumed that they were different bodies. We now know that both the evening star and the morning star are the planet Venus, which is large enough and close enough to be faintly visible in daylight at certain times in its movements around the sun.

Now think what this means. If a medieval astronomer had said, "The evening star is just identically the morning star," he would have been exactly right, but he would not have been able to prove that he was right without telescopes and other modern astronomical instruments. One of his fellow astronomers might have said, "If they are identical, then you ought to be able to tell that they are just by examining the meanings of the words in your assertion." But plausible though that would have sounded, it would have been wrong. The object named by the phrase "morning star" is identical with the object named by the phrase "evening star," but that fact must be discovered by science; it cannot be deduced merely from the meanings of the words. Philosophers refer to this as a *contingent identity*. J. J. C. Smart claims that the phrase "state of consciousness" names identically the same object or state of affairs as the phrase "brain state," but he says that the identity is a contingent one, and hence must be discovered by science, rather than merely deduced from the meanings of those phrases.

IV

In Chapter Seven, you will recall, we took a look at the two-centuries-long debate started by Descartes over the nature and limits of human knowledge. In one selection from his *Meditations,* Descartes puzzled over the nature of his knowledge of the physical world. Reflecting on a piece of wax which he found ready to hand, he finally concluded that his knowledge of the physical nature of the wax must be derived from the use of his rational powers, rather than from his sensory interaction with the wax. This question of the origin of scientific knowledge—whether from reason, from the senses, or from some combination—has continued to fascinate and trouble philosophers to the present day.

The rationalists—Descartes and Leibniz foremost among them—concluded that true scientific knowledge must derive from reason rather than from the senses. Earlier in this chapter, we saw that Leibniz rested all of our scientific and metaphysical knowledge on two fundamental principles: the Law of Contradiction and the Principle of Sufficient Reason. It is hardly surprising that philosophers like Descartes and Leibniz adopted this point of view. Their ideal models of knowledge were mathematics and the new mathematical physics, and both appeal to reason rather than to the senses in establishing their principles.

The most powerful attack on the rationalist account of scientific knowledge came from the Scots skeptic, David Hume. In the last chapter, you read his famous critique of the concept of causation. Hume showed that the causal principles on which science was founded could not be defended by reason alone. As Kant later put it, science could not be known *a priori*.

But Hume didn't leave the scientist much to hope for from sense-perception and empirical observation either. Scientific laws, he pointed out, assert the existence of regularities in nature. Now, the most that observation and sense-experience can teach us is that these regularities have occurred in the past. In order to turn that observation into true knowledge, we must generalize to the future as well (and also to other past causes which we may not have observed). But at this point Descartes' old question—can I be certain?—rears its head. Neither reason nor the observation of past instances justifies me in asserting that those regularities will occur in the future. So, as you already know, Hume arrives at the skeptical, pessimistic conclusion that we cannot *know* anything substantive about the world. Here is a passage from one of Hume's later works, the *Enquiry Concerning the Human Understanding,* in which he summarizes his criticism of scientific efforts to reason from experience.

Here then is our natural state of ignorance with regard to the powers and influence of all objects. How is this remedied by experience? It only shows us a number of uniform effects, resulting from certain objects, and teaches us, that those particular objects, at that particular time, were endowed with such powers and forces. When a new object, endowed with similar sensible qualities, is produced, we expect similar powers and forces, and look for a like effect. From a body of like colour and consistence with bread, we expect like nourishment and support. But this surely is a step or progress of the mind, which wants to be explained. When a man says, *I have found, in all past instances, such sensible qualities conjoined with such secret powers:* And when he says, *similar sensible qualities will always be conjoined with similar secret powers;* he is not guilty of a tautology, nor are these propositions in any respect the same. You say that the one proposition is an inference from the other. But you must confess that the inference is not intuitive; neither is it demonstrative: Of what nature is it then? To say it is experimental, is begging the question. For all inferences from experience suppose, as their foundation, that the future will resemble the past, and that similar powers will be conjoined with similar sensible qualities. If there be any suspicion, that the course of nature may change, and that the past may be no rule for the future, all experience becomes useless, and can give rise to no inference or conclusion. It is impossible, therefore, that any arguments from experience can prove this resemblance of the past to the future; since all these arguments are founded on the supposition of that resemblance. Let the course of things be allowed hitherto ever so regular; that alone, without some new argument or inference, proves not, that, for the future, it will continue so. In vain do you pretend to have learned the nature of bodies from your past experience. Their secret nature, and consequently, all their effects and influence, may change, without any change in their sensible qualities. This happens sometimes, and with regard to some objects: Why may it not happen always, and with regard to all objects? What logic, what process of argument secures you against this supposition? My practice, you say, refutes my doubts. But you mistake the purport of my question. As an agent, I am quite satisifed in the point; but as a philosopher, who has some share of curiosity, I will not say scepticism, I want to learn the foundation of this inference. No reading, no enquiry has yet been able to remove my difficulty, or give me satisfaction in a matter of such importance.

DAVID HUME, *Enquiry Concerning the Human Understanding*

The problem posed by Hume has been given a name by philosophers. It is called the Problem of Induction. The problem is this: How can we reason from a collection of particular observations to the truth of a general proposition? The difficulty, as Hume makes quite clear, is that the general proposition always says more than is said by the particular observations with which we begin. The statement, All human beings are mortal, certainly says that Caesar is mortal, that Socrates is mortal, that Cleopatra is mortal, and so forth. But it also says that every human being now alive will die, as will any human beings who may be born in times to come. Now, how can I possibly *know* that that is true? I can point out that there are, thus far, no known cases of immortal human beings. But that simply does not constitute a sufficient ground for saying, with scientific certainty, that all human beings are mortal.

One reply to this line of argument, put forward by many philosophers and pretty well accepted today by most scientists, is that while Hume may, strictly speaking, be correct, science can still carry on, because the modern scientist deals in probability, not certainty. The mortality of all past humans may indeed fail to establish with certainty that all humans are mortal, but— these theorists say—it very nicely establishes the *probability* that all humans are mortal. And for scientific research and explanation, probability, not certainty, is all we need or can hope for. In this way, a large area of investigation was opened up into the rules and principles of inference governing the derivation of probabilistic conclusions from collections of data. Philosophers refer to this field as the study of probability and induction. You may have encountered one branch of it in the form of statistics, which is the science of manipulating masses of observations so as to yield general conclusions to which some degree of probability attaches.

In this section, we are going to take a closer look at the way in which science uses its general laws to explain the physical phenomena around us, and we shall therefore leave aside the complex and challenging subject of probability and induction. But it is worth pointing out that Hume's original objections to old-fashioned rationalist science can, with a few minor adjustments, be turned into very powerful objections to the newer inductive reasoning of modern science. There are still many philosophers who believe that no answer has been found to Hume's skeptical critique, and that contemporary science, like its seventeenth- and eighteenth-century predecessor, lacks a firm philosophical foundation.

Let us suppose that we have somehow acquired well-grounded principles of physical nature, either from induction based upon observation or from some sort of process of rational analysis. Suppose, for example, that we are prepared to accept the general principles of physics. How do we use this knowledge either to explain some particular event that has taken place or to predict what is going to happen in the future? Science, after all, is ultimately an attempt to understand, explain, and predict the events of nature. Merely knowing general principles, such as $F = ma$ (i.e., force equals mass times acceleration, Isaac Newton's so-called First Law), is a long way from knowing why my car runs, or why a toy top will balance on a string so long as it is spinning.

The most influential and widely discussed analysis of scientific explanation in modern philosophical literature was put forward by Carl G. Hempel. He and Paul Oppenheim summarized the analysis in an essay entitled "The Logic of Explanation." Hempel and Oppenheim quite obviously have in mind the more mathematical of the sciences, such as astronomy and physics, but they claim that their analysis of explanation applies to every branch of learning calling itself science. Elsewhere, Hempel even tried to apply his model to explanations in history, an attempt that has provoked a vigorous debate among philosophers and historians for almost forty years. Here is the basic statement of the theory of explanation.

> . . . . We divide an explanation into two major constituents, the explanandum and the explanans. By the explanandum, we understand the sentence describing the phenomenon to be explained (not that phenomenon itself); by the explanans, the class of those sentences which are adduced to account for the phenomenon. The explanans falls into two subclasses; one of these contains certain sentences $C_1, C_2, \ldots, C_k$ which state specific antecedent conditions; the other is a set of sentences $L_1, L_2, \ldots L_r$ which represent general laws.
>
> If a proposed explanation is to be sound, its constituents have to satisfy certain conditions of adequacy, which may be divided into logical and empirical conditions. For the following discussion, it will be sufficient to formulate these requirements in a slightly vague manner. . . .
>
> I. *Logical conditions of adequacy*
>   (R1) The explanandum must be a logical consequence of the explanans; in other words, the explanandum must be logically deducible from the information

contained in the explanans, for otherwise, the explanans would not constitute adequate grounds for the explanandum.

(R2) The explanans must contain general laws, and these must actually be required for the derivation of the explanandum.—We shall not make it a necessary condition for a sound explanation, however, that the explanans must contain at least one statement which is not a law; for, to mention just one reason, we would surely want to consider as an explanation the derivation of the general regularities governing the motion of double stars from the laws of celestial mechanics, even though all the statements in the explanans are general laws.

(R3) The explanans must have empirical content; i.e., it must be capable, at least in principle, of test by experiment or observation.—This condition is implicit in (R1); for since the explanandum is assumed to describe some empirical phenomenon, it follows from (R1) that the explanans entails at least one consequence of empirical character, and this fact confers upon it testability and empirical content. But the point deserves special mention because certain arguments which have been offered as explanations in the natural and in the social sciences violate this requirement.

II. *Empirical condition of adequacy*

(R4) The sentences constituting the explanans must be true.

That in a sound explanation, the statements constituting the explanans have to satisfy some condition of factual correctness is obvious. But it might seem more appropriate to stipulate that the explanans has to be highly confirmed by all the relevant evidence available rather than that it should be true. This stipulation however, leads to awkward consequences. Suppose that a certain phenomenon was explained at an earlier stage of science, by means of an explanans which was well supported by the evidence then at hand, but which has been highly disconfirmed by more recent empirical findings. In such a case, we would have to say that originally the explanatory account was a correct explanation, but that it ceased to be one later, when unfavorable evidence was discovered. This does not appear to accord with sound common usage, which directs us to say that on the basis of the limited initial evidence, the truth of the explanans, and thus the soundness of the explanation, had been quite probable, but that the ampler evidence now available made it highly probable that the explanans was not true, and hence that the account in question was not—and had never been—a correct explanation. . . .

Some of the characteristics of an explanation which have been indicated so far may be summarized in the following schema:

$$\left.\begin{array}{l} \left\{\begin{array}{ll} C_1, C_2, \ldots, C_k & \text{Statements of antecedent conditions} \\ L_1, L_2, \ldots, L_r & \text{General Laws} \end{array}\right\} \text{Explanans} \\ \hline E \quad \begin{array}{l}\text{Description of the empirical phenomenon to be explained}\end{array}\right\} \text{Explanandum}$$

Logical deduction

Let us note here that the same formal analysis, including the four necessary conditions, applies to scientific prediction as well as to explanation. The difference between the two is of a pragmatic character. If E is given, i.e. if we know that the phenomenon described by E has occurred, and a suitable set of statements C_1, C_2, . . ., C_k, L_1, L_2, . . . L_r is provided afterwards, we speak of an explanation of the phenomenon in question. If the latter statements are given and E is derived prior to the occurrence of the phenomenon it describes, we speak of a prediction. It may be said, therefore, that an explanation is not fully adequate unless its explanans, if taken account of in time, could have served as a basis for predicting the phenomenon under consideration. . . .

It is this potential predictive force which gives scientific explanation its importance: only to the extent that we are able to explain empirical facts can we attain the major objective of scientific research, namely not merely to record the phenomena of our experience, but to learn from them, by basing upon them theoretical generalizations which enable us to anticipate new occurrences and to control, at least to some extent, the changes in our environment.

CARL G. HEMPEL AND PAUL OPPENHEIM, *The Logic of Explanation*

The theory of scientific explanation set forth by Hempel and Oppenheim is associated with the so-called Vienna Circle, a group of philosophers and scientists who gathered in Vienna between World Wars I and II. The title "logical positivism" is frequently given to the point of view, or doctrine, developed by these philosophers. In the development of the theory of science, some of the members of the Vienna Circle employed very sophisticated techniques of formal logic, but their fundamental, underlying conception of the workings of science is actually very simple.

First of all, there are the observations of nature, the *data*. Some of these observations are simple, direct sensory reports, such as that the sun rose this morning or that a pot of water boiled when put over a fire. Most of the observations, however, involve scientific instruments such as telescopes, thermometers, or spectroscopes. Some may require exceedingly complicated equipment—electron microscopes, cyclotrons, or what have you. But, however the mass of data is collected, and whatever the scientists use in collecting it, once it has been collected, it stands alone as a solid base on which theories may be built and tested.

After the data have been collected, scientists perform *inductions* on the data, generalizing their observations in the form of general laws. These general laws are not known with certainty, as the old rationalists mistakenly thought. Rather, say the positivists, they are known only with probability. Elaborate systems of laws may be constructed, with a pyramid or hierarchy of laws from the most general down to the least general, but all of the laws, of whatever sort, are generalizations from the base of data collected by observation and experiment.

Finally, with the system of general laws in hand, the scientist can attempt to *explain* or *predict* new particular events. In the case of explanation, the scientist focusses on an event or an object that has already been observed. In the case of prediction, the focus of attention is an object or event that has not yet been observed. But in either case, the logical structure of the reasoning process is the same. As Hempel and Oppenheim make clear, the central idea of the positivists is always to exhibit a deductive connection between the statement of the general law and of certain initial conditions on the one hand, and the statement of the event to be explained or predicted on the other.

Simple as this description of the structure of science is, it has some very powerful and controversial implications. In the next few pages, we will explore some of these implications, and then take a look at a recent challenge to them by another modern philosopher of science.

Let us look first at the notion of a *data base,* a collection of factual observation reports. These reports, as we have seen, are used for at least three different purposes in the development and application of scientific knowledge. First, they are the basis for the inductions which give rise to the general laws. Second, they are used as statements of initial conditions (to use Hempel and Oppenheim's term), which, taken together with the general laws, imply the occurrence of the events being explained or predicted. And finally, as observation reports come in, they either confirm or disconfirm the predictions of scientists. This in turn leads the scientists either to keep or to change their theories. The observation reports are then added to the data and serve as elements for new inductions and new predictions or explanations.

The absolutely crucial fact about the reports which make up the data base is that they are public, objective, unbiased, factual reports. They are checkable reports, reports which scientists anywhere in the world can confirm in their own laboratories and then use in their own inductions, predictions, and explanations. We are all familiar with the international character of science. Science, unlike religion, art, and politics, seems to know no ideology, no borders, no language barriers. A scientific discovery may be announced by a team of researchers drawn from a dozen different nationalities. It may be confirmed, half way around the world, by men and women from entirely different backgrounds. At scientific meetings, Russians and Americans, Chinese and Germans, Nigerians and Mexicans, can exchange theories and experimental results regardless of their political ideology or religious convictions.

According to the logical positivist theory of science, the explanation for this universal characteristic of science, as opposed to virtually every other human endeavor, lies in the logical structure of scientific explanation and theorizing. Since the data base consists of objective reports of observations, it is universally available to any scientists for their use in formulating or testing theories. Indeed, from the positivist point of view, there is no reason at all to limit the usability of the data base to the human species. If there are other sentient life forms in the universe, they too can use our data, and we theirs, in the mutual advancement of our science.

More important even than the non-ideological, non-political, non-religious character of scientific reports is their absolute neutrality with regard to the theories that scientists build on them. According to the positivists, the data reports are logically prior to the inductions or generalizations we call laws. That is to say, the laws are known (with probability only, of course) on the basis of the data, but the data are *not* known on the basis of the laws. The data are known by direct observation of nature, either with or without the aid of scientific instruments. It follows from this characteristic of the data, which we can call its *theory-neutrality,* that two scientists with opposed theories have a common ground for debate, namely the data base which they share with all other scientists. If Dr. Jones and Professor Robinson have incompatible theories of the causes of cancer, they—or other scientists—can test those theories by looking at the data. Perhaps Jones is using general laws that are not strongly supported by the existing data base. Maybe Robinson's theory leads to predictions which are not confirmed by further observations. To be sure, Jones and Robinson personally may have a great deal riding on the argument—scientific reputation, important jobs, large amounts of grant money. But since the data are public and the rules of scientific reasoning are logical rules available to everyone, the private, personal concerns of Jones and Robinson will necessarily be set aside, and the international scientific community will decide between their theories on purely objective, scientific grounds.

It should be obvious, from this summary of the positivist view of science, that the positivists (the early ones, anyway) viewed science as a positive human good. Many of the positivist philosophers of science were victims of the Nazi persecution in Germany before World War II. They firmly believed that the objective, international, non-ideological character of science would serve as a force for humanity in the world. They hoped that it would break down barriers between nations and overcome the murderous religious and ideological conflicts that were setting people against one another. Although you may find it a bit hard to see the connection between a theory of the data base and a hope for world peace, these philosophers genuinely thought that by demonstrating the absolute impartiality and neutrality of the foundation on which all science was built, they were also demonstrating the possibility for a truly humanity-wide science.

The theory-neutrality of the data base has a second consequence that is even more important in the philosophical analysis of scientific knowledge, although its political and humanitarian significance may be considerably less. Since the data are logically independent of the theories that are built on them, it follows that data can, logically speaking, survive the death of a theory. New data can kill a theory, of course. But new theories cannot kill data. The only thing that can call an observational report into question is a new, more refined observation report, or the inability of other scientists to repeat in their laboratories the experiment which gave rise to the original report.

Why is this important? Very simply because it implies that science is cumulative, progressive, always growing, always expanding. The more experiments scientists do, the larger the data base will grow. The larger the data base grows, the more powerful and the more highly confirmed the generalizations that can be built on that base. So unlike art, in which one fashion or fad sweeps away another, or politics, in which there is endless fighting among opposed factions, or religion, in which you either have the absolute and unchangeable truth once-for-all or you have nothing—unlike all of these non-scientific activities of the human species, science can grow steadily and inexorably, always building on its past, but always surpassing its past. In short, the positivist analysis of the structure of scientific knowledge directly implies that science is the one necessarily progressive activity in an otherwise strife-torn world.

The positivist picture of science was in part the result of a logical analysis of the epistemological status of scientific theories. As the selection by Hempel and Oppenheim makes clear, the positivists were interested in understanding the relationships between evidence and conclusion, just as Descartes and Leibniz and Hume were. But Hempel and Oppenheim are twentieth-century philosophers, not seventeenth- or eighteenth-century philosophers, and their analysis of the logical structure of scientific explanation is obviously very profoundly influenced by the actual, historical development of science between the seventeenth and the twentieth centuries. In Leibniz's time, pure physics was an almost entirely non-experimental enterprise carried on by brilliant individuals (like himself) in ambitious, system-building efforts. With the extraordinary success of Isaac Newton in producing, as a very young man, a complete theoretical explanation of the movements of the heavenly bodies and the behavior of terrestrial bodies, it was obviously easy to imagine that the truth of the fundamental laws of nature could soon be grasped in its systematic entirety.

By the time the twentieth century arrived, science had totally changed. It is now an industry, a way of life, an activity engaging hundreds of thousands of men and women, using millions of dollars of complicated equipment. The natural sciences, by this time, have a history stretching back at least three centuries, and a future that seems unlimited. In the late nineteenth and early twentieth century, a series of shattering discoveries and developments in the physical sciences destroyed the old belief that the basic laws were already known, and that only the applications remained. Maxwell's theory of electromagnetism, Einstein's theory of relativity, Planck's quantum theory—these and many other innovations convinced students of science that there is no end to the new laws that scientists may discover, no limit to the scope of scientific knowledge. The positivist picture of science—the data base, the general laws, the explanations and predictions—was an attempt to make sense of what science had become in the twentieth century.

One of the curious side-effects of the philosophy of science was a more serious scholarly interest in the history of science itself. At first, of course, science did not seem to have a history. Indeed, to the seventeenth-century rationalists, science was the very opposite of history. Descartes' rules of rational investigation told us to put aside the fruits of past investigations, and accept only what we could confirm directly for ourselves. But clearly by the twentieth century, science as an enterprise had acquired a history too long, too complex, and too fascinating to be ignored. Historians and philosophers of science began to take a new look at such half-forgotten theories as the ancient Ptolemaic belief that the earth was at the center of the universe, or the curious "phlogiston" explanation for combustion. These students of science wanted to see whether they could figure out why some theories failed and others succeeded; they were curious to discover the actual reasoning processes by which scientists gave up one theory, which they had believed and used for a long time, and adopted a new, quite different theory, which might require them to change the way they were accustomed to think. The most immediate consequence of this new interest in the history of science was, of course, a richer understanding and appreciation of the process by which modern science had come into being. But a rather unexpected result of the close study of major turning points in the history of science was a major challenge to the positivist theory of the structure of scientific explanation.

The challenge was posed by a young physicist, historian of science, and philosopher named Thomas S. Kuhn, in a short book entitled *The Structure of Scientific Revolutions*. Kuhn published his book in 1962, and by a rather odd trick of historical accident, it first appeared as a long monograph in a big, cooperative two-volume work called *Foundations of the Unity of Science*, organized and written by the leading logical positivists of the day. No single book in the philosophy of science has had a wider audience or a more far-reaching influence than Kuhn's *The Structure of Scientific Revolutions*.

Kuhn's basic idea, like that of the positivists, is rather simple, but his picture of the history, development, and logic of science is completely different from theirs. Kuhn started out to take a close, careful historical look at some of the great turning points in the development of the physical sciences, moments when one major theory, such as the Ptolemaic conception of the universe, was given up, and another, such as the Copernican (sun-centered) theory was adopted. Now, if we believe the positivist story, then we ought to expect to discover that the transition from one theory to another goes something like this: first, the old theory is widely accepted, on the grounds that it does a better job of explaining and predicting than any other available theory. Then some new observations are made, some new data are reported, which do not fit the old theory. As these deviant data pile up, new inductions are performed, changes are made in the formulation of general laws, and bit by bit the old theory gives way to a new, more successful explanation or prediction of the observed facts. In this process, the positivists lead us to think, rational scientists from opposing theoretical camps will be able to agree on the data and on the logic of explanation or prediction. Therefore, they will be able to resolve their disagreements by debate, rational argument, and if necessary, further experimentation. To be sure, there may be some scientists who hold out for the old, discredited theory, but we, with the advantage of hindsight, ought to be able to see that they are allowing their personal commitments to cloud their scientific minds. In short, the giving up of an old theory and the adoption of a new one ought to be an objective, rational, step-by-step process, in which the new theory wins out because it has the weight of the evidence on its side. I think it is fair to say that even today, most of us imagine that science progresses in just this way.

What Kuhn actually discovered was wildly different from this idealized picture. First of all, it turned out that the new theory was frequently no better at explaining or predicting data than the old theory. What is more, when one took a look at what scientists of the day actually said about the competing theories, it was clear that the defenders of the theories that lost out were quite often as clear-headed, as rational, as objectively scientific, as the proponents of the new, soon-to-be-successful theories. The defenders of the theory that the earth is at the center of the universe weren't dodos. The critics of Newton's new physics weren't hidebound conservatives frightened of new ideas. They were perfectly reasonable scientists who pointed to quite sound reasons for rejecting the new theories.

Kuhn claimed that science did not at all progress slowly, incrementally, step-by-step. Instead, he suggested, the picture was entirely different. In an odd way, it was more like the history of a country which went through periodic political upheavals. Hence his title, "The Structure of Scientific *Revolutions.*" The key to his new description of science was the notion of a *revolution* in scientific thinking and practice.

Briefly, Kuhn's account went like this. At most times in the development of a science like physics, scientists share a ruling conception of how the universe works, what the *significant* experimental data are, what the well-established theories are, and how to go about their business of scientific research. This shared conception is dominated by, and derived from, some very striking and powerful experiment or theory which serves as a model for their own research. Kuhn calls this model a *paradigm,* and in a postscript added to the second edition of his book, he suggests that it might be helpful to think of it in much the way that we might think of a very great painting, which influences later painters and serves as a model which they try to imitate or follow. During the time that a paradigm rules in a branch of science, scientists are engaged in what Kuhn calls *normal science.* What he means is that scientists conduct experiments, collect data, check predictions, all in the service of supporting, developing, and checking the dominant theory.

From time to time, however, a situation of internal theoretical conflict develops within the science. Data may be collected which fail to confirm the predictions associated with the dominant theory. Now, deviant data are always turning up, even during periods of normal science. There is nothing unusual about that. But for some reason (Kuhn cannot tell us precisely why), at certain times these deviant data come to be viewed as counterinstances to the ruling theory, as disconfirmations of it, not simply as messy observations to be tidied up by a variation on the ruling theory.

For a time, scientists plug on, trying to fit the deviant data into the ruling theory. They do this not because they are pig-headed or narrow-minded, but because for scientists, as for anybody, something is always better than nothing. A theory that has been doing a very good job of explaining and predicting for some time is not going to be tossed out when there is nothing to take its place.

Sooner or later, some brilliant innovative scientist does a crucial experiment, formulates a new theory, which makes those deviant data fall into place. By a revolutionary leap, this theoretical rebel puts forward a totally new and different account of the realm that the other scientists have been exploring. Now a period of theoretical conflict occurs, during which the new theory wins supporters who do theoretical battle with the defenders of the established paradigm. In this conflict, the facts and the arguments are by no means all on one side. The new theory may explain data which the old theory could not handle; but very possibly, it will fail to do as good a job of explaining well-known data which the old theory handled very nicely. Debates will take place over which data are the truly significant ones, and as you can imagine, each side will accuse the other of placing the greatest emphasis on the data that its theory can explain the best.

Eventually, either the new theory fails to win adherents, and is rejected, or it conquers the older theory and becomes itself the ruling paradigm. The students and disciples of the revolutionaries settle into a new routine, and once more normal science becomes the order of the day.

It is obvious that Kuhn's account of the development of science differs greatly, simply as an historical story, from the account we would expect from the positivists (who were not, themselves, very interested in the history of science). It is perhaps not so obvious how completely Kuhn's account undermines the positivist belief in the objective, rational, progressive, humanitarian, world-unifying mission of science in the modern world.

Consider first the foundation-stone of the positivist theory: the data base. As we have seen, everything in the positivist analysis of science rests on their claim that the observational reports making up the data base are objective, theory-neutral reports, equally available to, and usable by, all scientists of whatever theoretical persuasion. Kuhn's analysis of science, however, casts serious doubt on this description of the data base. If Kuhn is correct, then scientists operating with different paradigms will disagree about more than their theories. They will even disagree about what are the data! In that case, it would seem, there will be no way at all for opposed theorists to arrive at common agreement by rational debate. Here is the opening paragraph from the section of Kuhn's book entitled "Revolutions as Changes of World View."

> Examining the record of past research from the vantage of contemporary historiography, the historian of science may be tempted to exclaim that when paradigms change, the world itself changes with them. Led by a new paradigm, scientists adopt new instruments and look in new places. Even more important, during revolutions scientists see new and different things when looking with familiar instruments in places

they have looked before. It is rather as if the professional community had been suddenly transported to another planet where familiar objects are seen in a different light and are joined by unfamiliar ones as well. Of course, nothing of quite that sort does occur: there is no geographical transplantation; outside the laboratory everyday affairs usually continue as before. Nevertheless, paradigm changes do cause scientists to see the world of their research-engagement differently. In so far as their only recourse to that world is through what they see and do, we may want to say that after a revolution scientists are responding to a different world.

THOMAS S. KUHN, *The Structure of Scientific Revolutions*

So it would seem, if Kuhn is correct, that the data base does *not* grow steadily and progressively as science advances. At each revolution, new data will be added to the base, but some old data will be thrown out. Last-ditch defenders of outmoded theories will find themselves appealing to "data" that the rest of the scientific community no longer considers to be data at all.

What is more, during the revolutionary period itself, there will be no objective, rational, universally-agreed-upon principles for settling the dispute between competing paradigms. The battle will be fought out in the learned journals and the laboratories, with each side reporting the data it considers truly significant and decisive, and both sides disputing the proper interpretation of such data as they can agree mutually to accept.

Now, this does not sound like the grand march of non-ideological, humanitarian science! It sounds like a political fight between two ideologies, or a theological dispute between two religious camps. Despite Kuhn's very strong disclaimers, this theory seems to come perilously close to equating success with truth. The theory that wins out, and becomes established as the basis of normal science, Kuhn seems to be saying, is the right one *because it wins*. Could science simply go wrong for a century or two? Could some crackpot working in a dusty cellar actually be right, when all the world says nay? Kuhn apparently is telling us that we have no other criterion, no other test, save actual historical success.

The positivist picture of science is, in my opinion, a great deal more attractive than the picture painted by Kuhn. I am old-fashioned enough to want to believe in the progressive march of science, in the ability of rational men and women to come to agreement on the basis of facts and arguments. There is, from my point of view, only one thing to be said for Kuhn's account of the nature of science. It fits the facts better. When we actually look at the history of science, Kuhn's model of periods of normal science dominated by paradigms, interrupted by revolutions in which new paradigms drive out old, explains and predicts better than the positivist story of slow, steady data accumulation and piecemeal theory change. In other words, the positivist standards for accepting and rejecting theories tell us that Kuhn's theory is better than the positivist theory. So, if we accept the positivist theory, we ought to reject it!

Philosophy, Socrates tells us, begins in wonder. Perhaps a philosophy textbook ought to end with paradox. The rest is up to you.

The American logician and philosopher of language Willard van Orman Quine once observed, rather wryly, that the fundamental question of ontology could be expressed in three Anglo-Saxon monosyllables: What is there? The correct answer, he went on to point out, can be given in a single word: everything. But though that is undoubtedly a true answer, it is scarcely illuminating.

When we ask, What is there?—or, more ponderously, What are the fundamental constituents of being?—we certainly do not want to be told that there is "everything." Nor, quite obviously, do we want a laundry list of particular things. We don't want someone to answer, "Well, there is my coat, and there is the sun, and there is the number twenty-three, and there is Henry Robinson, and etc., etc." Pretty clearly, what we are looking for is some idea of the basic *sorts of things* that there are. Some philosophers, as we have seen, claim that there is nothing in the world but physical objects in space; others argue that there is nothing but ideas in some mind; still others say that there are two basic types of things: physical objects in space, and ideas in minds.

The technical term first used by Aristotle for a basic *kind* of thing is *category,* and a great many of the philosophical debates over the past two and a half millennia have been about what to include in the list of categories into which we can divide up all the things there are. It is for this reason that Clarence Irving Lewis, in the selection included here from his classic work *Mind and the World Order,* begins by saying that the problem of metaphysics is "the problem of the categories."

In this chapter, we have looked at the three-cornered seventeenth- and eighteenth-century dispute among the school of philosophers known as "materialists," who said that the fundamental category of being is "matter in space," the school known as "idealists," who said that the fundamental category is "minds and their ideas," and the school known as "dualists," who said that there are *two* fundamental categories, neither one reducible to the other, namely "matter in space" and "minds with their ideas."

All of the proponents of these various positions assumed, virtually without argument, that the fundamental question of ontology has a single objective answer, true for all times and all places. The task of the philosopher, therefore, must be simply to discover that answer, and work out its ramifications and implications. Immanuel Kant made a revolutionary change in the philosophical treatment of the problem of the categories by advancing the idea that the basic categories of our world derive from the mind itself, rather than from God, or from nature. He argued that the categories are, in fact, the most fundamental ways in which the mind organizes its experience. If this is so, Kant recognized, then two conclusions follow, one of which seems quite optimistic, the other rather pessimistic. The optimistic conclusion is that if the mind is the origin of the structure of the experienced world, then we ought to be able to overcome the skepticism into which Hume had plunged us with his critique of the knowledge claims of science and ordinary experience. We ought to be able to know certain very general things about the structure of the world, assuming that that structure owes its existence and its form to the mind itself. The pessimistic conclusion was that if what we know, when we know the world, is some structure which the mind itself has imposed upon its experience, then there is no hope at all that we can know the nature of things as they are "in themselves." In the language which Kant used, we can know things "only as they appear to us" in the order or under the form of the mind's own categories.

But though Kant drastically changed the traditional way of thinking about the problem of the categories, he still clung to the ancient assumption that the categories must be everywhere and always the same for all mankind. This followed from his quite unexamined belief that the basic structure of the mind must be fixed and universal. If the mind was the source of the categories, then there must be one and only one set of categories for all minds and all experience.

In the nineteenth century, a number of philosophers, deeply influenced by developments in society as well as in science, began to explore the possibility that human nature itself might change over time. They began to ask whether an historical, or developmental, approach to the analysis of nature, society, and human nature might be more appropriate than the traditional view that the fundamental nature of things was fixed for all time. In the philosophy of C. I. Lewis, the Kantian conception of the categories as the mind's own way of organizing experience came together with the more modern idea that the categories of reality might vary from time to time, or from one society to another. The result was the quite distinctive and sophisticated theory set forth in this selection.

Lewis is one of the two or three most important American philosophers. For the first three centuries of our history, American philosophy, like so much else in the New World, was imported from the old country, from Great Britain and the Continent. The single major philosophical school associated primarily with the United States is the school of thought known as *pragmatism*. The most widely read representative of the pragmatist school is William James, and the most influential, through his writings on education, has been John Dewey. But it is in the writings of C. I. Lewis that the pragmatist doctrines of meaning and truth receive their most sophisticated and precise philosophical elaboration.

Two points in this selection are worthy of special notice. First, Lewis rejects the reductionist tendency of the logical positivists, among others, and insists on a pluralist analysis of the concept of the real. He refuses, in other words, to say that there is just *one* basic category of reality to which everything else must be "reduced." In this respect, Lewis follows Kant and Aristotle, rather than Plato, or Leibniz, or Hobbes. For Lewis, the issue in metaphysics is not which single sort of reality (mental or physical, universal or particular) is to be identified as *the truly real;* rather, it is what *sorts* of realities there are, and precisely what the demarcations among them are.

The second point is, in its way, quite revolutionary. Breaking with the tradition of analyzing the categories of being and the nature of knowledge from the point of view of the isolated human mind, Lewis argues that it is our collective human interests, our social concerns, that shape the categories of being that come to be embedded in our thought and language. In adding this social dimension to metaphysics and epistemology, Lewis reflects the influence of the newer disciplines of the social sciences. His theories can be compared, in this respect, to those of the American social psychologist George Herbert Mead. Lewis' work also bears a significant relationship to the branch of social science called "the sociology of knowledge," although he himself would probably have been intellectually out of sympathy with that school of early twentieth-century thought.

It is perhaps worth noting that Lewis was a logician as well as an epistemologist, metaphysician, and value theorist. Most of the important thinkers in the Western philosophical tradition have been students of, and sometimes original contributors to, the discipline of formal logic.

. . . The problem of metaphysics is "the problem of the categories."* The reason for this lies in a curious complexity of the meaning of "reality." Logical validity is at bottom of one single type. And perhaps the good and the right are relatively simple in their ultimate nature. But the adjective "real" is systematically ambiguous and can have a single meaning only in a special sense. The ascription of reality to the content of any particular experience is always elliptical: some qualification—material reality, psychic reality, mathematical reality—is always understood. And whatever is real in one such sense will be unreal in others. Conversely, every given content of experience is a reality of some sort or other; so that the problem of distinguishing real from unreal, the principles of which metaphysics seeks to formulate, is always a problem of right understanding, of referring the given experience to its proper category. The mirage, for example, though not real trees and water, is a real state of atmosphere and light; to relegate it to the limbo of nothingness would be to obliterate a genuine item of the objective world. A dream is illusory because the dreamer takes its images for physical things; but to the psychologist, interested in the scientific study of the mental, just these experienced images, occurring in just this context of other circumstance, constitute a reality to be embraced under law and having its own indisputable place in the realm of fact. The content of every experience is real when it is correctly understood, and is that kind of reality which it is then interpreted to be. Metaphysics is concerned to reveal just that set of major classifications of phenomena, and just those precise criteria of valid understanding, by which the whole array of given experience may be set in order and each item (ideally) assigned its intelligible and unambiguous place.

So understood, the principles of the categories, which metaphysics seeks, stand, on the one side, in close relation to experience and can not meaningfully transcend it. But on the other side—or in a different sense—they stand above or before experience, and are definitive or prescriptive, and hence a priori.

Whatever principles apply to experience must be phrased in terms of experience. The clues to the categorial† interpretation—the correct understanding—of any presentation of sense must be empirical clues. If they are not contained within that segment of experience which constitutes the phenomenon itself, then they must be discoverable in its relation to other empirical fact. If the dream or illusion is not betrayed by internal evidence, then its true nature must be disclosed by the conjunction with what precedes or follows. But while the distinguishing marks of reality of any particular sort are thus experimental, the principles by which the interpretation or classification is made are prior to the experience in question. It is only because the mind is prepared to judge

---

* A more logical terminology would qualify this as the "categories of reality," and would distinguish these from the "categories of value."

† "Categorial" is used throughout with the meaning "pertaining to the categories." This avoids possible confusion with "categorical," meaning specifically "unconditional, not hypothetical."

it real or unreal according as it bears or fails to bear certain marks, that interpretation of the given is possible at all, and that experience can be understood.

It is through reflective examination of experience (more particularly of our own part in it or attitude toward it) that we may correctly formulate these principles of the categories, since they are implicit in our practical dealings with the empirically given. But they are not empirical generalizations in the sense that some later experience may prove an exception and thus invalidate them. They formulate an attitude of interpretation or discrimination by which what would be exceptional is at once thrown out of court. For example, no experience of the physical can fail to bear those marks the absence of which would bar the given content of experience from interpretation as physical reality. The formulation of our deliberately taken, and consistently adhered to, attitude of interpretation constitutes a categorial *definition* of "the physical." Such a categorial definitive principle forbids nothing in the way of experience; it prohibits neither illusion nor senseless dream. Thus such principles are not material truths: they can be a priori—knowable with certainty in advance of experience—precisely because they impose no limitation upon the given but, as principles of interpretation, nevertheless condition it as a constituent of *reality*. . . .

So conceived, the principles which formulate criteria of the real, in its various types, are a priori in precisely the same sense as are the canons of ethics and of logic. Experience does not itself determine what is good or bad, or the nature of goodness, nor does it determine what is valid or invalid, or the nature of logical validity. Equally it does not determine what is real or unreal (in any particular sense), or the nature of reality. Experience does not categorize itself. The criteria of interpretation are of the mind; they are imposed upon the given by our active attitude.

The main business of a sound metaphysics is, thus, with the problem of the categories; the formulation of the criteria of reality, in its various types. It is to the shame of philosophy that these problems, which by their nature must be capable of precise solution since they require only persistent regard for fact and self-conscious examination of our own grounds of judgment, have been so generally neglected. Just this common disregard of verifiable fact and mundane criteria of the real is largely responsible for that quagmire of incertitude and welter of the irrelevant and vague which at present bears the name of metaphysics. The problems of the categories admit of as much real progress as those of logic; in fact, they are problems of the same general type. . . .

The definition of the real in general, and the picturing of reality as a whole, are subordinate matters; and perhaps, as has been suggested, the second of these is not possible. The word "real" has a single meaning, of course, in the same sense that "useful" or any other such elliptical term has a single meaning. Nothing is useful for every purpose, and perhaps everything is useful for some purpose. A definition of "useful" *in general* would not divide things into two classes, the useful and the useless. Nor could we arrive at such a definition by attempting to collect all useful things into a class and remark their common characters, since we should probably have everything in the class and nothing outside it to represent the useless. Instead, we should first have to consider the different types of usefulness or of useful things and then discover, if possible, what it is that characterizes the useful as contrasted with the useless in all these different cases. We should find, of course, that it was not some sense-quality but a relation to an end which was the universal mark of usefulness. Similarly, to arrive at a general definition of "the real" it would not do to lump together all sorts of realities in one class and seek directly for their common character. Everything in this class would be at once real, in some category, and unreal in others. And nothing would be left outside it. The subject of our generalization must be, instead, the distinction real-unreal in all the different categories. What definition of reality in general we might thus arrive at, we need not pause to inquire. Obviously it would be found to embrace some relation to empirical givenness in general or to our interpreting attitude, or to something involving both of these, rather than any particular and distinguishing empirical characteristics.

That in any case a successful definition of the real in general would not carry us far in any cosmological attempt to plumb the deeps of the universe, is evident from the fact that it would delimit reality in intension only, and would leave quite undetermined the particular content of reality *in extenso.* The total picture of reality can be drawn only when the last experience of the last man, and the final facts of science, are summed up. Why cosmology in this sense should be supposed to be the business of the philosopher—or of anyone else—I cannot see. In the nature of the case, it must be a coöperative enterprise, and presumably one that is always incomplete. . . .

It is only in and through the general course of human experience that we have a content for our philosophic thinking, and the significance of philosophic truth lies always in its application to experience. But it is experience from a certain point of view, or a certain aspect of it, with which we are concerned. Ethics cannot tell us how much of life is good, what particular sins are committed, or what proportion of men are moral; nor does metaphysics describe the course of the universe or determine the extent and the particulars of the real. It is the logical essence of goodness, the canons of validity, the criteria of the beautiful, and likewise, the principles of the distinction of real from unreal, that philosophy may hope to formulate. These criteria and principles, the mind itself brings to experience in its interpretation, its discriminations, and its evaluation of what is given. Thus philosophy is, so to speak, the mind's own study of itself in action; and the method of it is simply reflective. It seeks to formulate explicitly what from the beginning is our own creation and possession.

However, I should not like to appear to defend the notion that such analysis is a simple matter or that it requires only to express in precise terms the principles of common-sense. As has often enough been emphasized, common-sense is itself a naïve metaphysics and one which frequently breaks down on examination. Just as naïve morality may become confused before the dialectical attack, so common-sense categories of reality fail in crucial cases to meet the tests of consistency and accord with intelligent practice. It is true in metaphysics, as it is in ethics and in logic, that while valid principles must be supposed somehow implicit in the ordinary intercourse of mind with reality, they are not present in the sense of being fatally adhered to. If they were, the philosophic enterprise would have no practical value. Self-consciousness may be an end in itself, but if it did not have eventual influence upon human action it would be a luxury which humanity could not afford. That we coincide in our logical sense, does not make logic a work of supererogation. No more does coincidence in our ultimate sense of reality and in our categories render metaphysical discussion nugatory. Just as the study of logic may conduce to cogency of thought, and ethics contribute to greater clarity and consistency in moral judgment, so too the elucidation of metaphysical problems may contribute to the precision and adequacy of our interpretation of the real; it may even serve, on occasion, to work improvement in the concepts of the special sciences. Philosophy cannot be merely a verbally more precise rendering of common-sense, nor a direct generalization from actual practice. Though it rises from what is implicit in experience, its procedure must be critical, not descriptive. So far as it is to be of use, it must assume the function of sharpening and correcting an interpretation which has already entered into the fabric of that experience which is its datum. Logical principles aim to replace the uncritical moral sense, ethics, our naïve morality, and metaphysics, our unreflective ontological judgments. Such an enterprise is no simple matter of formulating the obvious.

The reflective method must, of course, be dialectical—in the Socratic-Platonic, not the Hegelian, sense. It accords with the Socratic presumption that the truth which is sought is already implicit in the mind which seeks it, and needs only to be elicited and brought to clear expression. It accords, further, in the recognition that it is definitions or "essences" which are the philosophic goal. And it likewise recognizes that the hope of agreement between minds, to be reached by philosophic discussion, must rest upon the presumption that this accord somehow exists already.

Historically, however, the dialectical method has been overlaid with all sorts of addenda, and perverted by extraneous assumptions which are fallacious. So that I should choose the name "reflective" as less liable to unwarranted interpretation. It does not follow from the dialectical method that the basis of the accord between minds represents some universal pattern of human reason, apart from the world of sense in which we live; nor that the mind has access to some realm of transcendent concepts which it recovers, of its own powers, at the instigation of experience; nor that agreement of minds presumes initial principles which are self-evident. It does not even follow that the agreement which we seek is already implicitly complete in all respects. To all such notions there is an alternative, to account for this agreement between minds, which is simple and even obvious. The coincidence of our fundamental criteria and principles is the combined result of the similarity of human animals, and of their primal interests, and the similarities of the experience with which they have to deal. More explicitly, it represents one result of the interplay between these two; the coincidence of human modes of behavior, particularly when the interests which such behavior serves involve coöperation.

Our categories are guides to action. Those attitudes which survive the test of practice will reflect not only the nature of the active creature but the general character of the experience he confronts. Thus, indirectly, even what is a priori may not be an exclusive product of "reason," or made in Plato's heaven in utter independence of the world we live in. Moreover, the fact that man survives and prospers by his social habits serves to accentuate and perfect agreement in our basic attitudes. Our common understanding and our common world may be, in part, created in response to our need to act together and to comprehend one another. Critical discussion is but a prolongation of that effort which we make to extend the bounds of successful human coöperation. It is no more necessary to suppose that agreement in fundamental principles is completely ready-made than it is to suppose that infants must already have precisely those ideas which later they find words to express. Indeed our categories are almost as much a social product as is language, and in something like the same sense. It is only the *possibility* of agreement which must be antecedently presumed. The "human mind" is a coincidence of individual minds which partly, no doubt, must be native, but partly is itself created by the social process. Even that likeness which is native would seem to consist in capacities and tendencies to action, not in mental content or explicit modes of thought. That the categories are fundamental in such wise that the social process can neither create nor alter them, is a rationalistic prejudice without foundation. There is much which is profound and true in traditional conceptions of the a priori. But equally it should be clear that there is much in such conceptions which smacks of magic and superstitious nonsense. Particularly it is implausible that what is a priori can be rooted in a "rational nature of man" which is something miraculous and beyond the bounds of psychological analysis and genetic explanation. . . .

It is of the essence of the dialectical or reflective method that we should recognize that proof, in philosophy, can be nothing more at bottom than persuasion. It makes no difference what the manner of presentation should be, whether deductive from initial assumptions, or inductive from example, or merely following the order dictated by clarity of exposition. If it be deductive, then the initial assumptions cannot coerce the mind. There are no propositions which are self-evident in isolation. So far as the deductive presentation hopes to convince of what was not previously believed, it must either seek out initial agreements from which it may proceed, or—as is more frequently the case—the deductively first propositions must be rendered significant and acceptable by exhibiting the cogency and general consonance with experience of their consequences. If the method be inductive from example, then the principles to be proved are implicit in the assumption that cited examples are veridical and typical and genuinely fall under the category to be investigated. There can be no Archimedean point for the philosopher. Proof, he can offer only in the sense of so connecting his theses as to exhibit their mutual support, and only through appeal to other minds to reflect upon their experience and their own attitudes and perceive that he correctly portrays them. If there be those minds which find no alternatives save certainty, apart from all appeal to prior fact, or skepticism, then to skepticism they are self-condemned. And much good may it do them! As philosophers, we have something we must be faithful to, even if that something be ourselves. If we are perverse, it is possible that our philosophy will consist of lies.

Already this introductory analysis of method is too long. But the conception of the a priori here suggested is a novel one: a little further discussion may have its value by way of anticipating briefly what is to follow.

If Philosophy is the study of the a priori, and is thus the mind's formulation of its own active attitudes, still the attitude which is the object of such study is one taken toward the content of an experience in some sense independent of and bound to be reflected in the attitude itself. What is a priori is prior to experience in almost the same sense that purpose is. Purposes are not dictated by the content of the given; they are our own. Yet purposes must take their shape and have their realization in terms of experience; the content of the given is not irrelevant to them. And purposes which can find no application will disappear. In somewhat the same fashion what is a priori and of the mind is prior to the content of the given, yet in another sense not altogether independent of experience in general.

It is an error common to rationalism and to pure empiricism that both attempt an impossible separation of something called the mind from something else called experience. Likewise both treat of knowledge as if it were a relation of the individual mind to external object in such wise that the existence of other minds is irrelevant; they do not sufficiently recognize the sense in which our truth is social. Traditional rationalism, observing that any principles which should serve as ultimate criterion or determine categorial interpretation must be prior to and independent of the experience to which it applies, has supposed that such principles must be innate and so discoverable by some sort of direct inspection. If a canon of their truth is requisite, this must be supplied by something of a higher order than experience, such as self-evidence or the natural light of reason. The mistakes of this point of view are two. In the first place, it assumes that mind is immediate to itself in a sense in which the object of experience is not. But what other means have we of discovering the mind save that same experience in which also external objects are presented? And if the object transcends the experience of it, is not this equally true of the mind? The single experience exhausts the reality of neither. Any particular experience is a whole within which that part or aspect which represents the legislative or categorial activity of mind and that which is given content, independent of the mind's interpretation, are separable only by analysis. We have no higher faculty or more esoteric experience through which the mind discovers itself. And second, rationalism fallaciously assumes that what is prior to, or legislative for, the particular experience must be likewise independent of experience in general. Though categorial principle must, in the nature of the case, be prior to the particular experience, it nevertheless represents an attitude which the mind has taken in the light of past experience as a whole, and one which would even be susceptible of change if confronted with some pervasive alteration in the general character of what is presented. . . .

Though we bring the a priori principle, as criterion, to any particular experience, yet this legislative attitude of mind is clearly one which is taken because, our experience on the whole being what it is, this principle helps to render it intelligible, and behavior in accord with it is normally successful. The mind must bring to experience whatever serve as the criteria of interpretation—of the real, as of the right, the beautiful, and the valid. The content of experience cannot evaluate or interpret itself. Nevertheless the validity of such interpretation must reflect the character of experience in general, and meet the pragmatic test of value as a guide to action.

The fallacy of pure empiricism is the converse of that which rationalism commits. In seeking to identify the real with what is given in experience, apart from construction or interpretation by the mind, and to elicit general principles directly from the content of experience, empiricism condemns itself to a vicious circle. Experience as it comes to us contains not only the real but all the content of illusion, dream, hallucination, and misapprehension. When the empiricist supposes that laws or principles can be derived simply by generalization from experience, he *means* to refer only to *veridical* experience, forgetting that without the criterion of legislative principle experience cannot first be sorted into veridical and illusory. . . .

It is obvious that similar considerations hold for the other problems of philosophy. The nature of the good can be learned from experience only if the content of experience be first classified into good and bad, or grades of better and worse. Such classification or grading already involves the legislative application of the same principle which is sought. In logic, principles can be elicited by generalization from examples only if cases of valid reasoning have first been segregated by some criterion. It is this criterion which the generalization is required to disclose. In esthetics, the laws of the beautiful may be derived from experience only if the criteria of beauty have first been correctly applied.

The world of experience is not given in experience: it is constructed by thought from the data of sense. This reality which everybody knows reflects the structure of human intelligence as much as it does the nature of the independently given sensory content. It is a whole in which mind and what is given to mind already meet and are interwoven. The datum of our philosophic study is not the "buzzing, blooming confusion" on which the infant first opens his eyes, not the thin experience of immediate sensation, but the thick experience of every-day life.

This experience of *reality* exists only because the mind of man takes attitudes and makes interpretations. The buzzing, blooming confusion could not become reality for an oyster. A purely passive consciousness, if such can be conceived, would find no use for the concept of reality, because it would find none for the idea of the *un*real; because it would take no attitude that could be balked, and make no interpretation which conceivably could be mistaken.

On the other hand, we can discover mind and its principles only by analysis in this experience which we have. We cannot, unless dogmatically, construct experience from a hypothetical and transcendent mind working upon a material which likewise is something beyond experience. We can only discover mind and what is independently given to it by an analysis within experience itself. And it is only because mind has entered into the structure of the real world which we know and the experience of everyday, that analysis, or *any* attempted knowledge, may discover it.

In finding thus that the principles and criteria which philosophy seeks to formulate must be significant at once of experience and of our active attitudes, the reflective method inevitably is pragmatic also. Concepts and principles reveal themselves as instruments of interpretation; their meaning lies in the empirical consequences of the active attitude. The categories are ways of dealing with what is given to the mind, and if they had no practical consequences, the mind would never use them. Since philosophy seeks to formulate what is implicit in mind's every-day interpretations, we may test the significance of any philosophic principle, and pave the way for determining its truth, if we ask: How would experience be different if this should be correct than if it should be false? or, How differently should we orient ourselves to experience and deal with it if this should be so than if it should be not so? . . .

The totality of the possible experiences in which any interpretation would be verified—the completest possible empirical verification which is conceivable—constitutes the entire meaning which that interpretation has. A predication of reality to what transcends experience completely and in every sense, is not problematic; it is nonsense. . . .

To sum up, then: The reflective method is empirical and analytic in that it recognizes experience in general as the datum of philosophy. But it is not empirical in the sense of taking this experience to coincide with data of sense which are merely given to the mind. Nor is it analytic in the sense of supposing that experience is complete and ready-made.

Rather, it finds that philosophy is particularly concerned with that part or aspect of experience which the mind contributes by its attitude of interpretation. In thus recognizing that the principles which are sought are in some sense a priori, it is rationalistic.

It is not rationalistic, however, in the sense of presuming the mind as a Procrustean bed into which experience is forced, or as an initial datum which can be assumed or its findings known apart from sense-experience. Nor does it presume the "rational human mind" as something completely identical in and native to all human beings, or as a transcendent entity which, even if it lived in some other world of sense, would still possess precisely the same categories and pattern of intelligence.

The reflective method is pragmatic in the same sense that it is empirical and analytic. It supposes that the categories and principles which it seeks must already be implicit in human experience and human attitude. The significance of such fundamental conceptions must always be practical because thought and action are continuous, and because no other origin of them can be plausible than an origin which reflects their bearing on experience. . . .

The reflective method necessarily leads to the repudiation of any reality supposed to be transcendent of experience altogether. A true philosophic interpretation must always follow the clues of the practical reasons for our predications. A philosophy which relegates any object of human thought to the transcendent, is false to the human interests which have created that thought, and to the experience which gives it meaning. Philosophic truth, like knowledge in general, is about experience, and not about something strangely beyond the ken of man, open only to the seer and the prophet. We all know the nature of life and of the real, though only with exquisite care can we tell the truth about them.

TOPICS FOR FURTHER STUDY

1. According to Lewis, we must adopt the "reflective" method when we investigate the categories of reality. Like Socrates, he believes that the answers to philosophical questions lie in our own minds, not in the world. No amount of experience can settle for us the question whether an electron is a physical object, or what sort of reality dreams have. But then how can philosophers resolve disputes between opposed metaphysical camps? Must we simply give up, and conclude that the materialists, the idealists, and the dualists each have "their own point of view"?

2. Lewis's pragmatism comes to the fore in his statement that "our categories are guides to action." What does this mean? Could we have categories that were *bad* guides to action, as we might have a map that was a bad guide to the area in which we found ourselves? Would that show that our categories were wrong? Is it foolish to cling to categories that do not guide us efficiently? If the answer is yes, can we also say that it is foolish to cling to moral principles that make us uncomfortable or that tell us to do what is difficult and unpleasant? What is the difference in the two cases?

3. Our categories of reality, Lewis claims, are socially determined. But society is composed of diverse groups with quite varied interests. Are the believers in ghosts, for example, *wrong* to suppose that such things exist, or are they merely a social group with different collective interests and a different set of categories? Does Lewis's theory of categories permit us to make rational assessments of competing accounts of the nature of reality?

4. The metaphysicians of the seventeenth and eighteenth centuries (Descartes, Leibniz, Kant, and others) were concerned to give an account of the categories of reality that would make sense of the new physics and cosmology. The developments in the social sciences of the nineteenth and twentieth centuries created new conceptual and theoretical problems for the "theory of the categories." Should philosophers accept the natural and social sciences as our best guide to the nature of reality? What role should religious doctrine play in shaping our conception of the categories of reality?

SUGGESTIONS FOR FURTHER READING

Metaphysics

ARISTOTLE, *Metaphysics*

D. M. ARMSTRONG, *A Materialistic Theory of Mind*

G. BERKELEY, *Three Dialogues Between Hylas and Philonous*

A. FLEW (ed.), *Body, Mind and Death*

MARTIN HEIDEGGER, *What Is Metaphysics?*

IMMANUEL KANT, *A Critique of Pure Reason*

P. LASLETT (ed.), *The Physical Basis of Mind*

J. O'CONNOR, (ed.), *Modern Materialism: Readings on Mind-Body Identity*

GILBERT RYLE, *The Concept of Mind*

G. N. A. VESEY (ed.), *Body and Mind*

JOHN WISDOM, *Problems of Mind and Matter*

Philosophy of Science

ROBERT J. ACKERMANN, *The Philosophy of Science*

P. K. FEYERABEND and G. MAXWELL (eds.), *Mind, Matter, and Method*

N. R. HANSON, *Patterns of Discovery*

IMRE LAKATOS and A. MUSGRAVE (eds.), *Problems in the Philosophy of Science*

ERNEST NAGEL, *The Structure of Science*

KARL R. POPPER, *Objective Knowledge*

FEROME RAVETZ, *Scientific Knowledge and Its Problems*

GLOSSARY

Absolute theory of space   The theory that space exists independently of the things in space, so that it makes sense to talk about the absolute position or location or dimensions of a body in space

Alienation   The estrangement of individuals from the product of their labor, from the labor itself, from their own human nature, and from their fellow workers

Analytic proposition   A statement that merely spells out what is already contained in the subject of the statement

Anarchist   One who believes that no state has any right to rule and that governmental authority is illegitimate and undesirable

a posteriori   As a consequence of experience of objects—an adverb used to modify verbs of cognition, as "to know *a posteriori*" or "to apprehend *a posteriori.*"

Propositions are said to be knowable *a posteriori* when they are knowable only as a consequence of an experience of the objects they make assertions about.

a priori   Prior to, or independently of, experience—an adverb used to modify verbs of cognition, as "to know *a priori*." Propositions are said to be knowable *a priori* when they are knowable prior to, or independently of, any experience of the objects they make assertions about.

Argument from Design   The proof of the existence of God, employed by William Paley, that states that from the extraordinary intricacy of nature, it can be inferred that its Creator is an intelligent, purposeful, all-powerful Maker, who in His infinite wisdom has adjusted means to ends, part to whole, organ to organism, throughout the whole of space and time

Attributes   The characteristics, states, activities or features which predicates name or refer to

Capitalism   An economic system based on private or corporate ownership of the means of production and distribution of goods in a marketplace that determines prices and quantity of production by competition in a free market

Categorical imperative   A moral law that is absolute and universally binding

Cogito, ergo sum   "I think, therefore I am"—the phrase used by Descartes to prove his own existence

Copy theory of ideas   The theory that all our ideas are either copies of sense impressions or else combinations and rearrangements of copies of sense impressions

Cosmological argument for the existence of God   The argument, first stated by Aristotle, that infers the existence of a first cause, or first mover, or necessary being, from the fact that there are causes and effects, or bodies in motion, or contingent beings, in the observable world. The argument was developed and perfected by St. Thomas Aquinas.

Cosmology   The study of the nature of the world

Dialectic   The use of dialogue to attempt to discover the answer to a philosophical question

Dialogue   A process of question and answer between two people

Dualism   The theory that the universe is composed of two fundamentally different sorts of things: minds and bodies

Empiricism   The theory that all knowledge is derived from sense experience

Epistemological turn   A shift in philosophy from emphasis on metaphysics to emphasis on epistemology

Epistemology   The study of the limits and capabilities of the mind to acquire and understand knowledge

Ethics   The study of the rational grounds of right action

Fascism   A system of government that advocates that the goals of the nation and/or race take priority over those of the individual

Historical materialism   The Marxist theory that ideas and social institutions develop only as a reflection of a material economic base

Idealism   The theory that everything in the universe is a mind, and that bodies are to be analyzed as collections of, aspects of, or thoughts in, minds

Instrumental value   The worth a thing has as a means to an end other than the thing itself

Intrinsic value   The worth a thing has in and of itself

Irony   A mode of discourse by which the speaker communicates, to the real audience, a meaning opposite from that conveyed to the superficial, or apparent audience

Law of Contradiction   The fundamental principle of logic. It asserts that if a statement asserts a meaningful proposition, then the statement and its negation cannot both be true.

Law of the Excluded Middle   The principle that if a statement asserts a meaningful proposition, then either the statement is true, or its negation is true, and there is no third possibility

Logic   The discipline that investigates the correct principles of formal reasoning—sometimes characterized as the science of the laws of thought

Materialism   The theory that everything in the universe is a body, and minds are to be analyzed as collections of, or aspects of, or configurations of, bodies

Metaphysics   The study of the forms and nature of being and the structure of the universe

Method of doubt   The suspension of judgment in regard to knowledge claims until they have been demonstrated to be either true or false

Monad   A simple substance without parts—the fundamental element in the metaphysical theories of Leibniz

Natural law   A rational principle of order or a norm in accordance with which the universe has been created or organized. Both the physical universe and the moral order of human society are thought, by one major philosophical tradition, to be guided by natural law.

Neo-classicism   The philosophy of art that exalts order, proportion, and reason, and subordinates artistic creativity to objective principles of aesthetic taste

Ontological argument for the existence of God   An argument first put forward by St. Anselm, which claims to deduce the actual existence of God from the mere concept of God as that being than which no greater can be conceived

Popular sovereignty   The doctrine that ultimate political authority (sovereignty) belongs to the people who are governed

Principle of sufficient reason   A principle, stated by Leibniz, according to which no fact can be real and no statement true unless it has a sufficient reason why it should be thus

Proletariat   The class of industrial workers who, Marx believed, would eventually rise up against the ruling capitalist class and take control of the means of production

Rationalism   The doctrine that reason, as opposed to sense experience, is the primary source of knowledge

Relational theory of space   The theory that space is the totality of the relations of substances, so that it only makes sense to talk about the position or location or dimension of a body in space in relation to the rest of the system of other bodies

Repression   A process by which unacceptable impulses or desires are excluded from consciousness and left to operate in the unconscious

Romanticism   The philosophy of art that denies the supremacy of reason in art and holds that the power of creative imagination is the highest human faculty

Skepticism   The doctrine that certainty with regard to any principle or matter of fact is impossible

Social contract   A collective agreement, by the members of a society, concerning the fundamental, or constitutional, rules by which the society shall be governed

Socialism   The doctrine that the working class should, and will, collectively control the means of production and use them to satisfy human needs rather than to gain a profit

Social relationships of production   The system of relationships into which people enter by virtue of the role they play in the material production of goods and services in society

Solipsism   The doctrine that only I, the thinking self, exist, all else being merely ideas in my mind

Sovereignty   Supreme political authority. A right to rule that takes precedence over all else

State, the   The group of people who rule, give orders, run things, and enforce the rules of social groups within defined territorial limits or borders

Stoics   Ancient Greek philosophers who believed that the natural world exhibits an order that can be understood through rational inquiry

Substance   Anything that can have attributes predicated of it, but which itself cannot be predicated as an attribute of any other thing

Synthetic proposition   A statement that adds something to what is contained in the idea of the subject of the proposition

Tautology   A proposition that can be known to be true merely on the basis of the meanings of the words used in it

Teleology   A study of the purposes, or ends, of natural things—also, the belief that nature has a purpose or goal toward which it tends

Transcendence   A going beyond the given natural or social reality—in Marcuse, the imaginative leap beyond the given social world, with its repressions, oppressions, and its reality-oriented sacrifices, to the conception of possible future social orders in which some of the repressed libidinal energy has been liberated

Truth of fact   Truths that can be certified only by appeal to empirical evidence

Unity of consciousness   The connection, or unity, exhibited by all the contents of the consciousness of a single mind—according to Kant, the most fundamental feature of any consciousness at all

Utilitarianism   The ethical theory which teaches that in every situation, the right act is the act which is most likely to bring the greatest amount of pleasure to the most people

INDEX

Abortion, 83–84, 85–92
Abortion and the Concept of a Person, 85–92
Academy, the, 188–89
Adequacy
  empirical condition of, 344–45
  logical conditions of, 343–44
Alienation, 110–18, 159
Analogy, 240
  argument from, 236–37
Analytic proposition, defined, 249
Anarchists, 142
Anaximander, 15, 17, 20
Anaximenes, 15

Anselm, St., 236, 246–49, 251, 256, 262
Anthropology and the Abnormal, 58–59
Appearance *vs.* reality, 181–82
Apprehension, evil of, 71
Aquinas, St. Thomas, 188–89, 236, 241–44, 251, 256
Argument from Design
  David Hume on, 240–41
  weaknesses, 239–41
  William Paley on, 236–38
Aristotle, 77, 189, 276, 277, 317, 330
Art
  in Aristotle, 190–91, 193
  and change, 206

Art (*Cont.*)
  cognitive value, 212
  infectiousness of, 202
  intrinsic value of, 195
  negative, 209–10
  philosophy of, 178–220
  in Plato, 183–88, 193
  reason in, 197
  religious dimension, 203–5
  sincerity of, 202–3
  social function, 209–11
Atomic theory, of contents of mind, 294–95
Atomism, 15–16
Atomists, 318–19
Atoms, structure of, 18
Attributes, and substance, 317–18
Augustan Age, 197
Augustus, Caesar, 197
Aurelius, Marcus, 23–24, 77
Authority
  legitimacy of, 142
  limits of, 166
  and personal autonomy, 143
Autonomy, 60, 63–64
  loss of, 143

Bedau, Hugo, 168
Bell, Clive, 195
Benedict, Ruth, 58–59
Bentham, Jeremy, 66, 67–68, 71–72, 96, 195
Berkeley, George, 25, 181, 271, 290–91
Bourgeois culture, 227–28, 229
British empiricists, 285–86
Burke, Edmund, 153, 154

Capitalism, 98–100, 159
  and alienation, 117–18
  irrationality of, 115–16, 119
  as social force, 106
Categorical imperative, 59–62

Categories, 299, 353–54
Certainty, 283–84
Childhood and Society, 82
Chopin, Frederick, 198
Christianity, and Kierkegaard, 226–27
Civil disobedience, 167–76
Civilization, origins of, 207
Civilization and its Discontents, 207
Coercion, evil of, 71
Cogito argument, 282–84, 298–99
Collective ownership, 119
Communication
  and art, 218–19
  of feelings, 201–2
Communism, 119
Communist party, 166–67
Concept, defined, 306
Concerning the Human Understanding, 290
Concluding Unscientific Postscript to the Philosophical Fragments, 233–34
Consciousness, 298–99
  nature of, 336
Conservative, ideal, 111–12
Continental rationalists, 285–86
Contingent identity, 340
Contracts, and human experience, 153
Contradiction, law of, 287–88, 341
Copernican theory, 349
Copy theory, 294
Cosmological argument, 241–44
  refutation of, 244–46
Cosmologists, 276
Cosmology, 19–20
  defined, 13
  theories of, 14
Creation myths, 14
Criticism, 53
Critique of Pure Reason, 28, 231, 249, 250–51, 276

Data base, 346, 347–48
Death, inevitability of, 224
Delacroix, Eugene, 197
Democritus, 17, 333

Descartes, René, 17, 257, 262, 268–82, 284, 319, 331–33
de Tocqueville, Alexis, 100, 112–14
Dewey, John, 354
Dialectical argument, 9
Dialogue, 6–7, 180–81
Dialogues (Plato's), 180–88
Dialogues Concerning Natural Religion, 237, 239, 240–41, 245–46
Discourse on Method, 273
Distributive Justice, 125–33
Division of labor, 160
Doctrine of Fascism, The, 156–58
Doctrine of the people, 156
Double audience, 7–8, 10
Dreams
  interpretation of, 272–73
  and reality, 270
Dualism, 332

Economic order, 159
Economic–Philosophic Manuscripts of 1844, 117–18
Edman, Irwin, 51
Education, weapon of utilitarians, 98
Ego, origins of, 207
Ego integrity, 81
Electromagnetism, theory of, 348
Empirical observation, 341
End, distinct from means, 108–9
Engels, Friedrich, 159, 164–65
Enquiry Concerning the Human Understanding, 341–42
Entrepreneur, 98
Epicurus, 17, 333
Epistemological turn, 274, 276
Epistemology, 28, 271–72. *See also* Knowledge, theory of
  and interpretation of Work of God, 272
Erikson, Erik, 77, 81
Eros and Civilization, 207
Essay Concerning the Human Understanding, 286
Ethical relativist, 58
Ethical skepticism, 57–58

Ethics, 52–92
Euclidean geometry, 274
Euclidean theorem, 263
Evangelists, 226
Excluded middle, law of the, 287
Existence, cause of, 295
Existentialism, 223
Expressive form, 212

Faith, and existence of God, 251
Fascism, 153, 156
Fetus, as person, 84, 85–92
Findlay, J. N., 263
Form(s)
  abstract, 215–16
  and art, 190
  discursive, 217–18
  dynamic, 216
  expressive, 212–13
  logical, 216
  significant, 214
  universal, 191
Frankfurt School of Social Research, 206
Freedom, 112–14
  in social contract, 144, 148
Free market system, 99
Frege, Gottlob, 340
Freud, Sigmund, 81, 207, 252–55
  as rationalist, 253
Fromm, Eric, 77
Future of an Illusion, The, 254–55

Gassendi, Pierre, 333
Gell–Mann, Murray, 20
God
  attributes of, 239
  belief in, 224–26
  concrete existence of, 262–63
  contingent existence of, 261
  defined, 248
  impossibility of nonexistence, 259

God (*Cont.*)
  necessary existence of, 257, 261
  proofs of existence of, 235–36
    argument from design, 236–41
    cosmological argument, 241–46
    ontological argument, 246–51
  sources for beliefs about, 241
  unlimited being, 259
Good life, principles of, 76–77
Gorgias, 32–33, 182–84
Gravity, 327
Greatest Happiness Principle, 66, 71–76
Groundwork of the Metaphysic of Morals,
    62–63, 63–64, 65–66

Hegel, Georg Wilhelm Friedrich, 34, 228
Hegelian philosophy, 228–29
*Herr Eugen Dühring's Revolution in
    Science,* 164
Historical materialism, 159
Hobbes, Thomas, 333–36
Humanity, intrinsic value of, 195
Hume, David, 25–28, 57, 139, 149, 236,
    237, 271, 286, 290, 292, 341–43

Idealism, 332
Ideas, of God, 290–91
Identity crisis, 81
Ignorance, and enlightenment, 98
Imagination, as highest human faculty,
    197
Induction, 345
Industrialism, 155
  conservative reaction to, 114
Industrialization, 252
Instrumentalists, 202
Instrumental value, 193
Intentions, 196–97
*Introduction to the Principles of Morals
    and Legislation,* 67–68, 71–72
Introspection, 304–5
Irony, 7–10, 11

James, William, 354
Journal of Metaphysics, 231
Justice, 77
Just society, 123

Kant, Immanuel, 25, 50–53, 76, 137, 143,
    195, 236, 249–51, 257, 262, 263,
    265, 271, 276, 298
  categorical imperative of, 59–62
Kennedy, John F., 166
Kierkegaard, Søren, 22–34, 251
Kingdom of ends, 65–66
Knowledge
  by acquaintance, 303–4
  by description, 303, 306–7
  psychological criteria for, 287
  scientific, 340
  sociology of, 354
  sources of, 283–86
  structure of, 287
  test of, 197
  theory(ies) of, 24–25, 268–310
Kuhn, Thomas S., 349–52

Laissez-faire, 114
  doctrine of, 103–5
Laissez-faire economic theory, 98
Langer, Susanne K., 213–20
Language, 353
Law, obedience to, 142
Leap of faith, 229, 230–31, 232
Leibniz, Gottfried, 17, 256, 271, 272, 286,
    288, 312–13, 315–30
Leibniz–Clarke Correspondence, 325–26
Leviathan, 334–36
Lewis, Clarence Irving, 354
Liberalism, conservative reaction to, 114
Locke, John, 25, 150–53, 271, 286, 289–
    92
Logical positivism, 345
Logic of Explanation, The, 345
Lucretius, 15, 17, 333
Lyrical Ballads, 198–200

Majority rule, 147–48
Malcolm, Norman, 256
  Anselm's Ontological Arguments,
    258
Mao Tse-Tung, 165
Marcuse, Herbert, 206–11
Marx, Karl, 77, 98, 100, 114–22, 159–
    65, 229, 252
Material base, of society, 159–60
Materialism, 332–40
  defined, 337–39
Materialism, 337–39
Mead, George Herbert, 354
Meaning, theory of, 325
Meditations, 24
Meditations on First Philosophy, 269, 274,
    279–82, 284–85
Memory, 304
Mental illness, 81
Metaphysics, 191, 276, 312–64
  defined, 184
  meaning of, 313–15
  questions of, 314–15
Method of doubt, 274–76, 277–79
Method of inquiry, 274
Middle-class culture, 227
Milesians, themes of, 14–15
Mill, James, 98
Mill, John Stuart, 94–106
Mind and the World Order, 353
Mind–body interaction, 336
Modal concepts, 256
Model of social organization, 159
Monads
  concept of windowless, 328–29
  defined, 320
  harmony, 328
  interactions between, 327
  properties of, 322
  theory of, 320–21
Monadology, The, 288–89, 320–21
Moral agents, 61–62
Morality, 52–92
  cultural influence on, 57
Moral law, persons as authors of,
    60
Mussolini, Benito, 156–58

Nationalities, and political independence,
    155
Natural law, 23
Natural Theology, 237–38
Negation, 287
Negative thinking, theory of function of,
    208–9
Neo-classicism, 197
Neo-Platonists, 198
Newton, Isaac, 272, 292, 327
Normal science, 350

Oakeshott, Michael, 108–10, 193
Of the Original Contract, 149–50
Old Régime and the French Revolution,
    The, 114
On Civil Disobedience, 168
One-Dimensional Man, 120–21, 210–11
One-substance theory, 332
On the Nature of Things, 16–17
Ontological argument, 246, 256
  refutation, 249–51
Organic theory of state, 154–55

Paley, William, 251
Paradigm, 350
Pater, Walter, 195
Perception, 292
  unity of, 299
Person, concept of, 85–92
Personality development, 81
Phenomenological fallacy, 338
Phenomenology of Mind, 231
Philosophical Fragments, 231
Philosophical Perplexity, 36–48
Philosophy
  defined, 31, 34, 35
  range of, 20–21
Phlogiston theory, 349
Physical nature, principles of, 343
Physics, 277
Plato, 5, 9, 17, 77, 121–22, 155, 179–93,
    197–98, 252

Plato (*Cont.*)
 on art, 183–88
 philosophical theory, 182–88
Pleasure
 addition of, 66, 69
 and capitalism, 99–100
 as good, 67
 and utilitarianism, 97–98
Pleasure principle, 207
Poetics, The, 190, 191–93
Political obligation, 144–45
Political philosophy, 136–76
 defined, 140
Positivists, 347–48
Positivist theory, 351
Pragmatism, 354
Prime mover, 190
Principia Mathematica (Russell and
  Whitehead), 17
Principles of Political Economy, 103–4,
  105–6
Principle of Sufficient Reason, 288, 341
Principle of utility, 68, 75
 applied to social issues, 96
Problem of the Categories, The, 355–63
Problem of Induction, 342
Problems of Art, 213–20
Probability, 342
Production, role of economic, 160
Profit, and pleasure, 104–5
Proletarian revolution, 164–65, 252
Proslogion, 246–47, 258
Psychiatry, development of, 81
Psychoanalytic theory, 81, 252
Psychology and reason, 191
Punishment, unprofitable, 71–72

Quantum theory, 348
Quasi-contract, 152
Quine, Willard van Orman, 123, 353–54

Rational agent, 60–62, 108
Rational investigation, 348–49

Rationalism in Politics, 109–10
Rationalists, 109–10
 and scientific knowledge, 341
Rational philosophy, 229–30
Rawls, John, 124–33
Reality, knowledge of, 181–82
Reality principle, 207
Reason, 182
 in art, 198
 and existence of God, 251
 and knowledge of God, 241
 utilitarian concept of, 107–8
Reflections on the French Revolution, 154
Relativity, theory of, 348
Religion
 attacks on, 252–55
 decline of, 252
 Freud's view, 254–55
 philosophy of, 222–66
Religious revival, 252
Repression, 207–8
 necessary, 208
 surplus, 208–9
Republic, 11–13, 78–81, 184–88
Responsio editoris, 258
Restraint, evil of, 71
Revelation, and knowledge of God,
  241
Revolution
 in Marxism, 163–64
 proletarian, 164–65
Ricardo, David, 98
Romanticism, 197
Romantics, and Plato, 198
Rousseau, Jean-Jacques, 136–48, 271
Rule of translation, 216
Rules for the Direction of the Mind, 269
Russell, Bertrand, 17, 303–10

Schizophrenia, 330
Science
 impact on philosophy, 229–30
 philosophy of, 312–64
 positivist theory of, 346

Science (*Cont.*)
  Scientific Materialism and the Identity Theory, 339
Scientific Method, 273
Second Treatise of Civil Government, 150–51
Secularization, of Western society, 252
Self-knowledge, and happiness, 252
Sense-data, 303–5
Skepticism, 278, 298
  solution to, 300
Slavery, and utilitarianism, 73
Smart, J. J. C., 337
Smith, Adam, 98–99, 239
Social contract, 144–48. *See also* Contracts
  criticism of, 148–50
  and freedom, 144, 148
Social Contract, The, 143, 145, 146–47
Social justice, 124–33
Social philosophy, 94–133
Social relationships of production, 160
Socialism, 119
Society
  changes in, 163
  good, defined, 140
  as living organism, 154–55
  Marx's theory of, 161
  traditions of, 155
Socrates, 180–88, 352
  basic principles, 6
  life of, 2–5
  use of irony, 7–10, 11
Solipsism, defined, 283
Sovereignty, 143
Space
  defined, 322
  theories of, 323–25
Spinoza, Baruch, 181, 257
State
  authority of, 142–43
  characteristics of, 142
  defined, 140–41
  organic theory of, 154–55
  superstructure of, 162

Stoics, 77
  creed of, 21–22
  and natural law, 23
Structure of Scientific Revolutions, 351–52
Subjective principle, 62
Substance
  created, 319
  defined, 317
  of God, 319
  immaterial, 319
  interaction of, 328
  in metaphysics, 317–18
  nature of, 326–27
  theories of, 331–33
  uncreated, 319–20
Sufferance, evil of, 72
Summa Theologica, 241, 243–44
Superstition, and enlightenment, 98
Surplus repression, 208
Synthetic propositions, defined, 250

Tacit consent, and contracts, 152
Tautologies, 248–49
Teleology, 141
Tests of certainty, and structure of knowledge, 287
Thales, 14–15, 17, 20
Thomism, 241, 242
Thought, unity of, 299
Thought experiment, 284
Three Dialogues Between Hylas and Philonus, 291
Time, conceptions of, 324
Tolstoy, Leo, 200
Tradition, 107
  defined, 11
Transcendence, defined, 210
Treatise Concerning the Principles of Human knowledge, 291
Treatise of Human Nature, 27–28, 286, 292–93, 295–97
Truth
  and objectivity, 230
  and subjectivity, 230

Truths of fact, 288
Two-dimensional culture, 210
Two-substance theory, 332

Unconscious, the content of,
    207–8
Unity of consciousness, 299
Universe, as concentric spheres, 14
Urbanization, 252
Utilitarianism, 66–76
    defined, 66
    objections to, 70
    and social reform, 97
    strength of, 70–71
Utilitarianism, 101–2

Values
    instrumental, 193–94
    intrinsic, 193–95
Violence, effect on viewers of, 191

War and Peace, 200, 201
Wealth of Nations, The, 100
What is Art?, 203
White paper principle, 292, 294
Whitehead, Alfred North, 17
Wilde, Oscar, 195–97
Wittgenstein, Ludwig, 29–31, 35–36
Words, and ideas, 289–90
Wordsworth, William, 198–200
Working class, 155